RECONCEPTUALIZING THE LITERACIES IN ADOLESCENTS' LIVES

Bridging the Everyday/Academic Divide

Third Edition

Edited by

Donna E. Alvermann
Kathleen A. Hinchman

Routledge
Taylor & Francis Group

NEW YORK AND LONDON

Visit the companion website for this book
at www.routledge.com/cw/alvermann

Third edition published 2012
by Routledge
711 Third Avenue, New York, NY 10017

Simultaneously published in the UK
by Routledge
2 Park Square, Milton Park, Abingdon, Oxon OX14 4RN

Routledge is an imprint of the Taylor & Francis Group, an informa business

First edition published by Routledge 1998
Second edition published by Routledge 2006

Library of Congress Cataloging in Publication Data
Reconceptualizing the literacies in adolescent's lives : bridging
the everyday, academic divide / edited by Donna E. Alvermann,
Kathleen A. Hinchman. — 3rd ed.
     p. cm.
Includes index.
1. Language arts (Secondary)—Social aspects—United States.
2. Literacy—Social aspects—United States. 3. Critical pedagogy—United
States. I. Alvermann, Donna E. II. Hinchman, Kathleen A.

LB1631.R296 2011
428.0071′2—dc23   2011026130

ISBN13: 978-0-415-89291-9 (hbk)
ISBN13: 978-0-415-89292-6 (pbk)
ISBN13: 978-0-203-81728-5 (ebk)

Typeset in Bembo
by Cenveo publisher services
Printed and bound in the United States of America on acid-free paper by
Edwards Brothers Inc.

RECONCEPTUALIZING THE LITERACIES IN ADOLESCENTS' LIVES

The third edition of *Reconceptualizing the Literacies in Adolescents' Lives* recognizes that digital media and social networking phenomena are now central in adolescents' lives. What is different in this edition is the focus on bridging students' everyday literacies and literacy practices common to subject matter learning. Four chapters from earlier editions serve as touchstone texts, honoring youth's diverse experiences and illustrating how young people's literacies are enacted, situated, and mediated in various locales. Eight new chapters consider how these themes are lived in today's schools and in the rapidly changing world outside of school and show applications of key concepts in rural, suburban, and urban sites.

New in the Third Edition

- Heightened attention to multimodal meaning construction
- More discussion of practical implications in both online and offline environments
- Teacher commentaries at the end of each section
- Companion website—facilitates application of the text's key ideas through discussion questions, links to instructional activities, blogs, additional readings and viewings, interactive web pages, and videos

Donna E. Alvermann is Distinguished Research Professor of Language and Literacy Education at the University of Georgia.

Kathleen A. Hinchman is Professor in the Reading and Language Arts Center at Syracuse University.

CONTENTS

FOREWORD

Reconceptualizing Teacher Knowledge and Student Achievement

Randy Bomer

How and what would we teach if we really knew the young adults in our classrooms? If we knew about Javier's collection of *fotonovelas*, passed down to him by his father, and his deep and growing expertise about that literate form, what foundation might that provide for extensions of his literacy that we hope to sponsor? If we could see into the inner visions of possible identities that our students carry with them through their days, the powerful people they would like to become, how might we hitch our curricular wagons to those ambitions, boosting them each into a new self even as we extend what they can do in writing and reading? How might we teach, in other words, if we had evidence that our middle and high school students are not constantly in danger of falling short of standards but are actually already competent, well on their way to all the underlying practices of thinking, understanding, and crafting that make up our hopes for their achievement, in and out of school? This new edition of *Reconceptualizing the Literacies in Adolescents' Lives* helps us develop new, appreciative eyes for the assets adolescents have already developed in their literacy—and the energy of their striving toward new abilities—sometimes with our help and sometimes without it. It is a book that gives us eyes for what we, as their teachers, might learn from what our students are already doing and it informs our imagination about how we might support them in their expanding capacities.

The adolescents represented in the first edition of this book were kids of the 1990s. For adults whose lives have accelerated as we age and for whom time is striding hastily across the decades, that time seems like the day before yesterday. But adolescent lives and literacies—like those of adults and children, too—were markedly different then: the Internet, gaming, and mobile phones were only the merest suggestion of what they have become in the intervening years. The political and economic landscapes of 1996 have changed multiple times since, and history shows no signs of slowing down. A 15-year-old back then is in her early thirties as this new edition comes out, and perhaps she now looks at 15-year-olds on the city bus with less than perfect comprehension.

The world changes, and adolescence changes. The adolescence of the 1950s wasn't the adolescence of the 1970s, and today's adolescence isn't that of the 1990s. Individuals change through the life period we refer to as adolescence, and the meaning of that phase of life is in a constant state of transformation as well. This book is unusual in the ways it has mirrored that change across its editions, reflecting the dynamic and protean nature of its subject matter. For these authors, reconceptualizing literacy and adolescents is not something that is ever achieved once and for all. Reconceptualization is part of a continual process of coming to understand both literacy and adolescence, over and over again.

Many of the scholars in this volume are finding it useful to think of literacy as a practice that takes its shapes and meanings from the ways it is situated within the other things people are doing with one another. As we will hear throughout this book, literate texts don't *mean* completely independently; they don't act in isolation. They are always situated in a complex network of purposes, activities, and relationships. Teachers see this all the time, when they hear students protest in class their distaste for reading and writing but then notice that the same kids doing the complaining also carry around skateboarding and guitar magazines, check out particular websites every time they are near a computer, write songs, or send a thousand text messages every day. It takes a special kind of teacher knowledge to educate young people that their existing literacies count, and thereby to produce the conversational environments that give students permission to import their energetic practices into the classroom and use them in their expansions of their literate territories (Bomer, 2011).

This new edition draws upon (and contributes to) research in adolescent literacy that has developed in important directions during the years since the first and second editions. Rather than pointing out again and again that some adolescents seem not to be benefitting from school, scholars have instead hunted down the spaces in which adolescents enthusiastically engage in literacy practices, where they grow in their use of signs, language, and rhetoric every day (Christenbury, Bomer, & Smagorinsky, 2008). They have searched out strengths, with the express purpose of learning the essential elements of the settings, the defining features of the practices within which adolescents do not appear at all resistant, rebellious, apathetic, or any other patterned stereotype that seems to be continually reinforced when people represent adolescents in the contexts they have not chosen. It seems unarguable that it would be a better world for young people if the places we require them to spend time could have the features of the spaces in which they thrive, if we could design environments and curricula that inspired students to be their best.

This move in adolescent literacy parallels and contributes to developments in the field sometimes known as the Learning Sciences, a field that is presently driving our understandings about how adults and young people alike are learning in the rich spaces made available in a global society, a digital environment, and communities that value knowledge and innovation. Drawing from recent research in a wide variety of disciplines, Sawyer (2006) sees the Learning Sciences as advancing a collection of themes.

First, there is a focus on underlying conceptual understandings rather than facts and rote procedures, which are only useful when a person knows when to apply them, how to modify them, and what they mean. The work in this book on adolescent literacy likewise elevates the importance of underlying understandings about how texts of all kinds work in the real world, not the memorization of official vocabulary lists or formulas for writing. Second, in the Learning Sciences, attention is trained not just on teaching and its outcomes but on processes and actions of learning. Adolescent literacy research follows students into the environments in which they learn in order to develop insights that can inform teachers and help them recognize their students' approximations and capacities. Third, Learning Sciences concerns itself with understanding and creating learning environments, in just the ways I described researchers in adolescent literacy following students into the environments in which they voluntarily and enthusiastically develop literacy practices. Sawyer's fourth claim on behalf of the Learning Sciences is that learning always must be built upon existing knowledge, and perhaps this is the strongest connection to much of the out-of-school literacy research that readers will find in this book. That research helps teachers understand and imagine what students already know, the value of that knowledge, so that they can begin to construct ways of building upon it. Finally, Sawyer states that reflection, the learner's analysis and naming of his own state of knowledge, is important to students' learning. It may be that this project of involving adolescent students in naming their own practices and knowledge, mapping those particular competencies onto the whole continent of literacy that there is to learn, is the next step in building literacy curricula from the insights this research offers. And it is a special gift of this edition of this important book that it takes substantial steps in this direction, investigating the curricular possibilities that arise from a close look at what students already know and can do.

I think readers of this edition of *Rethinking the Literacies in Adolescents' Lives* will feel as grateful as if someone had just turned them on to a new kind of music. These authors help us to admire students just like the ones we see all the time in ordinary classrooms. Now as we walk past them in the hall or pull up next to them for a writing conference, we are even more eager to learn what they know and to show them the wealth they're already carrying in their pockets.

References

Bomer, R. (2011). *Building adolescent literacy in today's English classroom*. Portsmouth, NH: Heinemann.

Christenbury, L., Bomer, R., and Smagorinsky, P. (2008). *Handbook of adolescent literacy research*. New York: Guilford.

Sawyer, K. (2006). Introduction. In K. Sawyer (Ed.), *The Cambridge handbook of the learning sciences*. New York: Cambridge University Press.

INTRODUCTION

When the going gets tough, the tough get going. Shop-worn, maybe. But this maxim warrants some consideration, especially when used to reference the spirit in which six classroom teachers and a school media specialist accepted our invitation to respond to the third edition of *Reconceptualizing the Literacies in Adolescents' Lives*. Our invitation could not have arrived at a more inauspicious time. For two of the seven, a heavy coaching load had added considerably to the stress of closing out a school year. For two others, the invitation led to an unanticipated spring-break project, and for the remaining three, it simply served as a reminder that teachers do not receive gold stars for authoring chapters when high stakes testing is in full swing. Yet, to a person, the response was, "Yes, I'm in—you can count on me." And count we did. Some lively and insightful writing began arriving from the field, signaling once again that educators in the so-called trenches are not easily stymied.

Nor have zealously administered, achievement-directed policies squelched the passion and sophisticated, situated literacies celebrated throughout this text and two earlier editions. The text's three iterations actually align with the life span of much recent school reform. The first edition (Alvermann, Hinchman, Moore, Phelps, & Waff, 1998) was written as U.S. states and school districts responded to Goals 2000, federal legislation requiring states to develop "clear and rigorous standards for what every child should know and be able to do" with "district-wide planning and implementation of school improvement efforts focused on improving student achievement to those standards" (United States Department of Education, 1998). This edition explored generative sociocultural aspects of adolescents' literacies, along with instructional moves suggested by these explorations. So that instructional ideas would be valued as realistic by teachers grappling with the turn-of-the-century focus on achievement, chapter authors revised their drafts using feedback from practicing teachers during a weekend workshop in Athens, Georgia.

The second edition of our text (Alvermann, Hinchman, Moore, Phelps, & Waff, 2006) was similarly sociocultural in orientation. We developed it during initial implementation of the No Child Left Behind Act of 2001 (NCLB) (United States Congressional Record, 2002). The chapters included in this edition represented a more strident call for respecting young people's identity-making in connection with various literacies despite an emphasis on achievement-driven school contexts. Because of what we were learning from research on the situated nature of youth's literacies, both the first and second editions called for building bridges between in- and out-of-school literacies in newly productive ways.

When we first broached the idea of a third edition, we asked ourselves, "Can we really reconceptualize the literacies in adolescents' lives for a third time?" The answer to this question is explained in Randy Bomer's foreword: Adolescents and their contexts, media, and literacies continue to evolve, sometimes at breakneck pace, which suggests the need for ongoing reconceptualizing. Thus, this new, third edition shares the sociocultural orientation of its predecessors. However, unlike its predecessors, this text's call is not for building bridges between two contexts, in-school and out-of-school, per se. The contexts are now too complex to be attached with a single bridge suggesting only two sides. Instead, multiple bridges connect texts, purposes, tasks, identities, social affiliations, media, and settings, blurring simple demarcations to form myriad new literacies. Such literacies are demonstrated in texting, blogging, gaming, spoken-word poetry, fantasy fiction, video sharing, and various kinds of social networking, and in media that move onto and off the popular culture center stage in the wink of an eye: Wireless streaming replaced by Ethernet cables; Flip cameras exchanged for cell phone videos; digital teaching, textbooks, testing, used in blended public, private, and charter schools; and bestsellers appearing in hardback, paperback, Kindle, Nook, and iPad forms—even as bricks-and-mortar bookstores go out of business, libraries scramble, and schools struggle to reconfigure. These rapidly changing circumstances have engaged young people's passions in unprecedented ways.

There is no escaping that digital media and social networking have become central to our day-to-day existence. To ignore their influence on adolescents is to overlook the literacies that young people already possess or are in the process of acquiring. In locales where Internet access is available, youth need not move from their computer screens to interact with others, to engage with content that is linguistically, visually, and aurally rich in meaning, and to communicate on a global scale.

Yet for all this richness and variability, there are pockets of real concern. Some adolescents remain on the periphery of available social networks, whether due to discrimination related to race, ethnicity, economics, disability, a confluence of other social circumstances, or by choice. Others, including youth who emigrate with their families to resume schooling in a new corner of the world or become part of a transnational community, are at the very center of government- and life-changing events, but without the literacy skills needed to mediate those events. Still other young people are faced with the challenge of choosing career paths that are evolving so quickly it is hard to predict what literacies might be needed in their lifetime. After all, what does it mean to be a politician, car mechanic, teacher, banker, plumber, pharmacist, farmer, or policymaker in such a rapidly changing world?

Even so, in the United States young people will be required to pass new forms of literacy assessments associated with the newest reforms, the Common Core State Standards and Race to the Top (United States Department of Education, 2009). And as we write this, teachers are being introduced to workplace evaluations tied to their students' test scores. Whatever form these new literacy tests take, they will surely become anxiety producers that exacerbate hasty searches for instructional solutions, but without concern for the situated literacies that young people have already developed or will need.

This is the world within which we considered the task of reconceptualizing adolescents' literacies for a third time. To explore how young people's everyday literacies and subject-matter learning can be bridged in newly innovative ways suitable for youth, teachers, and schools, we organized the text into four sections. We also included four chapters from earlier volumes of this text, one per section, because they seemed especially emblematic of four key themes, explained in the section descriptions below, that extend across the time periods represented by all three editions. As such, these chapters serve as what Lorri Neilsen Glenn, in the first chapter, describes as touchstone texts. Two newly invited chapters complement the touchstone text in each section.

Part I, Understanding Youth's Everyday Literacies, begins with Lorri Neilsen Glenn's chapter, which explains how touchstone texts influenced the literate lives of two rural youth over time. In Chapter 2, Stergios Botzakis explores the role comic books played in the life-long reading habits and passions of one individual. Eliane Rubinstein-Ávila then describes, in Chapter 3, Latino/a youth's everyday Internet use, with an emphasis on their participation in transnational communities.

In Part II, Integrating Everyday and Academic Literacies, David O'Brien's touchstone chapter examines how multimediating helped youth who struggled with the school literacy curriculum to see themselves as capable. In Chapter 6, Barbara Guzzetti and Marcia Mardis explore forensic comics and graphic novels as supports for students' learning of scientific concepts, and in Chapter 7 Marcelle M. Haddix explains writing instruction that helped African American boys develop their writing abilities outside of school walls.

Part III, Addressing Sociocultural and Identity Issues in Adolescents' Literacy Lives, begins with Bob Fecho, Bette Davis, and Renee Moore's touchstone chapter on classroom action research that involved high school students in transacting with issues of race, culture, and language as they developed academic literacies. In Chapter 10 Kelly Wissman and Lalitha Vasudevan explore ties between identity and poetry of self-definition written by young women and men in two out-of-school settings. In turn, in Chapter 11, Gay Ivey uncovers and dismantles assumptions about using various forms of young adult literature in Appalachian classrooms.

Part IV, Changing Teachers, Teaching Changes, is introduced with Alfred Tatum's touchstone chapter tapping teachers' perspectives toward rethinking literacy instruction for students from diverse backgrounds. In Chapter 14, Eli Tucker-Raymond, Daisy Torres-Petrovich, Keith Dumbleton, and Ellen Damlich trace how a collaborative professional development group explored integrating critical media literacies in their teaching. In Chapter 15 in this section, Margaret Hagood describes a middle school professional development project whose goal was to design instruction that considered popular culture and web-based literacies.

As noted earlier, new to this edition is a discussion at the end of each of the text's four sections (Chapters 4, 8, 12 and 16), authored by classroom teachers, to share insights that resonated for them as they considered the three chapters in each section. An Afterword inquires into how institutional structures—buildings, college campuses, classrooms, and other nonphysical structures, such as curricular guidelines, policies, standards, and assessments—contribute to the invisibility of students' everyday literacies.

Finally, we've developed a companion website to accompany this text (www.routledge.com/cw/alvermann), including discussion questions that may be used or modified by book clubs, study groups, and classes that use the text, along with links to relevant instructional ideas, research articles, interactive web pages, and videos that support insights gleaned from each chapter of this new edition.

We would be remiss if we didn't tip an imaginary hat to our coeditors from the first two editions of this text, David W. Moore, Stephen F. Phelps, and Diane R. Waff, along with chapter authors too numerous to list here. As is often the case with collaborations, we made each other smarter in ways that helped us formulate new, productive conceptualizations. We are grateful to have had the opportunity to think with them about the important issues that situate adolescents' literacies. We also offer a heartfelt thanks to Naomi Silverman, our Routledge/Taylor and Francis editor who continues to help us reconceptualize each volume. Finally, thanks to our family members, Jack, Bill, Dan, and Amanda, who always point us in better directions.

We are excited about and energized by this third edition. The chapter authors provide rich accounts of how youth situate, mingle, and enhance their everyday and academic literacies, as well as how teachers and teacher educators collaborate to enact pedagogies that facilitate adolescents' uses of 21st century texts. The research-based examples they provide will undoubtedly serve as grist for reconceptualizing the literacies in adolescents' lives for years to come.

Kathleen A. Hinchman
Donna E. Alvermann

References

Alvermann, D. E., Hinchman, K. A., Moore, D. W., Phelps, S. F., & Waff, D. R. (1998). *Reconceptualizing the literacies in adolescents' lives*. Mahwah, NJ: Lawrence Erlbaum Associates.

Alvermann, D. E., Hinchman, K. A., Moore, D. W., Phelps, S. F., & Waff, D. R. (2006). *Reconceptualizing the literacies in adolescents' lives* (2nd ed.). Mahwah, NJ: Lawrence Erlbaum Associates.

United States Congressional Record. (2002). *No Child Left Behind Act of 2001* (Public Law 107–110). Washington, DC: United States Congress.

United States Department of Education. (1998). Executive summary. *Goals 2000: Reforming education to improve student achievement* (Archived Information). Washington, DC: United States Department of Education. Retrieved May 26, 2011, from www2. ed.gov/pubs/G2KReforming/g2exec.html.

United States Department of Education. (2009). Executive summary. *Race to the Top*. Washington, DC: United States Department of Education. Retrieved May 26, 2011, www2.ed.gov/programs/racetothetop/executive-summary.pdf.

PART I

Understanding Youth's Everyday Literacies

1

TOUCHSTONE CHAPTER
PLAYING FOR REAL

Texts and the Performance of Identity

Lorri Neilsen Glenn

> Old paint on canvas as it ages sometimes becomes transparent. When that happens it is possible, in some pictures, to see the original lines: a tree will show through a woman's dress, a child makes way for a dog, a large boat is no longer on an open sea….This is called pentimento…the old conception, replaced by a later choice, is a way of seeing and then seeing again.
>
> Lillian Hellman (1973), *Pentimento*

This chapter is in two sections: Adolescence, and Early Adulthood. The first section, Adolescence, is an abbreviation of an earlier chapter written for the first edition of this handbook (Neilsen, 1998b). The earlier chapter, written eight years ago, focuses on identity creation, and on what I call *"touchstone" texts* informing the lives of two adolescents in high school. These touchstone texts shape the lives of David and El in ways that suggest that reading in adolescence is an activity of interpolation—whether the texts are film, cultural practices, or literary works, they inhabit the reader and the reader, in turn, writes the texts into his or her life. This earlier chapter, "Adolescence," suggests that, as educators, we must learn which texts resonate for adolescents and why. Both the substance of "Adolescence" and the theoretical inferences have remained as they were 8 years ago in order to preserve the original data, analyses and theoretical perspectives of both the participants and the researcher in context at that time. The reader is encouraged to read this section as though he or she might be reading it 8 years ago.

The second section of this chapter is an update; here, in "Adulthood," we meet again the two friends, David and El, 8 years after high school and after their first conversation with the researcher. What are their textual preoccupations now? What role do they believe their readings have played in shaping their lives?

And what insights, given their experience, might they offer to educators today? This section, like the earlier chapter, invites an aesthetic as much as an efferent reading. Because much of our reading in school and the academy is efferent (and much writing is thus propositional, theoretical, and closed), this chapter offers the possibility of understanding research and scholartistry (Neilsen, 2002), which is, like texts, students, and data themselves, open to multiple interpretations.

Adolescence

Prologue

"Who am I?" is a question of central importance in adolescence. No longer children unselfconsciously acting out story in the school yard or playing dress-up in the basement, adolescents try on roles in their lives at school, at home, and in the community. Unlike the play of young children, however, adolescent play often is marked by the awareness of its purpose: to explore identities in order to find a place in the world. Although play at all ages is serious, adolescent performance-as–identity has a particular urgency and intensity. Eva Hoffman (1989) describes this intensity about life as being marked by "fire, flair, a holy spark of inspiration" (p. 154). Who will I be today, tomorrow, next year?

This study explored the role of text in the lives of two adolescents in a Nova Scotia rural community. Here the term *text* refers to sets of signifying practices and discourses available to us in local and larger discourse communities: a novel in English class, the conversation about that novel, teen zines, mall cultures, music videos, advertising, and television sitcoms, for example. The premise of this study is that our engagements with everyday texts help all readers and writers to shape and reshape our identities, but that adolescents, in particular, engage in more fluid, intentional and often more passionate identity-play in their encounters with such symbolic resources. These resources not only help the adolescent make sense of her or his experience, but also offer opportunities for trying on or taking up often multiple and conflicting roles or identities. In this way, a text is both role and reality. Adolescents, who typically demonstrate as much zeal in taking up roles as they do in resisting them, become at once the performer, the audience, and the theatre. By performing the texts of their lives, they are reading and writing themselves.

As researcher, mother, and community member, I have observed the participants, Eleanor and David, in a number of social, personal, and school settings since their first grade in school. The in-depth interviews about the role of key texts in their lives, however, were taken over two months late in their Grade 11 (junior) year in high school. Emerging from transcripts of six hours of individual and paired interviews is a recurring theme: the fluidity of text in performance and role-playing as Eleanor and David make and shape meaning in their lives through literacy. Their understanding and "scripting" of principal—or what I refer to as "touchstone"— texts in their lives is woven into their school and social behavior in a process of ongoing revision. Here the texts are the novel, *The Catcher in the Rye*, and the film, *Pulp Fiction*. Their motifs and influences shift, recede, and emerge, seeming at times like the phenomena of pentimento in painting (Hellman, 1978) or the layered scripts of a palimpsest. The text or texts, as the adolescents themselves, resist stasis and defy definition.

The Players

Eleanor

Eleanor and her older sister moved with their mother (a single parent) to this rural Nova Scotia community before Eleanor started school. She lives with her mother, the owner of a craft store, and her stepfather, a fifth-generation Nova Scotian, in a recently converted boathouse on St. Margaret's Bay.

Interviews with El took place just before she turned 17. El is independent, has traveled alone to Ireland to visit relatives, travels every other weekend to see her birth father, and works part-time at a local restaurant/coffee house and occasionally as a sign painter. She goes into Halifax regularly to see films, hang out in coffee houses, or to visit her current boyfriend, an art student.

El's dress is distinctive, what some might call "nonconformist." She wears several earrings, including a nose ring; her dark hair has sported many hairstyles. She is short, quiet, but not shy, and often questions her parents' and her teachers' decisions. Art, drama, English, and history are her favorite school subjects. She has attended school in the same school system since grade primary.

David

David, 17, moved to the community from western Canada 13 years ago with his parents, both of whom are educators. He has a 9-year-old brother. David and Eleanor have been close friends since Grade 1, but never romantically paired. David, like El, has been independent from childhood, and has traveled frequently out of Nova Scotia. He attended school in the same classes as Eleanor. Highly verbal, he performs in school settings (as class clown), has studied drama with the local theatre school, and served as a youth judge at the local film festival. David is on two baseball teams, has been an avid skater and snowboarder, and when not with his girlfriend, Cheryl, hangs out with El and other friends from school. Ross, David, Simon, and El have made several home videos based on material they have written or improvised.

David dresses in a style he calls unique ("I am not preppie, not jock, and not punk"), but is in the contemporary style of skateboarders (large shirts, long skirt-like shorts). Like El, David's heritage is European, largely Caucasian; his great-grandmother was Cree. His brown hair, once worn in a ponytail, is now short and dyed dark blond. David is tall and solidly built. El's and David's strong sense of justice is demonstrated in their ongoing challenge of what they see as sexist or racist practices of their teachers or the community. Both frequently "diss" the rural community for what they see as its provincial attitudes.

Researcher/Narrator

As a 13-year resident of the rural community, I have researched and written about the literate behavior of adults in the area (Neilsen, 1989). As David's mother and a volunteer in their schools, I have seen both David and El in a variety of literacy and schooling contexts over the 11-year period in which they have known one another. Having moved intellectually from an atomistic, functional notion of literacy and literacy research in the 1970s, I am now engaged in ongoing research into gender and literacy that might be characterized as phenomenological.

The Texts

The Catcher in the Rye

J.D. Salinger's 1951 story of a prep-school runaway is perhaps one of North America's most controversial and enduring novels. Typically described as the only novel to successfully "convey contemporary youth's dissatisfaction with adult society" (Benet's, 1987), it deals with the two days following Holden Caulfield's departure from school. Holden Caulfield is considered by many adolescent and adult readers to represent the voice of disaffected youth. Indeed, although readers in the 1950s were avid readers of the novel (the language was frank and racy enough for the times to ensure a wide readership), the work continues to attract succeeding generations of young readers.

Pulp Fiction

The controversial movie (Tarantino, 1994) about low-rent hit men won the 1994 Cannes Film Festival's highest prize, the *Palme d'Or*, and a 1994 Academy Award for Best Original Screenplay for the writer/director, Quentin Tarantino. Celebrated as the work of one of cinema's "*enfants terrible*," the movie also marked actor John Travolta's long-awaited return to the screen.

Like Salinger, Tarantino has been praised for his authentic, engaging dialogue and his originality. In Tarantino's case, the film is flagrantly derivative of other films and of pop culture narratives and, ironically, it is this derivative "*bricolage*" quality, in part, that wowed the critics. The term *pulp fiction* refers to the 5-cent novels popular a generation ago, and the movie is replete with pop culture images and references and allusions to well-known movies. The film disrupts the conventional narrative and linear plot line; viewers must piece together "what happened" through a series of flashbacks (and jumps forward). Martin and Porter (1996) describe it as a "trash masterpiece" in which the writer/director "spares the viewer little in this tale of the underbelly of Los Angeles where philosophizing hit men and techno-crazed druggies live on the thrill-packed edge" (p. 103). Vincent Vega (Travolta) and Jules (Samuel Jackson) are the hapless gangsters whom we follow on the trail of a suitcase, the contents of which remains a mystery.

The movie, like its director/writer, is not without its critics. Some have called the film "blaxploitation," claiming that actor Samuel Jackson's Afro and exaggerated sideburns (part of the movie's 1970s motif) make him just another Black stereotype, and that Travolta's "White negro" attitude, as well as the script's frequent use of the word "nigger," makes the movie both dangerous and racist. Feminists, in particular, have attacked the film for its graphic violence: heroin addiction, execution-style murder, male rape, and bondage.

Theoretical Backdrop

This study assumes that becoming literate is a lifelong process, and that literacy learning and literate behaviors are semiotic activities (Neilsen, 1989) in which we learn to read and write within value-laden code systems. Becoming literate is a process not only of acquiring functional skills of decoding and encoding printed material, but also of developing critical awareness and agency in one's own life.

Adolescents in particular draw from popular culture to "actively create and define their own social identities…'reading' and 'writing' popular culture are thus inherently social processes" (Buckingham & Sefton-Green, 1994, p. 108). As young people learn to see themselves in social and political terms, they have the opportunity to actively choose or to resist the discourses and roles available to them. Although it is true that choice itself is framed and shaped by myriad personal and social influences, it is also true that the more diverse and discrepant the choices provided for young adults, the greater the chance their choices will move them beyond the insular and the local. Buckingham and Sefton-Green (1994) offer this observation:

> Becoming critical could be seen simply as a matter…in Bourdieu's terms, of acquiring a kind of cultural capital…on the other hand, (it) could be seen from a Vygotskyan perspective…(emphasizing) the way in which critical understanding offers the individual a degree of power and control over his or her thought processes.
>
> *(p. 182)*

Adolescents supported in multiple opportunities to work with a range of texts, both school-sanctioned and popular, would seem, then, to be well positioned for growth in their critical literacy development.

Cherland (1993) and others have shown how young girls take up gender identities through reading as a social practice. Rogers' (1993) study of preadolescent
girls makes apparent that entry into adolescence creates for young girls a "crisis of
courage" (p. 290) in which they struggle to maintain their outspokenness and
strength in the face of pressures to assume societal roles and expectations for
feminine behavior. Finders' (1996a, 1996b) work on the "underlife" of junior
high school girls' literacy practices illustrates how social roles are shaped and
maintained through girls' reading and writing outside of school-sanctioned literacy practices. Humans, regardless of age, tend to resist an official view of who
they must be and what they must do (Finders, 1996a).

Boys, as much as girls, can be constrained by limited constructions of their
gender identities in school and society. Most work in gender over the last decade
has affirmed that cultural values about males and females are inscribed in literacy
practices and can reinforce strongly the stereotypical male/female polarities of
activity/passivity, dominance/submission, and public/private. Finders (1996a) calls
for opportunities that examine:

> the social, historical and cultural motivations of particular roles available—
> in texts, classrooms, and the larger culture—(that) will lead students to
> more critical awareness and thus, it is hoped, to the ability to revise those
> roles…Students, both male and female…need opportunities to practice
> dealing with intellectual uncertainties and political tension.
>
> *(p. 126)*

The texts of students' lives, regardless of the context, often undergo a process that
Jenkins (1992) calls "becoming real," whether the text is in the private or the
public domain. First the text—particularly if it is interesting to the reader/
viewer—is incorporated into lived experience; then it is reread and rewritten so
that it is more productive and more able to sustain its original appeal; and finally,
it is shared within social practices as assumed and tacit knowledge, particularly
among friends.

As this study shows, the touchstone texts that inform Eleanor's and David's
lives—*The Catcher in the Rye* and *Pulp Fiction*, respectively—undergo such a process of becoming real, culminating, finally, in the insertion of these texts into their
social world. In this way, whether it is a *Saturday Night Live* sketch seen alone at
home and then reenacted in the school hallway as a piece of shared text (and then
subsequently used as a "shorthand" reference for a social phenomenon), or
whether it is a touchstone novel or film that plays an important role in their lives,
these young people live the private in concert with the public. Each script, or
text, has the potential for reenactment in public in some form, whether the enact-
ment is explicit (in speech or writing) or tacit (changed behavior, for example).

To learn about the texts in their lives, I asked two questions of El and David:
"Tell me about your reading and writing in school" (I asked this question of

them individually, and together); and "Tell me about your favorite 'text' (book, movie)" (I explained my perspective on "text," and that my meaning included other media). Each talked with only my occasional prompting for further explanation. Because we know each other so well, the conversations were, at first, awkward, as though we each recognized the performative nature of such talk. For David, especially, knowing me as "Mom," interested in his learning and his academic progress, he seemed at times caught between what he wanted to say and what he thought I might want to hear, both as a parent and a researcher. As a researcher, however, I did not consider this wrinkle problematic: Issues of stance and disclosure, identity and performance adhere in most research interviewing, regardless of the relationship between the people involved. El and David seemed remarkably candid and willingly offered their thoughts. Later, they read transcriptions of our recorded conversations, made changes, then read and revised a draft copy of what became the chapter.

Presenting the data in this format is an attempt, like breaking down the fourth wall in theatre, to collapse the distinctions between text and audience (or text and reader)—to make this a reading event, not an object—and to move away from viewing our own interactions with text as an activity separate from who we are (Rosenblatt, 1978).

Eleanor

> Then I'd throw my automatic down the elevator shaft—after I'd wiped off all the finger prints and all. Then I'd crawl back to my room and call up Jane and have her come over and bandage up my guts. I pictured her holding a cigarette for me to smoke while I was bleeding and all.
>
> The goddam movies. They can ruin you. I'm not kidding....Holden Caulfield, *The Catcher in the Rye*
>
> *(Salinger, 1951, p. 104)*

Why El Likes Catcher in the Rye

I think it's just the way he goes on these spiels...there's this one chapter—I actually did bits of it for a monologue once in drama—and Holden's in this crap hotel, and he's in the lobby, in this, as he calls it, "vomity-looking chair," and all of a sudden he starts thinking about Jane, the girl he's still in love with, and it just goes off for the whole chapter about Jane—just the way he goes all over the place and he goes so deep into the way he's thinking, and you just relate to that, I mean that's how it happens in life...chapter eleven...here it is [she reads]:

> All of a sudden, on my way out to the lobby, I got old Jane Gallagher on the brain again. I got her on, and I couldn't get her off. I sat down in this vomity-looking chair in the lobby and thought about her and Stradlater sitting in that goddam Ed Banky's car, and though I was pretty damn sure

> old Stradlater hadn't given her the time—I know old Jane like a book—I still couldn't get her off my brain.
>
> *(Salinger, 1951, p. 76)*

and then he just goes on and on and on...

And this is probably my favorite part in the whole book...when they're out on the screened-in porch and it was the first time they had even got close to necking, and they didn't really, and it was raining, "raining like a bastard out" and

> all of a sudden this booze hound her mother was married to came out on the porch and asked Jane if there were any cigarettes in the house.... Anyway, Jane wouldn't answer him...she didn't even look up from the game.
>
> *(Salinger, 1951, p. 78)*

Jane just started crying. And he (Holden) talks about how this teardrop fell on a red square on the checkerboard, and how she just rubbed it in. And you can just see it so well, the way he describes it. So well. It makes me really feel the respect that he had for Jane, how he cared for her, I dunno. You almost think he doesn't have any respect for anything else but her...well, except Phoebe (El pronounces this "foe-bee"), his sister. I love to hear him talking about his kid sister, and how she dances, and the little things about her that make him happy.

Another scene that really gets to me is when he was in his sister's school, when he went to get Phoebe to tell her he was leaving, and he saw "fuck off" written on the wall, and he was so angry, he wanted to go and smash the guy who did it, that it was so horrible that little kids would see this....

On Seeing Catcher in the Rye *as a Film*

Never. No way. Because I have got it so clearly in my head if it was on film it would ruin it, unless I made the film....I mean the only thing anyone ever says about him is Sally, and she talks about his crewcut, so I don't know what he looks like. He's probably not big, cause he was worrying about old Stradlater stretching his jacket, and he's tall, I think, and he has a little bit of grey hair, it says that somewhere. I see him, like now, how he would dress now, because I don't know what the fashion was then. It does relate now, it's timeless, really.

I can't even think who I would have play him as an actor...I wouldn't. I couldn't. Because then it just turns all Hollywood. I don't want to see it like that. Yuk! Tom Cruise as Holden Caulfield? If it was going to be a movie it would have to be someone young, not big, who had never played anything before. Everyone else has a reputation and that takes over their character in a lot of movies. I could see people I know playing Holden Caulfield, but not anybody well known....I know he's tall, skinny, with short hair, not a crew cut, short at the back, kind of long at the front. With casual pants, button-up shirts. I can hear his voice in my head, but I could never describe it exactly. Kinda low, but not real deep.

Reading and Rereading

When I first read the book, I was in 7th grade, and I was, like, so sad. Just because I want this person to be alive, to really exist, so that I could know them....When I finished the book, I thought, what do I do now? Because I just felt like I knew this person....I wanted him to be around to talk to. I think I was a little in love with him.

But the more I read it—like the last time I read it through was a while back—and I was more distanced from it, I think. I just felt he was too pissed off at everything, and that bothered me. Nothing pleased him....I've heard people say it's a really depressing sort of book, I don't find it that way, but I think the more I read it, the more I get out of it. Maybe the first time I read it I didn't really understand what he was going through. It was just a story, he was just a cool guy who did whatever he felt like doing....

He couldn't relate to society because he thought it was all bullshit....A lot of people would like to have the guts that Holden did, just to say screw it and leave school, and get away, but they don't. I dunno, he just sounds like an adolescent sounds, even now. He says 'goddam' all the time. I just love that. He just says what he wants. And all these people he knows; they all represent different people in the teenage social structure. I know people like Stradlater. I'm friends with people like Holden. And I know people like Ackley—the guy with the mossy teeth—people who have disgusting fingernails and stuff. I know these people.

Sometimes I see all the negative stuff in Holden, and I just want to tell him to smarten up...other times it seems as though it's the complete truth. I think I reread it because it sounds realistic, and I would reread it just for the section on Jane and the tear on the checkerboard. That really struck me. It was just so obvious that he cared about her so passionately. That really gives him another dimension. And I reread that and wondered about the stepfather and Jane, whether we were supposed to take from that that there was some kind of abuse going on. It's subtle, but it's there.

And Holden's feelings of protectiveness toward Jane. If you didn't reread and see those things then he wouldn't be a good character, he'd just be a joke. So many people are like that. They'd never tell their little sister what they're thinking, like how much they really care about her. I remember the time at the end when he was so exhausted, and sick, I think, and he was watching Phoebe going around and around the carousel, he was so full of happiness he wanted to cry. He loved her but didn't say. He didn't talk to Jane the whole time even though he had the opportunity...he's deeper than you'd expect....

But last time I read it, I wondered actually if Holden was homophobic. Remember at the end when he leaves his drunk teacher's house so quickly? Who knows if the guy was making a pass at him, but I think Holden thought so....And something else I noticed the last reading. Remember how he went to see his teacher, Spencer, and old Spencer showed him his terrible essay on the Egyptians? Well, at the end of the book, he's in the museum, and he starts telling these little kids all about the Egyptians, like he actually knows something about them. It's as though he finally found a use for all that information in real life. He becomes the teacher. You know what I mean? It's like he's in between being a child and an adult.

On Playing

Every single person Holden meets is interesting. Like his professor, the woman on the train. I just laughed at him telling her all those lies about her son....Me and Nic have this routine that we do sometimes. It's sort of like Holden's. We act like I'm from Ireland and he's from Germany and we're just traveling around Nova Scotia, and we put on accents and have this great big story we tell people downtown. Remember when Holden was dancing with that girl and he told her she just missed seeing a movie star? That was so funny. I'd love to do that.

On Connecting With Male and Female Characters

I spend a lot of time with guys. I have friends who are girls, too, but I connect with guys more I think....For music I choose mostly women artists. Sinead O'Connor. But I like older music, mostly male artists. Like Donovan, The Doors, Cream, The Beatles, Neil Young, America. It was my sister, though, who suggested I read *Catcher*. And my science teacher just freaked out when she saw I was reading it—she didn't read it until she was in university. I think she was shocked because most people my age were reading the *Babysitter's Club* and *Sweet Valley High* books. I read those in Grade 5: they were, like, chewing-gum reading. I wish there was stuff for girls to read that wasn't so empty. Things that would also make you think a little bit, maybe learn something. Instead of living in Sweet Valley and wishing for a convertible. I like novels, and poetry, and stories where there is more interpretation and where your own experience comes into it.

On Pulp Fiction

I liked the way the story was told—the storyline all jumbled. I liked the cinematography and the dialogue. It was both vulgar and smart. I liked the way the dialogue got into detail about little things. Like Vincent and Jules get into this big thing about Mia and foot massage outside the door of where they're supposed to pick up the briefcase. It had nothing to do with what they were there for, they just went on a rant. Like the kind of rant that Holden would go on. I went not because of Travolta, but because everyone was raving about it. It scared me, actually, because of my reaction to the violence. Some of the violent scenes just were nothing, which made me wonder if I was overexposed to violence, they were brutal, but what got to me—when I really freaked out—was when Vincent was putting the needle into Mia's heart. You know, the adrenalin to revive her. I mean he was saving her life, not killing her like all the rest of the violence in the movie, but saving her, and that's the part that really affected me.

David

BUDDY: Hi I'm Buddy, what can I get 'cha?
VINCENT: I'll have the Douglas Sirk steak.
BUDDY: How do you want it, burnt to a crisp, or bloody as hell?
VINCENT: Bloody as hell. And to drink, a vanilla coke.
BUDDY: How about you, Peggy Sue?
MIA: I'll have the Durwood Kirby burger—bloody—and a five-dollar shake.
BUDDY: How d'ya want that shake, Martin and Lewis or Amos and Andy?
MIA: Martin and Lewis
Vincent takes a look around the place. The Yuppies are dancing, the diners are biting into big, juicy hamburgers, and the icons are playing their parts. Marilyn is squealing, the Midget is paging Philip Morris, Donna Reed is making her customers drink their milk, and Dean and Jerry are acting like fools.
MIA: Whaddya think?
VINCENT: It's like a wax museum with a pulse rate. (*Pulp Fiction*, Tarantino, 1994)

Why David Likes Pulp Fiction

I thought it was hilarious. And I really liked the way Tarantino messed with linear structure and chopped up the film…that was just not done in any movie I have ever seen. Plus I fell in love with John Travolta—he was just wicked; it was his comeback film. Plus the writing was really good. You know, dialogue about nothing.

Often in movies, every word that someone says is critically important, you know, very, very significant. This was just casual conversation between guys… what they said was important, because it added to their characters or added to the scene, but it didn't have life or death consequences. Like Travolta describing his trip to Amsterdam, saying to his partner:

You'd really like it cause you can get a glass of beer at McDonald's. And you know what they call a quarter pounder with cheese at McDonald's?

> You mean they don't call it a quarter pounder with cheese? No man, they got the metric system. They wouldn't know what the fuck a quarter pounder is. What do they call it? Royale with cheese. Royale with cheese? Yeah, Royale with cheese.

Later on, they go:

> You want some bacon? No man, I don't eat pork. What, you Jewish or something? No man, I just don't dig on swine. Yeah, but bacon tastes good, pork chops taste good. Yeah, it might taste like pumpkin pie, but I'd never know' cause I wouldn't eat the filthy motherfucker. Pigs eat and root and shit; pigs are filthy animals.

And they go on like that. This is right after Jules has found redemption because of some divine intervention where this guy hauled off and fired six shots from a hand cannon and missed them. But he's not talking about how he's found God, or how he's going to leave and find his true path, or nothing like that, he's talking about bacon…you know what I mean? It's really well done. It's really laid back. It's hilarious.

On Having Point

There's *Forrest Gump*. Where every word brought you closer to feeling compassion for Forrest Gump. Where you're really manipulated. But then there's TV, like *Seinfeld*, and all these new Generation X TV shows like *Friends* or the *Single Guy*, *Caroline in the City*, talking about nothing. Larry David and Jerry Seinfeld came up with the idea of a show about nothing, and it's made millions. And that's what it is. Just casual encounters and funny situations. It doesn't have to follow a direct plot line. It doesn't have to be boy meets girl, stuff like that. It's just everyday life. That's what it showed in *Pulp Fiction*. Just the everyday, underground life of two second-rate gangsters. They might be a little more philosophical than most, but….

I'm not part of Generation X, but I think these guys [Generation Xers] are sick of always having a plot line, or sick of things always having an inner meaning. I think every show has a point. But I don't think that it has to be a big one. I think life is like that. It doesn't always have a big point. Just lots of little ones.

On the Writer/Director

People just write what they know….I dunno, if you lived in Iceland you wouldn't write about the desert. Obviously Tarantino had a vast knowledge about certain kinds of movies. That's why he hasn't done a romance film, cause he really liked gangster films. He's like a geek. It's not the same old, same old, let's cast Arnold

Schwarzenegger where we can make a million dollars' cause it's a film where we blow up everything. And it's not a Disney cartoon borrowed from a book. He's coming up with original stuff. *Pulp Fiction* was never a book.

Pulp fiction…ten cents. Book format…cheap entertainment, you know? Maybe the movie has some similarities with those old novels. The entertainment value. They're second-rate gangsters.

On Fiction and Reality

I think it's a portrayal of that kind of life, but it's not real life,' cause real life isn't like that. People want to see real life, but they want to see it done more cleverly and more exciting. They don't want to see it done over the top—at least I don't—I want to see it as close to reality, but still far away. That's a paradox, isn't it. It's an impossible reality, I guess.

On Cultural Texts

I mean, I understood all those things in the restaurant scene. Mamie Van Doren, cherry cokes, all that. I mean, I didn't live in the 50s, so I don't really know it, but I think the media has taught me to know what all that is, even though I didn't live it. So I could place it right away.

On Viewing and Re-Viewing: The Text Becomes Real

It certainly boosted my interest in movie-making and being in films. About that time I was in a lull, I didn't know if I was going to continue in theatre or study film, and then seeing that movie…it was like, ohmygod, this is something entirely new. I liked it more when I got to see it more, talk about it more, share it more with my friends. I probably wouldn't have liked the movie as much if I was the only person I knew who saw it. My close friends and I got the sound track, which was a kick-ass soundtrack which also added to my love for the film because there were excerpts from the movie on the soundtrack, which I memorized. Gave me a greater appreciation for music at that time. One of Jules' lines, for example, is "That's all right…that's Kool n' the Gang."

We even went so far as to do our own *Pulp Fiction* movie, Simon and I. We took the video camera from Simon's house, went downtown to an apartment building and did the scene about the foot massage. We found a place on Queen that looked kind of 70s, carpeted and all that, went up to one of the floors and asked Simon's sister to film us. We walked around, we were dressed up, and then we went downstairs and did the scene about Royale with cheese.

Then we did the play at school, which I directed. It intrigued me. I loved that script. The dialogue made the characters and the characters were wicked. I found the script on the Internet, printed off sections I wanted. I would have printed off other sections but because it was for the school, it couldn't contain "mother-fucker" and all that. I had to be selective. It was too bad, because I had to leave out some of the best scenes, like the foot massage one because it was talking about, like, oral sex. Ross and I still want to put *Pulp Fiction* in its linear order and see what kind of movie it turns out to be. It could totally suck.

On Identities and the Future

There's always fantasy, like it would be cool to be Vincent Vega, to be like those guys. There's nothing more I want right now than to live in the big city. I want to live in a city, to know the goings-on, to be able to walk out my front door, and be there. But do it outside Canada. There's times when I would like to be Quentin Tarantino. To have made it.

I hate Canadian movies. I know they are deeper, have more meaning, win all these awards, but that's not the attraction for me....I mean if I were in Canadian music, I would stay here. Canadian music rules. Canadian music—that's where it's at nowadays. But not our movie industry. It's too boring. I'm attracted to the fame, I guess, and you won't get that in Canada. I'm not just talking about *Pulp Fiction* now. I'm talking about my life. I want my life to be exciting. To mean something.

On Performing

Quentin Tarantino seems like us. Hanging around making films, hanging out with friends. Our conversations are like that kind of dialogue. Or like Seinfeld. I mean, maybe we're mocking them, but...we joke around with each other. A lot of our dialogue we borrow from *Pulp Fiction*, from shows, and stuff—that's the way we live our interactive life with each other. I mean I might live differently with my parents, or with Cheryl, but when I'm with all my friends together I'm being myself but I'm also performing, and everyone is. We borrow from the film, argue about nothing and are funny. Like Ross will go, hey, I like your shoes, let's just say. And I go, yeah, man, they ARE the shoes. And Ross will say, Oh, they ARE the shoes. And then we just go off talking about shoes. Just think of a situation and we'd try to one up each other, playing, not like competition, but to try to come up with better lines. One up each other.

Adults have lived a lot of their life, and they've had time to mature, develop into a person, and I know they keep learning, but teenagers are so impressiona-ble. And we're borrowing from everything we see that we think is cool. I mean, like maybe this will fit on me. This will look cool on me; this kind of conversa-tion, this kind of attitude. According to what we think is cool at that time. Your favorite song might be from the 60s, but mine is still changing. Right now, I'm still picking my favorites. I'm trying out new personalities from different sources, and if I think it's cool, maybe I'll try it out. Maybe it will be me. Then again, maybe it won't be me, but it will stay with me, and so that adds to my personality, and so I also have that little facet of me, because I use it as knowledge. So by doing this my whole life I kinda gain a way of being.

I think certain attributes of mine are going to remain the same. I think I'm a funny person, and I know I'm not very good at listening. I've always talked a lot and I don't think that will change. I think you just change according to your surroundings, your age, your experiences, but that core personality that you start out with is still there.

I don't think you ever lose anything as a person. It all helps to make up who you are. Maybe, like with Travolta, you gain his coolness, but then by gaining the coolness you've added his arrogance, which means you've lost your kindness. But maybe it's not lost, maybe it's buried underneath there, underneath this John Travolta mask you're wearing. For a lot of time I even had my hair like Travolta. I don't think that 20 years from now I could look back on Vincent Vega, and say, how could I ever have liked him? I think he's super cool. If you can look back and it still intrigues you, still draws you in, still makes it happen for you then it's part of you. I couldn't think this way if it had been Tom Hanks.

On Catcher in the Rye

When I read that I walked around for a week annoyed at people because all they were doing was bullshitting. Everyone seemed to be so phony. Holden was a character I really liked but he didn't touch me personally, not like Vincent. Holden gave me an insight into how some teenagers live and think, but that's about it. I'm not a book kinda guy anyway. I don't like to read. I like movies and films. And music.

El and David on Teachers and Teaching: Selected Dialogue

DAVID: I learned a lot last year in history—about Roman times and that—but this year is so much more useful knowing how political and social things got to be the way they are because of events 50 years ago....

EL: Like I never knew what a Fascist pig was....

DAVID: I knew the name Mussolini, but until we had Mr. M., I used to think he was like this Italian mobster, from Sicily who killed guys....

EL: Amazing the conclusions you come up with yourself.

DAVID: I find out he was the first Fascist leader. And here I thought he was Jimmy Hoffa, or the Godfather....Mr. M. gives us amazing detail....

EL: Yeah, he's still so passionate about it. He's been teaching the same course for 16 years...and he still LOVES it....

DAVID: A teacher shouldn't be the kind of person who has the book with all the answers at the back. You know what I mean? The teachers' edition. You got to have Mr. M. who knows everything there is to know about modern history...and you need Ms. M. who is an actual artist—

EL: —who went to art school.

DAVID: And you need an English teacher like Ms. A. or Mr. H. and who have experienced life.... Mr. H. has been in Vietnam...he's been a hippie...he's seen world change...he was there when the Berlin Wall came down, for example—

EL: —Interesting experiences at least...a teachers' life shouldn't affect how we learn, but it does. When you know somebody has a flair for life, they obviously have a flair for other things.

Epilogue

Texts are symbolic resources for these two; they are imaginative possibilities, sometimes a costume, and sometimes a mask. Texts house dreams, too, and El and David have dreamed through *Catcher* and *Pulp Fiction*.

If we "read" them one way, we can read El's dreams as including the romance story; her reaction to the teardrop scene—through which Holden reveals his love for Jane—seems to indicate her wish to be loved the same way. (Nic, El's boyfriend, is known for his antiestablishment beliefs.) The admiration she has for Holden's love for his sister, Phoebe, also seems to show the centrality in her life of human values such as caring, preservation of the innocent, and the male's role as protector. Watching *Pulp Fiction*, El is struck most, for example, by the moment where Vincent's violent act (a needle plunged in the heart) revives Mia, the female playing a supporting role in the movie.

If we read El's dreams another way, we can imagine her wish to have the freedom and flexibility that Holden has—and perhaps which many males share— to live his life the way he wishes, if only for a couple of days. El's stated wish to live an exciting life is consistent with her enjoyment of a character who has created his own excitement. Yet we are left to wonder whether she sees herself playing the lead role in her life, as Holden seems to do, or to play a supporting role on stage with a man. Furthermore, is El forced, because of lack of options in school, to see life through the curtain of male protagonists and male leads?

El dislikes anything that has "gone Hollywood," a phrase she seems to associate with inauthenticity, phoniness. Her love for reading and writing propel her to use literacy to pursue what she believes to be authentic, particularly through journal writing and the reading of poetry and novels. But, left without adult support in this goal, she typically finds male-centred texts to fuel her interest; what would happen if she found similarly strong and vivid female characters? The English curriculum for her senior year does not look, at this point, to represent perspectives other than male Eurocentric perspectives, and so I will, as a result of these conversations, offer to pass along books or to assist her in any of her assignments.

David's dreams are made explicit: For this year, at least, he wants to be famous. He is unabashedly frank in his admiration of Travolta, Tarantino, and the character Vincent Vega, seeing them perhaps as role models to emulate, as symbolic resources to try on identities. Consistent with the social construction of masculinities, David dreams of having the power and control that his role models enjoy. David's observations seem to write the story of the hero, the master of his fate.

Although David espouses antisexist and antiracist practices in school and society, his rereading of the film does not include a condemnation of what others see as its racist or sexist elements. When David and I have a follow-up conversation, he claims that teachers, because of their role as sources of knowledge for students, must guard against racist and sexist practices. Film-makers, however, are merely "showing real life, and real life is sexist and racist."

Adulthood: 8 Years On

Looking is what saves us….Simone Weil, *Waiting for God*, p. 125

More than eight years have elapsed since I interviewed El and David about the texts that informed their lives. Although the two have undergone considerable change in their circumstances, they have remained in touch over the years. Both play on the same softball team that meets weekends on the Halifax Common; they get together socially now and then, and run into each other at local cultural events.

El, now 25, moved into Halifax after high school to complete a Bachelor's Degree in Art at the Nova Scotia College of Art and Design. She hosts a radio program on the local university network (spin handle: Miss Darla Kitty). She lives with Stephen, the technical director at the station, refuses plastic at the grocery store, and finds as many ways as she can as a citizen and artist to jam culture (interrupt the given cultural texts or undercut them; see www.adbusters.com for more information on culture jamming). El is now an artist, and has had several shows, one of which included a compilation video focusing on the gender stereotypes in a month of television advertising. For income, El works in a number of art galleries as a curator and administrator. Being in the field seemed a natural step: "My art teacher in High School helped me pull a portfolio together, my boyfriend was at the art college, and I was always hanging around with people in the arts community." Her program at the Nova Scotia College of Art and Design allowed her to do off-campus study and develop some of her own curriculum, one part of which was a "road trip" down from Canada around the perimeter of the United States:

> *That journey was instrumental in shaping the way I think about things, and the way I make art. Now that I've graduated, it's a struggle to keep going—to balance*

the art, the business of the art (getting grants and support), making enough for bread and butter. To find time to create. To develop my own work when part of my job is to curate others' work. I don't have kids, I don't have a mortgage; this is the time I can keep pushing the poverty line and try to keep my art at the forefront. You can't have it both ways, unless you're making something really commercially viable. Sometimes I get sucked into that whole cycle of wanting to be affluent, of wanting money. But then finally, I think, I don't care about money. I've been really fortunate to have a job in the arts community and do my art, instead of having to sling beer. Although I'm feeling the pressure, I'm resistant to having children—a lot of my friends are. My art is my baby....How do you balance those things in life?

David, now 26, is finishing a cultural studies degree at Mount Saint Vincent University, works as a chef at My Other Brother Darryl's, and as a DJ at "*whatever places will have me.*" He wants to travel to Ireland with his girlfriend after graduation, then return to finish a graduate degree. "*You can't do anything with a B.A., and besides, I'm really interested in the ideas.*" After enrolling in university after high school—"*basically, I went because my girlfriend at the time was going*"—he left before completing a year because "*I suddenly asked myself, what am I doing? This wasn't me. I broke up with my girlfriend and left the province.*" He moved to Alberta, where he worked in a series of McJobs in a tourist town in the Rockies, tried "*every experience available to me there...what's that saying? The paths of excess lead to the path of wisdom? Those years are blurry.*" He returned to Nova Scotia ready to resume his education on his own terms.

I was interested in visual communications of some sort. I tried theatre during high school and in my first year, and that was fine. But I read about this cultural studies program (the only one East of Toronto) and saw it was about visual and media literacy, and film and art. I was never a big reader, but now I read more than ever. Not fiction, though. Articles on culture, the semiotics of things. I watch a lot of film. Males generally are more visual, I think, when it comes to learning. It's funny. I'm still in the media, but no longer as the actor or player or director. Now, I'm in the role of critic, looking at the media and its influence. In a theoretical context—thinking more than doing.

Review: The Players Look Back at Themselves

DAVID: I feel like I've learned a hell of a lot, but it feels like no time at all. Don't feel old yet. That person eight years ago was a product of his generation. I took in what was there, reworked it as my own. We all latch on to something we think is our own at that age. *Pulp Fiction* appealed to me because it was different from the mainstream. Tarantino challenged the status quo. El and I have always been critical thinkers, when I think about it now.

We got into trouble in high school not for fights in the hall, but because we were always questioning authority. That photocopying scam—remember that? Matt's in grad school now—obviously turned him into a criminal (laughs). When I used to do the announcements at Sir John A (high school), I remember saying "Here at SJA, we put the 'fun' in funeral," and thinking that was hilarious. I regret that. I was an asshole. And I remember getting into trouble with the secretary because I announced over the intercom that "on this day"—however many years ago, I can't remember—"John Lennon announced that the Beatles were bigger than God." Oh, she was so upset and I just couldn't understand it.

EL: It's weird to see yourself like that. That was me, though. For yourself, you don't see the change. I have friends who are turning thirty—I can't believe it. But I can see how who I am now was always there. But back then we were so optimistic! Now we're jaded and depressed (both laugh).

Re-visioning: Texts in Lives

DAVID: I was so interested in the glamour of *Pulp Fiction* at that time. I was so impressionable. Now, I can't trust anything anyone tells me. Ever. There are some sources of authority, perhaps, but definitely not the media. In those days, I believed in Tarantino and his fresh way of storytelling—his fresh perspective. I think I wasn't caught up so much in the content of the movie as its presentation. Tarantino's passion, his energy. You just feel it. The teacher we talked about—Mr. McNair—same thing. We loved him because he was enthusiastic. I'm still drawn to that kind of enthusiasm.

EL: *Catcher in the Rye* is still the most important book for me. And it still changes, every time I read it. Never has been any other text I return to like that, except my art work. When I took a road trip on my own around the United States, I read all of Salinger's other work…he draws on the same contexts and people, which I find interesting. I was in New York recently and found myself in Central Park, thinking "Where is the carousel?" I wanted to do a Holden Caulfield tour.

DAVID: Holden Caulfield's New York.

EL: Exactly. When I was doing an independent study in art school, I went to Montreal and shot video of all the places Leonard Cohen hung out. When my friend Andrea went to school there, her class went to all the places mentioned in (Mordecai Richler's) *Duddy Kravitz*. That's what we need to do more of in schools. Nowadays, I don't read a lot of fiction. When I did my tour of the States I read and reread *A Picture of Dorian Gray*. That was significant for me. It's about morality, though, more than anything: The painting changes (his face) as he does things he shouldn't. It's still relevant. Usually, I read *The Guardian Weekly*. I want to do more reading about theory, like

David is now. I didn't pay a lot of attention to theory while I was in art school, and should have.

DAVID: When I was working in Canmore, something really hit me. It's about a larger text, I guess. It's a tourist town and I realized that people buy anything if you feed it to them properly. Eighty dollars for a t-shirt with a logo—insane. Now I make t-shirts on my own that send up corporate America, but I give them away as gifts. I know there is potential there for making money. But I can't do that to myself. John Berger's work really got me to understand how and why we look at each other, how we frame things, our gaze…men act, women appear, that sort of thing. When I put on those cultural studies glasses, well, I realized what we're immersed in. It wasn't a fish who discovered water. Even rereading the chapter you wrote about us, seeing Bourdieu's name, and now understanding, reading our pop culture articles, Adbusters, all that good material that keeps me interested, thinking.

EL: It's about being aware. Everything around us influences us. It wasn't until I traveled on my own—outside of Halifax without any support system—that I felt like I could really invent myself. I went to art school in part because Nic was going. Then, years later, when I broke up with another boyfriend, Keith, I didn't know what I'd buy at the fucking grocery store! I had not lived outside my parents' house long enough before I started dating him and having him influence my taste; that's a lot of the reason why we broke up. I can't live my life not knowing what I would do on my own, completely, by myself. That's why I think travel is important—like you did, David, going to Canmore for a couple of years. It allows us to invent ourselves outside of any context.

Rethinking Schools

EL: We're never really taught that saying yes to yourself is good. We're supposed to follow rules, what our parents want, what the school wants. We need to learn to find out what's best for us. Our associations restrict us, and we don't have a chance to figure out who we are. I'm my sister's sister, my parents' daughter, Stephen's girlfriend, and I play into those roles. I stay that way because people expect it of me. We need to encourage students to get outside school. They herd us into university right after school, and we have no time for reflection on what we might want to do with our lives. What we might study, if we might go at all? No one pushes trades or practical skills and we need people who know those things. Those are important jobs. We have a highly educated generation of people who went to university and can't get a fucking job: a B.F.A. means B.F.A.

DAVID: There is a big gap between what we learn in school and what we need in life. So much in life is trial and error. We could learn about credit, business, finances. Schools could teach more media literacy. I'd love to see a course in high school—"let's jam this billboard," that sort of thing. Creative ways of looking at the world. I don't think teenagers know, for example, that their music is completely constructed. The power that Disney has.

EL: Even in art school. When you're a practicing artist, a whole lot of it is about writing grant applications, getting a show ready, knowing how to be a business person for your own work. In art courses for our degree, we have great touchy-feely critiques, but we're not dealing with the nuts and bolts of getting your work out there. Skills like that are necessary. In high school, we teach skills but we don't allow kids to learn their applications. Math is useless for everyday. When Keith and I were in Mexico renting a car, he got out his calculator and did a parabola to figure out the best value. But he was a finance major.

DAVID: Shouldn't the everyday person know how to do that? Schools are teaching basically in the same way they did a hundred years ago. Nothing's really changed. And we're still teaching to produce doctors and lawyers, and to take one path and stay with it. My biggest concern in life is job security. People change jobs four, five different times or more in a life nowadays. Used to be a ladder, promotions, some kind of stability, having a pension. It's not like that now. I always feel I'm in a position where I have to sell out in order to survive.

Replay: Media as Text

EL: Horrific things are happening all the time everywhere. No one gives a shit about people dying of AIDS in Africa. It's not what's hip in the media nowadays. The media drives everything.

DAVID: When you think about the way we learn, though, no wonder we are all the same. We all read the same books, go to school, exposed to the same media events. We are only slightly different from one another. The media gets kids' attention more than parents do. Kids get more instruction from media than from teachers. Eight years ago, it was the same—I think I'm just more aware.

EL: I didn't watch as much TV when I was younger. It was always on in the house. I went into my room to draw or paint. Aside from *Kids in the Hall*, or *Saturday Night Live*, I never watched. Now I watch the news a lot because I'm much more interested in world events. I get angry at how political debate is covered, how they do "balanced" reporting but always show their political leanings. I'm almost addicted to watching it because I want to see what people are being told. It's important to be aware, so that I can formulate an opinion. I seek out other texts in my life that help me do that— newspapers, for example. So many people don't question what they watch. In fact, the media, as David said, is making the choice for us. Everything is presented in sound bytes, and black and white arguments. In terms of disasters, we're oversaturated with information, images, numbers—the death toll for the tsunami is rising, we see how horrific it is but we have no real sense or consequence of that, we're still here, whining…

DAVID: …in our own little worlds—Oh, I wish it didn't snow last night, or…

EL: Interviewing people from the comfort of their suburban couch makes me angry…people have no idea what reality is like. Or they're in their own safe reality.

DAVID: The media fascinates me. I know I could make money advertising, but I have an ethical problem with that. I could be Mr. Jingle Man, if I wanted, working for some radio station, making a hundred grand because I can alliterate—but I can't see myself pimping for the man. I'm angry about the way we are duped—who gets the voice, who gets left out, who gets represented and who doesn't. Whenever I'm watching TV I'm always studying, I'm not relaxing any more. I watch less than I ever have. I want to be in the industry, but I want to change it. When I was in high school, I watched everything. Unlike El, who just chose what she watched in high school, I was a passive watcher, into things like *Little House on the Prairie*, for God's sake, and *Saved by the Bell*. Now, who's speaking to me here? Half Pint? What does her life on the prairies have to do with me? I was just filling time. Escape, suspending reality. Out in Hubbards it was hard to have a social life like in the city, so a lot of times I just parked in front of the TV, and didn't think. A lot of bad things can happen when you don't think. At this point, I guess I can look at it as research—I pull out quotes now and then I can use—(laughs).

EL: The ads always do me in. I rent movies, or box sets of shows so I don't have to watch ads. The ads make me furious. I did an art piece about that in August—it was a video in which I had logged television ads for three months. Looking at the gender constructions in advertising—the women's products are always about a better face or better hair or cleaning the house, and men's are shaving and beer and they're always attached to virile sexuality. I'm shaving and then there's a hot chick right on me, or I'm having a beer and there's tits over there and tits over here. Women's beauty ads are all about I'm not sexy enough—so I have a hard time watching. They're absurd. The products and the wasteful attitudes we have. There's an ad about a disposable dish wipe. The soap is already in the dish wipe, you use it, and then you throw it away! And then she says "and there's plenty more where that came from." We are living in an unsustainable world. We're not making the association between our excess consumer habit—problem, addiction—with climate change and our environment failing.

DAVID: I'm free—I have a right to my SUV.

EL: Freedom becomes the right to choose from dozens of options. To me, freedom is having air to breathe, to be able to walk somewhere. We should be forced to use hybrid cars; someone should be forced to make them.

DAVID: People should be paying more at the pumps for starters.

EL: Go to Europe and try to buy gas. We like deals. We go to Wal-Mart so we can buy more stuff. The dollar store. Where did that come from? Whose back is that on? Nobody cares.

DAVID: We're appalled by the fact that Nike gets people in Asia to make their shoes. The person who just recently told me he was appalled by that is working at a call center. What are these call centers for? For big U.S. business in the U.S. They come in to the economically poorer places in the continent, lure people in with jobs—we live these contradictions. I do. I shop at Wal-Mart. I'm a student—I can't afford anything else.

EL: You can drive 500 miles every day and stay in the same hotels, eat the same meals, listen to the same station.

DAVID: A deejay I know came up to Reflections; he's a house legend from Chicago. Tommy, the owner of the bar, has $200.00 in his pocket, ready to take this guy out for a big seafood dinner, the downtown bars. No, no need to stop, this guys says, just take me to a Best Western and pick up a Big Mac meal on the way. Hey, no problem! $6.99. But think about it—in this culture we all stay in the same place and eat the same food. Cultural imperialism. It's safety.

EL: People are resistant to change right about now…we don't think we have to change, we won't give up our luxuries to save anybody else.

DAVID: The rest of the world doesn't expect to be happy, but we in Western society expect to be. A right to be happy. A tremendous amount of emphasis on the individual, rights, and free will.

Reality Bites

EL: It's hard to be able to live and keep your principles. I try to go to the grocery store and buy groceries without any plastic. Just try that. Fruits, vegetables. I remember in high school wanting to be an individual. Now I'm more interested in social issues, turning toward concern for one another.

DAVID: I wonder if what we had as youth was enthusiasm or ignorance? I'm taking a course in humor this year—let me tell you, nothing's funny anymore once you've analyzed it! Most of my sarcasm or general discontent or critical abilities come from the culture—take Michael Moore, his films are agenda-based, but he is also opening new perspectives on things. Or think of Noam Chomsky—in a democratic society we can't control what people do but we can control what they think. Manufacturing consent through images, texts, representations—the general effect is compliance. The older we get, the more we're aware. I still love learning, but things are more serious for me now.

EL: In art school, I was overwhelmed with what was possible, learning new skills; it was exciting to see what my peers and teachers were doing, what was happening internationally. Now, working at the gallery, very few students can get my attention with their work. I can't figure out where the change happened. Was it because I was so invested in the individuals behind the work when I was seeing it before? Knowing the creators? Was it that the quality was higher than it is now, or is it just that I am a lot more critical and not as involved with the student body? As I archive stuff, I find I can't remember what the work was. You also get so saturated with the imagery and with all the works and the magazines and whatever that you now only really get jazzed by something that's really exceptional. I'm more art literate now, I guess.

DAVID: Reminds me of that comment that knowledge kills curiosity…the earlier stuff, you were invested in, you were interested, and perhaps that suspends some kind of critical thought.

EL: People say that art school will teach the art right out of you because learning the history and contexts and technical information takes the enjoyment out. There's a split that happens in school: those who want to get into the critical side—contemporary thought, history; and then a whole other faction who just want to paint because they like it. And those are the people who get into a craft to support their art; keeps them doing the work without getting into the critical side of things. Art comes from a strictly personal place but it needs to transcend the personal. When you're in high school, you don't realize that. You think art is just about the expression and the creativity, not about the wider conversation. Now that's what's most important to me. The art I want to do is based in the populist—radio, video. I want to be able to talk to people in the medium that's most available to them. I want to have an expanded audience, not to be esoteric.

DAVID: Let's do this in another 10 years. Turn this into a reality program? (everyone laughs).

House Lights

This is a hermeneutic process—reading El and David, writing them, having El and David re-read themselves eight years later, talk about who they are now and what texts they engage with that shape or reconfirm their identity as young adults. Then—here, now—writing their words (condensed for this chapter, the essences remaining intact), and in so doing, reading what seems to be significant. Then, in a further act of interpretation, describing what I, as researcher and parent, see happening. What resonates for me, obviously, depends on what ideas and preoccupations are shaping my own reading of the world eight years later. Herakleitos was right—we can't step in the same river twice. Everything moves. There are no fixed meanings, and no answers. But there are points of illumination we cannot ignore. Rather than summarize what the conversations with El and David now and then "mean" (everything doesn't have to have a point, after all; it's only our Western desire for rationalist explanation that causes us to believe this), let me offer three among many connections I made as a researcher and educator. The reader of this chapter will, of course, have his or her own places of resonance.

- Desire is a form of seeking home—who we are in heart and mind. Reading and literacy are forms of desire. David and El's wish to be at home in the world (Neilsen, 1989) propelled them toward certain texts, texts that fed ontological desire: Who am I? Is this my identity? Is this how I write myself? That both of them first entered university influenced by peer group, familiar territory, and current love interest is not insignificant. These social factors and cultural offerings are texts as powerfully influential as any work of fiction. What do schools offer that incites desire in youth? What ways can schools be places where seeking home is encouraged?

- Literacy and reading are forms of inscribing ourselves into a landscape. As we move from beginner to apprentice to fully functioning reader (student, working adult), we develop a greater sense of agency: Yes, I can move this world. For El and David, participation in the art world and in cultural studies, respectively, years of induction into the landscape have made each of them more aware, more active, and more critically attuned to the field. El, in fact, sees the world from a feminist perspective. Each is critically aware—as Simone Weil says, "Looking is what saves us"—not only of their respective fields as texts, but of the world as larger text. The price for this awareness maybe the very idealism we, as educators, admire in the young. When does being aware and critical destroy the desire to move the world? When does critical awareness begin to destroy imagination?

- Schools have much work to do in Western culture, a culture that influences youth daily with films, television, video games, branding, and inscriptions into most everything we eat, drink, ride, read, or speak. We need to develop media literate readers and writers; but we need to accept the fact that schools are largely anachronistic and unwilling to accept the cultural texts that students engage with. We need to answer questions about relevance, engagement, social justice, and ways of knowing; we need to reduce our dependence on fundamentalism, intellectual safety, homogeneity, and control in reading—indeed, in all curricula. The terrible truth is that there is no single preferred reading of any text, no script that works for all, just as there are no basics and no magic formulae. There is only life, its complexities and insistent forces, and the love for learning and participating in the world we hope to continue to foster in youth.

Both El and David have become political activists in their own local, but significant ways—refusing plastic at the grocery store, resisting (and rewriting) labels on clothing, for example. Both feel trapped—wanting to pursue work they love, but knowing that to do so will compromise their principles. Each wants to resist being co-opted by corporate values, by American economic and political imperialism, by the thousand of little ethical compromises each of us makes when we do what we must do to live in the world as it is. Both these adults are playing for real now, trying to find place and balance: Cultural texts are juggernauts, and David and El invent their roles as they go, resisting, adapting, coming to a greater understanding both of their possibilities and their limitations (Neilsen, 1998a). It's bittersweet, this play, and as educators, we know it has had—and will continue to have—a long run. We live it ourselves.

References

Benet's reader's encyclopedia (3rd ed.). (1987). New York: Harper & Row.

Buckingham, D., & Sefton-Green, J. (1994). *Cultural studies goes to school*. London: Taylor & Francis.

Cherland, M. R., with Edelsky, C. (1993). Girls and reading: The desire for agency and the horror of helplessness in fictional encounters. In L. Christian-Smith, (Ed.), *Texts of desire: Essays on fiction, femininity and schooling* (pp. 28–44). London: Falmer Press.

Finders, M. (1996a). "Just girls": Literacy and allegiance in junior high school. *Written Communication, 13*, 93–129.

Finders, M. (1996b). Queens and teen zines: Early adolescent females reading their way toward adulthood. *Anthropology and Education Quarterly, 2*, 71–89.

Hoffman, E. (1989). *Lost in translation*. New York: Penguin.

Jenkins, H. (1992). *Textual poachers*. New York: Routledge.

Martin, M., & Porter, M. (1996). *Video movie guide 1996*. New York: Ballantine Books.

Neilsen, L. (2002). Learning from the liminal: Fiction as knowledge. *Alberta Journal of Educational Research, 48*, 206–214.

Neilsen, L. (1989). *Literacy and living*. Portsmouth, NH: Heinemann Educational Books.

Neilsen, L. (1998a). Exploring reading: Mapping the personal text. In *Knowing her place: Research literacies and feminist occasions* (pp. 63–85). San Francisco: Caddo Gap Press.

Neilsen, L. (1998b). Playing for real: Performative texts and adolescent identities. In D. Alvermann, K. Hinchman, D. Moore, S. Phelps, & D. Waff (Eds.), *Reconceputalizing the literacies in adolescents' lives* (1st ed., pp. 3–26). Mahwah, NJ: Lawrence Erlbaum Associates.

Neilsen Hellman, L. (1973). *Pentimento*. New York: Signet.

Rogers, A. G. (1993). Voice, play and a practice of ordinary courage in girls' and women's lives. *Harvard Educational Review, 63*(3), 265–295.

Rosenblatt, L. (1978). *The reader, the text, the poem: A transactional theory of the reading process*. Carbondale, IL: University of Illinois Press.

Salinger, J. D. (1951). *The catcher in the rye*. New York: Bantam.

Tarantino, Q. (1994). *Pulp fiction*. Miramax Films.

Weil, S. (2001). *Waiting for God*. New York: Harper Perennial.

2

BECOMING LIFE-LONG READERS

Insights from a Comic Book Reader

Stergios G. Botzakis

When literacy, for adolescents or otherwise, is discussed in typical U.S. educational policy, it is usually as a set of skills or knowledge to be acquired (e.g. Common Core State Standards Initiative, 2010). This study takes a different tack, building from the notion that reading is an activity not separate from but integrated and informative in people's lives. It has been remarked recently that the aims of education have been hijacked by accountability and assessment away from learning (Ravitch, 2010), and this study aims to draw attention back to those who engage in literacy and learning activities, not the curriculum or policies that can abstract their faces. If educators want to support adolescents in learning to read and write for the 21st century, it is time to look beyond the notion of basic skills culled from "fab five" lists, instructional pillars, essential keys, charter schools, or other magic bullets that offer singular solutions to the challenges educators and students face.

Educational research has long demonstrated literacy learning as a project requiring balanced and complex endeavors—a collection of small events, tasks, and concerns that must be attended to in order to support teachers and guide students to success (e.g. Street, 1984/1995). In this conception of learning, literacy is not a simple set of skills or a checklist of curricular items to cover but groups of people and the series of activities that shape and affect those who participate in them. This study, about one individual who reads comic books and what such reading offers those who engage in it regularly, is aimed toward rekindling the idea of literacy as a social practice by shedding light on what reading provides for those that read, lending insight into what is useful and meaningful about literacy for adolescents and anyone else involved in the educational enterprise.

Lives that Include Reading

As a "focal practice" (Sumara, 1996), reading is not simply an item added into people's lives. Reading rearranges their lives, and they become "involved in a life" (p. 9) that includes reading. Reading texts transforms people, places, and relationships; being a reader constitutes a different identity than being a non-reader, just as other activities might mark a person as a gardener, a dog-lover, or a dancer. With its palpable effects on people's lives, reading is an avenue for gathering ideas and using them as tools that could be incorporated into an "identity kit" (Gee, 1991, 1996). Reading has been variously described as involved in intellectual activity (Long, 2003) and physical sensation (Nell, 1988). These uses of reading have long been associated with the western idea of "mental discipline" where exercising and maintaining one's mind is regarded as important as doing the same with one's body (Tracey & Morrow, 2006). A common western notion about literacy is, as one participant remarked, "Reading anything, basically, is good for a person" (R. Antilles, Interview, April 12, 2004).

In *The Use of Pleasure*, Foucault (1985) described a history of particular western experiences by detailing how certain terms and practices have intermingled to create many commonsense notions, such as sexuality, insanity, or justice. He examined how the ideas of self-improvement and self-awareness have played out over time and become taken for granted. Although Foucault's (1985) work on the use of pleasure focused primarily on sexual practices, the practice of developing self-awareness and self-control through moderation has been incorporated into western discourses in many ways. Greco-Roman culture involved practicing "arts of existence" where people created "rules of conduct" and also sought "to transform themselves" into the best possible versions of themselves (Foucault, 1985, p. 10).

Accompanying these arts were the moral goals of trying to become self-aware while also changing the self into an "ethical subject" who would be the optimal citizen (Foucault, 1985, p. 28). These goals required that people "monitor, test, improve, and transform" themselves (p. 28) much in the same way that more recent practices of democracy have espoused (New London Group, 1996; Tyner, 1998). Key within these "arts of existence" was the practice of moderation; maintaining a mastery of one's appetites and pleasures was especially important so that a person would not get carried away and become unproductive but would "rule the desires and the pleasures" in their lives (Foucault, 1985, p. 70).

Foucault's arts of existence have been taken up by other scholars studying language and social phenomena. Gee (1991, 1996) expanded on how Discourses acted as sets of rules that linked language, institutions, and social relationships and how these rules allowed for individuals to enact particular identities. In his conception, "identity kits" included the functions that social institutions played in constructing what counted as literacy as well as in affecting how people spoke, wrote, and took on social roles. Such Discourses were not quickly assumed however; they could not simply be learned. Rather, they came to be formed by the process of acquisition, "a process of acquiring something (usually subconsciously) by exposure to models, a process of trial and error, and practice within social groups, without formal teaching" (Gee, 1996, p. 138). The acquisition of a primary discourse took place from a very early age and continued over time. By extension, "learning to read [was] always learning some aspect of some discourse" (Gee 1991, p. 6), and literate activity was very much bundled up in identity.

Reading books for pleasure and self-improvement has become one of the social practices closely associated with the arts of existence and identity development (Farr, 2004; Long, 2003; Nell, 1988). Furthermore, many thinkers and writers have delineated what should count as meaningful and productive reading material for legitimate reading purposes (Hirsh, 1988; Plato, 390 BCE; Rooney, 2005). The concepts of acquisition (Gee, 1996) and arts of existence (Foucault, 1985) relied on such hierarchical power relations. Acquisition was the process of developing a primary discourse, one that would be in a sense more central and dominant in a person's life. Arts of existence also involved decisions made about what constituted the best way to lead a live; such a course of action required that choices be made about which practices and beliefs were to be favored over others. Competing discourses created unequal situations: Non-dominant groups had to figure out ways to exist with dominant cultural situations, and sometimes these situations required appropriating features of the Dominant Discourse.

Because their reading preferences were typically shunned, comic book readers practiced arts of existence that allowed them to navigate such an unequal social situation. R. Antilles's (Interview, April 12, 2004) statement about the "good" in reading linked up with the idea of reading as a worthwhile, self-improving activity but in a more generically inclusive way that subverts typical tastes and hierarchies of worth (Fiske, 1989; Long, 2003; Rooney, 2005). His words pointed to how individuals had the ability to transform social frameworks to work to their advantage; they could act tactically (de Certeau, 1984).

Reading and the Practices of Everyday Life

In my analysis of how comic book readers dealt with this situation and performed their arts of existence, I found the work of de Certeau (1984) most informative. He delineated "practices of everyday life" using metaphors of conflict that drew on Marxist views that there were two forces at work, one "powerful" and one "weak," much like the bourgeoisie and proletariat. In this view, the powerful controlled the means of production; they tried to get the weak to go along with their views. They practiced "strategies." That is, the powerful disciplined the weak in a Foucauldian sense (Foucault, 1979). They tried to inculcate into the weak that the system was right and true, that this was the only way to live a life, and that the existing power structures were justified, natural, and decreed.

However, the weak were not powerless in this hegemonic environment. They had recourse to the strategies of the powerful in the form of "tactics" of their own. Recognizing that people could be "sly as a fox and twice as quick," de Certeau (1984) spoke of how people "made do" (p. 29) with limited resources or spaces. People could have been given spaces in which to live, work, and play but still subvert the prevailing culture. Students in school sat and appeared docile but were engaged in passing notes or in defacing textbooks or desks; office workers appeared busy but took company time to write personal letters or to take company materials such as paper and use them for non-work purposes. Various social groups engaged in tactics when they used spaces for purposes other than those for which they were designed.

De Certeau (1984) identified reading as a tactic and likened it to a form of poaching. He explained that "readers are travelers; they move across lands belonging to someone else, like nomads poaching their way across fields they did not write" (p. 174). Texts were tools for readers' use in this conception. Words on pages were not simply the province of the author. Readers were not just the simple recipients of the transformative material from texts; they had agency to act on their own behalf, using texts (or not) in the course of their lives. As will be discussed below, comic book readers acted as poachers when they chose to read and use texts for various purposes in their lives. Moreover, they acted tactically when they did this with texts that were often regarded as the "lowest level" of contemporary fiction (Rooney, 2005, p. 18).

With the relationship of strategies and tactics wherein non-dominant groups had to develop their own practices to get by, de Certeau's (1984) work forecasted Gee's (1991, 1996) "primary discourses." The literacy practices in one's primary discourse could lead to difficulties if those practices were not consistent with reading practices performed in formal school settings. Such a disconnect would require learners to take up other discursive practices. Whereas de Certeau (1984) called such activities "making do" or poaching, Gee (1996) used "mushfaking," a prison term meaning "to make do with something less when the real thing is not available" (p. 147). By mushfaking a Discourse, Gee meant that members of non-dominant social groups assumed some of the outward qualities of the Dominant Discourse, while retaining their primary Discourses as well.

Reading practices have occurred in a number of contexts and situations, and reading has been described as a solitary act or a withdrawal from social activity (Street, 1995, 2003). In one of the few research projects focusing on pleasure reading, Nell (1988) studied the psychology of pleasure reading by interviewing hundreds of people individually and in groups, conducting laboratory experiments, and gathering survey responses. He used the term *ludic readers* to describe his participants, emphasizing the Latin root *ludo* (I play) to highlight that the type of reading he was studying was primarily a play activity that people engaged in for its own sake. Ludic readers read at least one book a week and were frequent purveyors of "trash" such as westerns, fantasy, or romance novels (Nell, 1988, p. 5).

Comic book readers who have long kept up their reading habits on a daily or weekly basis fit Nell's definition of ludic readers. Additionally, he classified ludic readers into two types: type A, who read to escape reality; and type B, who read to reflect on their own lives.

In his laboratory studies, Nell (1988) attached nodes to monitor physical features such as heart rates and facial expressions of ludic readers who were engaged in reading extended texts. He found that ludic readers went into a state resembling a trance or a dream and also that they experienced moments of physical arousal when heart rates rose or facial muscles twitched into slight smiles or frowns. He equated ludic readers' experiences with drug or alcohol highs, mystical experiences, or meditative states. What all of these states have in common was what Nell (1988) called *alternate states of consciousness*. For these participants, reading provided easy access to a highly sought after consciousness experience. This study provided insight into the physical outcomes that readers poached from their interactions with texts.

I highlighted Nell's (1988) study because it demonstrated how literacy was simultaneously consumptive and productive. Institutions and discourses acted upon people in terms of setting up rules and values that affected behavior (Foucault, 1979; Gee, 1991, 1996), but individuals still were able to find spaces to gain advantages amidst social constrains and create their own rules of behavior (de Certeau, 1984; Fiske, 1989). Although institutional discourses, which de Certeau (1984) termed strategies, delimited and affected people's social actions, they did not totally dictate practice. The ludic readers Nell described took up the idea that reading was helpful in bettering one's mind, but they also practiced reading in individual ways for individual purposes, whether as an escape, a means of accessing a physical sensation, or a lens for reflection on themselves or the world. Their reading practices were a combination of global and local considerations and situations. I used a notion that literacy practices both engaged people and allowed them to engage in their worlds in a variety of ways to frame this study of comic book readers.

My Research Framework

My study focused on lifelong reading practices, so I sought out comic book readers who had engaged in reading a particular genre over a large portion of their lives. I gathered participants using a combination of purposeful sampling and snowballing (Patton, 2002), recruiting customers and their acquaintances from two local comic book stores.

Like many qualitative research projects, my data collection centered on interviews, field notes, a researcher's log, and artifacts (postcards, comic book images, written notes). I planned an interview cycle consisting of three components: two individual sessions and one focus group. Initially, participants took part in a one-hour interview with me. After transcribing those interviews and asking

participants to check over their interview transcripts, I planned for each participant to take part in a focus group interview. Finally, there was a third individual
interview with each participant where they commented on the research process
as well as the written reports I had generated. I transcribed these interviews, and
integrated their comments into my reports.

Aaron, My Focal Participant

Although I collected data from twelve participants, I focus here on one case,
Aaron (a pseudonym). I chose him in particular because he described a large
number, though not the largest among participants, of functions for reading in his
life, many of which were echoed by other participants in the course of their
interviews. By focusing on one particular participant, I can show more instances
of how reading was involved in a life and how reading practices shifted over time,
from childhood to adolescence to adulthood.

Aaron was about to begin completing his undergraduate degree in cultural
anthropology at the time of our initial interview. He described himself as a
36-year-old, white, married male, and he was also a father. In the past he had
worked as a web designer and as a cook. He described himself as being a relatively poor student growing up, but he had found success more recently as he
returned to school to complete his undergraduate degree. Aaron's interests
included watching Asian movies, playing role-playing games, playing computer
games, reading, cooking, and playing with his child. Aaron's reading interests
ranged across a number of texts, including magazines, *manga*, online comic
books, fiction, histories, science and anthropology books, and role-playing
game books.

Data Analysis using Meaning Interpretation

I analyzed Aaron's interview data using the meaning interpretation method,
where the researcher worked from a distance created by taking a "theoretical
stance, recontextualizing what [was] said in a specific conceptual context" (Kvale,
1996, p. 201). Put differently, the researcher made connections between the
contexts of the language of the interview and the contexts of theories in order to
create interpretations and different kinds of meaning. Meaning interpretation was
an additive exercise where researchers looked at "statements within broader
frames of reference. The context for interpretation of a statement may, for example, be provided by the entire interview or by a theory" (p. 193). This research
project was an example of poaching where I took ideas, theories, and practices
from the variety of texts—including data sources and theoretical writings—and
used them to analyze the statements in an interview. Using discursive practices
such as arts of existence (Foucault, 1985) and strategies and tactics (de Certeau,
1984), I connected literacy theories to Aaron's reading practices.

My analyses used the theories of Foucault and de Certeau as touchstones, but not in the "deeper" interpretations that Kvale (1996) mentioned. The theories of Foucault (1972) and de Certeau (1984) did not make reference to deep meanings but were more related to surfaces. My theoretical framework relied on the functionality of discourse (Bové, 1995), and not on essences or innate meanings to be found in language, and my analyses reflected Aaron's practices, not the reasons behind them. The purpose of my analyses was to describe how a comic book reader was a tactical poacher (de Certeau 1984) as he read.

Meaning interpretation (Kvale, 1996) resembled discourse analysis as defined by Gee, in that it was bound up in "what we [meant] and how others [interpreted] us" (Gee 2005, p. xii). Discourse analysis here hinged on the performative definition of discourse as "what people [were] doing with their talk or writing, what they [were] trying to achieve" (Burr 1995, p. 47). Discourse came from social realms and was linked to language and social activity. I enacted meaning interpretation as a kind of discourse analysis that used the theories of Foucault and de Certeau to examine Aaron's utterances. The purpose of my analyses was to explore the identities Aaron enacted through language, the connections he made via language, how the language he used privileged specific sign systems, and also how language worked when it was put into action.

An "Omnivorous" Reader

INTERVIEWER: How would you describe yourself as a reader?

AARON: Omnivorous, I guess.

INTERVIEWER: What does that mean?

AARON: I read lots of things. I'm always, I always have a book that I'm reading. I read lots of different kinds of things. I read a little bit of fiction, a little bit of history, science, some anthropology, lots of RPG [role playing games] books, magazines. (A. Burr, Interview, December 12, 2005)

From the onset, Aaron took up a particular discourse when speaking about his reading by using the word omnivorous. Omnivorous is a scientific term, typically used by biologists or zoologists to describe the eating habits of animals. An omnivore is a type of animal that eats a variety of food, a combination of plants and meat. By using this technical term, Aaron created a context where he set himself up as an expert, a knowledgeable person who used specialized vocabulary. This term pointed to a tactic he used when discussing popular culture texts; he melded the use of technical language and popular culture language to create a situation where both were of equal value.

Saying that he always had some text he was reading, Aaron likened reading to any activity that he engaged in as a matter of course, because he needed it for some purpose in his life, just as he needed to eat on a regular basis. He very clearly positioned himself as a consumer of books, but, as Fiske (1989) has noted, a consumer is not solely passive. Being omnivorous pointed to the great variety Aaron had in his diet of reading material, which he indicated as ranging from pleasure reading in various forms, to reading for a specific activity, to play role-playing games, to more formal scholarly works of science, history, and anthropology. Bundled within Aaron's descriptions of his preferred reading materials were a variety of functions reading served for him. In many ways, how he described reading throughout his life resembled de Certeau's (1984) conception of poaching, a practice of taking from a text only what was useful to the reader and where authorial intention fell by the wayside. What mattered more was not the content of texts but how readers took up and used that content to suit their own purposes. Depending on the context, Aaron found different uses for texts. He described the functions reading served for him in more depth throughout our interviews.

Reading's Different Functions for Aaron

Aaron talked about how at various points in his life he used reading for different purposes. Although he did not make the explicit connection, he talked about his life in some ways resembling Foucault's (1985) "arts of existence" in that he sought to find the best ways to function in the world. "Arts of existence" were bound up in the discursive practices that shaped a person's identity, the behaviors that were chosen to enact to be a certain type of person. Reading in particular was an activity that Aaron used to perform his various roles better. The particular purposes of those "arts of existence" necessarily shifted over time as Aaron took on different social roles. The shifts from child to student to worker to parent to university student were accompanied by different sets of behaviors and expectations. One constant across these shifting roles was reading. Aaron described himself as a lifelong reader; some of his earliest memories were of his father reading to him. However, the role of reading "has come to mean something very different" for him than it did ten or fifteen years ago (A. Burr, Interview, December 12, 2005). The following are some of the various functions of reading described by Aaron.

Inspiration

When asked what he got from reading comic books, Aaron responded,

> Mostly distraction. Occasionally inspiration. Like, *Transmetropolitan* is very inspiring. When I am done reading it, I just want to start a blog that comments ferociously on government or media or something like that. I mean, I guess there's, I guess inspiration. Worse case it's just some good times or some fodder to chat with other people about or game fodder.
>
> *(A. Burr, Interview, December 12, 2005)*

Transmetropolitan was a series of futuristic stories published by DC Comics from 1997 until 2002. Aaron described *Transmetropolitan* as "Hunter S. Thompson in a transhumanist setting." The lead character, Spider Jerusalem, was a gonzo journalist in a cyberpunk world where grafting multiple body parts and technology together was a norm. One storyline followed the outcomes from a presidential election, and the storylines in general had libertarian political overtones. This reading experience appeared to be an instance where fantasy materials often seen as inferior to "high culture" were incorporated into a life meaningfully, in ways that mirrored the reflections and explorations of book club members (Long, 2003), literature readers (Sumara, 1996), and *ludic* readers (Nell, 1988). It offered Aaron an opportunity for reflection on the political world, analysis of plot, characters, and symbolism, and a temporary diversion.

Chabon described that this incorporation worked because readers were "quite adept at taking the crappy material of the world-retailers and cobbling together, syncretizing them into something authentic and good" (in Jones, 2002, p. 229). Jones (2002) spoke of how "every successful children's action fantasy, like Pokémon, like Superman, [was] also an *organizing fantasy*" (p. 223) that played a role in helping them make sense of their world. He saw the need for children to become interested in different fantasies as they grew older to suit their changing needs. Aaron's reading of *Transmetropolitan* was described in a way that pointed to how that narrative became enmeshed in Aaron's political views, and how a fantasy world became infused with happenings in his lifeworld.

Aaron used the inspiration he got from pleasure reading in other ways as well. It was "fodder" for various types of personal interaction, from idle discussions to more creative moments of game playing. Aaron described how comic book stories sometimes "would be entirely their own inspirations for games, for the feeling of a game. Sometimes characters. Sometimes [he]'ll steal a character entirely for a game, especially superheroes" (A. Burr, Interview, December 12, 2006). His "stealing" was an unequivocal example of poaching (de Certeau, 1984). The characters and settings of some stories offered him the materials for creating a different environment, one adapted from the intended original, where he and his peers could engage in social activities and creative story telling. He used comic books as raw materials just as many of the fans used various media texts to create their own individualized texts (Jenkins, 1992). At other times in his life, Aaron described using texts for another purpose, as shelters.

A Hiding Place

Aaron's reading tastes as a child revolved around fantasy and science fiction texts, and he mentioned especially being a fan of the X-Men, Spider-Man, and Alpha Flight, superhero comic books published by Marvel Comics. As he got older, he became more engrossed in novels, particularly Tolkien's *Lord of the Rings* books.

He described being introduced to comic books around the age of 8, but he also said that he was 12 when he "started always having a book around to read" (A. Burr, Interview, December 12, 2006). As a child, Aaron said that "the person that I was then was the person that needed the safe place, the fantasy to hide in" (A. Burr, Interview, December 12, 2005). He indicated here that the type of reading he was engaged in then was a necessity; he said that it was something he "needed." Reading as a sanctuary was a much different conception of an activity that many other students, particularly those who were limited in their ability to read, have found to be threatening, frightening and something to avoid (Lee & Jackson, 1991). His familiarity and comfort level with reading caused it to be something reliable, even protective for him. As he stated when I asked him what role reading played for him, "when I was reading a whole lot, it was my escape, my protection place" (A. Burr, Interview, December 12, 2005). At a negative point in Aaron's life, as he transitioned from private to public school, reading served a protective function. In the present, Aaron noted that he could have chosen different options instead of retreating into books, such as seeking out different social relationships, but that he was unaware of alternative options at the time.

When I asked him what he was hiding from, he responded that "I was a geeky sensitive boy going to a public elementary school and a public high school. Hiding from social pain [Laughs], that was probably it. Hiding from failures, social failures, academic failures, hiding from academic failures, hiding from arguments with my family" (A. Burr, Interview, December 12, 2005). In this description, reading for him resembled Nell's (1988) Type A reader who used reading as a refuge from the world. In this sense, reading was not merely a solipsistic act of withdrawal but a coping mechanism that provided Aaron with something to help him navigate his social world; reading was a remedy for various hurts. Aaron used it medicinally to alleviate the "pains" that he associated with school, his peers, and his family situation. Time spent reading was a respite from social realities that troubled him. Tactically speaking, reading fantasy material helped Aaron reposition himself from being the "geeky sensitive boy." Reading took him to a realm where he had more control over situations, and that control allowed him to explore issues of social behavior and masculinity. While he was reading, he was not the same boy he had been in other contexts. Although he described himself as more confident and self-aware as an adult, Aaron still spoke of taking some respite through reading.

Popcorn

Even though he did not required as much protection in the past 10 to 15 years, Aaron did describe another way in which he still used reading as a reprieve from other activities and situations. Periodically he engaged in reading particular texts, including comic books, as a combination of entertainment and relaxation.

In describing his current reading habits, he looked ahead to his return to college coursework stating that "because a large chunk of my cognitive power is going to be taken up by reading the stuff for school, and I will just need my entertainment, my popcorn" (A. Burr, Interview, December 12, 2005). No longer seeking as much refuge from social pains, Aaron has shifted to using reading as a shelter from the mental taxation of his coursework. Reading comic books was described as a comfort food that was light, fluffy, and mostly devoid of substance.

Aaron likened the activity of reading for pleasure to television watching. "We don't really watch a lot of TV," he stated, "so the reading popcorn fills the same role" (A. Burr, Interview, December 12, 2005). Comic books were particularly attractive to him as diversions "because they're fun. They almost entirely fall into the popcorn. They are purely entertainment, they're mindless fun mostly" (A. Burr, Interview, December 12, 2005). Despite the figure of a vacuous practice, popcorn was not merely an empty filler; reading texts like comic books created the context for an alternate state of consciousness. Even though he called popcorn reading "mindless," Aaron also talked about how it occasionally sparked his thoughts in productive ways. It wasn't so much that he wasn't thinking while reading; it seemed rather he was thinking differently. Occasionally going into this alternate state of thinking helped him deal with other, more taxing activities and roles. Consuming popcorn was part of Aaron's regimen in maintaining his productive everyday practices.

Consumer and Consumed: The Comic Book Habit

In Aaron's descriptions of how he has used reading, he positioned himself at times being as much the consumed as the consumer. This consumerism came up particularly when he spoke about beginning to read comic books.

INTERVIEWER: Do you remember when you started reading comic books?

AARON: I remember being a kid, 10, 8, 10, 12 years old, and being visiting my mom's mom in Baton Rouge and going to the dime store and she buying me a couple of comics books. I wasn't "reading" reading comic books then. I wasn't collecting them. I didn't start my habit until I was in high school, when I had some money coming in on my own that I was buying them. I got pretty scary. I had a "habit" habit.

INTERVIEWER: You were buying tons and tons of them?

AARON: Yeah. Thirty bucks a week kind of thing. And this was back in the '80s. Thirty bucks a week was serious. [Laughs] Comics were…even the expensive ones only cost $1.75 back then.

INTERVIEWER: That's impressive.

AARON: That was scary. I quit when I went to college.

INTERVIEWER: Why did you quit?

AARON: Because I didn't have any money.

Reading and buying comic books became a habit for him. Aaron at one point felt the need to buy a lot of comic books and he spent a good deal of money on his habit. Part of his experience as a reader was linked to economic concerns. He had to support himself independently in terms of money, so he learned to prioritize products differently.

The term "habit" called to mind Nell's (1988) conception of reading as an addiction. Aaron's habit was an addiction to obtaining and consuming comic books, texts that he read in order to escape into different states of mind. In his usage of the term, the habit seemed pathological. Buying comic books precluded him from getting other things; it was a consuming drive. In using these texts to hide from particular happenings in his environment, Aaron ran the risk of becoming too disconnected from social situations. Being addicted to a particular kind of text has resulted in certain stereotypes about fans being divorced from reality to the point of being socially inept. Instead of leading to a broad disconnect between his personal predilections and his public functioning, Aaron's experiences with his comic book habit were a learning experience in dealing with finances. Eventually, he forewent buying comic books in order to buy other items. His needs for these texts were diminished, although he described still continuing to peruse comic books that his roommate owned. In his present circumstances as spouse, parent, and student, Aaron described buying a very limited amount of comic books, typically preferring *manga*, graphic novels, and trade paperbacks. He still read individual comic books by downloading scanned copies from the Internet. Aaron has learned to put other concerns ahead of his comic book habit. Instead of using reading as a retreat, he has moved more into a place where he was able to use his pleasure reading as a balance to his various taxing responsibilities. He still "poached" certain value from reading to help him in his everyday life (de Certeau, 1984). His reading, instead of being a habit, was more a salve that enabled him to use more energy in other avenues. One of these avenues involved learning about the world around him.

Teacher

Looking forward to completing his undergraduate degree and moving into graduate work, Aaron foresaw an opportunity to link his in- and out-of-school reading behaviors.

> I fully expect, when I go back into school actually, I 100% expect if I study what I want to be studying, cultural anthropology, in grad school, that comic books will be [included in my academic reading], because one of the things I am interested in is how we view Japan. And basically what people I know know about Japan, we know about Japan from *manga*, *anime* and movies. Pop culture, that's what we know. I've read a few novels, and maybe a few other people have read novels, but really we don't know

much else about, I mean, that's how we know about Japan, the culture, about how people live. But that's something I want to study is how, I'm learning this thing, I'm learning about Chinese culture that way, or expatriate Chinese culture, because almost all of the things, the comics, the movies, and the novels that I am reading now are from post-1949 China. So they are from Taiwan and Hong Kong and Singapore and they are from places where the Chinese who did not become the communist Chinese went to live.

(A. Burr, Interview, December 12, 2005)

Aaron attributed reading in a variety of contexts as a large part of his learning.

In describing his past reading practices, Aaron said that, "When I was reading a whole lot, it was my escape, my protection place," but more recently he added, "It plays the role of, I guess, teacher maybe, mostly now" (A. Burr, Interview, December 12, 2005). His description pointed to a more authoritative role of texts, and the learning he described took place both inside and outside of school contexts. "I kind of read where my interests are going," Aaron told me, explaining that on his own he studied Japanese and Chinese cultures through reading *manga*, watching *anime* and kung fu films, and studying historical and anthropological works as well as novels from and about those countries. His conceptions of reading and texts dovetailed with those of Jenkins's (1992) views about media texts in that a number of different media types were conflated. For Aaron, reading was described as an intertextual activity, involving a variety of texts and a variety of media. Reading was intertwined with a number of other often educational activities; it was part of a larger conglomeration of information, media, behaviors, and pastimes.

Within this student/teacher conception of reader/text, Aaron displayed an awareness of a number of roles. "Now [being a reader's] much more, it's just part of how I process information, how I gather information, and actually even in reading things how I expel information or regurgitate information or meld different pieces of information" (A. Burr, Interview, December 12, 2005). A reader entailed a number of different activities, combinations of being reception, creative, and connective. Being a lifelong reader was akin to being a student who has a number of activities to perform, and outcomes shaped textual interactions. Sometimes, he found it necessary to absorb and expel texts for papers and exams, but there was also a component of integrating texts together into a larger body of knowledge; Aaron described this type of reading as taking up "a large chunk of [his] cognitive power" (A. Burr, Interview, December 12, 2005).

Reading was also an opportunity for him to usurp the authority of texts to gain his own version of authority in a community of scholars. Aaron described his reading as research that contributed to his perceived role as an anthropologist. He used what could be considered frivolous, popular culture readings to construct an identity as an intellectual authority, one that conversed in a circle of peers.

Aaron wasn't simply reading comic books and watching movies; he was studying and analyzing cultures. He was an unaccredited academic, a consumer of texts who bended them to his purposes. Aaron had a name for such experts: geeks.

Geek Behavior

> I guess, I define, there are different kinds of geeks. But a kind of catch-all, somebody who might show up at Dragoncon. A fanboy about something that is not mainstream. Like, you know they put on television shows that make money for the companies. *Buffy* [*the Vampire Slayer*] would be a great example. That lots of people don't watch, but if you watch *Buffy* you're a geek. That's how I define it. A geek would be somebody who likes something a whole lot and is kind of unashamed about liking it, but it's not something that would be brought up at any party. At a party you could talk about it with another geek, even if it's not something, if it's something you don't like.
>
> *(A. Burr, Interview, December 12, 2005)*

Implied within Aaron's description of geeks was an element that shame was involved. Part of what could be considered shameful was acting like a "fanboy," a kind of naively devoted fan (Pustz, 1999). The activities and affections that these fans show can seem childish or immature, as if they were not developed. In Aaron's terms, being a fanboy was not something that one made public; it was not information that would be offered up willingly in a social gathering such as a casual party. Paradoxically, however, Aaron also mentioned how geeks somehow found each other in these settings and how the common experience of being a fan, regardless of the object of interest, created a social bond.

Aaron's definition of geek implied being a marginal type of fan. Being a reader, then, was tied into geek behavior where people exercise their popular culture choices (Fiske, 1989). He referenced Dragoncon, a science fiction/fantasy convention annually held in Atlanta. Dragoncon has attracted a variety of fan groups including comic book readers, science fiction aficionados, role game players, fantasy fans, movie buffs, and bondage fetishists among others. Many fans come dressed up as characters; actors and actresses from TV and movies come to speak and sign autographs, and vendors come selling specialty items from toys to rare DVDs to foam weapons to arcane jewelry and costumes. Dragoncon has been a general gathering place for a number of different fan groups. Many of the behaviors Jenkins (1992) described in his work on fans, including singing, sharing fan fiction, and engaging in discussion panels, occurred at Dragoncon. It was a type of party where geeks could unabashedly share their fandom.

Part of the attraction of Dragoncon, and of speaking with other geeks, was in the great crossover Aaron observed in geeks. Jenkins (1992) also observed this crossover when he noted that being a particular fan did not define someone completely because fans engaged in multiple texts and did not merely pigeonhole themselves. As Aaron put it, "when you hang out with gamers, you can pretty much guarantee that they've all read *Lord of the Rings*, they all keep on some comics, and they've all seen *Star Wars* and the *Matrix*" (A. Burr, Interview, December 12, 2005). Being a geek, according to Aaron, involved a certain amount of connoisseurship and common knowledge. This description of being a geek was the result of a process of acquisition much in the same way Gee (1996) described people acquiring secondary discourses. This acquisition also led to developing *intensive* and *extensive* knowledge that Gee described as being features of *affinity groups*, people involved in a common endeavor (Gee, 2003, p. 192). Members of affinity groups engaged in similar activities and behaviors that marked each other as "insiders" (Gee 2003, p. 27). Aaron spoke about how this process of acquisition sometimes was taken too far.

"There's a movement in the RPGs, in the RPG realm, circles, to discuss RPGs in an academic way. And I think that it, it almost saddens me to see people do that" (A. Burr, Interview, December 12, 2005). Being a geek was likened to being a type of scholar, but not totally equated with legitimate scholarship. He saw taking something like role playing too seriously as sad because it attributed too much status to a slight practice. He used the example of the professor who invented the field of "Hitler studies" in DeLillo's (1985) novel *White noise*. Aaron spoke about how that "joke realm of study" was taken too seriously in the novel and unnecessarily elevated as scholarship. The manner in which some academics studied and spoke about RPGs reflected the pomposity played out in the novel. According to Aaron, it seemed like "geeks trying to make themselves socially acceptable" at his proverbial party.

Staying true to his definition of geek, Aaron added that "I don't think there's any reason we have to make ourselves acceptable. We're socially acceptable within our society." Geeks, in other words, were invited to the party; they were not crashing it. There was no need for shame within this society, as it was not limited to a particular group of fans. The presence of multiple fans meant that geeks were "our little society, but I mean it's all over the place." In other words, there were multiple types of geeks at the party. He spoke of fan groups almost like parallel discourses that operated throughout social worlds (Gee, 1991, 1996). Geeks were like academics except that they were experts of disreputable knowledge. Hills (2002) made a similar link in his exploration of fan groups when he observed that academic analyses of readers and fan cultures revealed "cloaked versions" (p. 54) of academic researchers themselves. Different iterations of "geek" existed in multiple contexts in western culture. The major difference between them was the particular status in the type of knowledge each was expert. Geek has also entered into common parlance in similar terms as a kind of expert, particularly in relation to technology (Best Buy's "Geek Squad" advertising campaign was one example of this usage). Being a certain kind of geek, for example a computer programmer or a college professor, actually had social benefits.

However, using Aaron's examples, it was generally more socially acceptable to be an anthropologist of Asian cultures than it was to be an expert in RPGs.

What Aaron's Accounts Tell Teachers and Researchers

As an omnivorous reader, Aaron consumed a great variety of texts. His consumption had a number of functions for him, including inspiration for thought and action, fodder for personal interactions, popcorn to relax with, a teacher to relay him knowledge, and a habit that he had to learn to deal with. He took up various types of knowledge from texts in a way that de Certeau (1984) might have called poaching. He used *manga*, movies, magazines, and comic books to inform himself about other cultures, an endeavor that frequently led him to further research. Most of his inquiry took place outside of school, and only recently has Aaron incorporated his interests into a formal school environment, as he reported in our follow-up interview along with the news that he had achieved straight As for the first time ever in the first semester of his work in cultural anthropology (A. Burr, Interview, May 24, 2006). In addition to artifacts, he also used texts as shelters, reprieves, and fodder for social interactions as well as RPGs. Aaron likened his actions not to being a poacher but a geek, someone whose specialized knowledge helped him to function in certain social arenas. I likened Aaron's becoming a geek to Gee's notion of acquiring a discourse or joining an affinity group (Gee, 1991, 1996, 2003). Both Aaron and Gee spoke to how reading provided the materials, tools, and fodder for crafting a certain way of living. In this manner, being a geek resembled poaching materials (de Certeau, 1984) and tools for an identity kit (Gee, 1991, 1996). Reading gave Aaron a certain cache; it was an intimate part of his social context. It was through reading that Aaron gained expertise to work to his advantage; reading was his invitation to the party.

Poaching and School

Education research has suggested that regular and frequent engagement in reading has positive effects on learning and scholastic performance (Allington, 2006; Brozo, 2002; Schwanenflugel, Hamilton, Kuhn, & Stahl, 2004), but for Aaron being an able and involved reader did not always equate to school success. As a student, Aaron had experienced a number of academic failures even though he was an avid and involved reader. His abilities and expertise did not appear in the school environment, but reading did pay off in other arenas. Reading made it possible for him to cope with traumatic or troubling situations, to examine himself and his life. Additionally, he gained expertise and knowledge that he eventually incorporated into social activities. Nevertheless, Aaron's accounts do provide insights for educators.

Aaron's accounts speak to the potential for using a wide range of texts for various purposes in schools, even texts otherwise not recognized as academic.

His use of texts showed how they could affect multiple aspects of his life, and it would behoove schools to seek out ways to make such social connections with their students, beginning with the use of texts that could invite positive interactions. Aaron said that part of the reason for the disparity between the uses of reading in- and out-of-school was that his interests often were not recognized in school, and the set curricula were an unattractive alternative. Poaching was an exercise in using advantages, and if education did not seem particularly attractive or advantageous, even a skilled and able reader did not use his abilities to achieve school success. Having access to diverse texts and textual activities may have attracted his attention and activity earlier, and perhaps he might not have been so disengaged in school work.

The allure of good grades and school success does not motivate all readers. Aaron did not read simply for understanding or to do well on assessments; he read for his own purposes, whether to occupy his mind, to reflect on his life, to hide, to find material for his games, or to learn about his interests. The practice of poaching (de Certeau, 1984) shifted the centrality of institutions toward a greater role of the agency of individuals; people's concerns and actions became as important as those of the institutions, including churches, governments, and schools. Institutions like schools might have shaped conceptions of literacy as amassing knowledge and gaining expertise, but Aaron took those practices and transferred them to other spaces, using alternate texts to find meaning and demonstrating their knowledge and abilities outside of academic circles.

School's effects may not be seen until much later in life. For Aaron, school was not the be-all, end-all, and he sought success and validation in other places. However, schools and other social institutions influence people's interactions with texts, and in part Aaron reflects those global influences. When he read to find meaning or do research, he was taking part in mental exercises that have been valorized by various institutions for millennia as being part of a balanced "arts of existence" (Foucault, 1985) in the western world. Aaron was hardly a "renegade" (Worthy, 1998) when he engaged in reading to keep his mind active, to reflect on his life, and to amass knowledge. All of these behaviors have been part of what constituted a traditional conception of a life lived well that has been promoted by institutions such as governments, churches, and schools for thousands of years in the West. He just chose to undertake these behaviors using popular culture texts.

Poaching and Literacy Research

Aaron's accounts demonstrated how reading was as much bound up in social application and relationships as it was in skills and strategies. Contrary to much literacy research, school was not always at the center of his reading practices. Although numerous researchers stress the effects and importance of out-of-school experiences and literacy practices on students (e.g., Hull & Schultz, 2002), there remains a strong emphasis on autonomous models of reading in policies and standards (e.g., Common Core State Standards Initiative, 2010), which in turn affect how and what literacy research is conducted.

Coupling de Certeau's (1984) observation that people were not "fools" (p. 38) with Freire's (1970) observation that they also were not mere vessels to fill up with knowledge, I also wished to point out that reading was not something disconnected from people's lives on a local level. Reading was germane to Aaron's interests, social connections, and activities. He continued to read and get something out of reading because it was worthwhile to him, and what was worthwhile was partly determined through his individual needs or social interactions and not dictated from an authority. By looking at reading as a set of practices and not a discrete set of processes, I hoped to shed some light on how reading was something acquired and taught but also something that was adapted through social practice.

Striking about Aaron's descriptions of his reading was how he took up popular culture texts such as *manga*, comic books, and kung fu films and used them to gain expertise much like an anthropologist might. His use of such media for gaining content area knowledge points to the potential of local literacy practices leading to more global understandings of the world as well as to possibilities for using popular culture texts as educational avenues (Alvermann, Moon, & Hagood, 1999; Morrell, 2004; Xu, Perkins, & Zunich, 2005). Currently, the type of scientifically based research endorsed in the United States has shifted pedagogy and research about literacy to more global conceptions of reading that discount local influences (Shavelson & Towne, 2002). This move has also resulted in narrowed skills instruction and required texts that did not account for the full range of what reading can be and that alienated students from schooling (Meier & Wood, 2004).

However, literacy is not "a deterministic force nor a creation of local agents" (Brandt & Clinton, 2002, p. 338) but is the product of social practices that draw from global and local contexts (Gee, 1996; Street, 2003). Although literacy has cognitive aspects, it is also socially situated and its uses are highly contextual. Both social and cognitive characteristics must be considered by literacy researchers. Aaron spoke to the complexities and gradations of reading and, even though those features might need to be pared down in the interests of education from time to time, it would behoove educators, researchers, and learners to not let those pared down versions become definitive.

References

Allington, R. L. (2006). *What really matters for struggling readers: Designing research-based programs* (2nd edition). Boston: Pearson Education, Inc.

Alvermann, D. E., Moon, J. S., & Hagood, M. C. (1999). *Popular culture in the classroom: Teaching and researching media literacy*. Newark, DE: International Reading Association.

Bakhtin, M. M. (1986). *Speech genres and other late essays* (V. W. McGee, Trans.). Austin: University of Texas Press.

Bové, P. A. (1995). Discourse. In F. Lentricchia & T. McLaughlin (Eds.), *Critical terms for literacy study* (pp. 50–65). Chicago: University of Chicago Press.

Brandt, D. & Clinton, K. (2002). Limits of the local: Expanding perspectives on literacy as a social practice. *Journal of Literacy Research, 34*(3), 337–356.

Brozo, W. G. (2002). *To be a boy, to be a reader.* Newark, DE: International Reading Association.

Burr, V. (1995). *An introduction to social constructionism.* New York: Routledge.

Common Core State Standards Initiative. (2010). Common core state standards for English language arts and literacy in history/social studies, science, and technical subjects. Retrieved March 14, 2011 from http://www.corestandards.org/assets/CCSSI_ELA%20Standards.pdf

De Certeau, M. (1984). *The practice of everyday life* (S. Rendall, Trans.). Berkeley: University of California Press.

DeLillo, D. (1985). *White noise.* New York: Penguin Books.

Farr, C. K. (2004). *Reading Oprah: How Oprah's book club changed the way America reads.* Albany: State University of New York Press.

Fiske, J. (1989). *Understanding popular culture.* New York: Routledge.

Foucault, M. (1972). *The archaeology of knowledge and the discourse on language* (A. M. Sheridan Smith, Trans.). New York: Pantheon Books. (Original work published 1969.)

Foucault, M. (1979). *Discipline and punish: The birth of the prison* (A. Sheridan, Trans.). New York: Vintage Books. (Original work published 1975.)

Foucault, M. (1985). *The use of pleasure: Volume 2 of the history of sexuality* (R. Hurley, Trans.). New York: Vintage Books. (Original work published 1984.)

Freire, P. (1970). *Pedagogy of the oppressed.* New York: Continuum.

Gee, J. P. (1991). What is literacy? In C. Mitchell, & K. Weiler (Eds.), *Rewriting literacy: Culture and the discourse of the other* (pp. 3–11). New York: Bergin & Garvey.

Gee, J. P. (1996). *Social linguistics and literacies: Ideology in discourses* (2nd ed.). Philadelphia: Routledge Falmer.

Gee, J. P. (2003). *What video games have to teach us about learning and literacy.* New York: Palgrave Macmillan.

Gee, J. P. (2005). *An introduction to discourse analysis: Theory and method* (2nd ed.). New York: Routledge.

Hills, M. (2002). *Fan cultures.* New York: Routledge.

Hirsch, E. D. (1988). *Cultural literacy: What every American needs to know.* New York: Vintage.

Hull, G., & Schultz, K. (Eds.). (2002). *School's out! Bridging out-of-school literacies with classroom practice.* New York: Teachers College Press.

Jenkins, H. (1992). *Textual poachers: Television fans and participatory culture.* New York: Routledge.

Jones, G. (2002). *Killing monsters: Why children need fantasy, superheroes, and make-believe violence.* New York: Basic Books.

Kvale, S. (1996). *Interviews: An introduction to qualitative research interviewing.* Thousand Oaks, CA: SAGE Publications.

Lee, C., & Jackson, R. (1991). Faking it. Portsmouth, NH: Heinemann.

Long, E. (2003). *Book clubs: Women and the uses of reading in everyday life.* Chicago: The University of Chicago Press.

Meier, D., & Wood, G. (2004). *Many children left behind: How the No Child Left Behind Act is damaging our children and our schools.* Boston: Beacon Press.

Morrell, E. (2004). *Linking literacy and popular culture: Finding connections for lifelong learning.* Norwood, MA: Christopher-Gordon Publishers.

Nell, V. (1988). *Lost in a book: The psychology of reading for pleasure.* New Haven, CT: Yale University Press.

New London Group. (1996). A pedagogy of multiliteracies: Designing social futures. *Harvard Educational Review, 66*(1), 60–92.

Patton, M. Q. (2002). *Qualitative research and evaluation methods* (3rd ed.). Thousand Oaks: Sage Publications.

Plato. (390 BCE/1991). *The Republic of Plato* (A. Bloom, Trans. 2nd ed.). New York: Basic Books.

Pustz, M. J. (1999). *Comic book culture: Fanboys and true believers.* Jackson: University Press of Mississippi.

Ravitch, D. (2010). *The death and life of the great American school system: How testing and choice are undermining education.* New York: Basic Books.

Rooney, K. (2005). *Reading with Oprah: The book club that changed America.* Fayetteville: The University of Arkansas Press.

Schwanenflugel, P. J., Hamilton, A. M., Kuhn, M. R., & Stahl, S. A. (2004). Becoming a fluent reader: Skill and prosodic features in the oral reading of young children. *Journal of Educational Psychology, 96*(1), 119–129.

Shavelson, R. J., & Towne, L. (2002). *Scientific research in education.* Washington, DC: National Academies Press.

Street, B. V. (1995). *Literacy in theory and practice.* New York: Cambridge University Press. (Original work published 1984.)

Street, B. V. (2003). What's "new" in New Literacy Studies? Critical approaches to literacy in theory and practice. *Current Issues in Comparative Education, 5*(2), 77–91.

Sumara, D. J. (1996). *Private readings in public: Schooling the literary imagination.* New York: Peter Lang.

Tracey, D. H., & Morrow, L. M. (2006). *Lenses on reading: An introduction to theories and models.* New York: The Guilford Press.

Tyner, K. (1998). *Literacy in a digital world: Teaching and learning in the age of information.* Mahwah, NJ: Erlbaum.

Worthy, J. (1998). "On every page someone gets killed!" Book conversations you don't hear in school. *Journal of Adolescent and Adult Literacy, 41*(7), 508–517.

Xu, S., Perkins, R. S., & Zunich, L. O. (2005). *Trading cards to comic strips: Popular culture texts and literacy learning in grades k–8.* Newark, DE: International Reading Association.

3

LOW-INCOME YOUTH'S (PUBLIC) INTERNET PRACTICES IN SOUTH AMERICA

Potential Lessons for Educators in the U.S. and Other Post-Industrial Nations

Eliane Rubinstein-Ávila

As we enter the second decade of the 21st century, popular views of Millennials—Americans born between 1980 and 2000 (Howe & Strauss, 2000)—as information and communication technology (ICT) "wunderkinds" and "cyber-whizzes" are still prevalent. In fact, for at least the past decade, researchers have argued that such generalizations about the "digital generation" are not empirically based, and are grossly exaggerated (Facer & Furlong, 2001; Hargittai & Hinnant, 2008). The media seem to reinforce another popular belief: that children and adolescents are inextricable from ICT and the Internet in particular. However, the Pew Internet and American Life Project (Lenhart, Madden, Macgill, & Smith, 2007) found that young people between the ages of 18–24, are the most "connected" group. Nevertheless, viewing an age group as homogenous Internet users is problematic (Boonaert & Vettenburg, 2011). Multiple factors, such as social economic status (SES), which takes into consideration the educational level of parents, age, racial/ethnic background, geographical location, know-how, and to some extent gender, impact the ways in which youth use the Internet across the globe (Barzilai-Nahlon, 2006; Cheong, 2008; Furuholt, Kristiansen & Wahid, 2008; Livingstone & Helsper, 2007; Mills, 2010; Moje, Overby, Tysvaer, & Morris, 2008; North, Snyder & Bulfin, 2008).

There is little doubt that the global increase in Internet penetration has eased access; in fact, proliferation of Internet cafés (or cybercafés)—especially in developing and poor countries—has provided more opportunities for low-income youth to access the Internet for a reasonable fee. Still, for the poorest youth in some countries, access may be too costly (Furuholt et al., 2008). Even as Internet access rapidly expands, the digital divide has not entirely disappeared. If anything, the divide has become more nuanced and multifaceted (Furuholt et al., 2008) and is frequently referred to as "digital inequality." With issues of access per se no longer a major concern of researchers and policymakers, attention has turned to the ways in which (and purposes for which) young people are accessing the Internet. Increasingly, there is interest in understanding youth's online problem solving skills and web know-how, as well as the extent to which there are patterns of Internet use across groups.

Although middle and upper class youth and young adults across post-industrial nations are increasingly and simultaneously connected to ICT (Cotten, Anderson & Tufekci, 2009; Heim et al., 2007), we know relatively little about how and for what purposes nondominant youth, especially those in low-income groups, use the Internet (e.g., Facer & Furlong, 2001; Furuholt et al., 2008; Mills, 2010; Rubinstein-Ávila, 2006, 2009a). In fact, Boonaert and Vettenburg (2011) claim that "The point of view of the young people themselves is absent" (p. 59) across most studies about Internet use. This is particularly the case for low-income youth who live in developing nations where English is not the *lingua franca*.

This chapter focuses on low-income youth and young adults' Internet practices in public Internet cafés in three of South America's strongest economies: Brazil, Chile, and Argentina. Internet cafés are plentiful across developing nations because they provide fairly affordable Internet access to the masses. My purpose in writing this chapter is to push for greater awareness by educators and researchers of the social contexts of Internet practices among low-income youth and young adults, especially among those living on the periphery of the cyber revolution. Such awareness building is necessary if the online literacies of youth and young adults are to be understood and supported within and beyond school environments.

Research Addressing the Shift from Digital Divide to Digital Inequality

Recent findings across an interdisciplinary body of literature show that the rapid growth of broadband service and Internet proliferation on a global scale is neither geographically nor socially equitable. In fact, while Internet access in many metropolitan areas has multiplied exponentially, that has not been the case across poor, rural areas around the globe. Here, I provide a brief overview of some factors contributing to digital inequalities in our "post-access" era (Jung, 2008).

Researchers from various disciplines, including communication and media studies, information and technology, sociology, and economics, to name a few, are exploring the extent to which Internet use among youth and young adults yields social gains (Furuholt et al., 2008). Some studies found patterns of Internet use and purposes across groups (Hargittai, 2010; Hargittai & Hinnant, 2008; Jung, 2008). Social economic status (SES) seems to be a strong—if not the strongest—predictor of who will use which types of Internet practices and for what purposes. For instance, studies show that youth from middle and upper class homes are more likely than youth from lower class homes to access the Internet from a variety of settings (venues) and to engage in a broad range of Internet activities (Hargittai & Hinnant, 2008; North, et al., 2008).

Although Boonaert and Vettenburg (2011) have been critical of this notion, some online activities are considered to be more capital enhancing than other, in that they promote upward mobility (Hargittai & Hinnant, 2008). For example, accessing governmental and educational information, political participation, citizenship, job/career advancement, research, and financial and health services are thought to increase one's potential for achieving upward mobility.

Perhaps not surprisingly, coming from a higher SES background correlates with higher web expertise and problem-solving skills (Cheong, 2008). Access, or a lack of it, to the conventions of disciplinary knowledge is also associated with class. The results of Haras' (2011) survey of 290 low-income Latinos/as high school students (ages 14 to 18) living in the Los Angeles area, whose families were mostly from Central America, suggest that although students had Internet access, most were not proficient in retrieving the online information they needed to complete the assignment successfully. For example, most of the students provided a very rough and general description of how they would compare and contrast two cultures. Few provided a detailed plan as to how they would use Internet resources to conduct effective compare/contrast searches (Haras, 2011).

Similarly, in their study of 9th graders, Wilder and Dressman (2006) provided an example of the ways in which different experiences with academic literacy and Internet know-how played out in classrooms. The authors observed the ways in which six 9th grade students searched online for information in order to complete a cultural geography assignment. Compared to their middle class peers, lower-income students exhibited more difficulty searching for relevant information, distinguishing among credible and less credible sources, and skimming online texts effectively.

Finally, while the research literature on youth and young adults' Internet uses has expanded in the last few years, there have been few published studies on the Internet practices among South American youth. I found only one published report—by Carcamo and Nesbet (2008), in Spanish—on Internet uses among Chilean youth.

My Exploratory Study

I followed Boonaert and Vettenburg's (2011) and Takahashi's (2010) suggestions to take into account the voices that are usually absent in the research literature, and to explore the "social context in which…[youth] engage with media and ICT in the globalized world" (Takahashi, 2010, p. 455). Because youth in developing countries are most likely to access the Internet in public spaces (Borzekowski & Rickert, 2001; Furuholt et al., 2008), I recruited my participants in public Internet cafés in metropolitan areas, as well as in smaller towns, in Brazil, Argentina, and Chile. I am fluent in Portuguese and in Spanish; therefore, I did not need a translator. I provide a detailed reflexive account on conducting research across national, cultural, and linguistic borders elsewhere (Rubinstein-Ávila, 2009b).

The data on which this chapter is based were collected during 10 weeks of fieldwork. Data sources included 109 surveys/questionnaires completed by youth and young adults who reported being between the ages of 14 and 24; 15 in-depth conversations with a subset of the survey respondents; informal interviews with six Internet café attendants/managers; and ethnographic field notes that I wrote as a participant observer across six sites.

The term Internet café (in Brazil more commonly known as "LAN houze") was used for a range of establishments catering to different types of patrons. Because youth establishments differed from those geared toward the general adult population, I selected a couple of youth Internet cafés in each city or town—a total of five cafés and one federally funded youth center (in Chile), which offered free Internet access to youth. Most of the participants in my study were not from the poorest shantytowns (often on the edge of metropolitan areas). Due to travel time and personal safety issues, I sought Internet cafés that were in lower income neighborhoods with easy access to middle to lower middle class areas.

Once I negotiated entry and gained consent at each site, I began "hanging out" and "casing the joint(s)" (Dyson & Genishi, 2005), focusing on the social dimensions of each space, its energy, a feel for who the young customers were, and the most effective way of reaching out to them. I also began building rapport with the café managers/employees, but since there was rarely more than one person working at one time, there were many interruptions. Around my third visit at each site, I began participant observation and taking ethnographic field notes. I did not observe anyone carrying or using laptops in public; therefore, I used a paper pad on which I recorded field notes. I tried to transpose my field notes to my laptop on the same day that I collected them. On the days that I remained on site until closing time (around 10 p.m.), I transposed my field notes to my laptop the next morning.

Internet Cafés in Argentina, Brazil, and Chile

In this section I report on what I found pertaining to all 109 respondents and to a subset of those individuals with whom I spoke in greater depth. After providing an overview of the range of Internet cafés I visited, I address the following questions: a) What are the (public) Internet practices among low-income youth in Brazil, Chile, and Argentina?; and b) What can we learn about youth's (public) Internet practices to widen our understanding of Internet use among those who live in the margins of the Net Generation?

Across the South American cities and towns in which I collected data, Internet cafés were ubiquitous; however, they differed a great deal depending on the audience to whom they catered. Establishments that catered to the general adult population tended to be smaller and have fewer terminals than those that catered to youth. In addition to offering customers the opportunity to access the Internet for a fee (or increments), the Internet cafés offered services such as copying, faxing, and printing. Printers and faxing machines are a great deal more expensive in South America than they are in the U.S., and even families who own home computers are less likely than American families to own printers, fax machines, shredders, and so on. Although in 2007 there were already companies advertising "bundling" packages (e.g., cable TV, broadband Internet), a speedy web connection in homes was not widely accessible, which made the Internet cafés even more necessary.

The Internet cafés that catered mainly to tourists (large metropolitan areas only) were strategically located close to hotels and seasonal rentals, and offered phone cabins for long distance/overseas calls. These tourist-oriented Internet cafés differed from the general adult Internet cafés in that they were fully air conditioned, equipped with cushy office chairs that swiveled, had new terminals, displayed large posters on the wall highlighting each country's scenery, and charged more per hour.

The Internet cafés geared toward youth were different from the other two types of establishments. They were more spacious (yet grungy), had many more terminals (at least 12, and in large cities at least 20), and offered a wide range of games. Only the youth Internet cafés provided patrons with access to massively multiplayer online role-playing games (MMORGs). Given the dynamic, extremely engaging, and social aspects of MMORGs, it was not uncommon for boys and young men (mainly) to spend several hours around one particular terminal.

As one would expect, youth Internet cafés were definitely livelier and noisier, with plenty of competitive bantering—even swearing, as an expression of excitement. However, I never observed a fight break out between patrons, and I was told that fights were extremely rare. I mainly observed patrons communicating online with others, scrolling through photos, watching YouTube, and playing a wide range of online games (e.g., puzzles and sports—mainly soccer). The most common MMORGs I observed young patrons play were *Counter-Strike*, which had just been banned by the Brazilian government because of its violence, *Mortal Kombat*, and *World of Warcraft*.

Internet cafés that catered to youth were not easy to find. They were tucked away in old street malls, sometimes on the second floor, and not immediately visible to pedestrians on the busy city streets. Most of the youth Internet cafés played loud music, were equipped with snack/candy machines, and offered sandwiches and sodas for purchase. Coffee drinks were not offered at any of the sites. Although I occasionally spotted adult males who seemed to be over 25 years of age (with some well into their 30s) in youth establishments, they seemed to be known by other patrons as hard-core gamers. Interestingly, although the names of these youth Internet cafés were often in English (e.g., Speedy Net, Cyber Point, Web-Power, Cyber U), I did not hear patrons speak English in any of the sites I visited. In fact, patrons used Spanish (in Chile and Argentina) and Portuguese vocabulary (in Brazil) to refer to all software and hardware functions.

Internet cafés were more than just places for young people to go online; they also served as social "hot spots" for meeting local youth, especially in smaller towns where there were fewer venues geared toward youth. In larger cities, from 8 to 10 p.m., they functioned as places in which to see and be seen. It was not unusual for three or four friends to congregate around one screen. Many repeat patrons, especially those who came in on a daily basis, had seemingly developed friendships with others, and managers/employees at times seemed to function as guides to less-skilled patrons, especially to those who needed assistance when it came to MMORGs.

Insights Gleaned from Survey Responses

The 109 participants (between the ages of 14 and 24) who completed a face-to-face survey represented the following countries: 35 from Argentina, 36 from Chile, and 38 from Brazil. Overall, 60 participants (55%) identified as male, 44 (40%) identified as female, and 5 participants (5%) did not answer the question on gender. Seventy-nine (73%) reported being enrolled in a school (middle school, high school, or remedial night school to complete a secondary certificate). A handful of participants were enrolled in college, but none in the prestigious federal institutions of higher learning. Twenty-two (20%) reported not being enrolled in school, and 8 (7%) did not answer the question.

Most of the participants, 70 (64%), reported being between the ages of 14–18, and 39 (36%) reported being between the ages of 19–24. The mean age of the sample was 17.6 (s.d. = 3.0). Because I found fewer young women than young men in the Internet cafés across all three countries, on two occasions (both in Chile, which was the last data collection opportunity), I sought female partici-pants from a group that was congregating outside a church, and from a group of mostly female students on a school fieldtrip.

The face-to-face survey began with a series of predetermined demographic items that asked participants to circle if they were male/female or other, their age, enrolled (or not) in school, and so on. One survey item asked respondents who reported being enrolled in school to specify if the school was private or public. That item was meant to assess a young person's SES. Across South America, public school is a proxy for low SES; middle class and upper class SES families are not likely to send their children to K-12 public school systems. However, given the boom in private K-12 schools, especially in Brazil, with a vast range in tuition prices and quality, a binary such as public/private school attendance could be too simplistic for determining SES. Moreover, several of the participants in Chile were enrolled in a school that was partly funded by federal government subsidies (Arenas, 2004), despite being referred to as a private school. Due to the complexity of the survey item that asked about private or public schooling, responses to that item were not analyzed. Given my experience, the sites I selected, and my own contact with the participants, it is safe to assume that many, if not most, participants were low-income, but definitely not poor within the South American context.

Variables of interest included participants' breadth of Internet use (n = 23 different predetermined activities for respondents to check), the frequency with which they accessed the Internet and the time they spent online, whether or not they were enrolled in school, their preferred search engine, and from how many places they accessed the Internet. The Internet activities included instant messaging, chatting, surfing the web, downloading music, viewing YouTube clips, engaging with social networks, gaming, news, sports, homework, web-surfing, searching for general information, health-related searches, accessing porn sites, and so on. Although some of the young male participants mentioned that everyone knew how to get around the cafés' restrictions aimed at discouraging access to porn sites, I did not find that to be a common Internet activity across my observations.

On average, the participants reported engaging in seven to eight Internet activities out of the 23 listed. Few engaged in only one or two activities; similarly, very few participants reported engaging in more than 20 of the listed activities. One college student had designed his own website. Not surprisingly, the more years participants reported having accessed the Internet, the more often they continued to do so. In fact, youth who reported going online for over five years tended to go online on a daily basis. However, going online every day did not necessarily correlate with the breadth of activities in which they reported engaging. Across the sample, youth who reported using the Internet for less than one year were in the minority; most youth reported having been connected from three to five years. As expected, older youth between 19 and 24 typically reported using the Internet for the longest time. Despite the number of years participants reported being connected, most described themselves as still learning, or doing fairly well, as opposed to being proficient in using the Internet.

Summary and Explanation of the Correlations from the Survey Results

1. Those who engaged in a broad range of Internet activities were also likely to have conducted health related searches (e. g., searching for websites on topics such as nutrition, diseases, contraceptives, etc.). In statistical terms, participants' breadth of Internet activities was significantly correlated to their breadth of health related searches, $r(106) = .56$, $p < .001$.

2. The longer (more years) participants had been connected to the Internet, the more likely they were to access it from more than one place (not just the Internet café). Stated statistically, participants' length of time using the Internet was positively correlated to the number of places from which they

accessed the internet (i.e., home or from the homes of friends/family members) $r_{tb}(106) = .19$, p $<$ .05.

3. Participants who had been accessing the Internet for several years (five and over) were likely to go online daily. In other words, there was a positive correlation between the length of time participants had been connecting to the Internet and how frequently they used it, $r_s(105) = .516$, p $<.001$.

4. Age did not correlate highly with overall breadth of Internet activities. Although this finding may seem counterintuitive, it is possibly explained by the fact that many of the participants who reported being students also reported being enrolled in "night schools," which are typically remedial "catch-up" programs designed for older students who had dropped out of school and were pursuing their secondary diploma, something akin to a GED in the United States.

5. Among the participants who reported being students, few reported having access to the Internet at school. Except for two participants, the young people in my study did not find public Internet access to be excessively expensive.

Alternative Modes of Communication

An activity that I observed most often involved youth chatting online and accessing social networking sites (*Orkut* in Brazil, and mainly *Fotolog* in Argentina and Chile—occasionally Facebook, but not in Brazil). My field notes indicated that across sites, young people spent long periods of time (sometimes in small groups) browsing photos of friends and acquaintances, as well as their own photos. They seemed engaged in this activity more often than posting or reading their friends' posts—what Carcamo and Nesbet (2008) call "cybervoyeurism." When asked what motivated them to do so, a common response was to spy on other's people's lives. As one young Brazilian woman explained:

> It's like being a little gnat in someone's life. You see without being seen.... You can poke holes at their stories. If my boyfriend says he was at his grandmother's last Sunday, I can say...you liar! I have proof! You were out with friends!

To some extent the participants' online lives seemed to be an extension of their offline lives, even if the connection was not as seamless as Leander and McKim (2003) found among middle class youth in post-industrial nations. A lingering question, of course, is to what extent does an alternative mode of communication such as the Internet enhance young people's desire to stay in touch socially? Similarly, what is the tradeoff when the Internet becomes a tool for merely sedating young people or makes "spying" on social relationships easy?

Among my participants, the Internet offered alternate modes of expressing themselves and connecting. Several stated that instant messaging had become their favorite way of communicating because it was "very different" from talking on the phone with a friend "and a lot more fun." Instant messaging was often perceived as being easier and less expensive than placing a call. Most of the youth with whom I spoke had "pay as you go" cell phones and were often "too broke to buy a card." To obtain an emic, or insider's perspective, on my participants' preference for messaging, I asked them to explain what that term meant to them. A 16-year-old young woman, whom I will call Patricia, engaged in a conversation with me that yielded the following anecdote.

Patricia had just been contacted by a couple of her girlfriends, who were at another Internet café in town. She was laughing convulsively as she shared what she remembered from a recent online interaction with some female friends. "They wrote to me: Hey little cow [*vaquinha*]! Are you going out tonight?" Patricia (who had a perfect figure) was laughing so hard I thought she was going to choke. "Oh! Really?" I said, not quite getting the joke. "Ok…So how did you respond?" Patricia barely stopped laughing for a few seconds: "I said [typed] MOOOOOOOO!" and then she burst out laughing once more. This brief exchange illustrates what messaging meant, in part at least, to Patricia: namely, having a space in which to be creative and playful in communicating with friends.

Personal online communication among other participants in my study ranged from the most trivial and playful to potentially life-changing decisions. Several youth shared that the Internet provided them with a chance to keep in touch with family members who had left the country to work abroad (Canada, United States, Germany, and Italy). Edmilson's email exchanges with his Brazilian uncle in Germany provide a good example. Edmilson was a tall 19-year-old, dark-skinned Brazilian who worked as an "office boy"—a dead-end job that included delivering documents on foot and preparing and serving coffee to clients. Like many low-income young people across South America, Edmilson had not completed secondary school. He had considered going to Germany to join his uncle who had been living and working there for years. However, Edmilson told me that following a recent, steady stream of online communications with his uncle (mostly through email, and occasionally through Skype), he had changed his mind about going to work in Germany:

> My uncle loves it there, and he may never come back, who knows?… But…I don't really think it's for me [*cara*] man! [*Sei la!*]

I probed further, for I was very curious as to what may have led him to make such an important decision, and to what extent the opportunity to communicate with his uncle online had had an impact on his decision. He said:

> I don't know…you gotta work VERY hard, and the cold…is SERIOUS (laughs out loud). And the Germans…well…they're…[*Sei la!*]

(Laughs some more). *Cara!* [Man!] How could I leave this here (raising both his hands, signaling the space around us)...our *calor humano* [human warmth], our music, the beach, these beautiful golden women—it's too much to [*abrir-mao, cara*] give up, man! [*Sei-la!*]....What is money for, if you can't have THIS? [His arms up in the air again—a huge grin on his face.]

I thought Edmilson was done sharing, when he suddenly looked straight ahead (away from me), and added:

It was a good thing we had the opportunity to [*trocar ideas*] [exchange ideas] *cara!*...For me...it would have been...[*Sei la!*] a mistake...no doubt *cara!* No doubt!

Because Edmilson did not have a home computer in the small one-bedroom apartment he shared with his older, married sister, Internet cafés were the only places he could connect. Edmilson's Internet use was what one would describe as narrow; he dabbled in a few simple games and YouTube (mostly to view soccer clips of his favorite team). He did not feel confident about his Internet skills, nor was he confident about posting or communicating (in writing) with strangers. Like many low-income Brazilians with little formal schooling, Edmilson was ashamed of his ability to write "correctly." As Bartlett's (2007) work in Brazil pointed out, "the belief that a single, 'correct' Portuguese exists and that it is learned at school [has] distinct consequences for youth and [young low-income] adults" (p. 13). Edmilson only felt comfortable exchanging instant messages and emails with a few close friends and family members. In fact, despite the opportunity to reach out to people around the globe, most of the youth I talked to claimed to communicate only with those who were part of their offline community.

Internet Practices of Users on the Fringe of the Cyber Revolution

An analysis of the survey data showed that across my sample few young people used the Internet for fewer than three years, and few reported being occasional Internet users. After conducting the analysis, I realized that Ronaldo and Daniela, two of the participants with whom I had in-depth conversations, were in fact statistical outliers (i.e., data points at either extreme that are distant from where the majority of the data points clump together). Ronaldo's and Daniela's "stories" can teach us about the needs and the affordances of youth who are on the fringe of the so-called cyber revolution. Neither had had the opportunity to complete their secondary education. Daniela was a White 24-year-old, single mother who lived in a mid-size city in Chile; Ronaldo was a Black 22-year-old married man and the father of two young children who lived in a large city in Brazil. Their Internet practices and purposes for using the Internet could not have been more different from the sample as a whole.

Daniela told me she had been an occasional Internet user for three main reasons: money, time, and lack of need (purpose)—until recently, that is. Daniela explained that as an unemployed single mother, with no job prospects, she did not have the time or the means to "explore the Internet." In contrast to most young people in my study, Daniela said she could not afford to go to Internet cafés. Instead, she took advantage of free Internet access at a local youth community center (funded by the Chilean government) when she was able to have that time away from her daughter.

Further, Daniela explained that until recently she had no real need, or purpose, to go online. However, since she found out that she and her daughter had an opportunity to apply for citizenship in Spain (through family blood line laws), she was intent on finding the information she needed online. According to Daniela, leaving Chile for Spain legally and being able to work and support her daughter was her only opportunity to lead a healthy and productive life.

While Daniela was grateful for the opportunity the community center offered to access the Internet for free, the 30-minute limit (at a time) was extremely frustrating: "It takes me so long to find any information; when I finally find something, time is up." Given that there was no Spanish embassy in her city, the Internet was her "life-line"—the information she was able to obtain online was essential to her. She also mentioned being confused as to how and where to search for the information she needed. She did not feel that she knew people who could genuinely guide her.

Ronaldo was a choir director for a small Evangelical church in a large Brazilian city. He had resisted the Internet for years because he used to think that the Internet was "pure evil." When we talked, Ronaldo had been using the Internet for a little over a year because his younger brother had convinced him to give it a try. Ronaldo soon discovered that through YouTube he was able to obtain clips of historical recordings of famous old-timers singing a range of religious tunes. Ronaldo:

> It has really made a difference in my work; I learn so much from the old-time heroes, some that…died before I was even born. That changed my life, really! I am now teaching myself about the roots of Brazilian religious hymns—it's fascinating! Yes; there is a lot of evil in the Internet….It's like life in the world—one *can* and *must* choose good over evil.

Daniela, in Chile, and Ronaldo, in Brazil, accessed the Internet relatively infrequently, and for limited purposes. However, these two young adults, seemingly in the fringes of the cyber revolution, defy what we know about the ways in which, and purposes for which, low SES youth use the Internet. Daniela was seeking information that was essential to her plan to obtain Spanish citizenship for her daughter and herself, and to embark on a course what would hopefully lead to a more productive existence. Ronaldo not only accessed a type of professional development that enhanced his job in the church choir, but he also engaged in self-directed learning on a topic about which he was passionate. Can Daniela's and Ronaldo's Internet practices be categorized as "socially gainful (online) activities," and "capital enhancing" (Hargittai & Hinnant, 2008)? I contend that both Daniela and Ronaldo enacted agentive Internet practices, which had transformative, capital-enhancing potential.

Conclusion

Our current knowledge about youth's online literacy practices has been largely based on research conducted in post-industrial nations (mainly English-speaking countries), and often from middle class backgrounds. However, as we are reminded by Bean and Harper (2008), "to teach [and conduct research] in New Times, with new communication technology, at a time of intensifying globalization, means to engage difference, particularly social, cultural, and linguistic differences" (p. 6). Therefore, the voices of young people portrayed in this chapter help fill a gap in available information on the Internet practices and purposes of nondominant youth in non-English speaking contexts. Moreover, the online engagement of the youth I highlighted in this chapter may force us to broaden the practices subsumed under those in the socially enhancing category.

There is no doubt that "Adolescents' online literacies have implications for the research and teaching of literacy" (Alvermann, 2008, p. 16). The exploratory study of youth and young adults on which I report in this chapter also underscores a statement made by Stevens (2006) in a chapter she contributed for the second edition of *Reconceptualizing the Literacies in Adolescents' Lives*: "Educators and policymakers should be continually engaged in…types of questions…that inquire about the lives of young people, the worlds they are living in and likely to find themselves living in, and how to mediate the connections between these two" (p. 304). This is still a challenge—five years later.

Despite the proliferation of Internet cafés across South America, which has eased issues of access, many low-income youth and young adults in developing countries still lack access to formal secondary and tertiary education, and to opportunities that require complex ICT skills. Overall, the participants in my study seemed to partake in the consumption rather than the production of Internet-mediated practices; most were unlikely to compose or engage in the complex remixing of multimodal texts, or to engage in extensive identity, civic/political work (Knobel & Lankshear, 2008). On the other hand, youth in the margins of the cyber revolution, such as Daniela and Ronaldo, were engaged in agentive online activities as they attempted to transform their lives. Therefore, I contend that both Daniela's and Ronald's Internet practices were socially enhancing because they actively pursued them in order to better their lives and their future social standing.

Implications for Educators

Educators' assumptions or fears that youth's online expertise is likely to surpass their own is not always founded. As this chapter makes clear, many youth and young adults—especially from nondominant groups—are *not* accessing the Internet for a broad range of purposes or in ways that are the most effective or productive. Young people are likely to need more guidance as to the many ways in which the Internet can enhance their formal educational journey and their informal life-long learning. Many youth would benefit from the guidance of peers and adults who may be more knowledgeable about the web, especially when it comes to evaluating sites and the resources they retrieve. Even what is typically thought of as "unstructured" online time (e.g., after-school programs) may be taken up as an opportunity to engage young people in pursuing online creative activities, personal interests, civic participation, and identity work. In fact, schools with a high percentage of low-income students could integrate guided Internet access into the school day (including recess). Issues such as online authenticity, privacy, and ethics are particularly important to explore with youth as they expand their breadth of Internet practices.

Peer-to-peer scaffolding in schools could provide a collaborative environment in which to push youth with various levels of know-how into the role of digital producers rather than just consumers. It is imperative that, as educators, we do not use technology only in ways that provide greater benefits to those who are already digitally privileged, thereby inadvertently encouraging disadvantage among students who are already at a (digital) disadvantage. All students, especially students from nondominant groups, need instruction and guidance about the many affordances of critical online engagement. Because we now know that higher online skill levels are associated with a broader range of socially enhancing activities (Hargittai, 2010; Hargittai & Hinnant, 2008), teachers in kindergarten through grade 12 and college instructors will need to carefully consider their role in providing students with nuanced digital opportunities—especially for youth who may be on the margins of the cyber revolution.

Finally, it is important for educators to understand that technology is not "a thing" nor is it neutral. In fact, North et al. (2008) stress that "technology is a performative function...embedded in relations of power" (p. 207) and "can never be detached from its place in a social, cultural and historical context" (p. 907).

References

Alvermann, D. E. (2008). Why bother theorizing adolescent's online literacies for classroom practice and research? *Journal of Adult & Adolescent Literacy, 52*(1), 8–19.

Arenas, A. (2004). Privatization and vouchers in Colombia and Chile. *International Review of Education, 50*(3), 379–395.

Bartlett, L. (2007). Literacy, speech and shame: The cultural politics of literacy in Brazil. *International Journal of Qualitative Studies in Education, 20*, 1–17.

Barzilai-Nahlon, K. (2006). Gaps and bits: Conceptualizing measurement for digital dive/s. *The Information Society*, *22*, 269–278.

Bean, T., & Harper, H. (2008). Literacy education in New Times: In these times. *Journal of Adult & Adolescent Literacy*, *52*(1), 4–6.

Boonaert, T., & Vettenbeurg, N. (2011). Young people's Internet use: Divided or diversified? *Childhood*, *18*(1), 54–66.

Borzekowski, D. L. G., & Rickert, V. I. (2001). Adolescents, the Internet, and health: Issues of access and content. *Applied Developmental Psychology*, *22*, 49–59.

Carcamo, U. L., & Nesbet, F. A. M. (2008). Nativos digitales Chilensis: Los jóvenes, al sur de la Internet. *Revista Latina de Comunicacion Social*, *63*, 22–30. Retrieved from http//:www.Ull.es/publicaciones/Latina/_2008/03_Carcamo_y_Nesbet.html

Cheong, P. H. (2008). The young and the techless? Investigating Internet use and problem-solving behaviors of young adults in Singapore. *New Media & Society*, *10*(5), 771–791.

Cotten, S. R., Anderson, W. A., & Tufekci, Z. (2009). Old wine in a new technology, or a different type of digital divide? *New Media & Society*, *11*(7), 1163–1186.

Dyson, A. H., & Genishi, C. (2005). *On the case: Approaches to language and literacy research* (National Conference on Research in Language and Literacy). New York: Teachers College Press.

Facer, K., & Furlong, R. (2001). Beyond the myth of "cyberkid": Young people at the margins of the information revolution. *Journal of Youth Studies*, *4*(4), 451–469.

Furuholt, B., Kristiansen, S., & Wahid, F. (2008). Gaming or gaining? Comparing the use of Internet cafés in Indonesia and Tanzania. *The International Information & Library Review*, *40*, 129–139.

Haras, C. (2011). Information behaviors of Latinos attending high school in East Los Angeles. *Library and Information Science Research*, *33*(1), 34–40.

Hargittai, E. (2010). Digital na(t)ives? Variation in Internet skills and uses among member of the "Net Generation." *Sociological Inquiry*, *80*(1), 92–113.

Hargittai, E., & Hinnant, A. (2008). Digital inequality: Differences in young adults' use of the Internet. *Communication Research*, *35*(5), 602–621.

Heim, J., Brandtzaeg, P., Kaare, B., Endestad, T., & Torgersen, L. (2007). Children's usage of media technologies and psychosocial factors. *New Media & Society* *9*(3), 425–454.

Howe, N., & Strauss, W. (2000). *Millennials rising: The next great generation*. New York: Vintage Books.

Jung, J. (2008). Internet connectedness and its social origins: An ecological approach to postaccess digital divides. *Communication Studies*, *59*(4), 322–339.

Knobel, M., & Lankshear, C. (2008). Remix: the art and craft of endless hybridization. *Journal of Adult & Adolescent Literacy*, *52*(1), 22–33.

Leander, K. M., & McKim, K. (2003). Tracing the everyday "sitings" of adolescents on the Internet: A strategic adaptation of ethnography across online and offline spaces. *Education, Communication & Information*, *3*(2), 211–240.

Lenhart, A., Madden, M., Macgill, A. R., & Smith, A. (2007, December). *Teens and social media*. PEW Internet & American Life Project. Washington, DC: PEW Charitable Trusts. Retrieved May 23, 2011 from www.pewinternet.org/PPF/r/230/report_display.asp

Livingstone, S., & Helsper, E. (2007). Gradations in digital inclusion: Children, young people and the digital divide. *New Media & Society*, *9*(4), 671–696.

Mills, K. A. (2010). Shrek meets Vygotsky: Rethinking adolescents' multimodal literacy practices in schools. *Journal of Adolescent & Adult Literacy, 54*(1), 35–45.

Moje, E. B., Overby, M., Tysvaer, N., & Morris, K. (2008). The complex world of adolescent literacy: Myths, motivations, and mysteries. *Harvard Educational Review, 78*(1), 107–154.

North, S., Snyder, I., & Bulfin, S. (2008). Digital tastes: Social class and young people's technology use. *Information Communication and Society, 11*(7), 895–911.

Rubinstein-Ávila, E. (2006, December). Exploring the nature of low-income youth's technoliteracies. Paper presented at the annual meeting of the National Reading Conference, Los Angeles, CA.

Rubinstein-Ávila, E. (2009a, December). Metered online literacy practices among low-income youth in South America. Paper presented at the annual meeting of the National Reading Conference, Albuquerque, NM.

Rubinstein-Ávila, E. (2009b). Reflecting on the challenges of conducting research across national and linguistic borders: Lessons from the field. *Journal of Language and Literacy Education, 5*(1), 1–8. Retrieved August 1, 2011 from http://www.coe.uga.edu/jolle/2009_1/reflecting.pdf

Stevens, L. P. (2006). Reconceptualizing adolescent literacy policy's role: Productive ambiguity. In D. E. Alvermann, K. A. Hinchman, D. W. Moore, S. F. Phelps, & D. R. Waff (Eds.). *Reconceptualizing the literacies in adolescents' lives* (2nd ed., pp. 297–309). Mahwah, NJ: Lawrence Erlbaum.

Takahashi, T. (2010). MySpace or Mixi? Japanese engagement with SNS (social networking sites) in the global age. *New Media & Society, 12(3)*, 453–475.

Wilder, P., & Dressman, M. (2006). New literacies, enduring challenges? The influence of capital on adolescent readers' Internet practices. In D. E. Alvermann, K. A. Hinchman, D. W. Moore, S. F. Phelps, & D. R. Waff, (Eds.), *Reconceptualizing the literacies in adolescents' lives* (2nd ed., pp. 205–229). Mahwah, NJ: Lawrence Erlbaum.

4

TEACHER RESPONSE

Lessons Learned from Young People's Everyday Literacies

Anne Bulcher and Margaret Moran

Margaret (Midge) Moran and I (Anne Bulcher) are middle grades teachers with extensive and varied experience in education. Between us we have taught for about 60 years and are still going strong. Currently we teach next door to each other at a large suburban middle school (1,250 students). Midge teaches Spanish to 6th, 7th and 8th graders, and I am a math and reading interventionist using a scripted program—The Academy of Reading and Math. We spend a lot of time together, eating lunch in my classroom, discussing our views on technologies and our current thoughts on books from our ladies' book club.

Our views of the world are very different, based upon our experiences. In some ways we are opposites. Midge is liberal, and I am conservative. Yet despite these differences, we are close friends. We agree on one thing: we are here to provide the best possible education for our students. As a result, we constantly try to keep up with new ideas and trends in education. We challenge each other to improve skills by taking classes and by sharing winning strategies. That is what led us to the New Literacies classes taught by Dr. Margaret Hagood at the College of Charleston. In these classes, we've explored how literacy is not confined to just books and resources. Literacies include so many other sources of information, embracing all technologies—smartphones, tablets (iPads), notebooks, computers, Flip videos, and so on.

Our comments on the chapters authored by Lorri Nielsen Glenn (*Playing for Real: Texts and the Performance of Identity*), Stergios Botzakis (*Becoming Life-Long Readers: Insights from a Comic Book Reader*), and Eliane Rubinstein-Ávila (*Low-Income Youth's (Public) Internet Practices in South America: Potential Lessons for Educators in the U.S. and Other Post-Industrial Nations*) are offered in the context of our experiences and of the knowledge and practices we acquired by participating in Dr. Margaret Hagood's New Literacies classes.

Playing for Real: Texts and the Performance of Identity (Glenn)

I (Midge) love the reference to *"touchstone"* texts in this chapter. The "touch" part of it reminds me of how teachers, friends, texts can "touch" the lives of others. I found in reading the current interviews with David and El that their perspectives are not so different from my own. I am a product of education in the 1950s and 1960s; I attended college during the height of the Vietnam War. My primary education was certainly cookie cutter. But the world was in upheaval during my college years. We learned more by protesting and rallying than from writing papers. It seems both David and El viewed the majority of their primary education as generally unremarkable.

This was an interesting study as it was centered on two individuals, one of whom was closely related to the author. The profanity in this chapter was initially offputting. The use of the "f" word, not once but twice, disturbed me (Anne). While I realize the author was directly quoting El in both instances, I believe she could have conveyed the idea without actually using the word. I was also offended by the use of the word "shit", again in a quote by El. This is a textbook. I do not expect to see these words so explicitly stated. Perhaps I am old fashioned in my view of inappropriate language. We are bombarded by such language in the mainstream media, movies, and overheard conversations every hour of every day. In many ways, I think that textbooks should be a refuge from such profanity.

In addition to recognizing the texts that appeal to my students, I (Midge) need to recognize the themes/issues that are on their minds. Using these two elements, I can overlay the language/grammar I want to teach them. The third element of the formula is what the student will take from what is presented. I come away from this chapter with many insights. High on the list is that students are individuals, they may have multiple interpretations, and everything they are given will have some impact (miniscule as that might be). Students are not just learning to read—they're learning to be themselves.

It was interesting to me (Anne) to compare El and David's views about life and what defines them. I had difficulty understanding their reluctance to succumb to commercialism when it meant being able to provide necessities, like food and a roof over their heads. They felt they were compromising their principles.

I (Midge) continue to connect a random thought to this chapter: The medium is the message. This mantra was a phrase used during my college years. The phrase was introduced in Marshall McLuhan's most widely known book, *Understanding Media: The Extensions of Man*, published in 1964. I wonder if today's media (texting, Facebook, voicemail, email, and whatever is to be invented) might be the message now? Sometimes I feel overwhelmed to think that no matter how much I try to keep abreast of the texts in students' lives, I am doomed to remain hopelessly behind. Sometimes I think that "mothering" is a New Literacy strategy—we don't view ourselves as reading teachers, we're just arranging for life experiences. When thinking about how/what we are teaching with regard to literacy, I need to remember that we all change over time. What my students walk away with today will be re-digested multiple times and be a part of what they become.

Becoming Life-Long Readers: Insights from a Comic Book Reader (Botzakis)

When I (Anne) first read this chapter, my reaction was, "So what?" It is a gender-biased article. No big deal. More women should have been included by looking at what they read. However, after further reflection, I realized that I had totally missed the point. It occurred to me that the message was that knowledge can be gained even from seemingly non-traditional sources that were previously discounted because information/knowledge, to be legitimate, must come from a textbook or a reference source. In other contexts, the fact that Aaron learned much about Japanese and Southeast Asian cultures would have been dismissed because it was obtained from a less than authentic source. Over the years I have found, by trial and error, that it is easier to engage reluctant readers (particularly boys) by offering them reading material that is meaningful and of interest to them. Books and magazines about sports generally have high appeal value. Graphic novels are very popular with my students—again more so with the boys than with the girls.

This chapter reminds me (Midge) that literacy learning is definitely a collection of small events, tasks, and concerns. I think of what I've learned from my New Literacies classes. I have come to appreciate the value of Flip videos (and lament learning of their demise), YouTube, etc. I am reminded to engage students, not to teach in the same old way. When their eyes glaze over, it's time to re-strategize. Blogging might be a way of making the learning more social. Hmmmm... I wonder: Is there a chapter on how I can do all of this in 45 minutes? Whether reading to escape reality or to reflect on their own lives (Nell's definition of ludic readers), I'm reminded to just be glad that students are reading. It's nice to know why, but probably not necessary. This chapter confirmed for me that, for sure, school is not always the center of my students' reading practices.

For a long time I (Anne) was of the opinion that supermarket tabloids were only a source of sensational and unsubstantiated stories about famous people. I found out differently. Along with the sensational and lurid stories they do publish some articles that are informative and factual. I learned it is very possible to acquire useful, factual knowledge even from non-traditional sources. As a teacher this has helped me to validate more and more of my students' work and choices in reading material. As educators we need to teach our students to verify their knowledge and information and not be so quick to judge and discount on the basis of how and where it was acquired. An example from my own life comes from my learning about wikis. Initially, I was quick to judge them. I didn't think that they were of interest or of use in my already busy life. I thought that because a group of people publish wikis and edit them collaboratively, they would be inaccurate and biased sources of information. Again I was mistaken. Now I find myself consulting wikis on a frequent basis.

Low-Income Youth's (Public) Internet Practices in South America: Potential Lessons for Educators in the U.S. and Other Post-Industrial Nations (Rubinstein-Ávila)

Well, for sure, I (Midge) think this study needs to be done right here in Mount Pleasant! We have students whose needs aren't being met and whose computer access rivals that of those in this study. Only we don't have Internet cafés! I'm not sure how parallels (and subsequently strategies/recommendations) can be made between this chapter and what I'm dealing with here in the U.S. I was intrigued by this chapter because I taught in Honduras for two years from 2000–2002 and I see many similarities to my own experiences. Nearly all of the students I taught had no access to computers, other than the ones at school. And that was very limited. As a teacher who heavily relies on technology and its many literacy applications, I can see in retrospect how limited my ability to motivate, captivate, challenge, and enrich my students was. I did not even have textbooks. One thing I did have was a suitcase full of children's books. I brought this to class on Fridays. We sat outside on the covered walkway, and students could read these books (in English). It was probably one of the most successful strategies I had—the illustrations helped reinforce the meaning of the words and reveal the story line.

It was difficult to relate to this article as I (Anne) wondered, why is this important to me as an educator in the U.S.? It is predictable that young people—regardless of their location in the world and regardless of their financial circumstances—will find ways to access the Internet and benefit from the entertainment value (games) it provides. I suppose parallels can be drawn between inequalities that exist in the U.S. and South America as it relates to education and to Internet access. Some of the students I currently teach do not have Internet access at home because of financial constraints or they have no computer. If I were an educator outside the U.S.—particularly in South America—I'm sure my reaction to this article would be different. I would be inclined to not dismiss these findings as quickly. Certainly poverty has many faces—fewer opportunities for education and employment, which impact one's access to technology. It appears that the cafés provide a much needed service. However, much of the activity in the cafés is social and the use of Internet time is used for playing games. Very few use this opportunity to enhance their knowledge and skills in ways that could lead to employment.

On the topic of digital inequality, I (Midge) am a pragmatist. Even if this inequality is fixed, another inequality will replace it. The best we can do is to expose our students as best we can, providing at least a glimpse of what is possible, and encouraging them to reach for the stars. We can accept the ways in which they branch out. We can reinforce their attempts, dreams, and preferences. We should walk a mile in their shoes, not because we should be on that level, but so that we truly understand the challenges from their perspective. At times we may need to step back and view a situation from a different perspective. I think most students can "catch up" and "catch on" if we provide those opportunities. Recognizing, assessing, and providing those opportunities are part of what makes New Literacies so appealing and rewarding to me. I can begin to see successes with students right away.

Final Thoughts

Midge and I (Anne) have become better teachers and are engaging our students in more interesting activities as a result of the New Literacies classes we have taken and technology we have learned to incorporate. Neither of us is young. We love to see the look of surprise on our students' faces when they see that we are perfectly comfortable with using and teaching with the new technologies. With the plethora of technology (gadgets, applications) one has to be aware that one cannot use it all and one cannot apply it all, especially when state standards are a crucial part of the way we deliver instruction. Teaching with new literacies sometimes takes longer to apply, but doing so provides more meaningful projects and engaging lessons for our students. I feel privileged to have been asked to review these three chapters. The content was varied. Some was more appealing and resonated with me. All were informative and highlighted issues of education and educational needs. It is clear that regardless of years in education and regardless of chronological age, it is imperative to keep learning and perfecting our craft. Standing still or maintaining the status quo is not an option.

It's probably predictable that my (Midge's) final thoughts would be different from Anne's. We enrich and complement one another when it comes to education, gaining perspectives that we may not have had on our own. The sharing of ideas, research, and hypotheses will give us the needed flexibility to adapt to a very rapidly changing field. Whether the information comes from a book such as this one or from collaboration in a New Literacies class, we need to share what works and prepare for what comes next. Providing opportunities for our students to engage demands that we ourselves keep learning. I thank the authors for giving me more to think about.

PART II

Integrating Everyday and Academic Literacies

5

TOUCHSTONE CHAPTER
"STRUGGLING" ADOLESCENTS' ENGAGEMENT IN MULTIMEDIATING

Countering the Institutional Construction of Incompetence

David O'Brien

Prior to writing this chapter, I explored digital literacies as a set of New Literacies practices for so-called "at-risk" adolescents (O'Brien, 1998, 2003; O'Brien, Springs, & Stith, 2001). The work focused on how those practices expand our conceptions of literate competence while helping the students, many of whom have been disengaged from school for years, redefine their own competence. In this chapter, I extend this work by looking more closely at how current conceptualizations of literacy practices involved in using and creating digital media change adolescents' perceptions of their own literate competence by using examples from two projects.

In order to set the stage for looking more closely at literate practices involved in using digital media, I provide a brief background of my previous work and discuss and contrast traditional or "print-centric" and newer "digital media-centric" notions of literacy competence. I then define the newer competence through a framework called *multimediating* (Doneman, 1997; Lankshear & Knobel, 2003), using vignettes from the two projects. Finally, I discuss the future implications of the work in schools.

Background

From 1992 to 1997, I worked with school-based colleagues to set up a program for "at-risk" high school students—the Lafayette Jefferson High Literacy Lab (O'Brien et al., 2001). In the years between the end of the project and now, we continued to analyze data, working to make sense of how the program engaged the students enrolled in it and studying how that engagement contributed to both their sense of agency and actual improvement in achievement (O'Brien, 2001, 2003). Our initial goal was to better assess the students so that we could provide them with strategies that would improve their comprehension. After the first year of this work, it was apparent that fostering effective strategies was a necessary but insufficient way to address the problem.

What unfolded was a complex syndrome: Low achievement led to low perception about abilities, which resulted in increasing disengagement from reading, which, in turn, resulted in lack of practice, low fluency, lagging decoding skills, and the absence of strategies. These Literacy Lab students lost ground each year in relation to peers, and believed that the plight they faced was beyond their control, leading to "learned helplessness" (Seligman, 1992). When students discover, early in their academic careers, that they are not doing well in reading (it could be any school discipline), and they *attribute* success to stable factors outside of their control (e.g., the texts are too hard, effort doesn't yield results, the teacher is hard, they just don't have the ability), success is perceived as unattainable, universal, and permanent. Helplessness is learned as a response to something you can't explain—something that you don't have control over. When you see that you are not improving, even though your peers are, you assume that you lack ability (perceived as a stable, unchangeable factor). Yet, you might rationalize the failure to external factors like the teacher, or luck—for example, the teacher did not like me or it was just an unlucky day. As time goes on, though, the rationalizations don't help, and you continue to fall behind, you are less motivated to read, you avoid reading, and the more you avoid it, the less practice you have, and you fall further behind. When I met the Literacy Lab students, most of them read little; most considered themselves poor readers and viewed print as all but inaccessible. About half of them had a profound dislike of school. No wonder.

Toward the end of the first year of the project, we started to study and implement ways to motivate the Literacy Lab students so that they would engage with literacy practices in ways that boosted their perceptions of their abilities. We decided to engage them with digital media because, on the surface level, we thought it would, in and of itself, "motivate" them. We soon discovered that this was an oversimplification and quickly corrected. We set out to design tasks that, when completed, enabled the students to attribute success to actions within their control; this sense of agency was unlikely during years of failure with print-based tasks. The approach was later rooted in a considerable body of research in achievement motivation, a lot of which had not been written at the inception of the project (e.g., Alderman, 1999; Wigfield, 1997; Wigfield & Guthrie, 1995, 1997) but at the time was mostly informed by the then-emerging engagement theme of the National Reading Research Center at the Universities of Georgia and Maryland (Alvermann & Guthrie, 1993).

In a nutshell, we "discovered" in the Literacy Lab setting what had already been substantiated in controlled interventions: When students perceived that they were successful, and they could set personally relevant goals and see that they were improving, they would read and write more, build fluency, and decide to persevere, even on tasks that they perceived as being difficult (Anderman et al., 2001; Pintrich and Schunk, 1996). Coupled with the motivation of choosing topics and tasks and using popular media (Alvermann, 2004; Alvermann, Moon, & Hagood, 1999; Kellner, 1995, 2002; Sefton-Green, 1998; Semali & Pailliotet, 1999) this proved a powerful way to both reengage the disengaged, and to change their perceptions of themselves as not only literate, but highly so given an expanded notion of what it means to be literate.

Specifically, we set up an inquiry-based approach in which students selected topics of their choosing (with broad topical guidelines) and used a variety of tools, including media-authoring hardware and software, to construct projects associated with tangible goals. For example in a major project, which we termed the *Violence Project*, students selected from among film and TV media to show how the violence in each medium impacted adolescents. They were required to use a variety of media, including print, to make their case, and the goal was to present the final project for parents on open house night.

In a current project, we are studying seventh-grade students' literacy practices in a two-year, media-rich, language arts class offered at Hawthorne, a suburban middle school. The students engage in a range of literacy practices including reading, writing (print and media authoring), web browsing, and playing video games, to attain personally relevant goals through the use of tools they control and connect to outcomes. Students engage in media-rich inquiry projects resulting in presentations about topics of their choosing and play video games in both "free form" game play as well as with participation structures we set up. For example, students learn the digital and conceptual tools related to urban planning and living similar to the SIMs video games and engage in an activity of designing a community.

In the current study (O'Brien, Beach, & Scharber, 2005), we are looking at how media-rich activities help learners connect their various lived worlds, some of them virtual rather than actual. Among other things, we are studying how these activities transform the students' senses of competence and agency, particularly as it has been defined in relation to print-based activities. In all of the work, we are continuing to address two key questions: First, why do adolescents who "struggle" with reading print text—a complex processing act, but not as complex as reading and writing a range of media—competently engage in these media-rich practices and choose to engage in them? Second, what is the nature of that competency and how is it connected to engagement?

At the core of the issue is how competencies are defined within the traditional "print-centric" world in comparison to how they are defined in the newer digital "media-centric" world. The caveat here is that these worlds are not distinct. Youth and adolescents navigate in and out of them seamlessly, but the literacy that officially counts is the print-centric one—the one that is formally assessed, the one they get feedback on from day to day in school, and the one that, in their minds, is the sole measure of their literate competence. In the next section,

I present vignettes from the two projects to accentuate how students lacking in print-centric competence according to formal tests, succeed with media tasks. As a follow-up, I compare and contrast print-centric and media-centric literacies. Finally, I elaborate on media-centric competence by looking closely at some more activities in the two projects with a focus on the process of using and creating media rather than on the media themselves—a process that has been termed *multimediating*.

Frameworks for Thinking About Competence and Engagement

In these vignettes, adolescents classified as "at risk" or "struggling," labels they usually acquire early in their academic careers, competently engage in media-centric tasks, most of which involve using media as well as engaging in traditional literacy practices. As you read the two vignettes, note the literate practices the struggling adolescents engage in and think about why they might consider themselves competent using the practices in these tasks.

The Literacy Lab: Eddie and Ron

In the Jefferson High Literacy Lab, students identified as most at risk in reading were scheduled into an English elective that was actually a special reading class. The focus of the class was on using media to engage the struggling readers (at that point, they were referred to as "at-risk" learners) and to improve their reading achievement.

Eddie and Ron, both freshmen, were self-selected project partners in the Literacy Lab. Each, when assessed with standardized tests and content reading inventories, read at about third-grade level. Both of them devoted limited attention to reading and writing activities in school and neither expressed much interest in reading and writing related to school tasks. Both boys expressed a range of interests when given the choice of picking project topics. Football was one of those topics.

When given the opportunity to work on a media project, they delighted in their shared interest in Jim Harbaugh, the star quarterback of the Indianapolis Colts at the time. They decided to create a website honoring their football hero, planned it, storyboarded it, and divided up tasks. Eddie found images of Harbaugh in the *Indianapolis Monthly* magazine, which was running a feature story on Harbaugh. Ron located video clips of some of Harbaugh's best plays from television sports highlights he had taped, saved these into files, and wrote captions for them. Eddie rounded up some biographical information and news stories about Harbaugh from the *Indianapolis Monthly*, *Sports Illustrated*, and other sources and synthesized the material.

As Eddie and Ron worked together, they continued to sort out the text and images and modify their plan for Web pages. They collaborated using SuperCard©, an authoring package they were both learning at the time that allowed them to mock-up the web pages with displays of text, pictures, and video clips. Eddie looked up information in the SuperCard documentation to help Ron as Ron used menus to explore button options, select background colors, and put hyperlinks on pages. Eddie served as the format editor, double-checking Ron's layouts of the objects on each page. The final product was a SuperCard stack that logically and aesthetically displayed text and pictures about Harbaugh's personal life, the evolution of his career, and key plays that played as video clips in windows on separate pages with captions and descriptions.

The Reading and Writing Intervention 7 Class: Darnell, Arthur, and Jonathan

This seventh-grade class, team-taught by an English teacher and a reading specialist, is designed for the struggling readers and writers in Hawthorne middle school. The class of about 15 adolescents meets once per day and is organized around both traditional and media-centric activities designed to improve the students' reading and writing skills. This scenario comes from an after-school video game club for students in the reading class.

Darnell, Arthur, and Jonathan, who show varying interests in reading and writing, but struggle with traditional school reading and writing tasks, joined the after-school video game club set up by Brock and Cassie, our doctoral students. The boys started out by playing, *Harry Potter and the Chamber of Secrets*, but after 10 minutes they became disinterested in it because it is a single player game (you get to be Harry Potter). It was clear that they viewed the game club as a social group. Darnell told me that he liked to play the Harry Potter game on his own. When I queried him about the relations between the game and the films, he said that you could do better in the game if you understood the "storyline" from watching the Harry Potter films.

While I talked with Darnell, Arthur and Jonathan had already migrated over to the other side of the room where Brock was setting up a Game Cube© and the game *Symphonia*, a multiplayer option Role Playing Game (RPG) in which two worlds, unaware of each other, share Mana, the same life force. Darnell left the Harry Potter game and joined them. Darnell and Arthur said they had played *Symphonia* before. They swapped the controllers, and whoever did not have a controller was willing to help the person with the controller to strategize. The discourse during gameplay was a mixture of fun, razzing, and offering strategy advice as the game progressed.

As they played, I asked them about reading the narrative text on the screen—when the story is presented in text or when the text is presented with oral narration. They said that they read the narrative text when it contains something crucial to playing the games, but don't read it when it does not. When the storyline text came up, if they viewed it as important they paused to read and listen.

If they already knew it, they were frustrated with the screen time taken up by it. I asked them if they read any of the printed documentation for the games they play and they said that they didn't—but they noted that they used such references as a last resort. I also asked about the "strategy" magazines for games and Jonathan said that he has them but seldom uses them for strategies. He said that he uses them as a last resort if he gets stuck, but admitted that he reads the reviews of new games or revised games to see what the best new games will be.

Reconceptualizing Competence

Eddie and Ron are the classic struggling readers who seldom engage in reading and writing in school. Yet, when given an opportunity to choose both a topic (Jim Harbaugh) and task (designing a website) based on interest, they planned a composition (the storyboard of the site), read sources (both visual and print-based), synthesized texts—not just print but all media—and put all of the media together. In the process they used a range of tools, including reading, writing, and a media-authoring tool on a computer, while overcoming a series of challenges. The media project they produced included print texts they could write and read, even though those print texts exceed the level at which they are supposed to competently read and write based on traditional reading assessments like the Stanford Diagnostic Reading Tests. Also, students like Ron and Eddie, who spent a lot of engaged time on projects, improved in reading as assessed on the state standardized tests.

Darnell, Arthur, and Jonathan, although more capable readers than their counterparts in the Literacy Lab project, did not do well on reading and writing in comparison to their same-age peers. The video game vignette shows that they are more than happy to read narratives that they believe will help them use tools (game controls, strategies) they need. They understand story lines in games and how those story lines connect to strategies. The game organizes a discourse community in which the boys are adept at using a range of social and strategic practices. They talk about the game, about their relative prowess with different genres of games (e.g., RPGs, shooter games, strategy games, simulations). They are also quick to offer advice about strategies to peers with the controllers while the game is being played. When playing another game, *WarioWorld*, they laughed, almost in synchronicity, at the same points in the game when a particularly interesting or surprising thing happened. The discourse was about familiarity with the game—the game, as a media text genre, is a given. As in all of the games, the boys automatically swapped controllers, and less knowledgeable peers, who haven't played a particular game, easily slid into controlling it with help from their more adept companions. Contrary to gender and discourse studies that indicate how males have conversational goals that place ultimate value on maintaining status (whereas girls and women use discourse to achieve connection and intimacy), for example in knowing things and knowing how to do things (e.g., Kendall & Tannen, 2003; Tannen, 1990), the boys in the video game club seemed willing to take advice from peers and to assume the position of being less knowledgeable than peers.

As the two vignettes show, literate competence is not a static, universal phenomenon. Rather, it is socially constructed, and relative to the use of certain tools, to complete certain goals. In terms of the reconceptualizing theme of this book, this is a New Literacies perspective (Gee, 1990; Lankshear & Knobel, 2003; Street, 1993). That is, it deviates from the traditional psychological notion that targets the processes and processor rather than practices, it situates the practices in the context of particular events in which they are used to complete a goal, and it relies on new tools like digital technologies that redefine texts and literacies. The vignettes show "reading" and "writing" as multidimensional and situated (Barton, Hamilton, & Ivanic, 2000; Street, 1993).

A Print-Centric View of Competence

The predominant processing definition of "struggling" adolescent learners is that they lack the skills and strategies that competent readers possess. They are struggling to be like their more competent peers. Just as the term *struggling* was starting to catch on, policymakers decided that "struggling" is too negative: Struggling readers are helplessly, hopelessly floundering; when we hear the term struggling, we see the "remedial" readers we have taught looking into hallways from "special" classrooms where they stay forever and never catch up with their peers. These kids were relabelled *striving* readers by the Bush administration (Long, 2005) because striving connotes moving forward rather than floundering. The formerly struggling readers are now seemingly reaching for lofty goals; they are optimistic, making progress, and self-assured that they will not be left behind. "Progress" in terminology aside, I use the term *struggling* readers because it was still the predominant term when this chapter was written, and messing with shades of meaning changes little about how labels affect the students.

Adolescents who struggle started out as primary-age readers who likely had trouble with decoding and fluent word recognition, including recognizing sight words; they were also kids unable to connect ideas in running text and make inferences (e.g., Pressley, 2002). They have been characterized as having "core linguistic deficits," something attributable to all struggling readers, particularly with weaknesses in phonological processing and word recognition (Moats, 2001). The affective correlate of this deficit view is that struggling adolescent readers, because they have been unsuccessful early in their academic careers, have not "practiced" reading because once they realized they were not good at it (because of deficits and poor instruction), they avoided it.

One instructional complement to this deficit view is that these older struggling readers would likely have ended up on a more positive academic trajectory if they had more effective instruction when they were in primary grades

(Lyon, Fletcher, Torgesen, Shaywitz, & Chhabra, 2004). Hence, the solution to their deficit is that they need more and better instruction on the things that they didn't learn in the first place so that they can catch up to "grade level" where their more competent peers reside. If they catch up, they will learn to like to read, they will do it more often, and through this practice, get better and better at it. The evidence indicates that these kids are not likely to ever catch up to their more competent peers (Allington & Walmsley, 1995; Juel, 1988). From about fourth grade on, in addition to fluent decoding and word recognition, competence also means being able to comprehend increasingly complex texts that are inaccessible to even some competent readers. Competence means that readers need to self-regulate, automatically drawing on a repertoire of skills and strategies and monitoring their understanding of written discourse that is increasingly disconnected as texts become compendia for more and more information (Jetton & Alexander, 2004). High school students and teachers I work with now on literacy coaching and academic literacy support say that many of the texts they try to use are so difficult that even the most competent readers are unlikely to tackle them.

In school, by the time you leave the primary grades, you believe that you have ability or you don't, and this self-appraisal is usually related not only to specific disciplines but to specific tasks within those disciplines (Anderman et al., 2001; Pintrich & Schunk, 2002). Even second-graders will render honest appraisals of their academic prowess by saying, "I am a good reader but I am not good at math" or "Marlene is better at reading than me." From the print-centric view, your perception of your competence in reading is based on what Street (1984, 1993, 2005) termed the *autonomous* view of literacy. Autonomous literacy, as defined in national and international campaigns, is a sort of decontextualized, "homogenized," absolute set of skills one is supposed to attain; the skills are assessed statistically and linked to technical and economic consequences. Literacy, in and of itself, autonomously, will exert predictable effects on social and cognitive practices. High stakes testing, meeting standards, reading texts in approved core curricula, completing assignments in which you recall questions about sections of textbooks, are all articulations of autonomous literacy. This relatively narrow, print-centric literacy has been most recently termed the "deep grammar of schooling" (Lankshear & Knobel, 2003, p. 30).

Within the secondary school as institution, perception about ability is also tied to labels and "special" programs to which one is assigned, and the institution, in labeling students as "at-risk" (substitute "struggling" or "remedial"), usually unwittingly abdicates ultimate responsibility for helping them (O'Brien et al., 2001). This is not to say that we set up programs so we don't have to help them; rather, the special programs provide a way of helping them that lets us off the hook in terms of providing experiences and opportunities that are afforded other students, particularly academic track students.

In the next section, I discuss a media-centric view of competence. Although the second definition of competence is supported by the work in multimediating presented in the two vignettes, that work, based on our research and that of others, has the potential to positively change learners' sense of competence from the frameworks supported by both definitions—with both print and media.

A Digital Media-Centric View of Competence

Even though literate competence is defined almost exclusively by national, state, and local standards related to facility in processing print, adolescents are developing new competencies as they increasingly use and create a range of electronic print and media texts. A national survey conducted by the Kaiser Family Foundation (Rideout, Roberts, & Foehr, 2005) unsurprisingly found that both children and teens are spending more and more time engaged with a variety of "new media" including computers, the Internet, and video games, and that during a quarter of their media use time (26%) they use more than one medium at a time. Even 10 years ago, 71% of teens said that they used the Internet as their primary source of information for completing school assignments (Lenhart, Simon, & Graziano, 2001). To date, in an analysis of Internet use across generations, 93% of teens (ages 12–17) report going online (Zickuhr, 2010). Clearly, the Internet is *the* new academic text, and being able to read it will be crucial to academic success in the years ahead.

Adolescents, along with the larger population, are developing new literacies in order to negotiate their media worlds. I like the term, *multimediating* (Doneman, 1997; also discussed in Lankshear & Knobel, 2003) as a way to define this new competence with digital media. It captures the complexity of simultaneous use of multiple media. Rather than *multimedia*, which focuses on the noun, the *production* of media, Doneman opts for the verb to capture the active processes of engaging in a variety of media environments. Multimediators move seamlessly in and out of the real world and virtual worlds, rapidly and automatically using various technologies that they embrace as extensions of themselves. As I discuss shortly, some of the processes used in multimediating are New Literacies.

Adolescent multimediators can work on a paper using a word processor with multiple IM windows open, some windows for conversations with peers also working on the assignment, some windows for social conversations, while listening to MP3 music files, intermittently looking aside from the computer screen to check a cell phone for text messages. In fact, researchers in the Kaiser Family Foundation study already cited (Rideout et al., 2005) found that youths, who spend on average 6½ hours per day using media, do not displace older media with new media—they simply spend more time with all media and use multiple media simultaneously; in short, they engage in multimediating.

Multimediating involves not only a simultaneous allocation of attention to different tasks, it also involves multimodal channel switching and/or simultaneous channel use plus rapid attention shifts, some self-initiated, some as automatic responses to a media field (e.g., pop-ups and banners on web pages, audible signals of information coming into email and text messaging). We have typically explained this shifting—which the Kaiser Family Foundation report, I think erroneously, termed *multitasking*—to the resource allocation flexibility of the cognitive processor. I say more about this misconception later. The New Literacies, in this paradigm, would be part of this efficient cognitive processor that has simply adapted to multimediating. There is another, perhaps more compelling and certainly more futuristic, explanation for how multimediators develop new competencies: cyborg theory.

Cognitive scientists, philosophers of mind, and neurologists are exploring the likelihood that the cyborg human brain is adapting to the expanding mediasphere, not by fine-tuning resources allocation but by rewriting its neural networks. Clark (2003), one of the breed of "new humanists," who is a philosopher and cognitive scientist, states that we should never underestimate the plasticity of the human brain, which, he contends, is always adaptable and modifiable to environmental "props and scaffolds" so as to be ready to grow into extended "cognitive and computational architectures" (p. 67). The cognitive and linguistic adaptations the brain may be making to permit multimediating could mean that reconceptualizing literacies is not only academic, it is neurobiological.

This cyborg theory rings of science fiction creepiness; the Borg on *Star Trek* chant in unison as they "assimilate" entire races, "Resistance is futile!" Yet, it is a perfectly good *partial* explanation for why adolescents who have grown up with computers and related technologies have developed and enhanced new ways of interfacing their brains and language systems with digital media. The multiliteracies and multimediating are the result of a brain "upgrade." Restak (2003), a neurologist and neuropsychiatrist, has actually coined the term the *New Brain*, which helps to partly explain what new media literacies are. Like the philosophers of mind, except in taking the route of neuroimaging rather than intellectual argument, he contends that media and technologies can permanently alter, although sometimes in harmful ways, the human brain. Like Clark, he supports the notion of brain plasticity, the ability of the neurobiology of the organ to adapt and, in a major split with traditional neuroscience, contends that brain plasticity does not stop at adolescence. Rather, Restak contends, plasticity continues throughout one's life. Although we know relatively little about the neurobiology of these new digital media literacies, it is incumbent upon us to find out more.

Multimediating and the Mediasphere

As I noted, traditional learning theorists might want to classify multimediating as a form of multitasking. The synthesis of media use in the Kaiser Family Foundation study cited previously (Rideout et al., 2005) characterized it just that way. In my view, that parallel is inaccurate. Multimediating is not the purposeful juggling of multiple tasks. Multimediating is constructing and reconstructing the community we live in—a community that, itself, melds the real with the virtual in the data-sphere or mediasphere (Rushkoff, 1996). It involves using media, producing media, and engaging in literate practices as a way of fitting in the world (Lankshear & Knobel, 2003). The new competencies subsume the old ones of processing print text but are more complex.

The *millennials*, students we teach who were born between 1980 and 2000, have also been referred to in the last 10 years by a variety of techno terms like the *Internet Generation* and the *Digital Generation* and, most recently, *Generation M* (M for mediacentric) because of their increasing facility with digital media and ICTs as a routine way of life. They are constantly immersed in the mediasphere and they negotiate it seamlessly.

The competencies adolescents are developing with these new media texts, if tapped and applauded, should drastically change our conceptions of what literacy means. More importantly, it will change adolescents' perceptions of their literacy abilities. And perceptions of abilities, particularly for adolescents who have been disengaged and have viewed themselves as incompetent with print texts since about second or third grade, may be as important, or even more important, to their future engagement, perseverance, goal setting, than either strategies or skills instruction alone (Anderman et al., 2001; Guthrie and Wigfield, 2000; Wigfield, 2004). The significance of the multiple "new" literacies in this reengagement of disengaged youth is just starting to unfold (Lankshear & Knobel, 2003).

In the remainder of the chapter, I explore multimediating more directly using additional vignettes from both the high school and middle school literacy projects. I also use some specific multimediating literacy frameworks to better explicate how the latest reconceptualizations of adolescent literacy, in the realm of multi-mediating, are redefining struggling adolescents' literate competence.

Another View From the Field: A Closer Look at Competence in Multimediating

Some of these vignettes are selected and adapted from some previous work with a new analysis based on the multimediating frameworks. Others are so new that they are still evolving, but I render an analysis of them as I understand them now. As before, read each with an eye for what these adolescents who struggle with print in typical schooled literacy tasks do when they are multimediating.

Katie: The Virtual Life of the Grateful Dead

Unlike Eddie and Ron and most other students in the Literacy Lab, Katie was a relatively high achiever but lacked "motivation," although she was about two grade equivalents behind her peers in reading. The slight lag could be attributable to her disengagement. We found out that she was interested in the Grateful Dead, a band she discovered via her parents' music collection. She was particularly interested in the band following the death of band leader Jerry Garcia. My colleague, Dave Stith, talked with her about the music. Being a musician himself, Dave facilitated her interest in the topic and she decided to do a media project on the Dead. For several weeks, Katie read everything she could find about the band in Rolling Stone and other music publications. Via her reading, she became fascinated with images of the band, both pictures and the various symbols the band used. She scanned in pictures of Garcia working with the band and relaxing at home. She integrated symbols into her print text, appropriately selecting San Francisco font to write text for her documentary. One day when we were videotaping various projects, she presented some of her work, talking very passionately about the band and their music and enthusiastically explaining how she used various hardware and software to create the project.

Denise and Lynn: CSI on CD

When I met her, Denise had been in the Literacy Lab for two years. She was mostly positive about her academic accomplishments, but thought that she struggled in reading because she didn't concentrate enough and viewed reading as erratic. "Some days I just can't read—I like, can't get it." Lynn was more typical of the Literacy Lab students with a lower achievement profile across subject areas. But Lynn was always upbeat and ready to work to improve herself. Denise, on the other hand, noted that she was fulfilling her promise to her parents to get Cs so she could continue to play basketball. Both Lynn and Denise were slow starting, but Lynn had more difficulty finding topics that interested her. Both girls reported that they thought they were reading better because of the Literacy Lab. The two girls were friends and liked to work together. The project that I became interested in studying was not a media project they worked on but something they did when they finished their main project tasks for the day—playing a CD-based mystery game, *Who Killed Elspeth Haskard: The Magic Death* written by Shannon Gilligan, an acclaimed author and producer of the "Who Killed…" interactive multimedia series. In the game, the players, Denise and Lynn, assumed the role of police detectives. They went to a virtual crime scene and gathered evidence (this was well before the popular *CSI* TV series), they accessed lab reports to check blood evidence and combed through telephone logs, they went through videos of interviews with suspects whose records they also pored over. As they became overwhelmed with evidence, they took copious notes and classified information in several ways to cross-check it. At one point, they even discovered that the CD contained conflicting information— for example, listing two different blood types for the same person in different places. When they solved the game, they decided to author one themselves, and over a period of about four weeks constructed a murder mystery with them, their friends Lynn and Raylene, and teachers (Dave, Rebecca, and me) as characters.

Tania: Multimediating a Minnesota Tradition

One of several activities we studied at the Hawthorne middle school focused on why and how the seventh graders put together media productions—why they picked the topics they did, what they were thinking as they constructed them, who the audience was. The vignettes were constructed from interviews we conducted using a retrospective think aloud format in which we elicited responses as the students showed us their productions. Tania's was atypical (although maybe not so unusual in Minnesota) in that she chose a male-oriented game about a male-oriented sport—deer hunting. She created a PowerPoint presentation on *Deerhunter*, a PlayStation® format game about hunting—getting gear, setting up a deerstand, picking the weather (a truly amazing virtual option), lining up a shot, and bagging "a big buck deer." She selected it because, like her dad, she was "addicted" to playing it. It was the way she could hunt with her dad before she was old enough for the real thing. And for the last year, as she played it, she said she was preparing to join the affinity group (Gee, 2003) of hunters—she noted excitedly that next year will be her first season in the real deer blind.

To show me a mockup of the actual virtual experiences, she assembled a set of slides showing how the deer looked in the rain, fog, snow, sun—she showed me what the deer looked like from a view in the game through binoculars and then through the scope of the rifle just before you bag him. Tania put the PowerPoint slides together by capturing screens from the game and from the game website. She didn't know where to look so she went to Google and typed in "images deer hunter" and, of the 50 pages that came up, some were from *Deerhunter*. She downloaded the images and placed them so that they would appeal to her intended audience—deer hunters, potential hunters, and her dad—whom she was trying to impress. She wrote the text for the images "mainly from memory" but pulled some text from the web. Tania classified media writing as easier than regular report writing because you have pictures; however, she noted that the visual composition that precedes the writing can be difficult because you have to think carefully and plan what features you want to show—and do it one slide at a time.

Mapping the Space of Multimediating

One of the focus group interview activities we did with the Hawthorne students involved drawing maps about the different worlds they live in and talking about the maps. These places that the kids inhabit represented geographical space, social/cultural spaces, and the so-called third space (Leander & Sheehy, 2004; Lefebvre, 1991; Soja, 1989) in which they engage in different discourses and enact various identities over space and time. In the focus group session, the kids also talked about pictures they took of various places, describing them, talking about why they took them. Some of the stories were linked to history or neighborhood stories about the places, like building features or natural features like important trees. Some were of family places. Some were of school, mostly social spaces (seeing friends between classes) and extracurricular activities like sports.

In a related activity, they drew maps of ideal communities, collaborating with peers to include all of the things they thought they needed or would like in such a community. The maps included neighborhoods for "richies" by the lake, houses with convenient shopping spaces, health clubs, and restaurants. One team constructed an elaborate school campus in one corner of their town where all of the schools from kindergarten through a four-year college were located. They said they did this so you can "get all of the education you need and never have to leave home." Another group I interviewed about their map planned an ideal community, with all of the amenities in other maps, except it included no schools. When I asked them about it, they simply said, "In an ideal world, there is no school."

As you can see in the vignettes, multimediating involved a variety of literacy practices and a range of purposes. But the common feature across vignettes is that it is part of what the adolescents did naturally in completing projects to help explain themselves, their interests, their pleasures, and the worlds they inhabit or would like to inhabit. In the next section, I delve further into what sorts of New Literacies practices were enacted in the multimediating vignettes and what they mean.

Literacy Frameworks for Critiquing New Literacies Competencies

In this section, I use a few of the many New Literacies frameworks to critique the vignettes of struggling readers engaged in or talking about multimediating, with a focus on redefining literate competence. These frameworks or conceptualizations, which are rapidly evolving, sometime overlap but also offer differing angles or important nuances on what multimediating is, what processes it involves and, by implication, what competencies it entails.

Multimodality

Kress's (2003; Kress & Van Leeuwen, 2001) framework of multimodality explores how representation of ideas using different semiotic modes (e.g., modes of representing knowledge and modes of practice) distributes meaning in new ways beyond representation with print or even traditionally linguistic means. According to Kress, we have moved from the page to the screen. The shift is not merely modal; rather, it is spatially more compelling. In two dimensions, I might use a print text description of a lesson I planned. In three dimensions I might use a video clip showing what I did during the lesson so viewers might read my plan and see how it actually played out. Based on careful planning or design, I can show a video accompanied by a narrative text and present a video and allow viewers/ composers to extend text by writing what they see in the video. I can use techniques such as framing (or lack thereof) to set off elements in different semiotic modes or to try to seamlessly merge them. Semiotic modes are subject to respective grammars or ways of saying things in different modes and knowing what can be said in each. The production, the articulation of the semiotic event, and distribution, the selection of the media, are interlinked and dictate how different media work together.

Katie designed her Grateful Dead documentary to maximize the use of different semiotic modes. She not only used print text and pictures but selected a font with regional significance to the band. What is more, she appropriated the band's own semiotic system by incorporating their symbols into her production. She exploited the spatial and modal dimensions of both print text and visual texts by juxtaposing them to create a more powerful message than the respective modes could carry alone in their original, linear form. Hence, Katie exhibited competence with framing the elements (e.g., a picture of Jerry Garcia relaxing, next to a picture of the band performing, accented by narrative about both photos with San Francisco font and embedded band symbols).

Denise and Lynn moved from the screen (the *Magic Death* CD) to the page and back to the screen as they used the media on the CD to construct notes and used notes to check the information on the CD. They negotiated various semiotic modes (videos of the crime scene, printed information telephone logs, and lab reports) and audio texts (interviews of the suspects) to synthesize what they learned into notes.

Tania composed her project on *Deerhunter* by carefully selecting images that highlighted what she believed to be the most compelling aspects of the game, and she both transposed text from Web sites and wrote text to accompany the images. Like adolescents in the other vignettes, she explored the respective grammars of the modalities she used and used them to fit her goal of producing something to convince others to play the game.

Focus group interviews that probed the various worlds these adolescents represented in their media productions and on their multimediating experiences, showed that they transition easily from the page to screen, from geographical space to virtual space and easily appropriate the literacies needed to succeed in virtual space. As consumers, they are adept at using the semiotic systems of each space they inhabit.

Textured Literacy

Yancey (2004) defines textured literacy as the ability to comfortably use and combine print, spoken, visual, and *digital* processes in a multilayered composition of a piece of writing. Essentially, this perspective can be used to characterize multimediating as a form of composition. The composition involves decisions about which media and artifacts to select to represent what one *knows* and wants others to know or feel. Ultimately, it also means using interactions with peers in constructing new, negotiated texts in which the media artifacts are expanded and critiqued.

Denise and Lynn tried to recreate the text of the CD-ROM *Magic Death* games in their own CD. Their composition is a good example of textualizing and intertextuality (Bloome & Egan-Robertson, 1993) as a cross between schooled and nonacademic literacy. The texture of their new media included the medical, technical, and law enforcement discourses Denise and Lynn experienced in the *Magic Death* game, photos they took of friends and teachers who became characters in the game, and storyline scenarios from Denise and Lynn's immediate social and school worlds. Both Tania's and Katie's productions were also sophisticated, textured compositions that involved decisions about which media to use, how much of each to use, and how to organize the print and visual media to impact an intended audience.

Technoliteracy and Literacies of Technology

Unlike the previous two frameworks, I use this one to focus on what we as teachers do to *provide educationally sound opportunities* for students to engage in multimediating rather than on what students do when multimediating. Both technoliteracy and the literacies of technology frameworks seem to address the thoughtful use of technologies in education.

Selfe & Hawisher (2004), in discussing the literacies of technology, have found it necessary to move beyond the oversimplified practice of literacy tied to particular tools like computers (hence, "computer literacy") to the notion of literacies of technology that more broadly connects social practices, people, technology, values, and literate activity within a larger "cultural ecology." Lankshear and Snyder's (2000) technoliteracy project explores the integration of technologies and literacy in useful ways while also presenting some caveats: First, there is pressure to technologize education in ways that may be detrimental; second, using technologies effectively requires a concerted effort to think deeply about literacy, learning, and technology together in critical, cultural, ways.

Technoliteracy and *literacies of technology* refer to an understanding of how literacies and technologies as implicitly integrative and mutually transformative practices come together when knowledgeable teachers use them in the arena of schooling. Unlike the other constructs used to critique New Literacies practices of students, this one allows a critique of the way teachers construct multimediating experiences for kids.

Katie's Grateful Dead project was one of many in a series of inquiry projects in which students in the Literacy Lab were to select both topics and tasks, using media authoring tools (hardware, software, collaborations with tech-savvy peers) to produce something they constructed to meet a personally relevant goal. The requirement was that the students include a range of media, not that they complete certain tasks with the media. Tania's *Deerhunter* project was similar, except her tools were a little more limited—using PowerPoint to display the inquiry and picking a topic within the realm of video games. Both of these projects were designed to allow the students to transform their understanding of literacy practices like reading and writing, rather than to focus on a tool like the computer to make something.

Denise and Lynn's video game playing was something that emerged out of the open structure we provided in the Literacy Lab where students had free access to the technologies. Playing games was transformed by them into a focused intermedial project—they wanted to make something like the *Magic Death* game. The intensity of their work on the project surprised both them and us, but they pursued it not because they were trying to use certain tech tools or to create something for an assignment; rather, they worked and watched what evolved out of their interest and perseverance.

Finally, the mapping spaces activity shows that kids intuitively understand technoliteracies as they understand other literate practices. For example, they are aware of the projective identities they have in video games (Gee, 2003) and how these identities need to be separated from their real-world identities; they matter-of-factly talk about IMing and text messaging as ways of being in the world— they do not stop to reflect on the technoliteracies that enable them to do these things. This is the very essence of the transformative nature of these technoliteracies. The pedagogical lesson from these literacies enacted outside of school is to look at how kids' engagement in these practices, and their feelings of competence, can be designed into school to bring out the best of what they can do, not with traditional print-centric literacies alone but with multimediating.

The Future of Multimediating in Schools

The New Literacies practices morph so rapidly that it is impossible to step back and say, "So this is what literacy is now"; rather, we must constantly retool, redefine, and figure out what to attend to during the evolution (Leu, 2000, 2002; Leu, Kinzer, Coiro, & Cammack, 2004). Multimediating is reshaping our traditional notions of literate competence at the same time it critiques the print-based notions of literacy tied to schooled practices. These practices have recently been referred to as the deep grammar of schooling (Lankshear & Knobel, 2003) and characterized as institutional practices and artifacts of the Institution of Old Learning, IOL for short (O'Brien & Bauer, 2005). The IOL protects and nurtures print-centric notions of literacy; it supports both assessment and instructional practices that keep schooled practices significantly behind what adolescents are engaging in outside of school. As in that cited article, I want to emphasize that the IOL is the *institution*, with its deeply held, historically grounded, organizational routines and practices, not the *teachers* within the institution. Many teachers are engaging in exciting New Literacies practices, but, overall, nationally, teachers can only progress as far as the IOL and national policy allow them.

The current "schooled literacy" response to New Literacies is to teach, model, coach, and provide practice in print strategies that struggling readers have never learned—more of the same, in spite of the fact that the approaches, for a host of reasons, did not work earlier in these adolescents' academic careers. While this often ineffective institutionalized practice is occurring in school, these same adolescents spend more and more time outside of school engaged in multimediating. As they do so, they build fluencies with the texts and technologies, develop positive perceptions about their abilities to engage in these New Literacies practices to meet personally relevant goals, and attribute much of their success to factors they control, based on their interests and connections to popular culture.

These multimediating adolescents are developing a very clear self-regulation of complex linguistic, cognitive, technical, and social skills and strategies. Few of the literate practices they master in multimediating are ever officially sanctioned in school as literate competencies. For example, the digitally rich inquiry projects, Internet use, IMing, and playing video games, all of which involve complex literacies, are typically viewed as either unimportant in school or as detractors from print-centric schooled literacies.

Research on how and why these new literate competencies develop is in its infancy. We need to design multidisciplinary studies that wed frameworks like socio-cognitive theories of motivation and engagement (which informs most of the engagement work in reading) and offer suggestions for how multimediating, which now occurs mostly outside of school settings, can be used in school not only to support adolescents' literate practices with print, but also to address the largely neglected "affective" dimensions of years of failure.

References

Alderman, M. K. (1999). *Motivation for achievement.* Mahwah, NJ: Lawrence Erlbaum Associates.

Allington, R. L., & Walmsley, S. R. (1995). *No quick fix: Rethinking literacy programs in America's elementary schools.* New York: Teachers College Press.

Alvermann, D. E. (2004). Media, information communication technologies, and youth literacies: A cultural studies perspective. *American Behavioral Scientist, 48*(1), 78–83.

Alvermann, D. E., & Guthrie, J. T. (1993). *Themes and directions of the National Reading Research Center* (Perspectives in Reading Research, No. 1). Athens, GA: National Reading Research Center, Universities of Georgia and Maryland.

Alvermann, D. E., Moon, J. S., & Hagood, M. C. (1999). *Popular culture in the classroom: Teaching and researching critical media literacy.* Newark, DE: International Reading Association.

Anderman, E. M., Eccles, J. S., Yoon, K. S., Roeser, R., Wigfield, A., & Blumenfeld, P. (2001). Learning to value mathematics and reading: Relations to mastery and performance-oriented instructional practices. *Contemporary Educational Psychology, 26,* 76–95.

Barton, D., Hamilton, M., & Ivanic, R. (Eds.). (2000). *Situated literacies: Reading and writing in context*. London: Routledge.

Bloome, D., & Egan-Robertson, A. (1993). The social construction of intertextuality in classroom reading and writing lessons. *Reading Research Quarterly, 28*, 305–333.

Clark, A. (2003). Natural born cyborgs? In J. Brockman (Ed.), *The new humanists* (pp. 70–77). New York: Barnes & Noble.

Doneman, M. (1997). Multimediating. In C. Lankshear, C. Bigum, & C. Durant (Eds.), *Digital rhetorics: Literacies and technologies in education—current practices and future directions* (Vol. 3, pp. 131–148). Brisbane, AU: QUT/DEETYA.

Gee, J. P. (1990). *Social linguistics and literacies: Ideology in discourses*. Hampshire, UK: Falmer.

Gee, J. P. (2003). *What video games have to teach us about learning and literacy*. New York: Palgrave Macmillan.

Guthrie, J. T., & Wigfield, A. (2000). Engagement and motivation in reading. In M. L. Kamil, P. Mosenthal, P. D. Pearson, & R. Barr (Eds.), *Handbook of reading research* (Vol. III, pp. 403–422). Mahwah, NJ: Lawrence Erlbaum Associates.

Jetton, T. L., & Alexander, P. A. (2004). Domains, teaching, and literacy. In T. L. Jetton & J. A. Dole (Eds.), *Adolescent literacy research and practice* (pp. 15–39). New York: Guilford.

Juel, C. (1988). Learning to read and write: A longitudinal study with 54 children from first through fourth grades. *Journal of Educational Psychology, 80*, 437–447.

Kellner, D. (1995). *Media culture*. London: Routledge.

Kellner, D. (2002). New media and new literacies: Reconstructing education for the new millennium. In L. Lievrouw & S. Livingstone (Eds.), *The handbook of new media* (pp. 90–104). London: Sage.

Kendall, S., & Tannen, D. (2003). Discourse and gender. In D. Schiffrin, D. Tannen, & H. E. Hamilton (Eds.), *Handbook of discourse analysis* (pp. 548–567). Malden, MA: Blackwell.

Kress, G. (2003). *Literacy in the new media age*. London: Routledge.

Kress, G., & Van Leeuwen, T. (2001). *Multimodal discourse: The modes and media of contemporary communication*. London: Edward Arnold.

Lankshear, C., & Knobel, M. (2003). *New literacies: Changing knowledge and classroom learning*. Buckingham, UK: Open University Press.

Lankshear, C., & Snyder, I. (2000). *Teachers and techno-literacy: Managing literacy, technology and learning in schools*. St Leonards NSW, Australia: Allen & Unwin.

Leander, K. M., & Sheehy, M. (Eds.). (2004). *Spatializing literacy research and practice*. New York: Peter Lang.

Lefebvre, H. (1991). *The production of space*. Cambridge, MA: Blackwell.

Lenhart, A., Simon, M., & Graziano, M. (2001). *The internet and education: Findings of the pew internet and american life project*. Available: http://www.pewinternet.org/Reports/2001/The-Internet-and-Education.aspx (accessed July 14, 2011).

Leu, D. J. (2000). Deictic consequences for literacy education in an information age. In M. L. Kamil, P. Mosenthal, P. D. Pearson, & R. Barr (Eds.), *Handbook of reading research* (Vol. III, pp. 743–770). Mahwah, NJ: Lawrence Erlbaum Associates.

Leu, D. J. (2002). The new literacies: Research on reading instruction with the Internet. In A. E. Farstrup & S. J. Samuels (Eds.), *What research has to say about reading instruction* (pp. 310–336). Newark, DE: International Reading Association.

Leu, D. J., Kinzer, C. K., Coiro, J. L., & Cammack, D. W. (2004). Toward a theory of new literacies emerging from the Internet and other information and communication technologies. In R. B. Ruddell & N. Unrau (Eds.), *Theoretical models and processes of reading* (5th ed., pp. 1570–1613). Newark, DE: International Reading Association.

Long, R. (2005). New year, full agenda. *Reading Today, 22*(4), 28.

Lyon, G. R., Fletcher, J. M., Torgesen, J. K., Shaywitz, S. E., & Chhabra, V. (2004). Preventing and remediating failure: A response to Allington. *Educational Leadership, 61*(6), 86–88.

Moats, L. (2001). When older students can't read. *Educational Leadership, 58*(6), 36–39.

O'Brien, D. G. (1998). Multiple literacies in a high school program for "at-risk" adolescents. In D. E. Alvermann, K. A. Hinchman, D. W. Moore, S. F. Phelps, & D. R. Waff (Eds.), *Reconceptualizing the literacies in adolescents' lives* (pp. 27–49). Mahwah, NJ: Lawrence Erlbaum Associates.

O'Brien, D. G. (2001). "At-risk" adolescents: Redefining competence through the multiliteracies of intermediality, visual arts, and representation. *Reading Online, 4*(11). Available: http://www.readingonline.org/newliteracies/obrien/.

O'Brien, D. G. (2003). Juxtaposing traditional and intermedial literacies to redefine the competence of struggling adolescents. *Reading Online, 6*(7). Available: http://www. readingonline.org/newliteracies/obrien2/.

O'Brien, D. G., & Bauer, E. (2005). Essay book review. New Literacies and the institution of old learning. *Reading Research Quarterly, 40*, 120–131.

O'Brien, D., Beach, R., & Scharber, C. (2005, December). *Struggling middle school students' multimediating: Countering institutionally defined notions of incompetence.* Paper presented at the Annual Meeting, National Reading Conference, Miami, FL.

O'Brien, D. G., Springs, R., & Stith, D. (2001). Engaging at-risk students: Literacy learning in a high school literacy lab. In E. B. Moje & D. G. O'Brien (Eds.), *Constructions of literacy: Studies of teaching and learning in and out of secondary schools* (pp. 105–123). Mahwah, NJ: Lawrence Erlbaum Associates.

Pintrich, P. R., & Schunk, D. H. (1996). *Motivation in education.* Englewood Cliffs, NJ: Merrill.

Pintrich, P. R., & Schunk, D. H. (2002). *Motivation in education: Theory, research, and applications* (2nd ed.). Englewood Cliffs, NJ: Merrill.

Pressley, M. (2002). *Reading instruction that works: The case for balanced teaching* (2nd ed.). New York: Guilford.

Restak, R. (2003). *The new brain: How the modern age is rewiring your mind.* New York: Rodale.

Rideout, V. J., Roberts, D. F., & Foehr, U. G. (2005). *Generation M: Media in the lives of 8–18 year-olds.* Menlo Park, CA: Kaiser Family Foundation.

Rushkoff, D. (1996). *Media virus.* New York: Ballantine.

Sefton-Green, J. (Ed.). (1998). *Digital diversions.* London: UCL Press.

Selfe, C. L., & Hawisher, G. E. (2004). *Literate lives in the information age: Narratives of literacy from the United States.* Mahwah, NJ: Lawrence Erlbaum Associates.

Seligman, M. (1992). *Helplessness.* New York: Freeman.

Semali, L., & Pailliotet, A. W. (Eds.). (1999). *Intermediality: The teachers' handbook of critical media literacy.* Boulder, CO: Westview.

Soja, E. W. (1989). *Postmodern geographies.* New York: Verso.

Street, B. V. (1984). *Literacy in theory and practice.* Cambridge, UK: Cambridge University Press.

Street, B. V. (Ed.). (1993). *Cross-cultural approaches to literacy.* Cambridge, UK: Cambridge University Press.

Street, B. V. (2005). Recent applications of New Literacy studies in educational contexts. *Research in the Teaching of English, 39*(4), 417–423.

Tannen, D. (1990). *You just don't understand: Women and men in conversation.* New York: Ballantine.

Wigfield, A. (1997). Children's motivations for reading and reading engagement. In J. T. Guthrie & A. Wigfield (Eds.), *Reading engagement: Motivating readers through integrated instruction* (pp. 14–33). Newark, DE: International Reading Association.

Wigfield, A. (2004). Motivation for reading during the early adolescent years. In D. S. Strickland & D. E. Alvermann (Eds.), *Bridging the literacy achievement gap in grades 4–12* (pp. 56–69). New York: Teachers College Press.

Wigfield, A., & Guthrie, J. T. (1995). *Dimensions of children's motivations for reading: An initial study* (No. 34). Athens, GA and College Park, MD: National Reading Research Center, Universities of Georgia and Maryland.

Wigfield, A., & Guthrie, J. T. (1997). Relations of children's motivation for reading to the amount and breadth of their reading. *Journal of Educational Psychology, 89,* 420–432.

Yancey, K. (2004). Using multiple technologies to teach writing. *Educational Leadership,* October 2004, 38–40.

Zickuhr, K. (2010). *Generations 2010.* Pew Internet and American Life Project, Washington, DC: Pew Research Center.

6

THINKING WITH FORENSIC SCIENCE

A Content Analysis of Forensic Comic Books and Graphic Novels

Barbara Guzzetti and Marcia Mardis

Imagine a school in which teachers are committed to bridging adolescents' everyday literacies with the literacy practices common to subject matter learning. Now, focus on a hypothetical science classroom in that school. What would the teacher in that classroom need to know about the everyday texts adolescents use that may have potential for connecting with their interests while simultaneously supporting the science curriculum? We had those questions in mind when we designed the study that is at the heart of this chapter.

Students' interest and achievement in science are under increased scrutiny in the United States due to their consistently poor achievement in science (NCES, 2011), particularly when compared to students' science achievement in other nations (OECD, 2010). Lagging performance has led science educators and policymakers to explore ways to improve learners' motivation and performance in science. In response, new science education standards in this country encourage teachers to focus on connecting students' preferences for social, interactive, and media-rich learning (AAUW, 2002; Guzzetti, 2009) to subject-matter instruction. This blend of knowledge and process is intended to develop and refine students' scientific inquiry skills while increasing their knowledge of scientific concepts (Ansbacher, 2000).

Simultaneously, similar concerns have been raised about students' proficiency in literacy in the United States (OECD, 2010). Increasing adolescents' ability and motivation to read, write, and talk like scientists has become a recent focus in the effort to improve their science achievement (Saul, 2003). The preteen and teen years are key times to spark students' interest and motivation because academic achievement often begins to decline during the middle-school years (Eccles et al., 1993). In many cases, this decline has been linked to students' inability to relate to course material.

Personalizing science by integrating literacy may be particularly beneficial for adolescents who begin to lose interest in science and choose non-science courses and careers (Yerrick & Ross, 2001). An instructional approach that draws on adolescents' preferences for everyday texts may have potential to interest young people in science while supporting the science curriculum. Therefore, we set out to examine how the content of science-related comic books and graphic novels convey science concepts that could complement and support science instruction.

Comics and Graphic Novels as Contexts for 21st Century Skills

The development of 21st century skills depends on deep engagement with content through multiple literacies. Becoming literate in contemporary times equates to effectively engaging with a variety of modes and texts (Rycik, 2008). For example, the ability to critically view and create images is increasingly needed in the 21st century. As a result, visual literacy has become a core learning skill (Mitchell, 1995). Visual literacy has been described as transformational because it allows learners to juxtapose words and images in new and personal ways (Abilock, 2008; Felten, 2008). Visual and print literacies are foundational to media literacy and literacy in content areas.

Informational text can be a source of visual literacy. A visually appealing book with a blend of words and images supports students' acquisition of conceptual knowledge by offering students additional opportunities to engage with concepts from many points of interest. These include interest in the content, interest in the images, and interest in the combination of the two. With these kinds of texts, students are more likely to spend time gaining vocabulary, being exposed to new concepts, and reflecting on questions and ideas (Duke, 2004). The confidence they gain by learning material in informational texts through multiple modes encourages students to ask more questions and think and write deeply about the subject (Filipenko, 2004).

Comic books are one of the most popular types of media texts used by young people (Guzzetti, 2010). They communicate narratives through a combination of text and sequential illustrations. The term comic book is actually a misnomer; they are not books, and they are often not comical (Wright, 2001). Comic books can be nonfiction as well as fiction and may contain easy narratives alongside challenging content (Meier, 2007).

Graphic novels are an extension of comic books and depend on images, text, and white space to convey meaning (McCloud, 1993; Rourke, 2010). Graphic novels incorporate sequential art and an ordered narrative with integrated images and text (Meier, 2007). Dresang (1999) described the graphic novel as a natural evolution from books for students in an image-rich culture. Because today's adolescents interact with so much visual media, they are comfortable using both images and text to create meaning, and graphic novels are credited with being the ideal vehicle for fostering students' visual and print literacy (Gillenwater, 2009).

Vivid depictions in graphic novels appeal to a variety of learners, including students with learning disabilities and language challenges (Chun, 2009; Smetana, Odelson, Burns, & Grisham, 2009). Educators can use graphic novels to increase students' motivation in school (Griffith, 2010) and for a lifetime (Botzakis, 2009b). These everyday texts are thought to promote better reading skills and improve students' comprehension because young people are interested in engaging in the content, and as a result may be inspired to write and think about the information presented (Frey & Fisher, 2004).

Like comic books, not all graphic novels are fiction. Those that are nonfiction can be used to support mastery in content areas like science, history, and social studies (Schwarz, 2002). Graphic novels are often informational texts that address political, social, historical, and personal issues in ways more powerful than other textual forms. Incorporating popular culture texts, such as comic books and graphic novels, helps to bridge the gap between students' literacy pursuits and popular culture interests outside of school and their in-school instruction, which they often view as unrelated to ordinary life (Morrison, Bryan & Chilcoat, 2002).

Forensic Science as Content for 21st Century Skills

Informed by the popularity among young people of television programs like *CSI*, *CSI NY*, *CSI Miami*, *The New Detectives*, and *Forensic Files*, forensic science has been integrated into the secondary school curriculum; these classes have become among the most popular ones that schools offer (Angier, 2009). Forensic science is the application of scientific knowledge to solve legal problems (Dillon, 1999). The study of forensic science has become a popular approach to teaching scientific thinking and inquiry skills because it promotes problem identification, question formation, data collection and analysis, and interpretation—all core components of scientific inquiry (Duncan & Daly-Engel, 2006).

Due to the popularity of forensic science television shows and movies, this active, integrative approach to instruction is deeply rooted in popular culture and appeals to and motivates adolescent learners in science (Harrison, 1999; Howitt, Lewis, & Waugh, 2009). Incorporating forensic activities into classroom instruction has resulted in students' increased engagement in science activity (Learner, 2003) and enthusiasm for science (Colgan, 2002). Forensic activities have helped students to think critically like scientists by analyzing the world around them (Dickie & Percival, 1986) and to increase their scientific inquiry skills (Guzzetti & Bang, 2011). Teachers who incorporate forensic activities in their science curriculum report that students view these activities as science in everyday life for problem solving (Brooks, Green, Kleck & Muench, 1995).

Forensic Comic Books and Graphic Novels

Recognizing that adolescents tend to prefer the types of ordinary texts found outside of school (Guzzetti, 2002; Worthy, Moorman, & Turner, 1999), publishers have begun to offer comic books and graphic novels that deal with forensic science at the secondary school level (e.g., Saferstein, 2008). Many titles from this new genre of alternative instructional materials (Guzzetti, 2010; Mardis 2006) can be found on LibraryThing.com (www.librarything.com). Other comic book series and graphic novels associated with *CSI*, *CSI NY*, and *CSI Miami* can be found on the website of IDW Publishing (http://CSI.wetpaint.com/page/CSI+Comic+Book).

One of us (Guzzetti, 2010) conducted a content analysis of these texts to determine their utility as supplementary materials for literacy-based science instruction and for teaching concepts in forensic chemistry. In that earlier study in which students were observed reading them in high school chemistry classes during a forensics unit, Guzzetti (2010) examined *CSI* comics and graphic novels for their format and content, particularly in relation to the teacher's forensics curriculum and lesson plans. Nearly one half of the content terms in the *CSI* comic books and graphic novels related to forensic evidence. Other terms represented eight forensic processes used in the forensics curriculum, while the remainder included two types of forensic technology or equipment used in chemistry instruction in secondary schools. These terms were introduced and used within the context of a story, but were not defined or explained.

Guzzetti's (2010) analysis of students' reports demonstrated that they were able to infer the meaning of the terms from the context, as well as gain working familiarity with, or reinforcement of, the terms for academic learning. Her findings also showed, however, that while young people can benefit from a wide range of relevant popular culture texts, these resources do not always contain sound science and concepts that reinforce the curriculum. Many of the scientific activities depicted in media texts of television programs and movies perpetuate misconceptions about forensic science, such as the widespread availability of DNA and fingerprint evidence, and the rapid processing time of evidence analysis (Bergslien, 2006).

Continuing the Exploration of Comic Books and Graphic Novels

As researchers, we were curious to investigate further the potential usefulness of forensic media texts in infusing literacy in science instruction. We also wanted to compare the usefulness of nonfiction comic books to fiction comic books and graphic novels. We anticipated that this comparative analysis would provide a more complete picture of the appropriateness of alternative texts in science instruction. Specifically, we wanted to know the degree to which forensic-related nonfiction comic books are useful for teaching science. For example, what science concepts might students learn from these everyday texts? What are the narrative elements and format features of forensic comics that may motivate adolescents to learn science? We also wanted to know how nonfiction forensic comic books compare to fiction comic books and graphic novels in terms of conceptual content, story elements, and format features.

Our Perspectives

Two complementary perspectives guided our study. The first of these views literacy as a social practice (Gee, 2003; Street, 1995). This view recognizes that literacy practices occur in situated, or specific, contexts (Street, 1995). It also posits that students have a literate life outside the classroom, and that they engage with others in their own explorations of literacy. The second perspective, which is based in the New Literacies Studies (Gee, 2003; New London Group, 1996), makes use of an expanded definition of what counts as text to include visual images as well as oral, written, or electronic messages. Taken together, these two perspectives account for literacy as a social practice by recognizing the multiple texts (visual, digital, and print) that students read in- and out-of-school in various social settings. They also recognize the interrelationships between the literacy skill and knowledge used in interactions with texts in both in- and out-of-school settings (Gee, 2003).

Choosing and Examining Forensic Science Graphic Novels and Comic Books

To explore the usefulness of comic books and graphic novels for teaching science, we focused on those that were forensics related due to the recent addition of forensic science to the curriculum in secondary schools (Guzzetti, 2009, 2010; Guzzetti & Bang, 2011). Our primary sample for this analysis was a convenience sample of six nonfiction forensic comic books in the series *Graphic forensic science* published by Rosen Publishing Group. We classified these books as nonfiction because of their classification as nonfiction by the Library of Congress catalogue (www.catalog.loc.gov) and because of the publisher's claim that these were true stories.

We chose this series due to the books' recent publication date, the series availability, the publishers' intended audience of middle school and up ages (www.rosenpublishing.com), and recommendations from independent reviewers published on Amazon.com and on Timberdoodle.com (www.timberdoodle.com/graphic_Forensic_science_Set_P1239-210.htm). We were also intrigued by the publisher's description of the books as containing "historical and scientific background, gripping photographs, and detailed annotated diagrams." The comic books in this series included the titles *Autopsies: Pathologists at work* (Jeffrey, 2008a); *Solving crimes with trace evidence* (Jeffrey, 2008b); *Detective work with ballistics* (West, 2008); *Crime scene investigators* (Shone, 2008a); *Corpses and skeletons* (Shone, 2008b); and *Solving crimes through criminal profiling* (Shone, 2008c).

A second set of forensic comic books and graphic novels we used for comparison were those in the fictional *CSI* series published by IDW Publishers. Although the individual comic books contained some nonfiction supplementary material, such as letters to the editor and ads for other related media, we classified these texts as fiction because a check of the Library of Congress catalogue revealed that the Library of Congress has classified each of the *CSI* titles as fiction. We also classified them as fiction due to the publisher's disclaimer on the title page of the compendium of three graphic novels, *CSI: Case files* (Collins, 2006b) that "any similarities to persons living or dead [in the stories] are purely coincidental."

This convenience sample of books had originally been selected for a prior content analysis (Guzzetti, 2010) based on their availability in comic book stores and public libraries, their popularity with young people, and their recent copyright dates. The usual publication format of these stories was to appear as a continuing episode with an instalment of the story in each comic book that was published monthly for five months. A total of five comic books in the series presented a complete story and were bound together as a graphic novel.

These titles were obtained and analyzed as either comic books or graphic novels by focusing on the terms used in the comic book stories and by examining their format features. Two titles, *CSI: Secret identity* (Grant, 2005) and *CSI: Dying in the gutters* (Grant, 2006) were analysed as a series of five individual comic books for a total of 10 comic books. Another title, *CSI: NY: Bloody murder* (Collins, 2005) was billed by the publisher as a graphic novella. Three other graphic novels were bound together as one book, *CSI: Miami* (Mariotte, 2005a). The graphic novels in this compendium included *CSI: Miami: Smoking gun* (Mariotte, 2005b); *CSI: Miami: Thou shalt not* (Oprisko, 2005b); and *CSI: Miami: Blood/Money* (Oprisko, 2005a). Another three graphic novels, *CSI: Serial* (Collins, 2006c); *CSI: Bad rap* (Collins, 2006a) and *CSI: Demon house* (Collins, 2004a) represented the first three *CSI* comic books that were published in a series form and later compiled into one volume, *CSI: Case Files* (Collins, Rodriguez & Wood, 2006).

A third series we considered, *Crime scene club*, published by Mason Crest, was not included in our examination because the books in the series did not fit our definition of a comic book or graphic novel. Despite the publisher's claim that "graphic novel illustrations add to the stories' excitement and appeal while color photographs clearly illustrate the concepts discussed in the non-fiction text" (www.masoncrest.com), the books did not integrate text and images in comic-book style. Instead, the text was accompanied by occasional illustrations in a traditional chapter format. Each book in the series concluded with an informational section, including forensic vocabulary and explanations of the forensic science techniques used in the story. This format, billed by the publishers as "fact and fiction" (Mason Crest Publishers, 2011), did not offer similar format and style elements for comparison to the other two series we included in this analysis.

How We Examined Our Forensic Science Comic Books and Graphic Novels

We conducted a content analysis to determine the usefulness of nonfiction comic books on forensics for facilitating students' conceptual learning in science. We also examined these nonfiction forensic comic books to determine if there were appealing features that could motivate students in content learning. In doing so, we examined the subject matter concepts they contained, as well as their features and formats.

We used a recognized way to analyse the conceptual content by examining the vocabulary in the nonfiction texts of the *Graphic forensic science* series as in a prior analysis of the *CSI* fiction series (Guzzetti, 2010). We focused on examining the vocabulary in these texts because in academic disciplines, concepts are represented by content vocabulary (Alvermann, Phelps, & Gillis, 2010). Mastery of academic vocabulary is crucial to comprehending content area texts (Pearson, Hiebert, & Kamil, 2007). Wide reading and multiple exposures to words can help students expand their vocabulary (Blachowicz, Fisher, Ogle, & Watts-Taffe, 2006). Students who master academic vocabulary are enabled to talk and write like members of a discipline (Nagy & Scott, 2000).

Hence, we identified the occurrence and frequency of vocabulary terms from forensic science that represented major ideas or supporting details in these stories. We noted those terms in the comic books that are commonly found in forensic curriculum materials, glossaries, and lesson plans, including those available online from the Shodor Educational Foundation (www.shodor.org/workshops/forensic/lessons) and TruTv (formerly called Court TV) available at www.trutv.com/foresncis_currriculum. We also noted vocabulary terms in the comic books that had been introduced in a forensic unit in chemistry classes observed in a prior study conducted by one of us (Guzzetti, 2009, 2010; Guzzetti & Bang, 2011).

To determine the potential appeal of these nonfiction comic books to secondary students, we analysed the books for their format and content in ways similar to how the fiction comic books had been examined (Guzzetti, 2010). First, we searched for topics currently popular among adolescents that might help to draw students into science. Second, we examined the narratives for referents to other media texts, such as websites, TV programs or other media that enhanced the comic books' storylines. We also looked for any authors' devices that might facilitate predictability of a reader's resolution of the problem, which in turn could provide practice with inductive and deductive reasoning or inquiry skills. Finally, we examined the format features by describing any additional texts or textual features included in the comic books aside from the main stories.

We analysed these data through matrix analysis (Miles & Huberman, 1994). We began the analysis by first reading through each comic book in its entirety. We then reread the texts, searching for vocabulary that represented forensic concepts commonly found in a forensic curriculum, listing the forensic terms that were used in the stories, as well as those in the expository introductions and the glossaries of the nonfiction series. By reading and rereading these lists, we discovered categories that represented distinct types of forensic terms. We then placed these terms within their respective categories and tallied their frequency within these classifications within and across titles.

We conducted an additional analysis for the nonfiction comic books. Since these titles included both expository and narrative texts, as well as glossaries, we conducted percentage tallies of where these terms appeared and noted where they appeared most frequently. In addition, we noted if and how frequently the terms were repeated across sections. We conducted this analysis for the individual titles, as well as across the titles.

In addition, we conducted other comparative content and format analyses. For example, we noted format features, settings for forensic nonfiction stories, predictive plots, and referrals to other media texts to support conceptual learning. We compared these elements and forensic terms in the nonfiction comic books to those in the fictional *CSI* series from the prior analysis of the *CSI* texts (Guzzetti, 2010).

The Potential of Forensic Comics and Graphic Novels for Teaching Science

Format Features of the Nonfiction Comic Books

The six hardcover comic books in the nonfiction series, *Graphic forensic science*, followed a uniform format. Individual books each contained a table of contents, followed by the first main section of the book. This section consisted of two to four pages of introductory expository text in which background information was provided, such as the history or development of that aspect of forensic science. Terms were defined and explained that related to the forensic topic of the book.

The next section, which was the longest, included three short stories that presented and illustrated in graphic form tales of actual forensic cases. These cases sometimes dated back to the 1800s, as well as more recent cases from the 20th and 21st centuries. The stories ranged in length from 8 to 20 pages each. In each of these stories, only one suspect was presented.

The last main section of the nonfiction comic books consisted of two pages of one-paragraph descriptions of four other famous cases, briefly described. These included cases such as Jack the Ripper, the Unabomber, and the Zodiac Killer depicted in *Solving crimes through criminal profiling* (Shonet, 2008). Supplementary material followed the last main section. For example, there was a page that listed professional organizations and their websites that related to the topic of the comic book, such as The American Academy of Forensic Science (www.aafs.org), the American College of Forensic Examiners (www.acfei.com), the International Crime Scene Investigators Association (www.icsia.org), and the National Forensic

Science Technology Center (www.nfstc.org). Each book also included the publisher's website for that book (e.g., see www.Rosenlinks.com/gfs/dfte for *Solving crimes with trace evidence* (Jeffrey, 2008b)). Following the supplementary material was a glossary, which included forensic science terms as well as other terms that were used in the stories, such as legal proceedings or the parts of a gun written about in *Detective work with ballistics* (West, 2008).

Content Vocabulary in the Nonfiction Comic Books

In examining the vocabulary across these sections, we found there were four kinds of conceptual vocabulary related to forensic science in the nonfiction comic books. These included three types of terms that were also found in the fiction graphic novels—terms related to forensic evidence, forensic processes, and forensic technology or equipment. A fourth type of term was found only in the graphic nonfiction. These terms represented various titles of forensic personnel. Each is discussed below.

Forensic Evidence

As in the fiction texts that had 44% of terms related to forensic evidence (Guzzetti, 2010), the most common type of vocabulary in the nonfiction forensic comic books was related to forensic evidence. About one half (58%) of the scientific terms were words that related to forensic evidence commonly found at crime scenes. There were 71 forensic evidence terms, 16 of which were repeated at least once across the six titles for a total of 101 forensic evidence terms used these texts. The most frequently occurring of these were prints (fingerprints, lip prints, and footprints), blood samples, and corpses. These types of evidence were found across five of the six titles.

This trend of presenting most of the forensic vocabulary as terms that related to evidence that was seen across the comic books was also evidenced in the individual titles. For example, 26 of the 48 forensic terms (54%) that were presented in *Autopsies: Pathologists at work* (Jeffrey, 2008a) related to evidence commonly found at crime scenes. These included terms that represented evidence on a body, such as trace evidence, toxins, and hair follicles. Many of these terms related to the condition of a corpse, such as skin mottling, rigor mortis, lividity, contusions, and lacerations. In two other titles, *Solving crime scenes with trace evidence* (Jeffrey, 2008b) and *Corpses and skeletons* (Shone, 2008b), terms related to forensic evidence constituted 50% of the forensic terms used in these texts.

These terms represented forensic evidence relevant to forensic science curriculum. Eleven of these terms, including footprints, fibers, fingerprints (and their classifications of arches, whorls and loops), lip prints, blood spatter, bite wounds, and dental impressions were types of evidence analyzed in high school chemistry labs during an earlier study (Guzzetti, 2010). All of these terms appeared in the forensic curriculum guides and lesson plans found online.

Forensic Procedures

Like the fiction comic books where 27% of the forensic terms related to forensic procedures (Guzzetti, 2010), about one quarter (22%) of the terms used across the six nonfiction comic books were terms related to forensic processes. These were the second most common types of forensic terms used in both the fiction and nonfiction comic books. Thirty-eight terms that represented forensic procedures appeared 54 times across the six nonfiction comic book titles. The most frequently occurring of these terms were photographs, dental plate records, and autopsy, forensic processes that were included in at least three of the six titles. Ten of these processes (i.e., fingerprint dusting, examining dental records, labelling, bagging, and tagging evidence, tape lifting, chemical testing, imprinting, crime reconstructions, and walk throughs) were addressed both in the forensic curriculum found online and in chemistry instruction observed in a prior study (Guzzetti, 2010). This tendency for forensic procedures to represent the second most common type of forensics term used across the six texts was also evidenced in five of the six individual titles in the series. For example, in *Crime scene investigation* (Shone, 2008a) 15 of the 41 forensic terms (37%) related to forensic procedures. These included terms like zonal search, autopsy, tool mark analysis, criminal profiling, and archiving. In *Detective work with ballistics* (West, 2008), 11 of 41 terms (27%) related to forensic processes, including such verbs as cast, catalogue, and cordon off. In *Solving crimes with trace evidence* (Jeffrey, 2008b), seven of the 32 terms (22%) represented forensic procedures, including the Henry System, serology, and post-mortem exam.

Most of these terms (e.g., post-mortem exam, exhumation, facial reconstruction, and autopsy), however, were introduced only in the comic books. These terms did not appear in curriculum guides or lesson plans, nor were they forensic processes used as activities or demonstrated in classroom instruction in the prior study (Guzzetti, 2010). These terms represented forensic procedures that are typically not conducted in secondary schools for pragmatic reasons.

Forensic Technology and Tools

Unlike the fiction comic books where 29% of the terms related to forensic technology and tools, only 11% of the forensic terms used in the six nonfiction books related to this aspect of forensic science. There were 16 terms that appeared 21 times across the six titles. These included scientific vocabulary, such as infrared light, x-ray, spectroscopy, automated fingerprint identification system (AFIS), pathology, and ultra-violet light. This trend for forensic technology and tools to be terms that were less likely to appear across the six titles held for the individual titles, as well. For example, only two terms out of 29 (7%), x-ray and infrared light, were used in *Corpses and skeletons* (Shone, 2008b) and only one term (MRI) was used in *Solving crimes through criminal profiling* (Shone, 2008c). The title that included the most forensic terms related to forensic technology and tools was *Solving crimes with trace evidence* (Jeffrey, 2008b). It included terms such as spectroscopy, dactyloscopy, microscopy, and AFIS.

Terms that were related to forensic terminology and tools were less likely than the other types of forensic terms to appear in curriculum guides or lesson plans. Only two of these terms (microscope and spectograph) were tools mentioned in curriculum guides and/or observed in forensic science instruction (Guzzetti, 2010). Most of these terms represented types of forensic technologies or tools not readily available in secondary schools. Hence, they had little relevance to the forensic science curriculum.

Forensic Personnel

A new genre of terms related to forensic personnel, which was not found in the fiction comic books (Guzzetti, 2010), was present in the six nonfiction comic books. Of the 19 terms related to forensic personnel, nine were repeated at least once across the six titles for a total of 33 appearances. These terms represented 16% of the forensic terms used across the six titles.

The most common term that was used in all six titles (and also found in the earlier *CSI* fiction study) was CSI, or crime scene investigator. Other terms included forensic anthropologist, forensic toxicologist, forensic odontologist, pathologist, medical examiner, ballistics expert, criminal profiler, and criminalist, all of which were used in the forensics curriculum. Only a few forensic roles (e.g., coroner, forensic entomologist, and forensic artist) were not present in available instructional materials.

Examination of the individual titles in the series revealed how less frequently these terms were used than other forensic terms. For example, only six of the 48 forensic terms used in *Autopsies: Pathologists at work* (Jeffrey, 2008a) were titles of forensic personnel, such as pathologist, coroner, forensic toxicologist, CSI, and county or chief medical examiner. In *Corpses and skeletons*, (Shone, 2008b) seven of the 29 forensic terms represented forensic roles, such as forensic anthropologist, forensic entomologist, forensic odontologist, and criminalist.

This type of forensics vocabulary is useful in the curriculum for explaining and promoting careers in forensic science. The terms were used to differentiate role responsibilities in solving crimes. Their inclusion can facilitate raised awareness of career opportunities and possibilities in forensic science.

Presentation of Forensic Terms

Results of our analysis of the presentation of terms in nonfiction comic books demonstrated that most of the conceptual terms related to forensics were not reinforced within the context of the narrative stories. Across the six titles, only about one-third (39%) of the forensic terms were used in both the introductory expository text and stories, or were included in both the glossary and the stories. Approximately one-fourth (27%) of the scientific terms were used only in the storylines. About another quarter (28%) of the forensic terms were introduced only in the introductory expository sections while 6% were included only in the glossaries. Nine terms (4%) were used both in the glossary and expository section but did not appear in the narrative stories.

This lack of reinforcement of forensic vocabulary in the nonfiction storylines was in sharp contrast to the *CSI* fiction comic books where all of the forensics terms were used in the narratives (Guzzetti, 2010). It was unclear why terms were included in the glossaries that were not used in the narrative stories or in the expository sections. Unlike the *CSI* comic books and graphic novels studied earlier, forensic terms in the nonfiction texts were usually defined within the context of the narratives or included in the expository sections. One example of this appeared in a section on crime scenes in *Crime scene investigators* (Shone, 2008a):

> The first on the crime scene are usually the police. A detective is put in charge of the case. CSI-Crime Scene Investigators are sent for and an ME-Medical Examiner or Coroner is informed. The ME may well visit the crime scene to examine the body and is in charge of the crime scene evidence. The CSI team carries out a detailed examination of the scene, gathering evidence as well as making a record of the scene with photographs, sketches and notes.
>
> *(p. 4)*

This paragraph was followed by a diagram illustrating the steps described in the expository text. The diagram depicted arriving at the crime scene, gathering evidence, examining evidence in the crime lab, and consulting archives to match evidence, such as fingerprints found at the crime scene. Interactive arrows demonstrated how CSIs moved back and forth among the crime scene and the crime laboratory.

Narrative Features and Storylines

We analyzed the nonfiction comic books for the presence or absence of three reoccurring narrative features within storylines found in the fictional *CSI* stories (Guzzetti, 2010). These elements included stories that contained predictable plots or hints that facilitated a reader's ability to predict and problem solve; high interest settings or story elements that had current appeal for adolescents; and referrals to related media. Each of these elements is described below.

Predictable Plots and Author Devices

There were several devices and story elements that differed between the nonfiction *Graphic forensic science* series and the fictional *CSI* stories. The inclusion of only one suspect and the brief presentations of the stories in the nonfiction comic books did not facilitate inferential thinking through deductive or inductive reasoning that could lead to prediction and the reader's resolution of the problem. The brevity of the stories did not promote the kind of inferential thinking that was facilitated by presentation of multiple suspects and fleshing out of the evidence and suspects' motives in the fictional *CSI* comic books.

In addition, the storylines in the nonfiction series did not make use of the types of authors' devices found in the *CSI* fiction series (Guzzetti, 2010). In the *CSI* series, an author sometimes coached readers in ways that helped them identify the culprit and resolve the crime. For example, in *CSI: Demon house* (Collins, 2004a) readers were given advice to "follow the evidence" (p. 49) and use their knowledge of copycat crimes.

Because the nonfiction stories were so short (nine of the 18 stories in the six titles were only 8–10 pages), the nonfiction plots were not well developed. The authors of the nonfiction stories did not attempt to activate a reader's schema for knowledge of specific genres of crimes, such as the ones found in the *CSI* fiction series of serial killings, ritual slayings, or drive-by shootings. These familiar plots can provide some degree of predictability to help students resolve fictional crimes.

High Interest Settings and Story Elements

Other narrative elements varied between the fiction and nonfiction series, as well. The *CSI* comic books and graphic novels contained treatment of issues that are popular among adolescent readers. These included settings or topics related to youth culture, including comic book conventions, music venues, haunted houses, and custom car shops. The fictional stories took up high interest topics, such as manga, anime, video gaming, and skateboarding, and vampires. Protagonists and characters in the *CSI* series were relatable ones for young people, such as middle-school teachers and college students who appeared in the stories as victims or perpetrators of fictional crimes. In contrast, none of these settings or topics appeared in the nonfiction series, and no students or teachers were suspects or victims in the nonfiction series.

Related Media

In the *CSI* series, mention of related media enhanced the plots. These media represented a range of textual forms, including video games, trade books, films, paintings, music, television programs, and comic books. All of these forms are easily recognized by youth in today's society.

By contrast, the nonfiction stories in the *Graphic forensic science* comics did not reference related media. One possible reason for this absence was that the nonfiction stories were often set in earlier times. For example, Henry Goddard and the First Ballistics Case in *Detective work with ballistics* (West, 2008) was set in 1835 and described how a butler fabricated a story of his involvement with burglars in hopes of getting a reward from his employer. When the *CSI* stories alluded to earlier times, such as the Depression Era or the Golden Age in *CSI: NY: Bloody murder* (Collins, 2005), such references related to the story events and settings, thereby enhancing the plot line.

Format Features

Photographs and Illustrations

Perhaps the most appealing elements of both the fiction comic books and graphic novels and the nonfiction comic books were the photographs and illustrations. In both series, the covers had multi-color photographs of forensic personnel. In the *CSI* series, these photographs were of the *CSI*, *CSI: NY* or *CSI: Miami* actors from the television series. In the nonfiction *Graphic forensic science*, cover photographs were of forensic personnel, technology, tools and evidence.

The illustrations in comic books and graphic novels are considered vehicles for promoting inferential thinking because they lack accompanying narrative explanations (Ivey, 2008). In both series, readers were required to infer an artist's intentions by closely examining the details in the drawings. For example, in *Solving crimes with trace evidence* (Jeffrey, 2008b), an illustration shows an impression of a fingerprint on a screen. The reader must infer that a latent fingerprint (a term defined in the glossary) is one that is accidentally left at a crime scene. In *CSI: NY: Bloody murder* (Collins, 2005), an illustration depicted a murder victim with short and deep slashes on her arms and legs, a drawing that prompted the reader to infer that an animal with claws had attacked the victim.

Interactive Text and Immersive Media

One of the most striking contrasts between the fictional *CSI* forensic comic books and graphic novels and the nonfiction *Graphic forensic science* series was in their incorporation of interactive texts and immersive media. The comic books in the *CSI* series provided interactive text, such as a letters to the editor column in *Issue two* of *CSI: Secret identity* (Grant, 2005). This column invited readers to communicate with the creators of the comic books and enter a contest to create a title for the column. Readers wrote fan letters, posed questions, and wrote reviews of current issues. There were no interactive texts like these in the nonfiction series.

We defined immersive media as those additional texts that supplemented or extended readers' interest in forensics. While the *CSI* series included multiple supplemental texts, such as short stories, ads for other comic books, action figures or *CSI* merchandise and apparel, and references to additional forms of media to promote community among fans (Hyman, 2004), the nonfiction comic books did not provide these kinds of immersive media. However, the publisher of the nonfiction series provided links to its web page for each comic book. For example, the link for *Solving crimes with trace evidence* (Jeffrey, 2008b) at www.rosen-links.com/gfs/dfte contained excerpts from the book, including a bibliography of recommended books for further reading on the topic. Each of these web pages also included links to other websites related to forensics, such as http://science.howstuffworks.com/csi.htm, www.crimescenceinvestigator.net, and www.nlm.nih.gov/visibleproofs/index.html.

What Our Findings Mean

Ideally, science instruction should provide opportunities for students to read, write, and discuss scientific ideas as they form and represent their understandings using the language and literacy skills deemed essential for science learning (OECD, 2010). Science teacher education programs now include courses related to improving students' literacy through engagement with scientifically sound and visually appealing resources (Downey, 2009). Like other researchers (e.g., Tatalovic, 2009), we have documented the appeal of comic books and graphic novels for enhancing science content. Natural phenomena are visual, and mastery of scientific content is closely linked to learners' capabilities with both print and visual texts (Smolkin & Donovan, 2005). Because comic books and graphic novels contain unique and interesting combinations of text and graphics, they have been found to support the science (Cary, 2004; McTaggert, 2008; Smetana et al., 2009).

Professional organizations also recommend incorporating a variety of texts, such as comic books and graphic novels, in science instruction. The National Science Education Standards (National Research Council, 1996), the National Science Teachers Association (2003), and the American Association for the Advancement of Science (AAAS, 1990) have emphasized that science teachers should not depend solely on direct, teacher-led instruction to convey science concepts. The use of multiple alternative texts enables science educators to integrate science content and literacy instruction (Shanahan, 2003). Such integration holds potential for readers to learn science concepts, engage with text, and think in reflective ways (Botzakis, 2009a).

At the same time it is worth noting that the two series we examined had the potential to perpetuate misconceptions about the science of forensics. For example, the frequent inclusion of latent fingerprints as evidence in many forensic science-related stories runs counter to their status as rare sources of clear or reliable evidence (Zabell, 2005). Likewise, some of the scientific analyses performed on physical evidence may be improperly conducted or include conclusions based on data retrieved from databases that do not yet exist (Bergslien, 2006).

The stories can also present an inaccurate view of the criminal justice system because a common thread in comics and graphic novels is the presumption of guilt; rarely will a story focus on establishing a character's innocence (Duncan & Daly-Engel, 2006). This has been referred to as "the CSI effect" (Campbell, 2006). Thus, we recommend that teachers provide opportunities for students to discuss comic books and graphic novels related to everyday forensic science texts.

Besides being powerful vehicles for applying the scientific method, forensic science stories can be used to explore topics of laboratory safety, scientific ethics, and the criminal justice process. We agree with other researchers (e.g., Howitt et al., 2009) that comic books and graphic novels have the potential to engage reluctant learners. Our study extends their findings by showing how these everyday texts can support students' familiarity with scientific concepts, develop their critical thinking skills, and inspire their explorations into further study of and careers in science.

References

Abilock, D. (2008). Visual literacy: Reading a documentary photograph. *Knowledge Quest, 36*(3), 7–13.

Alvermann, D. E., Phelps, S. E., & Gillis, V. R. (2010). *Content area reading and literacy: Succeding in today's diverse classrooms.* Boston, MS: Allyn & Bacon.

American Association for the Advancement of Science [AAAS]. (1990). *Effective learning and teaching.* Retrieved March 15, 2011 from www.project2061.org/publications/sfaa/online/chap13.htm.

American Association of University Women [AAUW] (2000). *Tech-savvy: Educating girls in the new computer age.* Washington, DC: American Association of University Women Educational Foundation.

Angier, N. (2009, May). A hit in school, maggots and all. *The New York Times.* Retrieved March 15, 2011 from www.nytimes.com/2009/5/12/science/12angi.html?_r=1%scp=48a9=forensics&5+=cse.

Ansbacher, T. (2000). An interview with John Dewey on science education. *The Physics Teacher, 38,* 224–227.

Bergslien, E. (2006). Teaching to avoid the "CSI Effect": Keeping the science in forensic science. *Journal of Chemical Education, 83*(5), 690–691.

Blachowitz, C. L. Z., Fisher, P. J., Ogle, D., & Watts-Taffe, S. (2006). Vocabulary: Questions from the classroom. *Reading Research Quarterly, 41,* 524–539.

Botzakis, S. (2009a). Adult fans of comic books: What they get out of reading. *Journal of Adolescent & Adult Literacy, 53*(1), 50–59.

Botzakis, S. (2009b, December). *Insights into lifelong literacy from adult comic book readers.* Paper presented at the meeting of the National Reading Conference, Albuquerque, NM. Retrieved March 15, 2011 from www.nrconline.org/cgi/conferencelibraray.cgi?downlaod=59th_Annual_Mtg/Botzakis_Paper_Adultcomicsreaders.doc.

Brooks, D., Green, P., Kleck, K., & Muench, D. (1995, May). The great tape robbery. *Science and Children, 32,* 22–24.

Campbell, A. (2006). What is the CSI effect? Retrieved March 15, 2011 from htttp://www.what-is-the-csi-effect.com.

Cary, S. (2004). *Going graphic: Comics at work in the mutlicutlral classroom*. Portsouth, NH: Heinmann.

Chun, C. W. (2009). Critical literacies and graphic novels for English Language Learners: Teaching Maus. *Journal of Adolescent & Adult Literacy, 53*, 144–153.

Colgan, C. (2002). Teaching forensics, then and now. *The Education Digest, 68*(1), 59–61.

Collins, M. A. (2004a). *CSI: Demon house*. San Diego, CA: IDW Publishing.

Collins, M. A. (2004b). *CSI: Double dealer*. San Diego, CA: IDW Publishing.

Collins, M. A. (2005). *CSI: NY: Bloody murder*. San Diego, CA: IDW Publishing.

Collins, M. A. (2006a). *CSI: Bad rap*. San Diego, CA: IDW Publishing.

Collins, M. A. (2006b). *CSI: Case files*. San Diego, CA: IDW Publishing.

Collins, M. A. (2006c). *CSI: Serial*. San Diego, CA: IDW Publishing.

Collins, M. A., Rodriguez, G., & Wood, A. (2006). *CSI: Case files*. San Diego, CA: IDS Publishing.

Dickie, S., & Percival, S. (1986). The break in at Skool Kem. *Science and Children, 24*, 20–23.

Dillon, H. (1999). Forensic scientists: A career in the crime lab. *Occupational Outlook Quarterly, 43*(3), 2–7.

Downey, E. M. (2009). Graphic novels in currriculum and instruction collections. *Reference & User Services Quarterly, 49*(2), 181–188.

Dresang, E. (1999). *Radical change: Books for youth in a digital age*. New York: H. W. Wilson.

Duke, N. K. (2004). The case for informational text. *Educational Leadership, 61*(6), 40–44.

Duncan, K., & Daly-Engel, T. (2006). Using forensic science problems as teaching tools. *The Science Teacher, 73*(8), 38–43.

Eccles, J. S., Wigfield, A., Midgley, C., Reuman, D., MacIver, D., & Feldlaufer, H. (1993). Negative effects of traditional middle schools on students' motivation. *The Elementary School Journal, 93*(5), 553–574.

Felten, P. (2008). Visual literacy. *Change, 40*(6), 60–63.

Filipenko, M. (2004). Constructing knowledge about and with informational texts: Implications for teacher-librarians working with young children. *School Libraries Worldwide, 10*(1 & 2), 21–36.

Frey, N., & Fisher, D. (2004). Using graphic novels, anime, and the Internet in an urban high school. *English Journal, 93*(3), 19–25.

Funkhouser, J. & Delisch, B. J. (2000). Integrating forensic science. *The Science Teacher, 67*(60), 32–35.

Gee, J. P. (2003). *What video games have to teach us about learning and literacy*. Palgrave Macmillan.

Gillenwater, C. (2009). Lost literacy: How graphic novels can recover visual literacy in the literacy classroom. *Afterimage, 3*(72), 33–36.

Grant, S. (2005). *CSI: Secret identity*. San Diego, CA: ISW Publishers

Grant, S. (2006). *CSI: Dying in the gutters*. San Diego, CA: IDW Publishers.

Griffith, P. E. (2010). Graphic novels in the secondary classroom and school libraries. *Journal of Adolescent & Adult Literacy, 54*(3), 181–189.

Guzzetti, B. J. (2002, September). *"This place has no atmosphere": Secondary students' reports of and suggstions for literacy in science*. Paper presented at the International Conference on Science and Literacy: Ontologoical, Epistemological, Linguistic and Pedagogical Considerations of Language and Science Literacy: Empowering Research and Informing Instruction. Victoria, BC: Canada.

Guzzetti, B. (2009). Thinking like a forensic scientist: Learning with academic and everyday texts. *Journal of Adolescent & Adult Literacy, 53*(3), 192–203.

Guzzetti, B. (2010). A content analysis of foreniscs comic books and graphic novels: Implications for science instruction. In R. T. Jimenez, V. J. Risko, D. W. Rowe, & M. Hundly (Eds.), *Fifty ninth yearbook of the National Reading Conference* (pp. 90–101). Oak Creek: WI: The National Reading Conference.

Guzzetti, B. J., & Bang, E. J. (2011). The impact of a litercay-based forensics unit on secondary students' atittudes and achievement in science. *Literacy Research and Instruction, 50*(1), 1–24.

Hand, B., Alvermann, D. E., Gee, J. P., Guzzetti, B. J., Norris, S., Phillips, L., Prain, V., & Yore, L. D. (2003). Message from The Island Group: What is literacy in science literacy? *Journal of Research in Science Teaching, 40*(7), 607–615.

Harrison, C. R. (1999). Spinning a web around forensic science and senior biology. *Australian Science Teachers' Journal, 45*(3), 17–20.

Howitt, C., Lewis, S. W., & Waugh, S. (2009). Analysis of an exemplary scientists in schools project in forensic science: Collaboration, communication, and enthusiasm. *Teaching Science, 55*(3), 46–51.

Hyman, P. (2004). *Video game companies encourage "moders"*. Retrieved March 13, 2011 from www.hollywoodrpeorter.com/hr/search/articledisplay.jap.

Ivey, G (2008). Intervening when older youth struggle with reading. In K. A. Hinchman & H. K. Sheridan-Thomas (Eds.), *Best practices in adolescent literacy instruction* (pp. 247–260). NewYork: The Guilford Press.

Jerffrey, G. (2008a). *Autopsies: Pathologists at work*. New York: Rosen Publishing Group.

Jeffrey, G. (2008b). *Solving crimes with trace evidence*. New York: Rosen Publishing Group.

Learner, S. (2003, September). Let's get practical. *The Times Educational Supplement, 4548*, 24.

Lemke, J. (1990). *Talking science: Language learning and values*. Norwood, NJ: Ablex.

Lynch, B., & Urru, F. (2006). Spike asylum. In S. Grant, *Dying in the gutters*. San Diego, CA: IDW Publishing.

McCloud, S. (1993). *Understanding comics*. Northampton, MA: Kitchen Sink Press.

McTaggert, J. (2008). Graphic novels: The good, the bad and the ugly. In N. Frey & D. Fisher (Eds.), *Teaching visual litearcy: Using comic books, graphic novels anime cartoons and more to develop comprehension and thinking skills*. Thousand Oaks, CA: Corwin.

Mardis, M. A. (2006). It's not just whodunnit, but how: "The CSI effect," science learning and the school library. *Knowledge Quest, 35*(1), 12–17.

Mariotte, J. (2005a). *CSI: Miami*. San Diego, CA: IDW Publishers.

Mariotte, J. (2005b). *CSI: Miami: Smoking gun*. San Diego, CA: IDW Publishers.

Mason Crest Publishers (2011). *Mason Crest series: The Crime Scene Club*. Retrieved May 14, 2011 from www.masoncrest.com/catalog_series.asp?sid=0030313B-1EB7.

Meier, J. (2007, October). *An exciting experiment collecting graphic novels in the sciences*. Retrieved May 14, 2011 from www.personal.psu.edu/jjm38/sciencegraphicnovels.pdf.

Miles, M., & Huberman, M. (1994). *Qualitative data analysis: An expanded sourcebook* (2nd ed.). Thousand Oaks: CA: Sage.

Mitchell, W. J. (1995). *Picture theory: Essays on verbal and visual representation*. Chicago, IL: University of Chicago Press.

Morrison, T. G., Bryan, G., & Chilcoat, C. (2002). Using student generated comic books in the classroom. *Journal of Adolescent & Adult Literacy, 45*(8), 758–767.

Nagy, W., & Scott, J. (2000). Vocabulary processes. In M. Kamil, P. Mosenthal, and P. D. Pearson (Eds.) *Handbook of Reading Research* (Vol. III, pp. 269–284). Mahwah, NJ: Erlbaum.

National Center for Education Statistics [NCES]. (2011). *The nation's report card: Science 2009.* Retrieved May 14, 2011 from http://nces.ed.gov/nationsreportcard/pdf/main2009/2011451.pdf.

National Research Council [NRC]. (1996). *National science education standards.* Washington D.C.: National Academy Press.

National Science Teachers Association. (2003). *Beyond 2000: Teachers speak out.* Retrieved May 14, 2011 from www.nsta.org/pdfs/PositionStatement_Beyond2000.pdf.

New London Group. (1996). A pedagogy of multiliteracies: Designing social features. *Harvard Educational Review, 46,* 60–92.

OECD. (2010). *PISA 2009 results: What students know and can do: Student performance in reading, mathematics and science* (Volume I). Retrieved May 14, 2011 from http://dx.doi.org/10.1787/9789264091450-en.

Oprisko, K. (2005a). *CSI: Miami: Blood/money.* San Diego, CA: IDW Publishers.

Oprisko, K. (2005b). *CSI: Thou shalt not.* San Diego, CA: IDW Publishers.

Pearson, P. D., Hiebert, E. H., & Kamil, M. L. (2007). Vocabulary assessement: What we know, what we need to learn. *Reading Research Quarterly, 42*(2), 282–296.

Rourke, J. (2010). *The comic book curriculum: Using comics to enhance learning and life.* Santa Barbara, CA: Libraries Unlimited.

Rycik, J. A. (2008). A decade of adolescent literacy. *American Secondary Education, 37*(1), 62–64.

Saferstein, R. (2008). *Forensic Science: An introduction.* Upper Saddle River, NJ: Pearson/Prentice Hall.

Saul, W. (2003). *Crossing borders in literacy and science instruction: Perspectives on literacy and practice.* Newark, DE: International Reading Association.

Schwartz, G. E. (2002, November). Graphic novels for multiple literacies. *Journal of Adolesent & Adult Literacy, 46*(3). Retrieved May 18, 2011 from www.readingonline.org/newltieracies/lit_index.asp?HREF=/newltiearcies/JAAL/11-02column/index.html.

Shanahan, C. (2003). *Using multiple texts to teach content.* Learning Point Associates: North Central Regional Educational Laboartory. Retrieved Februrary 7, 2010 from www.learningpt.org/pdfs/literacy/shanahan.pdf

Shone, R. (2008a). *Crime scene investigators.* New York: Rosen Publishing Group.

Shone, R. (2008b). *Corpses and skeletons.* New York: Rosen Publishing Group.

Shone, R. (2008c). *Solving crimes through criminal profiling.* New York: Rosen Publishing Group.

Shonet, R. (2008). *Solving crimes through criminal profiling.* New York: Rosen Publishing.

Smetana, L., Odelson, D., Burns, H., & Grisham, D. L. (2009). Using graphic novels in the high school classroom: Engaging deaf students with a new genre. *Journal of Adolescent & Adult Literacy, 53*(3), 228–240.

Smolkin, L. B., & Donovan, C. A. (2005). Looking closely at a science trade book: Gail Gibbons and multiodal literacy. *Language Arts, 83*(1), 52–62.

Street, B. V. (1995). *Social literacies.* New York: Longman.

Tatalovic, M. (2009). Science comics as tools of science education and communication: A brief, exploratory study. *Journal of Science Communication, 8*(4), 1–17.

Vygotsky, L. (1978) *Mind in society.* Cambridge, MA: Harvard University Press.

West, D. (2008). *Detective work with ballistics.* New York: Rosen Publishing Group.

Worthy, J., Moorman, G., & Turner, M. (1999). What Johnny likes to read is hard to find in school. *Reading Research Quarterly*, *34*(1), 12–27.

Wright, B. W. (2001). *Comic book nation*. Baltimore, Maryland: Johns Hopikins University Press.

Yerrick, R. K., & Ross, D. L. (2001, July/August). I read, I learn, iMovie: Strategies for developing literacy in the context of inquiry based science instruction. *Reading Online*, *5*(1). Retrieved July 14, 2011 from: www.readingonline.org/articles/art_index. asp?HREF=/articles/yerrick.index.html.

Zabell, S. (2005). Fingerprint evidence. *Journal of Law and Policy*, *13*, 143–179.

7

RECLAIMING AND REBUILDING THE WRITER IDENTITIES OF BLACK ADOLESCENT MALES

Marcelle M. Haddix

In this chapter, I describe the teaching and learning that took place during a summer writing institute for middle school Black adolescent males. This description is offered as a counternarrative to the dominant representations that exist in educational research about the social and academic experiences of Black adolescent males. It is well documented that Black males are disproportionately placed in special education, school suspensions, and expulsions and leading in school dropout rates, unemployment, and juvenile incarceration (e.g., Davis, 2006; Noguera, 2008; Polite & Davis, 1999). The recent 2010 *Yes we can: The Schott 50 state report on public education and Black males* reported that in some of the largest school districts in the country, including New York City, Philadelphia, and Detroit, 75% of African American males do not graduate from high school (Holzman, 2010). There is an increasing correlation between low graduation rates and high incarceration rates for Black males (Howard, 2008). Black males outnumber all other ethnic groups in the prison population and have a rate of incarceration five times higher than that of White males.

However, simply highlighting such reports is counterproductive. The overrepresentation of statistical and policy reports that place Black males and low academic and social outcomes in the center of the frame risks further reifying and perpetuating deficit constructions of Black youth (Haddix, 2009). Without explicit attention to how the issues surrounding the social and academic experiences of Black adolescent males are framed and complicated, we risk reinscribing normative and universally accepted definitions of what it means to be Black and male (hooks, 2003). The question remains, how do we do the work of correcting the educative and social experiences of Black adolescent males without furthering stereotypes and misrepresentations of Black masculinity?

Given all that is known and documented about the social and academic experiences of Black males in public education in the United States, a greater emphasis must be on what is being done to effectively and systematically change outcomes of social and academic failure and move toward promise and success. Through the description of curricular and pedagogical choices and the analysis of student produced work, I aim to make visible the language and literacy practices of Black boys that are often times ignored and not valued in official school contexts. In doing so, I offer recommendations for curricular and pedagogical choices that support the literacy achievement of Black boys in schools.

Educational Discourse on Black Adolescent Males

According to Davis (2006), studies on young Black males are steeped in two discourses: a discourse on the "Black male crisis" and "a discourse of academic failure" (pp. 291, 293). The discourse on Black males in educational research focuses on problems, primarily identifying pathologies rather than promoting promise. Black male adolescents have been constructed as a group whose cultural attributes, attitudes, values, and behaviors are fundamentally different than most students. These perceived differences undermine an academic achievement gap, of which the negative consequences are widely known. For decades, a prominent research inquiry in the educational research community has been to uncover factors contributing to academic achievement and failure for Black youth, and in particular, Black males (see Polite & Davis, 1999). Kunjufu (1982) identified the "fourth grade failure syndrome" for Black boys, citing low teacher expectations, boys "no longer cute," lack of parental involvement, peer pressure, and the lack of male teachers and role models, as reasons contributing to academic underachievement of Black males. Noguera (2008), in *The trouble with black boys*, cites parallel reasons, pointing to the growing rates of homicides and suicides, HIV/AIDS contractions, incarcerations, infantile deaths, declining life expectancy, unemployment, poor academic performance, poverty, and the lack of social and cultural capital. Beyond naming the harmful environmental and cultural forces that impede so many Black male youth's attainment of academic and social success, both Kunjufu and Noguera devise strategies for countering these forces. Noguera begins by turning the mirror on himself and other Black men whose lives contradict this dominant narrative, and he asks the question, "What explains why we are doing so well, and so many brothers like us are not?" (p. 20). He reframes the question of why Black males are failing, to why Black males are succeeding.

Given that it appears that a greater emphasis is on how to control them and socialize Black males for the pipeline from the educational system to the prison system (Ferguson, 2000), the dominant discourse of failure persists and serves to position Black males as scapegoats for failed academic efforts (Haddix, 2009). While it is extensively documented that Black males are falling behind academically, fewer research initiatives highlight the kinds of contexts that successfully prepare

Black males for navigating within and beyond the academic terrain. Further, few empirical studies look beyond how Black adolescent males perform on school based literacies, as determined by standardized test scores, and take into account other measures of effective literacy learning and engagement, including those that occur outside the school context. The emphasis in educational research must shift to a systemic investigation of the kinds of practices that sustain both in and out of school literacies (Hull & Schultz, 2001) of these youths to avoid further reifying deficit constructions of Black adolescent males and their prowess for intellectual performance in research, policy, and practice (Haddix, 2009). More research is needed that challenges the failure discourse by tapping into the everyday language and literacy practices of Black male youth.

Black Adolescent Males, Literate Identities, and the Teaching of Writing

In her research on teaching writing to culturally diverse communities, Ball (2000) argues that there is still great need for research projects that have an explicit aim to understand the development of voice in students of color, to explore the ways students of color access technology to communicate, and to ask how racially, culturally, and linguistically diverse youth use multimodal tools to communicate their lived experiences via writing. What we know about writing in schools predominantly comes from standardized measures of achievement, and national and state writing assessments consistently report that Black adolescent males are performing lower than other groups. In 2007 the National Assessment of Educational Progress (NAEP) writing assessment was administered to a nationally representative sample of more than 165,000 8th and 12th graders from public and private schools; 17% of Black male students scored at or above grade level on writing assessments. This reality is complicated by the fact that many young people are not given enough opportunities to develop writing in American schools (Applebee & Langer, 2009; Coker & Lewis, 2008). In secondary schools, legislative policies, like No Child Left Behind and now Race to the Top, have shifted the focus in writing instruction toward preparing students to write for state assessments alone (Newkirk & Kent, 2007; Shelton & Fu, 2004). As the context of American schools becomes increasingly racially, linguistically, and culturally diverse, there is a great need for research that goes beyond standardized measures and toward an explicit understanding of how the multiple literacies of all students, including but not limited to digital, visual, and cultural literacies, impact their development in and outside of the writing classroom.

When literacies are viewed as social practices, or individual actions within larger social and cultural processes, literate identities are viewed as being shaped and invented by experiences in particular contexts. Developing the kind of knowledge that comes from the schooling process requires that students learn to use language in new ways, in other words acquiring literate discourses.

Gallego and Hollingsworth (2000) define these school-based literacies as those that are needed to "adapt socially to school and other dominant language contexts, and the use or practice of those processes in order to gain a conceptual understanding of school subjects" (p. 5). The notion of school-based literacies as an "apprenticeship" into a particular social group suggests that literacy is used to solidify a social hierarchy and maintain social norms. Because many young people in American schools are not given enough opportunities to be agentive writers in American schools, the potential for young people to view themselves as writers in the school context is lessened. In his work with urban youth, Morrell (2007) encourages young people to become sophisticated, active ethnographers in their own academic practices as a way to overcome academic literacy limitations. In his work on the literacy development for Black adolescent males, Tatum (2005) calls for curriculum, teaching, and school leadership reform that maintains the centrality of the experiences and the voices of Black males in the reading classroom. Through active, personalized inquiry and projects, reading and writing styles of young people change, especially when students are encouraged to shape and reshape their literate identities (Alvermann, 2001).

In my work in community writing projects with Black adolescent youth, I am often struck by the responses I get from young people when I ask the question, "Are you a writer?" More often than not, they answer "no" because they make an immediate connection between writing and school sanctioned literacy practices. That question, however, assumes negative possibilities. That is, based on the way I frame the question, young people are left to answer either "yes" or "no." Because of the limited responses my question yields, I encourage more dialogue about multiple ways of writing and expression and writing for multiple purposes and contexts. With further exploration, young people identify as writers in self-sanctioned literacy practices, such as writing online via networking sites like Facebook or Twitter and/or writing poetry and lyrics. Writing for school is defined by timed writing tasks for standardized exams or the demonstration of the conventions of writing, and many of the young people I work with feel inept in such tasks. Our literate identities are the understandings of ourselves based on the discourses of which they are a part. In order for young people to take on identities as writers, they have to be apprenticed into writing communities. When I introduced myself to the boys participating in the summer writing institute that I will describe in this chapter, I identified first as a writer and I asked, "How do you complete the statement, *I am a (blank) writer?*" Eliminating the negative responses, everyone took on the identity of being a writer, whether they saw themselves as a good or bad writer. From there, we established a starting point for developing their writer identities.

Rebuilding Men in a Summer Writing Institute

During the summer of 2010, I developed and facilitated a 19-day summer writing institute for 5th to 8th grade boys in an urban middle school in Syracuse, NY.

The writing institute was designed to align with the school's Building Men program, an academic and social intervention program for predominantly Black middle school boys. A physical education teacher started the program because he noticed that many of his male students were engaged in athletics and competitive sports yet struggling academically in their core subject classes. He decided that he needed to do something to offset the dominant messages that his male students were receiving about their future aspirations—that they needed to either excel in sports or get into hip hop in order to be successful. The program met during and after school and focused on mentoring, social and leadership skills development, and literacy development.

As an extension of the Building Men program, I was asked to develop and implement an innovative literacy curriculum with an intense focus on writing. Initially, I had many concerns. One, the majority of students were required to participate in the summer institute; that is, I would be working with middle school boys who were at risk of failing academically and who needed to successfully complete the summer institute in order to progress to the next grade. Second, the program was for middle school boys who attended a K-8 school that was closing at the end of the school year. I was concerned that building their capacity to transfer any academic gains made over the summer to the academic school year would be disrupted and undermined by the impending closure of their school. A lot was at stake.

Going into this, despite having a great deal of experience working with teachers and students throughout this school district, I had never met the particular group of students that I would be working with. I was concerned that I would have limited time to develop trusting and caring relationships with these students, a condition that is critical for fostering literacy development (Camangian, 2010). I did know that the graduation rate was hovering at 50% and for Black boys, the percentage was considerably less, averaging 25%. This reality is reflected statewide. According to the 2010 Schott Report (Holzman, 2010), out of 10 of the lowest performing states for Black male high school graduation, New York was number one with a mere 25% of Black males graduating compared to 68% of White males. This is exacerbated by the lack of statistical data reporting middle school promotion of Black males in the school district; anecdotal data from school teachers and guidance counselors suggest that there is a growing number of Black male students who do not advance to high school. While data about high school graduation rates are available, less is known about the number of Black male students who do not advance beyond middle school or the number of Black male students that enter 9th grade and drop out of school before the 12th grade. Many Black male students fall through the cracks.

As I prepared for the summer institute, I met teachers and staff who worked with many of the boys during the academic school year. When they learned that I would be working with this particular group of students, many felt it was their duty to forewarn me about what I was getting myself into, almost to signal that

I should run for my life. I would get warnings like, "Oh my god, that kid is terrible! All the teachers have a nickname for him" and "Good luck, those boys are hopeless." The present and future lives of many of the boys had already been "figured" (Luttrell & Parker, 2001); they had been identified as the throw-aways, the disposables, and the finished. In putting forth a plan for working with these students, I did not promise teachers and administrators that I would improve test scores; my focus would be on reviving the spirits of Black boys who were cast off as socially unacceptable and unwelcome failures, the hopeless with no future. What I set out to do in 19 days was to let the boys know that they belonged, and as author Ishmael Beah (2008) has said about boy soldiers in war torn countries, "they are not finished" (n.p.).

Because the majority of the students were required to attend the summer institute, the first task was to attempt to disrupt the preconceived ideas that they would have about "going to summer school." By having a theme, the goal was to tap into possible interests of the students and to reengage them into schooling experiences. The theme of the summer writing institute was "Writers = Superheroes, MCs, Jedis, and Warriors" (see Figure 7.1). The curriculum was organized into four weeks, each focusing on a different subtheme. The two primary academic goals for the four weeks were to: 1) work with students in the abovementioned writing areas via the development of a writing portfolio and other ongoing writing tasks (e.g., the use of the Writer's Notebook) and 2) teach students strategies that foster greater reading comprehension and critical thinking skills. The program was geared toward helping students articulate their writing processes for academic writing tasks. Another objective was to help students attain a repertoire of comprehension and critical thinking strategies to employ when reading print, online, and media texts.

At the beginning of the program, to attain some baseline information, I asked each student to complete a writing assessment. The assessment asked the students to write a three- to five-paragraph essay answering the following questions:

- Who is the most influential person in your life and why?
- What special contribution has this person made to the world?
- How has this person influenced you?
- How has this person inspired who you will be in the future?

To contextualize the assessment, I read aloud a children's story about influential figures in American Black history. Then, I showed the students a digital story produced by local high school students showcasing contemporary influential figures in Black history. The digital story was set to a song by hip-hop artist, Nas, "I Know I Can Be What I Want to Be." Essentially, I did not want the students to come into the first class, sit down, and respond in writing to an administered assessment. Instead, I incorporated this assessment into the context of an entire literacy lesson on influential people in Black history. The objective was to give

FIGURE 7.1. Summer writing institute flyer.

students an opportunity to think about and discuss potential answers to the questions and to be more prepared to respond to the writing prompt. Most students responded to the writing prompt. A few responded with one- or two-paragraph answers addressing the questions. Most wrote a few sentences addressing the questions. A few left the writing task sheet blank. From general analysis of the writing assessments, influential persons in students' lives were parents, athletes, and in a few cases, musicians or artists. Analysis of the writing samples also showed that areas for improvement included: use of subject–verb agreement, use of commas and other punctuation, spelling, word choice/vocabulary, and use of details. In developing the curriculum, lessons also targeted developing students' command of these conventional grammar rules.

Reclaiming Writer Identities in a Summer Writing Institute

In the following sections, I describe the teaching and learning that took place during this summer writing institute. My instructional team consisted of myself, a university professor; a doctoral student, another Black woman teacher and school library/media specialist; and a teaching assistant who was a Black male preservice teacher from the university. Thirty-two male students enrolled in the summer institute; because the institute targeted Black male students, the majority were African or African American. In our group, we also had English language learners from 10 different countries, mostly African, Spanish speaking, or South Asian. During this summer, the students and my instructional team worked together to create a community of readers and writers.

In the sections that follow, I provide thick description of our curricular and pedagogical choices during the four weeks, and I focus specifically on the participation of Black adolescent males. What I describe is presented as a counterstory (Solórzano & Yosso, 2002) to the dominant representations of Black males in educational research. Specifically, I look at how the validation and support of African and African American linguistic and rhetorical traditions (Dyson & Smitherman, 2009), spoken word traditions (Fisher, 2007; Kinloch, 2005), critical and hip hop literacies (Hill, 2009; Morrell & Duncan-Andrade, 2004), and other non school-sanctioned literacy practices can foster positive learning outcomes for Black adolescent males in the writing classroom and counter environments that reify notions of failure and low expectations. I include examples from student writing, and where I do so, student writing is presented "as is" without the correction of errors in spelling, grammar, or punctuation. I do this because one of the things that I stressed with the students was the importance of getting it down on paper and of recognizing errors as learning opportunities. I also highlight and discuss where I draw on critical, visual, and hip-hop literacies as well as culturally relevant theories as frameworks for curricular and pedagogical decisions.

Week One: Superheroes

The theme for the first week of the program was "Superheroes." The plan for this week was to highlight the genre of comic books, graphic novels, and the role of visual literacies (Frey & Fisher, 2008). Visual literacy describes "the complex act of meaning making using still or moving images" (p. 1) and just as with other texts, "visually literate learners are able to make connections, determine importance, synthesize information, evaluate, and critique" (p. 1). Yet, visually mediated texts, like comic books and graphic novels, are contested and viewed differently by school boards, curriculum directors, parents, and teachers alike, specifically in relation to whether or not these are appropriate genres for classroom instruction. We needed a starting point that would welcome each student, despite his academic history. While the pre-assessment gave us some baseline data, it did not tell us whether students were engaged or disengaged with writing. We aimed to make the pre-assessment as open-ended as possible to stress the importance of developing relationships with students and of learning with and from them about their experiences with writing. Focusing on visual literacies immediately countered any concerns students brought about academic writing and offered a greater chance for each student to participate.

The first literacy activity during Week One was the decoration of Writer's Notebooks. We gave students composition notebooks and informed them that these notebooks would be used for a variety of purposes. For example, in each class, students participated in large and sometimes small group discussions relative to the day's topic. To cultivate discussions, students were asked to respond to texts in writing in their Writer's Notebooks. After reading or viewing print, media, or online texts, we asked students to pose questions, write reflections, and identify quotes and key ideas that resonated for them. Through ongoing reflective writing activities, we hoped to move students toward the internalization of writers' identities. Another main intention of the Writer's Notebooks was to provide students with a safe space to practice and acquire the language and ideas of their new discourse community. In Bakhtinian (1981) fashion, we think and write in conversation with our selves and we make meaning through conventionalized, socially, and culturally determined uses of language. In a Bakhtinian sense, when students wrote in their notebooks, they were provided a space to articulate their thoughts and ideas and to acquire a sense of how language is used within the discourse community, before voicing their thoughts out loud. In this way, it was important that students personalized their Writer's Notebooks. To do this, I brought in a stack of magazines, from sport themed to news media to music themed, scissors, and glue sticks. I asked students to cut out images from the magazines that represented who they are and what it means to be young and male today from their perspectives and lived experiences. Across the group, the selected images could be organized into four main categories—sports, music, women, and dogs. Their visual self-representations served as personal narratives and compositions.

During the week, we read comic strips and discussed the difference between DC and Marvel Comics superhero and villainous characters. Students were assigned a comic book character to research and to use in writing a character biopoem. Based on their research of DC and Marvel comic book characters, students were also challenged to create their own characters and to compose a comic strip introducing their new characters. Each Friday of every week, students had an opportunity to showcase their work, and this particular week there was a competition for the "most creative" superhero character, voted by the students. The use of comic books helped students to pose questions about how words and images together produce meaning, and it encouraged them to engage in the search for this meaning. Our reading of comic books and their own compositions of superhero characters expanded their understandings about what counts as literacy.

Week Two: MCs

There were two writing tasks for Week Two—a spoken word poetry performance and the critical analysis of music lyrics or a music video. The aim of this week was to look at the power of our words and to fashion new words and thoughts through oral expressions, such as with spoken word poetry. One exercise that we did at the beginning of this week was to talk about the language practices of today's youth. We invited students to brainstorm the words that characterize their generation. We asked them to list words and phrases that would be considered "slang terms" that they used in their everyday interactions. Some of the "Words of Your Generation" list included "Goin in hard"; "That's sick"; "Beastin"; "Whats gud ma"; "Roll out"; "Shut up nigga"; and "Whats puppin." They also listed "No homo," a phrase that has become more popular with the animated sitcom of the Aaron McGruder comic, *The Boondocks*. Their list also included numbers like 730, 373, and 252. I had to admit to the students that I was not familiar with most of the words on their list. So they allowed me to ask questions, and I asked students to provide definitions for these words. I learned that the numbers referred to gang zones in our local community. This prompted me to ask the question: Do we have the ability to "give words power" based on how we used them or do certain words have certain meanings regardless of how they are used? I explained how, for me, the numbers represented nothing and how I doubted that my reference of these numbers would put me at risk or dangers, merely because I am not a part of the gang culture. Language is always spoken or written out of a particular social identity (Gee, 1996). Through their use of vernacular forms of discourse, in this instance, these students spoke themselves into existence. Helping students to position themselves in their writing may be the most important task for teachers of writing, and embracing the voice of our students "legitimates and affirms the students' social and cultural identities" (Campbell, 1997, p. 69).

After we discussed and defined their words, we then delved into further discussion about the N-word. We asked the students to define their use of the term "nigga" and students represented two sides of the issue on this highly contested term. For some, "nigga" represented a best friend, a "homeboy," or it was a term that is used when individuals are "playing" with one another. However, students said that when someone uses the term "nigger" they are being racist, they are an enemy, or "someone you don't like." They made a clear distinction between the term "nigga" versus "nigger" with supported claims and reasons, most with which I disagreed. The discussion was a great segue into viewing clips from the documentary, *The N Word*, where students were able to listen to varying perspectives on the use of this term by celebrities like Chris Rock, Russell Simmons, and

Whoopi Goldberg. The students did not seek to agree with me, but instead, to persuade me to understand the issue from their point of view. This critical engagement fostered both depth and breadth in their exploration of a singular issue. This was one of many instances where we drew from a critical literacy framework (Luke, 2000; Stevens & Bean, 2007) to think about, question, study, and critique many popular and controversial issues that were of great interest to the students. For example, they were eager to write about and lend their voice and opinions to questions about dog fighting, school violence, and the commercialism of hip hop. We had conversations about whether or not phrases like "no homo" were problematic and the relationship to the bullying culture that persists in many schools and communities. Critical literacy is most often considered in terms of providing young people with tools to critique and question the world around them as they make sense of texts, including those mediated by the school environment and by popular and media texts. Morrell (2007) points out that because of the realities many urban youth confront on a regular basis and because of the dominant stereotyping of urban poor or people of color that persists within popular media and texts, young people will constantly have to interpret and critique texts. They are uniquely positioned to take on critical literacy as praxis, to take an activist stance toward challenging and changing such representations.

Given that critical literacy incorporates and subsumes traditional literacies frequently taught in schools, urban literacy classrooms become ideal locations for critical literacy education that supports young people in their move toward engaged citizenship and personal emancipation (Haddix & Rojas, 2011). According to Luke (2000), a central aim of critical literacy is to foster classroom environments where students and teachers *together* work to reconstruct their worlds, cultures, and identities through reading and rereading texts. This was particularly evident during our lessons on hip-hop culture. Within mainstream American culture, hip-hop culture has the transformative power to engage Black males in their struggle for emancipation (Davis, 2006). The MC (or emcee) is one of the four major elements of hip-hop culture, the others being deejaying, break dancing, and graffiti writing. The MC is the voice of hip-hop culture. When we introduced the theme of MCs for the second week of the institute, we explained that this week we would focus on the forms of expressions of hip-hop lyricists and spoken word artists. There is a risk in bringing hip-hop music into the classroom space, as with any music or other popular culture texts. One of the assignments for this week was the critique of music lyrics or a music video. I gave directions for the assignment by using the song "The People" by Common. I selected this song because I view Common to be a popular hip-hop artist, one that most students would know, and the song had a positive, socially conscious message. I brought in an example that I was familiar with and one that I could research, study, analyze, and critique prior to teaching the lesson. I was prepared for students to select mainstream hip-hop artists who were popular and whose lyrics I felt represented violent and misogynistic images and messages. What I was not prepared for was that the majority of the students wanted to critique the music of a local hip-hop group, Felony Set. I was cautioned by the name alone, specifically the reference to crime and violence. I learned quickly that the members of Felony Set were local neighborhood heroes for many of the students. Because I did not want to ignorantly censor their choices, I had to ask students for information about the group and together we viewed a couple of YouTube videos for further discussion, decentering my authority in the classroom. When preparing to critique the music video, I asked the students to write in their Writer's Notebooks their thoughts about the role of violence in the media and in music videos. We discussed whether or not violence influences the video or if the video influences violence. One student, Steven (all students' names are pseudonyms), wrote,

> There is a lot of violence ~~because~~ in the media because lots of rappers talk about violence in their raps and it influence people. I think that stuff they were talking about is true. And that were used to the violence.

Taking a critical literacy and culturally relevant stance (Ladson-Billings, 1995), rather than the voice of one authority, knowledge was constructed through reciprocal dialogue between the teacher and the students. The students called into question the inclusions and exclusions based on my definitions of what constituted hip-hop music and culture. Their music represented new literacies, a new discourse community, that they were creating and helping to promote.

Week Three: Jedis

One of the challenges that I faced working with the summer writing institute was that the students were in Grades 5 through 8. This meant that they represented a wide range of writing experiences. This impacted the selection of topics, texts, and writing tasks. In addition, many of the boys were required to attend the writing institute because they did not perform well enough to advance to the next grade level. Their participation and performance in the summer institute was being used as a determinant for whether or not they would graduate to the next grade that fall. The reasons cited by their teachers for low performance and lack of promotion included inconsistent attendance and absenteeism (as one teacher said, "they just don't show up") and lack of completion of assignments. One teacher shared how he knew that students would work on assignments, but at the end of the day, "They just didn't turn them in." Knowing this led me to speculate further about the significance of peer pressure and its impact on these boys' decisions to check out of school. The issue was not that they couldn't do the work; for some, they were deliberately choosing not to do it. For some, it challenged socially accepted norms of what it means to be Black and male (hooks, 2003). From a social constructionist approach, what it means to be Black and male is operationalized by specific behavior, attitude, affect, style, disposition, and belief (Davis, 2006). Such normalized discourses of masculinity shape and often dictate Black males' identities.

In considering how Black males reconstruct, conform to, challenge and negotiate masculinity, both traditional and alternative forms of schooling are needed to provide multiple avenues of success. To account for the variance of academic experiences represented in the group, I created a Jedi completion chart where by completing each of the assigned composing tasks, students could advance from younglings to Jedi high masters (see Figure 7.2). Upon entering the institute, students were told that they were "Jedis-in-training." I adopted the metaphor of "Jedis-in-training" from the *Star Wars* trilogy, of which most of the students were familiar. In *Star Wars*, the main objective of a Jedi is to become one with "The Force" which can ultimately increase a person's physical and mental abilities. A Jedi's aptitude is not in question but challenged through a series of activities that foster the necessity to act using mind, voice and hands. Even though the outcomes of their actions are not guaranteed, the steps to complete any task are never attempted as merely a "good try". "Jedis do, they do not try," so actions are thought out and intentional. Similarly, as the young men participated in our simulated galaxy, their minds would have to organize both task and action toward each phase of their Jedi apprenticeship. I explained to them that, like a Jedi's "lightsaber," their tools for defense would be both pencil and keyboard and their Writer's Notebooks.

Jedis-in-training
Completion chart

Task completed	Rank earned	Teacher initials & date
Decorate writer's notebook & exercises	Jedi youngling/initiate	
Comic strip OR superhero character biopoem	Jedi padawan/apprentice	
"I AM" poem	Jedi knight	
Music video presentation	Jedi master	
Spoken word poetry or music lyrics	Jedi council member	
Short story or personal narrative	Jedi high general	
Digital story	Jedi high master	

FIGURE 7.2. Jedi completion chart.

During the four weeks, students were to complete eight writing tasks and include them in their writing portfolio. Once successfully completed, students earned a new Jedi ranking. Criteria for successful completion of writing tasks included: 1) responding to teacher and peer feedback; 2) exhibiting few to no errors in grammar, spelling, and punctuation; and 3) revising/editing for each task. Eleven students completed all eight writing tasks and had substantial work to display in their writing portfolio; this earned them the status of Jedi High Master. All of the students achieved at least Jedi Knight status or better. This marker of student growth was critical given that the dominant narrative for the students in the summer institute was that they did not complete their work. The Jedi completion chart documented their personal growth and successes and helped to facilitate a feeling of accomplishment. This form of assessment provided a different story of the achievement gap. I would argue that the constant highlighting of achievement gap data that show the underperformance of Black males potentially lets us off the hook and allows for the acceptance of a culture of academic failure.

In addition to having issues with completing tasks, the students also avoided revising their work. It was apparent that students had not been a part of a writing culture where they were asked to revise. For some, revising was a new concept. This was an opening for us to discuss what it means to have composing processes and how these processes can be aligned with a genre or purpose for writing. My goal was for students to understand writing as an ongoing process, one that is never completely finished. The students' inexperience with the revising process was due in part to the fact that writing in school consisted mostly of timed writing on demand for standardized state exams. This was further complicated by the absence of the teaching of writing. During the third week, students were given the choice to write a personal narrative essay or a fictional short story. After reading examples and deconstructing the main elements of both genres, students worked on their individual pieces during writing workshop time. Seventh grader James decided that he wanted to write a personal narrative. Below is his first draft.

THE STORY OF MY LIFE
The Story Of My Life People Will Say He Was A Kind Person He Was Loving And He Would give You His Shirt Off His Back He would Give You His Shoes Off His Feet When You Are Mad Or Sad Me He Would Make It All Better

My main goal for developing writing skills was to provide students with a forum for expressing their views without first having to master academic conventions. For James, that was important because without permission to ignore those conventions initially, he might have stared at a blank page. For many of the boys, it was apparent that they were hesitant to write in fear of being wrong. In our institute, errors were viewed as positives. I explained that "errors" invited opportunities for learning new information. For example, James' first draft prompted mini-lessons about writing sentences and paragraphs, capitalization, punctuation, and adding details. After working one-on-one with James in writing conferences, he produced this second draft.

> THE STORY OF MY LIFE
>
> [Name of Grandfather] was an important part of the Syracuse community and he was my grandfather. He lived to be 91 years old. I would help him when he was alive. I went to his house and watched TV with him. I helped him with his yard. I helped him because he was old and I know he couldn't do things by himself. He passed away last year.
>
> When I pass away, people will say, "[He] was a kind person. He was loving and he would give you his shirt off his back. He would give you his shoes off his feet when you are mad or sad. He would make it all better."

In his second draft, James provided more details by contextualizing the content in his first draft. In our writing conference, James told me that he wanted his personal narrative to be about what he learned from having the opportunity to spend time with his grandfather, who had recently passed away. Through talk, he was able to further articulate details for his narrative and to expand on his first draft. Talking is an integral part of learning to write; as Dyson (2005) proposes, "Speech, or more accurately, situated voices are rich resources for composing and performing" (p. 153). When the school culture promotes behavior management and control, limited time is provided for students to interact with teachers and with each other about their work. I explained to all of the students that this was just the beginning. I wanted to illustrate through their examples how writing evolves and improves with revision.

Week Four: Warriors

The theme for the fourth week was "Warriors" because students were actively engaged in writing workshop, composing and revising various pieces for their writing portfolio. They became writing "warriors," all wanting to achieve their highest level on the Jedi completion chart. My main goal for the four weeks was to encourage the boys to see themselves as writers capable of achieving in school-based literacies. For this to happen, we needed to tap and validate their everyday literacies and literate identities. It is erroneous for Black males to identify as non-writers because of standardized test scores or achievement gap data. Further, it is wrong for Black male students to accept and adhere to social norms that suggest that being academically successful makes them less male and less Black. As cultural critic and scholar Michael Eric Dyson (2003) writes,

> One of the things we have to see is that it's a deeply racist moment to suggest that writing (as opposed to orality) is about a tradition external to

African American culture....We have to figure out a way to highlight the link between writing and the articulation of Black culture, which is where, for me, questions of authenticity are introduced. And right away, one comes up against the bulwark of racist assumptions about Black being and intelligence: It's not authentic for Blacks to speak articulately. It's not authentic for them to engage in intellectual performances.

(p. 30)

As an example of being negatively influenced to take on the identity of an underachieving student, Adrian wrote about personal challenges in this narrative:

"Fall and get back up"

I grew up as a child that always had it easy because I was little I was always spoiled. I had good grades and got rewarded for it. Everyone always talking about, "[He] is going to be something when he gets older." Everything was going good until I got to the seventh grade.

I was saying that I was going to do a good job. But it's easy to say that I'm going to do a good job but the hard part is doing it. So when I got to the seventh grade, I had a good start then I drifted away from doing good because I started to hang out with the wrong people. This is why I failed the seventh grade. So I got to come to an institute which turned out to be immensely fun. So what my title and this story means is that you will have down points in your life but when you fall from them you have to learn how to get back up. When you get back up, try not to make that mistake again!!!!

Here, Adrian articulates his own struggles with succumbing to what he deemed as poor personal choices (e.g., "hang out with the wrong people") that thwarted his trajectory of academic success. In some ways, this was his message to other students who had similar experiences. He wanted them to know that they could overcome failures and "get back up."

Another writing task during the last week was the "I AM" poem. I shared several examples of I AM poems and "Where I'm From" poems, including my own, to give the students an idea of the structure and form. For this writing task, I asked them to write poems that were autobiographical and that were real. In analyzing their poems, I observed that students wrote themselves into existence and claimed their future aspirations. For example, in Jared's "I AM" poem, he wrote:

I am
I am the one that graduate from college
I am the one that got a great job as a store owner
I am the one that got 2 cars a wife and kids
I am gone to die by oldness not gang related

In this poem, Jared dispels misconceptions of what it means to be a Black male adolescent, and he challenges the dominant framings of Black boys in school. He positions himself counter to the statistic that only 25% of Black males graduate from high school in New York State, and to a gang related death. In some ways, the "I AM" poem was a liberating force for Jared, as it was for many of the boys.

The Promise of Everyday Literacies in School Spaces

Our four weeks together was not enough time. As soon as I began to see some of the boys turn the corner in terms of their fears and "hang ups" around writing, the institute ended. While I might not have significantly increased students' test scores nor tackled every area of writing instruction in four weeks, I did observe writer identities emerge. Even more importantly, some of the boys began to experience school as a place where they, along with their language, their culture, their interests, and their ideas, belonged. Boys who had significant absenteeism during the academic school year attended each day of the institute. Students who teachers warned did not complete assignments attained Jedi High Master status. My time with the boys only complicated the many questions that I had about teaching writing in schools and the educational experiences of urban youth, and particularly Black boys. I questioned what might be hindering this kind of writing instruction and practice during the regular school day? What makes such practices impossible? As I said goodbye to my boys, I wondered, was that enough to sustain them as they started a new school year? Would what they had learned that summer carry over into the school year? If the writing curriculum didn't look like this, would they be okay?

One of my final messages to the young men who participated in the summer institute was for them to see their own potential, even when others didn't. Ultimately, the responsibility was on them, as individuals, to withstand and overcome any obstacles in order to become successful. While I do not underestimate the resiliency of Black boys to overcome significant odds, the power of their agency should not be over-estimated to the extent that we ignore the social and political forces that impact their schooling experiences. As Noguera (2003) writes,

> It would be naïve and erroneous to conclude that strength of character and the possibility of individual agency can enable one to avoid the perils present within the environment or that it is easy for individuals to choose to act outside the culture milieu in which they were raised. Even as we recognize that individuals make choices that influence the character of their lives, we must also recognize that the range of choices available are profoundly constrained and shaped by external forces.
>
> *(p. 440)*

Noguera claims that because Black boys can resist, subvert, and react against cultural and structural forces that shape identities, their perspectives are essential to combating these forces that also surround academic achievement. For example, Black male adolescents' voices and perspectives must be a part of the discourse that constitutes effective reading and writing instruction. There is a place and a need to understand and value youth culture in school. It is imperative that efforts to help Black youth be guided by ongoing attempts at understanding the cultural forms they produce and the ways in which they respond and adapt to their social and cultural environment (Noguera, 2003). It is problematic when current educational reform is more about what schools should do to bridge the achievement gap than about the role of students and their experiences in those efforts. While we work to rebuild and reclaim the writer identities of Black boys and support their agency and individual choice, we must still work against the external forces that aim to maintain the subjectification of Black males in U.S. society.

The outcomes from the summer writing institute reinforced the importance of building community level support for Black youth. However, I ended the summer program questioning its real impact on the academic trajectory for each student; four weeks was not enough time to compensate for the failings of formal schooling year round. The example that I describe only served 32 students during a short time period. In analyzing this example, I encourage viewing these kinds of curricular and pedagogical practices as possibilities for transforming the traditional school spaces and the incorporation of everyday literacies of Black males in ways that bolster their literacy learning in school. At the end of the program, we asked students to complete an evaluation about their experiences in the institute. One of the questions was, what has changed about your view about education after participating in this program? One student responded, "Good cuz it help people like kids like me." Another student commented, "I learned more from Ms. Marcelle." Such responses represented for me a shift in their understandings of literate identities and teacher–student relationships. Several of the boys' teachers from the academic school year labeled these students as "terrible", "hopeless", and without promise. In fact, these boys refigured their worlds and reclaimed their literate identities as individuals capable of learning with teachers and with each other and hopeful that people—their teachers, administrators, parents, and the larger community—would see "kids like me" as full of promise and potential.

References

Alvermann, D. E. (2001). Reading adolescents' reading identities: Looking back to see ahead. *Journal of Adolescent and Adult Literacy, 44*(8), 676–690.

Applebee, A. N., & Langer, J. A. (2009). What is happening in the teaching of writing? *English Journal, 98*(5), 18–28.

Bakhtin, M. M. (1981). *The dialogic imagination: Four essays* (M. Holquist & C. Emerson, Trans.). Austin, TX: University of Texas Press.

Ball, A. F. (2000). Empowering pedagogies that enhance the learning of multicultural students. *Teachers College Record, 102*(6), 1006–1034.

Beah, I. (2008). *A long way gone: Memoirs of a boy soldier.* New York: Farrar, Straus, & Giroux.

Camangian, P. (2010). Starting with self: Teaching autoethnography to foster critically caring literacies. *Research in the Teaching of English, 45*(2), 179–204.

Campbell, K. (1997). "Real niggaz's don't die": African American students speaking themselves into their writing. In C. Severino, J. C. Guerra & J. E. Butler (Eds.), *Writing in multicultural settings* (pp. 67–78). New York: MLA.

Coker, D., & Lewis, W. B. (2008). Beyond writing next: A discussion of writing research and instructional uncertainty. *Harvard Educational Review, 78*(1), 231–251.

Davis, J. E. (2006). Research at the margin: Mapping masculinity and mobility of African-American high school dropouts. *International Journal of Qualitative Studies in Education, 19*(3), 289–304.

Dyson, A. H. (2005). Crafting "the humble prose of living": Rethinking oral/written relations in the echoes of spoken word. *English Education, 37*(2), 149–164.

Dyson, A. H., & Smitherman, G. (2009). The right (write) start: African American Language and the discourse of sounding right. *Teachers College Record, 111*(4), 973–998.

Dyson, M. E. (2003). *Open mike: Reflections on philosophy, race, sex, culture, and religion.* New York: Basic Civitas Books.

Ferguson, A. A. (2000). *Bad boys: Public schools in the making of black masculinity.* Ann Arbor, MI: The University of Michigan Press.

Fisher, M. T. (2007). *Writing in rhythm: Spoken word poetry in urban classrooms.* New York: Teachers College Press.

Frey, N., & Fisher, D. (Eds.). (2008). *Teaching visual literacy: Using comic books, graphic novels, anime, cartoons, and more to develop comprehension and thinking skills.* Thousand Oaks, CA: Corwin Press.

Gallego, M. A., & Hollingsworth, S. (2000). Introduction: The idea of multiple literacies. In M. A. Gallego & S. Hollingsworth (Eds.), *What counts as literacy: Challenging the school standard* (pp. 1–23). New York: Teachers College Press.

Gee, J. P. (1996). *Social linguistic and literacies: Ideology in discourses* (2nd ed.). Bristol, PA: Taylor and Francis.

Haddix, M. (2009). Black boys can write: Challenging dominant framings of African American adolescent males in literacy research. *Journal of Adolescent & Adult Literacy, 53*(4), 341–343.

Haddix, M., & Rojas, M. A. (2011). (Re)framing teaching in urban classrooms: A poststructural (re)reading of critical literacy as curricular and pedagogical practice. In V. Kinloch (Ed.), *Urban literacies: Critical perspectives on language, learning, and community* (pp. 111–124). New York: Teachers College Press.

Hill, M. L. (2009). *Beats, rhymes, and classroom life: Hip-hop pedagogy and the politics of identity.* New York: Teachers College Press.

Holzman, M. (2010). *Yes we can: The 2010 Schott 50 state report on Black males in public education.* Cambridge, MA: Schott Foundation for Publication Education.

hooks, b. (2003). *We real cool: Black men and masculinity.* New York: Routledge.

Howard, T. (2008). Who really cares? The disenfranchisement of African American males in prek-12 schools: A critical race theory perspective. *Teachers College Record, 110*(5), 954–985.

Hull, G., & Schultz, K. (2001). Literacy and learning out of school: A review of theory and research. *Review of Educational Research, 71*(4), 575–611.

Kinloch, V. F. (2005). Poetry, literacy, and creativity: Fostering effective learning strategies in an urban classroom. *English Education, 37*(2), 96–114.

Kunjufu, J. (1982). *Countering the conspiracy to destroy black boys.* Chicago, IL: African American Images.

Ladson-Billings, G. (1995). Toward a theory of culturally relevant pedagogy. *American Education Research Journal, 32*(3), 465–491.

Luke, A. (2000). Critical literacy in Australia: A matter of context and standpoint. *Journal of Adolescent & Adult Literacy, 43*(5), 448–461.

Luttrell, W., & Parker, C. (2001). High school students' literacy practices and identities, and the figured world of school. *Journal of Research in Reading, 24*(3), 235–247.

Morrell, E. (2007). *Critical literacy and urban youth: Pedagogies of access, dissent, and liberation.* New York: Routledge.

Morrell, E., & Duncan-Andrade, J. (2004). What they do learn in school: Hip-hop as a bridge to canonical poetry. In J. Mahiri (Ed.), *What they don't learn in school: Literacy in the lives of urban youth* (pp. 247–268). New York: Peter Lang.

Newkirk, T., & Kent, R. (Eds.). (2007). *Teaching the neglected "R": Rethinking writing instruction in secondary classrooms.* Portsmouth, NH: Heinemann.

Noguera, P. A. (2003). The trouble with black boys: The role and influence of environmental and cultural factors on the academic performance of African American males. *Urban Education, 38*(4), 431–459.

Noguera, P. A. (2008). *The trouble with black boys....And other reflections on race, equity, and the future of public education.* San Francisco, CA: Jossey-Bass.

Polite, V. C., & Davis, J. E. (Eds.). (1999). *African American males in school and society: Practices and policies for effective education.* New York: Teachers College Press.

Shelton, N. R., & Fu, D. (2004). Creating space for teaching writing and for test preparation. *Language Arts, 82*(2), 120–128.

Solórzano, D. G., & Yosso, T. J. (2002). Critical race methodology: Counter-storytelling as an analytical framework for education research. *Qualitative Inquiry, 8*(1), 23–44.

Stevens, L. P., & Bean, T. W. (2007). *Critical literacy in the United States.* New York: Peter Lang.

Tatum, A. (2005). *Teaching reading to black adolescent males: Closing the achievement gap.* Portland, ME: Stenhouse Publishers.

8

TEACHER RESPONSE

Bridging Everyday Literacies with Academic Literacy

McKenzie Weaver

Everyday literacies have found their place in the academic classroom. After look-ing at the chapters by O'Brien, Guzzetti and Mardis, and Haddix, five main concepts were brought to the forefront: identity, literacy, motivation, engage-ment, and bridging the gap between school and life beyond its walls. Each of these concepts was explored in various settings, with different populations of adolescent students, and for its own reasons. Through a program for "at risk" high school students, O'Brien examined multi-mediating practices in relation to students who had struggled in the past with traditional print-centric media assign-ments. Guzzetti and Mardis took an in-depth look at the incorporation of popu-lar media into the study of forensic science with students from a suburban setting. Additionally, Haddix opened our eyes to the effects of negative stereotyping on the identities, motivation, and writing practices of Black adolescent males in an urban school. All authors focused on the convergence of everyday literacies with traditional school content.

As a school media specialist, I see my role as helping bridge the gap between the traditional literacies used in an academic environment and the "new" digital media often used by students and faculty outside of school. My particular gradu-ate degree is in Learning, Design, and Technology. With this background, I have been specially trained to design instruction based on the learning needs of audi-ences while incorporating various technologies as applicable. My students have taught me a great deal more about blogging, gaming, and creative commons materials. Additionally, I enjoy collaborating with classroom teachers to adapt their lessons to include various digital media literacies. As an educator in an ever-changing digital environment, it would be a disservice to not provide our stu-dents with the literacy skills necessary for them to succeed. Therefore, I look to the authors of these chapters for additional insight into ways to help bridge the gap between the school and social literacies of my adolescent students.

O'Brien and Haddix began by looking at students' views of themselves. Some of the students they encountered felt as though they were struggling academically or that they were not writers. These students did not possess the identity of being successful in school or of feeling competent in an academic area such as writing composition. The students in O'Brien's chapter, however, viewed themselves as competent users of digital media. While creating projects where the topic and media were of their choosing, these students were able to create end products that gave them a sense of success and accomplishment. The decision-making opportunities available to them during the projects also provided an increase in their engagement with the material. Guzzetti and Mardis also looked at identity when discussing the supplemental materials available to students with the *CSI* fiction series of graphic novels in a forensic science class. This connection to fan communities provided additional opportunities for students to express themselves, share views and experiences, and provide critiques with others in a supportive environment of people with similar interests (Black, 2009).

Although O'Brien and Guzzetti and Mardis briefly discussed the concept of identity or multiple identities, it was Haddix who looked at this issue in depth. After mentioning the "perceived differences" in Black adolescent males due to standardized test scores and misrepresentations in popular media, Haddix moved on to depict the battle between the multiple identities and the social communities in which they exist. Through the workshop portfolio project, Haddix was able to introduce her students to the idea of multiple literacies and multiple identities. Through a discussion of slang terminology in which she used role-reversal and allowed the students to teach her and form persuasive arguments for the use of certain terms, she was able to emphasize the relationship between social identity and "word power." Although it appeared that Haddix was able to move her students toward identities as writers, it would be beneficial to know how the various elements of the four-week summer writing workshop would transfer to the regular school environment and its associated norms and/or peer pressures.

Considering O'Brien's "feeling of competence," one wonders how much of our identities are developed around our successes and failures. Traditionally, a successful student is able to competently navigate print-based content materials and assessments. However, new views of literate competence, including new digital media and technologies, allow students to engage in and express themselves in various media simultaneously. The project options O'Brien offered not only provided students with a choice of end product but also allowed them to choose a method of expression in which they felt competent. Why not allow students to express what they have learned in various formats? Although standardized testing still exists in the traditional print format for most students, teachers need not require practice with such a format one hundred percent of the time. Students need opportunities to apply content in ways that are meaningful to them.

Test-taking strategies and skills become even more important to learning when content area teachers are able to incorporate them in their specific disciplines. When this occurs, students are more likely to read, write, and discuss content knowledgeably and confidently. They are also more likely to engage in appropriate discussions with subject-matter teachers, other professionals in the school or a community-based project, guest speakers, and producers of video/podcasts. Students benefit from discussions about the layout of a text, how to best decipher various diagrams or scenarios, how to identify relevant vocabulary, and how to find additional resources. Students need to be reminded that vocabulary development and comprehension of complex concepts come not only from the highlighted words in a printed text but also from inferences about images and sounds. For example, Guzzetti and Mardis showed us how students' engagement with comic books and graphic novels can have a place in the science classroom when used as tools for improving content area literacy and subject matter mastery.

Everyday media, such as comic books and graphic novels, might also prove beneficial to students who do not self-identify as competent readers of traditional science texts. They might also assist in the writing process, especially when used with students who enjoy engaging with familiar media to produce written materials. The connection between students' uses of everyday media and standardized test-taking is not well understood, at least not presently. Haddix addressed this disconnect by arguing that standardized testing is unable to assess students' multiple literacies. There is a finite amount of content that can actually be assessed with the most widely used standardized tests. Thus, Haddix recommended that schools form something analogous to "apprenticeship" communities in which teachers model the acquisition of skills necessary for accessing subject-matter knowledge. This type of educational community would have its own social norms not unlike those that currently exist in schools.

One issue that needs consideration when attempting to incorporate everyday media into a particular school setting is the possibility that doing so will alter existing social norms and create confusion for all concerned. As a school library media specialist, I have been fortunate to work in an atypical school wherein leisure reading is viewed as "cool" by the majority of students and teachers. However, I have also taught in schools and attended classes in other places where this was not the case. Although I have never been one to pay undue attention to peer pressure, I know that my practice of reading for fun has not been viewed as a "cool" thing to do in the past.

However, teachers and school media specialists have the potential to influence change in schools and how students identify (or not) as "cool" readers and writers. Educators who are responsible for instructing young people in the upper grades have an opportunity to improve student motivation and engagement. O'Brien introduced us to one of the biggest factors in successfully motivating and engaging adolescents in literacy learning—student choice. Through his inquiry- and project-based learning approaches, O'Brien advocated for students having a voice in choosing topics, deciding on what tools to use, and designing the end product. He believed they were able to creatively engage in learning while feeling motivated to complete an assignment because it was of interest, under their control, and within reach of being integrated into the regular curriculum. The students were in a situation where they were supported, encouraged to show what they could do, and most likely assessed by how successful they were in conveying their ideas rather than in how well or poorly they did on a traditional print-based assessment.

I have heard arguments that some adolescents' lack of motivation in the middle grades and at the high school level is due to too much testing, too much subject-area busy work, and various leveling practices, such as tracking. It is likely that students facing a lifetime of remedial track classes would have low self-esteem and lack motivation unless their teachers were unrelenting supporters and advocates. So, what can we do?

Haddix provides some potential answers. She explored Black adolescent males' lack of engagement in school-sanctioned writing activities. Although the summer workshop Haddix designed for the boys was required by their school, that intensive four-week session provided an opportunity to work with popular media and to showcase successes, however small. It also provided a means for influencing how the boys felt about themselves as writers. By emphasizing the need for her students to learn from their mistakes and to view their writing errors as opportunities for learning, Haddix impressed upon the boys that achieving success in academic writing was ultimately their responsibility.

When students are able to experience success in an academic endeavor, they are gaining competence and confidence. Guzzetti and Mardis showed us that students also gain confidence by learning through multiple modes (e.g., still and moving images interspersed with print, gestures, and sounds). Comic books and graphic novels can motivate students by bridging their everyday world with the challenging academic texts that the curriculum requires. While one mode of instruction is sufficient for one student, another student may benefit from seeing a diagram or video simulation in order to better understand the content. As a school library media specialist, I know that there are many good resources available in various formats; thus, teachers need not feel tied to traditional print texts.

Having said that, it is important that everyday media used in the classroom support the goals of the school, the curriculum, and the information literacy goals set forth by the American Association of School Libraries and Association for Educational Communication and Technology (AASL, 1998) well over a decade ago. When looking to adopt new materials, teachers should feel welcome to collaborate with their school library media specialist, who can assist in the creation of lesson plans, professional development, and the submission of new materials for approval by the media committee. For example, teachers who initially might feel uncomfortable introducing a *CSI* graphic novel series in their classrooms will find that this committee's approval is a safeguard in the event of a parental challenge.

To summarize, the authors of the three chapters I was invited to review focus on instructional approaches that provide adolescents with options and choices for bridging everyday literacy practices with traditional school content. While not assuming that all students are competent readers and writers, these authors are, nonetheless, optimistic in their view that it is entirely possible and worthwhile to celebrate the small successes of *all* students.

References

American Association of School Libraries, & Association for Educational Communication and Technology. [AASL]. (1998). *Information power: Building partnerships for learning.* Chicago: American Library Association.

Black, R. W. (2009). English-language learners, fan communities, and 21st-century skills. *Journal of Adolescent & Adult Literacy, 52*(8), 688–697.

PART III

Addressing Sociocultural and Identity Issues in Adolescents' Literacy Lives

9

TOUCHSTONE CHAPTER
EXPLORING RACE, LANGUAGE, AND CULTURE IN CRITICAL LITERACY CLASSROOMS

Bob Fecho, Bette Davis, and Renee Moore

The specific circumstances may have been different, but for each of us—Bob, Bette, and Renee—our explorations into issues of race, language, and culture began with what Bob has called teachable/researchable moments. Bob's moment hinged around a class reading of a Nikki Giovanni (1971) poem, "Beautiful Black Men." Feeling the poem to be a celebration of African American slang, language, and culture, Bob imagined that day's lesson with his high school class of African American juniors to be a romp through a discussion of vibrant imagery before moving to other work. However, what slowly emerged on that day were concerns and questions raised by his students about how they felt Giovanni was mocking Black dialect and, on learning that she was African American, how she was even betraying the African American community. Spurred by his own working-class concerns about language, his students' issues raised by the Giovanni poem, and a growing popular and academic zeitgeist around the ways language and culture transacted, Bob urged his class to begin collecting examples of dialogue around them so that the class could explore the power of language up close and with personal connections and context.

For Bette, her teachable/researchable moment is less a particular instance in time and more a collection of events centered around a teaching activity she has called "classtalk," spontaneous or framed discussions that focus on issues of language and grow from her needs as a teacher and the expressed needs of her students. In particular, Bette recalled a moment in a college freshman composition class she was teaching where students had come to the course with higher levels of critical language awareness than she might have anticipated. However, a few African American students expressed negative attitudes toward their most intimate language, even as they spoke it. In *Voices of the Self*, Keith Gilyard (1991) characterized such views as "eradicationist." Other African American students adamantly defended their home codes, at times voicing some aversion to code switching. Many of these comments surfaced during online exchanges with students in other regions of the United States participating in a Bread Loaf School of English online discussion about language issues. Specifically, one student whom Bette calls *E* complained online about having to switch to the linguistic code of the culture of power for any reason. From this planted seed branched a diversity of rich and insightful dialogue and exploration by Bette and her students into issues of race, language, and culture.

Renee's teachable/researchable moment surfaced in the late hours of the evening as she was grading papers. In a frustrated outburst in her teaching journal, Renee wrote the following about her rural Southern, mostly African American high school English classroom:

> The first semester is over and it is time for serious reflection and preparation. We [the English Department] have decided to launch the new grading scale. We will use it to penalize students uniformly for the most common grammatical errors after we distribute the departmental grammar handbook....I approach this with a good deal of anxiety. Will it achieve the desired results, or will we simply frustrate the students and make life miserable for everyone? One grim omen has been the grammar diagnostic that I used at the start of the school year. This past week, I had my accelerated 9th-grade class take the same test again as a post-test. I've only made it about halfway through the scoring, but the results so far are depressing; most of the students' scores improved only slightly, several stayed the same, and some dropped! This is after a solid semester—two grading periods—of intense grammar instruction! So what now?
>
> *(12/23/91)*

On the eve of holiday break, Renee resolved to launch herself and her students into a systematic study of race, language, and culture, one that was not about penalties, but about opportunities.

These incidents are significant because, in many ways, they are microcosms of what happens daily in urban, suburban, and rural classrooms across the United States. Students and teachers had run smack against problems of language and seemingly innocent transactions had left them bewildered, angry, frustrated, and betrayed. What was evident was that home codes, street codes, generational codes, and mainstream power codes had collided in our classrooms and had shattered opinion in many directions, none of which could be counted on to focus our discussion, yet all of which offered tantalizing possibilities for learning. As Lindfors (1999) indicated, inquiry is impositional and, although daunted by these language transactions, our students and we were also shaken from our complacency and compelled to investigate these issues.

Given this backdrop, two African American women and a European American man argue that all students, even those for whom school replicates their home codes, need to learn about the cultural complexities of language and to become critically aware of the role language plays in all our lives. However, for students whose home codes differ markedly from the mainstream power codes, such approaches to language learning are crucial. What we mean by language learning is that students need to be invited into the academic conversations about the social and political issues inherent in language—that unless learners have clear understandings of the import of code switching, for example, they will make ill-informed decisions regarding the impact of language on their lives. Therefore, creating a classroom where critical inquiry is the foundation presents one peda- gogy of possibility wherein students and teacher can delve into the nature of the mainstream culture while coming to some greater understanding of the diverse cultures present in the room. Furthermore, if student agency is to be respected, then such classrooms need to be sites where multiple perspectives become the fabric of the curriculum.

This chapter builds upon the foundation of the chapter Bob wrote for the first edition of this book, but it is expanded and deepened by the addition of the work of Renee and Bette. As such, we construct our argument by first creating a theoretical framework based on the work of Delpit, Rosenblatt, Freire, Gee, Bahktin, and Gordon. The aim of this framework is to provide a lens for considering both our research and our pedagogy. Furthermore, we build on this theoretical framework as we discuss the teaching, research, and policymak- ing implications of our work. Between this framework and our implications, we—Bob, Bette, and Renee—provide brief, but rich sketches of the teaching and research that occurred in our classrooms, particularly focusing on literacy events that complicated our discussions of language and the roles it plays in our lives.

Theoretical Framework

At the time of our work, we were all English teachers with over 50 years of com- bined teaching experience. Yet we were all at metaphysical places where our traditional charge of teaching students what some have called standard English was conflicting with what we knew about how language played out in our class- rooms, and in the lives and communities of our students. Therefore, we were teachers with conflicted goals. We wanted our students to be fluent in main- stream power codes because we, as Delpit (1995) noted, had seen too often how ignorance of those codes nullified otherwise bright and vibrant lives. On the other hand, those who too readily embrace mainstream power codes run the risk of forsaking their culture and the dialect that ties them to that culture. Most importantly, we wanted our students to understand the beauty and power inher- ent in a deep grasp of mainstream power codes, but we also wanted them to find the opportunities to express the beauty and power of their home and other per- sonal codes. The rub, however, was, and remains, that limitations of time, resources, and an overarching curriculum required that we make terrifying choices among these options.

The theoretical keystones of our framework are three concepts for which Delpit (1995) argued:

1   All students must be taught mainstream power codes because not to do so will further marginalize those who are already marginalized from access to social, economic, and political power venues.
2   Teachers must find ways to legitimize, validate, and celebrate the home and other personal codes students bring to the classroom. Not to do so is to create a gulf among the child, his home, and the school.
3   Students need to be taught the mainstream power codes in ways that critique those codes and open them to further expansion and greater inclusion. Only through critique will the codes become more representational and equitable.

It is our belief that any sound pedagogy in a literacy classroom is built on these concepts. Also, these concepts take on greater significance when they transact with the work of Rosenblatt (1995), Freire (1970/1993), Gee (1996), Bakhtin (1981), and Gordon (2000). The work of the first three theorists is familiar to the field of education. Rosenblatt's (1995) transactional literary theories, Freire's (1970/1993) theories of praxis and dialogue, and Gee's (1996) theories of learning and acquisition all expand or illuminate Delpit's three concepts.

However, with the work of Bakhtin being less accessible to teachers and the work of Gordon being less well known in educational literature, we felt an expanded discussion was warranted. In the case of Bakhtin (1981), we think the concept of what he calls *heteroglossia* provides the larger picture of support for Delpit's three concepts. Bakhtin used *heteroglossia* to describe an ongoing transaction between centripetal, or unifying forces of language, and centrifugal, or diversifying forces of language. On one hand, the centripetal forces, largely through dominant social control, are constantly trying to stabilize and ultimately reify language. On the other hand, the centrifugal forces, primarily through personal interpretation, are always diversifying language, possibly to the point of anarchy. Neither extreme is desirable, and Bakhtin argues that it's the balance of these tensions—their points of transaction—that makes for a healthy, living language. We believe such a scenario is exactly what Delpit's three concepts realize—classrooms at the nexus where home and personal codes transact with mainstream power codes toward the reshaping of new codes.

Furthermore, this transaction of theories needs to be seen through the existential lens provided by Gordon (2000), a Caribbean American philosopher. He posited that all attempts at meaning making are existential acts and that the more one is marginalized from mainstream power codes due to random events of birth, the more one needs to make meaning of the chaos he or she encounters. In particular, he averred that Blacks, due to the long-term and ongoing effects of racism, have particular need to write about and make sense of their lives, to find purpose beyond the reality. As Gordon cited, autobiography has dominated Black literature because, on one hand, it refuted racist arguments that Blacks were not fully human and lacked point of view. To write about one's life is to speak for one's humanity and perspective. On the other hand, such literary work also provided insight into the nature of being Black, particularly in an oppressive culture. Therefore, literacy practice is an existential act, that is, when we teach students to transact with language, we give them tools on which all future meaning will rely.

When backlit by Delpit's concepts, Gordon's existential perspectives and Bakhtin's concept of *heteroglossia* create an urgency for language learning in classrooms. Reading is less a handy academic tool or skill and more a primal necessity for negotiating one's sense of self and place in society. Furthermore, the import of cultures transacting with literacy and language to support identity creation become prominent; the idea that we use reading, writing, speaking, and listening as a means to position ourselves in relation to the greater world around us, regardless of how rational or irrational our transactions with that world may seem, takes hold.

Three Attempts to Reconceptualize Language Learning

Bob's Classroom

As a high school teacher in an urban northeast classroom, I was first daunted and then challenged by Delpit's complex charge—to create a classroom that taught the mainstream power codes, honored home and other personal codes, and invited students to critique their learning through those codes. Encouraged by the work that emerged from my students who had called Giovanni's poem into question, in subsequent years I sought to develop deeper, more systematic investigations into language. The key was to envision a classroom where critical inquiry could be enacted, one in which language became an object of study open to question by students but remained mindful of the traditions and conventions that currently held sway. By investigating and calling into question the language around them, my students would be given opportunities to both understand and accept the mainstream power codes, also coming to know the many dialects in use in the classroom and the extent to which those language codes affected their lives. The intent was to neither teach mainstream codes nor dialect directly, but instead to create academic situations in which students could look at the way language transacted with their lives and the lives of others and then speculate what future encounters with language might hold in store. At base, I would be inviting students into the political, social, and academic discussions about language that seem to exist in the courts, legislatures, corporate boardrooms, and academic conferences across the United States—everywhere, it seems, except language arts classrooms.

Faced with a mix of students whose success in school varied widely and wishing to incorporate Grades 9 through 12 in all language arts classrooms, my small learning community within a larger high school sought focus within this diversity. We found it by centering around one essential question—How does learning connect you to your world?—from which I keyed on language and created a curriculum that evolved through three inquiry projects. The first third of the year focused on raising issues and questions about the nature of language. Using literature as a base from which to work, students read texts such as Wilson's (1986) *Fences*, Gibsons's (1957) *The Miracle Worker*, and "Girl" by Kinkaid (1993), in each case being mindful of what each had to say about language and the ways in which language was used to further the needs of the story. Through discussions and activities centered by these works, themes that would drive the curriculum for the whole year began to emerge.

It was during this opening project that language was first connected to race when a discussion ensued, invited by the text of *Fences*, about the appropriateness of the racial invective nigger. Any teacher of African American students knows that although nigger is the worst racial slur and should be shunned by all White speakers, it is used by many Black adolescents as an inclusive greeting. My middle-class African American colleagues generally tend to frown on any use of the word in any context, as do many of the parents of the students I taught—yet, others of both groups model usage of the word. So when one student expressed concern that the main character used *nigger* too often and another student called that hypocrisy because his perception was that all the students used the word, we had stumbled into our first public display of the range of opinion that existed in the classroom regarding language.

With issues and questions emerging at a steady pace, it occurred to me that my students needed to somehow make a personal connection to these ideas about language. Consequently, the second third of the year was consumed by an autobiographical inquiry into language. Using models such as the movie of Christy Brown's (1989) *My Left Foot* and literary works like Angelou's (1970) *I Know Why the Caged Bird Sings* and Wright's (1945) *Black Boy*, students then wrote autobiographies, four chapters in length, of which at least one chapter had to deal with a way in which language had affected their lives. It was during this project that students broke through many of the barriers presented when an Eastern European American man teaches an African American student population. If revelations about language and connections to personal life had been lacking as the year started, they came out with depth and richness through the autobiographical writing. Language themes relating to family turmoil, profanity, racism, disempowerment, empowerment, and popular culture permeated the writing. Ways in which students were victimized by words ("The first sentence of the letter just made me put my head down and cry") or used words to victimize others ("I was also satisfied that he was hurt because of my words") were imbedded in thoughtful and descriptive tales of urban life.

Four major themes began to dominate our discussions that would propel us into the year-ending investigation. Through writing, debate, and mutual inquiry, concerns about the nature of standard English, Black English,[1] slang and profanity, and code switching continued to weave throughout the warp created by our investigation. These four themes eventually led to individual investigations into language. Students developed questions such as "What happens when the language of rap music is studied for what it says about Blacks in America?" and "What happens when an African American speaks standard English?" Armed with questions that they generated, students set about collecting data through interviews, journal keeping, note making, and electronic recording. In research reports and essays, students made tentative assertions, raised intriguing questions, and made empathetic pleas based on their analysis of the data.

For many students dealing with investigations into slang and profanity, the pervasiveness of these language forms seemed overwhelming. As one student put it, "Everywhere you look, you see profanity. Everywhere you go, you hear profanity. Profanity is everywhere, even in your home." She then used the assertion, based on the feelings of mothers she had interviewed, to argue that something so unavoidable should ultimately be embraced. Another student who had chronicled student–teacher classroom confrontations, concluded by noting that, "Until now, I really never cared about how profanity affects others…but I believe it's not appropriate in the classroom or toward teachers." In either case, although the assertions differed, the arguments were based in part on the information gathered through the personal investigation into language.

The student inquiries into code switching often showed sophistication in terms of what students knew about shifting language based on audience and social expectations. As one student noted in discussion about her study:

> When I'm with my mother and we get to talkin', we just havin' our own time, we're speakin' Black English. Like if I go around my grandmother's way, they're White, and she has a certain way of speakin'. And I talk a different way around her. When I'm with my friends I talk slang…Right here [in school], I'll talk standard….What I really speak is Black English. Cause that's what I'm used to—Black English and slang. That's what I mainly grew up around.

It is clear by these words that some students are fairly savvy about code switching and do so with some degree of intention and purpose. All too frequently, however, students also expressed resentment that they needed to shift into language forms that, for one reason or another, did not seem to represent them as they wanted to be represented to the world.

Most often, the resented switch was into standard English, and studies into the impact of standard and Black English abounded. Each term brought its share of controversy, passion, and divided opinion to the table. Perhaps this range is best embodied by the following observation, also taken from a discussion of the student's personal inquiry:

> My aunt on my dad's side, she speaks standard English all the time. And when I go over there, she corrects me all the time. "It's not you ain't, it's *you're not.* If I had a dime for every time you said you *ain't,* I could be the richest woman on this earth." And she even makes fun of how we speak. [unclear] and laughs about it. I don't think it's really funny, for real for real. I think she's lost her whole background. It seems like when I see her, I don't see a Black aunt, I see a White aunt. That's what I see. A creation of learning back in her day.

It may not be true that this student's aunt "lost her whole background," and it is prudent to consider that what constitutes Blackness or Whiteness is not limited to language. But this student showed strong evidence of using her investigation into language to gain deeper and more complex understandings of the way language played out in her life.

What stood out most from these discussions based on the student investigations into standard and Black English was the range of opinion about both concepts. Within my classroom, students found facets of both that were beneficial and problematic. Rarely were we able to gain much consensus on either topic, except to agree that both were not going away and would continue to affect the lives of us who studied them.

Although the frame around which we worked remained of my doing, the students had developed questions for inquiry, gathered and analyzed data, and arrived at conclusions that suited their needs and concerns. Over the course of the year, a loose and superficial set of queries had coalesced into areas of inquiry that were investigated through a variety of questions that were both challenging and meaningful to the student inquirers. As Delpit (1988) and Freire (1970/1993) both recommended, the codes of power were brought under scrutiny by those who have something to gain, but also something to lose, through acquisition of those codes. In naming the nature of the impact language held on our lives, we had brought our inquiry, if not to a conclusion, then to some plateau from which we could momentarily contemplate the view.

Bette's Classroom

"The spontaneous dialogues helped me a lot," a former student responded when, some three years after her course with me, I asked her what single feature of the class had contributed most to her development as a writer. These not-always-so-"spontaneous dialogues," which students and I call *classtalk,* have become a fixture in my courses at a small private liberal arts college in South Mississippi, where I have taught for nine years.

Many years before, when I taught public high school in the same town, I had begun exploring new ways of enhancing students' language development. This exploration grew out of my frustration that too many of my students left my class writing the same way they had when they entered. And while my experiments led to a variety of approaches that helped students create more substantive texts, we have continued to struggle in adapting language for various contexts. In addition, many reluctant writers in my classes have expressed to me their sense of inadequacy as speakers and writers, recalling how they had been silenced or ridiculed in school settings because they spoke and wrote in dialects that did not conform to academic standards.

Thus, two crucial questions guided our search:

1   How do we create a class community wherein students, their teacher, and their peers value the dialects they all bring to the classroom?
2   How do we assist one another in adapting our written language codes for a variety of audiences and purposes?

Fortunately, through study with Dixie Goswami, professor of English emerita at Clemson University and director of the writing program at Bread Loaf School of English, I learned of the benefits of teacher research in addressing these questions. Four important theory-based assumptions underpin this study. To start, I believe that well-facilitated conversations in a multicultural classroom can help "ensure the kind of equal-status interactions from which positive attitudes across...differences can grow" (Cazden, 1988, p. 135). Closely connected to this idea is my notion that contextualized talk is the primary mode of language acquisition, that we learn language through ongoing transactions with others (Bakhtin, 1981). I also believe that classtalk can provide a less threatening means of elevating students' critical language awareness (CLA), raising their consciousness of the power and politics of language (Clark & Ivanic, 1998). Throughout *Other People's Children*, Delpit (1995) expresses a similar view, stressing that children need to be instructed in the codes of the "culture of power." Finally, conversation provides a way to build on shared experience in developing written texts. If students are going to acquire "the language of education" (Martin, 1983, p. 9), they must be able to bring the knowledge and the language they gain in their homes and communities to school.

In addressing inquiry questions, I have documented selected classtalk events in a freshman composition class. The total class population included 10 low to upper income European American students and five low to middle income African Americans. By recording these sessions, I was able to gain an understanding of the range of response to these issues and to observe connections among the dialogues and theories cited earlier.

As mentioned in our introduction, my class became particularly engaged in discussion of language issues when an African American student (*E*) from our online discussion expressed his resistance to switching to standard American English. Although this transcript excerpt of our conversation in response to E's comments is long, I am including it in its entirety because it not only gives a sense of the range of perspective this classtalk brought to the surface, but it also holds potential for shaping future teaching and learning practices.[2]

WS: I can identify with his opinion. But I still feel that everybody ought to learn standard English and use it in the proper situations. But I still do not approve ridiculing people who speak a different dialect. It's important to have a common dialect among a similar group of people, because this is one aspect of what makes up culture.

DP (AFRICAN AMERICAN MALE): I wouldn't change my language for no one. Cause I'm gonna talk the way I talk anyway. [Some girls giggle.]

BR (EUROPEAN AMERICAN FEMALE): I think people should be allowed to express themselves in their own way. But I do believe that if you're going to school you should learn standard English. I'm not African American, but I was raised in a family with a strong Southern drawl, so when I started to school my teachers corrected me about my speech, and I don't feel that learning standard English took away from my culture or background…. [some students, African American and European American, indicate agreement].

GT (AFRICAN AMERICAN FEMALE): Yeah, he said something about losing his dignity when he change his dialect. But it don't have nothing to do with losing your dignity. It's just normal for you to change your speech according to who you talking to. And it's not just Blacks—it's Whites, too.

AN (EUROPEAN AMERICAN FEMALE): E needs to understand that everyone does not live in his community. Everybody is not Black and they don't know the dialect. Standard English is a universal language, and the majority of people understand it. While E was growing up, he shoulda wanted to learn—like the big words—like if it was a word he didn't know, they told us to go look it up…. [Exchange of stares among a few African American students; longer interval before next speaker.]

WS (AFRICAN AMERICAN MALE): He is saying there is a point where we cross over….It's not like we have to be White. And I disagree about a universal language—I don't think there is one universal language. [Silence, but some African American students nod in agreement.]

BD: I think we're on our way to some important insights. All of you have made very significant points. Let's get back to them and think further about this whole matter. We're running out of time, but I want you to do some further thinking—careful and honest thinking on paper—about these questions. I'd like to see your responses, but you don't have to share them with anyone else. It's your choice. [I write questions on board, saying them aloud as I write]: Are using "standard English" and using big words the same thing?

Try to give examples to back up your response. Do you always find it easy to code switch in situations requiring a formal—or standard—usage which you don't routinely use? Here I mean speaking or writing. Is standard English a "universal language?" Are you comfortable with your language practices? If so, what factors make you comfortable? If not, what makes you uncomfortable? How might we—teacher, student peers, and you—work together to enhance your effectiveness in using language?

In sum, most students admitted to having some trouble code switching from informal to more formal language, although some said it was easier to accomplish in writing than in speaking. All, including the student who initially made the claim, denied that standard English was a "universal language," while most expressed some discomfort with their language practices.

AS, who had made insightful contributions to the conversation, described what she considered to be her deficiencies as well as how we might best address them:

> I need to do more brainstorming before I write and take more time to get my verb tense right. Also when I slow down I catch myself when pronouncing things wrong. I believe reading the articles aloud in class make us pay more attention to the proper language, also we can read our papers aloud to each other and correct each other's mistakes....

The written responses, like the conversation, reflected some tensions often conducive to introspection and potential change: the African American male "identifying" with *E*, asserting the necessity of using "standard English...in the proper situations," but insisting, "it's not like we have to be White"; the gradual acknowledging of the discomforts of code switching. All these perspectives would help direct our further inquiry.

In addition, through close and recurring analyses of these classtalk events, including observations of student coresearchers and of colleagues, as well as my own, I have noted the following most important developments in our inquiry:

1   Students across racial and economic backgrounds display a strong sense of the role of audience and purpose in language choice. Therefore, they agree generally on the necessity of occasional code switching, or register shifting.
2   Although students recognize the strong impact of family and social traditions on individual language patterns, they also see that appropriating the language of another culture does not necessarily mean adopting an entirely new set of values.
3   Through carefully facilitated talk, students work toward their own understandings of complex language matters—understandings that challenge assumptions based on ignorance and bigotry. They confront the reality that

such assumptions transcend race, as noted in BR's comments about her "Southern drawl," although this accent does not necessarily imply "non-standard" usage. Students of all ethnic and economic backgrounds come to resist the notion that race, region, or any dialect necessarily reflects intelligence or that "English is the universal language."

This elevated awareness contributes to "equal-status interactions" and "positive attitudes" that Cazden (1988) considers important to language growth.

As students gain new insights on the complex and controversial issues surrounding language, some of them, like AS, assume greater roles in questioning and revising their own linguistic practices. Even where such agency is not evident among students, appropriations of particular new language patterns—new ways of representing ideas in speech and writing—surface. Students whose dialects often deviate from mainstream quickly add terms such as *context, code switching*, and *appropriation* to their vocabulary, applying them effectively in their conversations and written texts. Obviously, they acquire some of these new codes from the teacher, but they learn others from peers. Granted, these new patterns do not always include verbs or pronouns; however, they offer encouragement for further inquiry. And although we cannot discount the effects of other class events—the readings, direct instruction, the actual writing process, the careful observation—our inquiry calls attention to the potential of class conversation in heightening awareness of language issues, fostering positive attitudes toward dialect diversity, and promoting students' agency in adapting their language for various contexts.

Renee's Classroom

As I started a decade-long inquiry to construct a response both to Delpit's challenge and my own concerns about the need to teach mainstream power and home codes in my rural Mississippi high school classroom, I used a variety of means to get a range of perspectives on what such a classroom should look like. In collegial discussions, my former department head pointed out, "Everybody likes this teaching grammar through writing stuff because all it requires is doing a little 5-minute review of something we assume the students already know; then showing them how they can use it to improve a particular piece of writing. But somebody has to do the dirty work of teaching the concepts the first time, and that's the job nobody wants." In truth, most of us were teaching grammar skills as if every time were the students' first time being exposed to the topic. After these generally unsuccessful lessons, we would commiserate over how little the students knew or remembered from the last time they had studied the topic.

Continuing to inquire, I selected the group of students and parents who would work with me in the research process. I chose as my research assistant a high school senior, Sheila (not her real name), whom I had taught for the two previous years. I had a more difficult time choosing the students who would make up the focus group for my research interviews. I wanted a mix of males and females and of ability levels in grammar and usage. Also important were their parents or significant adults, who would make up the adult focus group. I deliberately chose students whose parents I knew would be more cooperative and likely to participate until project's end.

With the help of my online partners from Bread Loaf Teacher Network, I engaged my students and parents in discussions of the question, "What makes a good English teacher?" I knew from previous experience that students from our small, closely-knit community often expressed themselves more freely to distant online peers than they would to me or to their classmates. In a typical response, CA, a student from Mississippi noted:

> A good English teacher is a teacher that has a good relationship with their students. Not only do they teach their students but they talk to the students about things other than the things that are supposed to be taught. Good teachers take time out and speak to students like they are your friends. They never give up on any student no matter how much a student does not understand the work, the teacher always keeps their patience and tries to help the student no matter what.

I was surprised at the commonality in opinions among my rural students and their more urbane, online counterparts in East Orange, New Jersey.

My parents' group also provided rich perspectives. When I asked one parent during a Saturday morning conversation, "Why are our students so resistant to learning and using standard English?" he looked straight at me and said:

> English has a way of degrading you. Talkin' is s'posed to be natural. I feel angry. I'm angry about this. This deals with my self-esteem. They always tell us we're shiftless; we're lazy. I passed ENG 101 class at junior college, but the teacher flunked me and wrote on my last paper that is was because I "talked funny." English is a weapon of oppression. Just another tool to keep me in my place. Even if I master the language … [trails off].

His passionate response caught my attention because he had so eloquently captured the language dilemma with which I was struggling within the classroom, and indeed had struggled throughout my own education and professional life.

I also began to mine the rich body of work on language, race, and culture, studying such educators as Geneva Smitherman (1983), Ladson-Billings (1992), and Delpit (1995) among the over 70 research sources into which I tapped. In particular, Ball's (2000) study of female African American teachers reminded me of the importance of community. As Ball noted, "Discourse practices that take place within [the African American community] contribute to the building and sustaining of a sense of community and support a pedagogy that takes advantage of the cultural and linguistic knowledge that students bring to the learning environment" (p. 1008).

I put all these perspectives to work as I began to construct a vision of my classroom that employs an approach to language teaching I call Culturally Engaged Instruction (CEI). Over the course of my research, I've come to see CEI as *empowering language arts instruction in a dynamic practice shaped by informed and collaborative analysis of the particular cultural experiences, strengths, and learning goals of a specific group of students within a particular community.* Using CEI as my guide, I refined my preassessment process and developed individualized communications skills portfolios for each student, which required the participation of a significant adult member of the community. I have always used some kind of preassessment, but I also realize that my earlier preassessments had been too long and had too many separate parts, making the analysis very time consuming. I had learned it was more important that the students and I be able to draw some immediate conclusions from this early assessment, so we could begin working in a more personalized way sooner in the school year. Based on my hypothesis, an early, accurate, and detailed knowledge of the students is vital for culturally engaged instruction. Certainly, such knowledge is important for all good teaching; CEI is simply good teaching for a particular population of students.

My preassessment process revolved around having students demonstrate through performance their abilities in reading, writing, listening, and speaking. Only reading and writing are tested in the district or statewide assessments; however, I included the oral skills not only because they are part of the state framework, but also because they are highly valued communication skills within the local African American community and the ones in which the students tend to be strongest.

We began with a short, carefully chosen reading passage by or about an African American, preferably someone with whom they were not familiar. First, we did a timed reading to determine their speed. Then, they were allowed to read the article in full, set it aside, and free write what they remembered from the article. Next, I had them listen to an audiotape of a professional speaker on a motivational or inspirational topic, such as how to be a better reader. They were required to take notes during the tape. Scanning these later gave me an idea of their skills at listening comprehension. Finally, they used their notes from both exercises to draft an essay. I made sure to give the essay an I-Search twist, such as "What, if anything, did you get from the reading and/or the lecture that might help you this school year?" These essays became our writing and grammar samples. All this took a few days to complete.

After the first week of school, we started analyzing the results together and developing personal learning plans (PLPs). The PLP was the first requirement in the communications skills portfolio for my class. I spent at least one full class period introducing the portfolio. There were several points in the portfolio that were negotiable, both initially and as the school year progressed. The final step was for them to take the PLP and the portfolio checklist home.

Each student had to identify a significant adult of his or her choice (e.g., parent, neighbor, teacher, church member, etc.) who was willing to act as a mentor for the duration of the school year. The mentor's role was to encourage the student to keep up and complete his or her portfolio. Students had to explain the portfolio to the mentors and get them to sign a contract. I contacted the mentors as soon as I knew who they were to introduce myself, answer questions, take suggestions for adjustments in the PLP or portfolio, and open the door for communication throughout the year. All these steps helped us create a culturally engaged learning environment.

Applying what I have learned from my research specifically to the teaching of grammar instruction has led to several meaningful changes in my classroom practice. First, I made a decision to talk with my students honestly and often about why we are required to study and master standard American English. Second, I used what I have learned about the students throughout the language instruction, starting with the extensive preassessment. Taking the time to learn about them and using that information as we learn about language and how to use it has incredible benefits for all of us.

Over time, I realized I was searching for a more empowering approach to language arts instruction. I wanted to teach the language arts in such a way that each student not only became technically proficient or skilful, but also became cognizant of the effects of language on others. Just as important, I wanted my students to understand how language arts/communication skills could be used to project one's own ideas and to assess more critically the ideas of others.

Conclusion

What, then, is the nature of an English classroom where language is the subject of critical inquiry? What occurs there? What do students do? What is the teacher's role? What issues get raised, discussed, and explored? What is the atmosphere that is conducive to such inquiry, and how is that atmosphere created? What is the work of such a classroom, and how is that work negotiated? In theory, according to Freire (1970/1993), such a classroom would engage students and teacher in a dialogue about the nature of the world, would help students to problem pose and problem solve for themselves, would encourage the oppressed to name a world that is other than the world of their oppressors, and would develop a means for inquiring into the world as a co-investigation between teachers and students. Delpit (1988) would add that such a classroom must acknowledge, celebrate, and use the culturally inherent expertise of the students in the classroom, while informing those students about the codes of power so they may both utilize and critique those codes. These studies give us three separate, yet similar visions of what those combined theories could look like in practice.

Implications

As Bob has argued elsewhere (Fecho, 2004), making separate recommendations for separate stakeholders is problematic for a number of reasons. To begin, such practice implies that a suggestion for one stakeholder applies only to that stakeholder and no others, thus creating a kind of tunnel vision. Nor does this stance of separate recommendations encourage dialogue across stakeholders; instead, each assumes that if they take care of their concerns, all the pieces will come together. And, too often, in listing separate stakeholders, some key group is left out. All groups need to take responsibility for collaborative solutions. Therefore, in this section, we will argue that the implications of our work have mutual relevance for teachers, researchers, policymakers, and all other groups who hold vital interest in the education of our children.

Recognizing the Political Nature of Language Study

It is our contention that educators shouldn't go on teaching mainstream power codes to students of varied cultures and dialects as if acquisition of that privileged dialect had no impact on student cultural and familial identity; to do so is tantamount to burying our collective heads in the chalk dust. As teachers of children from cultures other than our own, we need to understand the importance of the home language, the language of peers, and any other language codes our students have acquired in their education both in and out of school. We should acknowledge that choices in subject–verb agreement and other seemingly neutral grammar constructions have at least partial connection to personal identity and an eventual impact on the way that students see themselves as members of racial, ethnic, regional, and class-based communities.

Yet, by admitting that we place students in awkward situations when we ask them, even at very young ages, to choose between the language of the home and that of school, we open ourselves to pedagogies of possibility that might enable such choices to be done with more grace and less loss. All stakeholders need to acknowledge the oppressive nature of mainstream power codes while affording students the opportunity to become fluent in those codes. In doing so, we can create pedagogy and educational policy that responds to Delpit's challenges and creates schools that are more inclusive of a wider range of cultures, as well as devising research that will help us to better understand how to do so wisely.

Recognizing the Need for Agency on the Part of All Stakeholders

As we showed through our classrooms, the voices of students, teachers, parents, researchers, and community members generate rich and multiple perspectives when entered into dialogue with each other and the voices of policymakers. This is a very Bakhtinian notion. Although we acknowledge the need for policy on language that helps to stabilize it and the ways it is learned, current policy is, instead, reifying language and language learning, encasing them in cement. Educators need to make room for centrifugal tension provided by local input into how we learn language, what counts as the range of language, and what meaning and import is derived through language. We're not asking for an either/or situation, but instead seek a dialogue around language and language learning that honors the input of more than one stakeholder.

By listening to our students and opening ourselves to the wider educational community, we—Bob, Bette, and Renee—created classrooms where students were engaged in language learning rather than merely complying with the process. They came to see language learning as something for which they had input and options, and we have come to further appreciate the multiple insightful perspectives students bring. If the educational community continues to operate as if no choices about language and language learning exist, we will continue to foster the false belief that some students cannot learn the mainstream power codes, when in reality these students often elect, either consciously or subconsciously, not to use those codes, despite their capacity to learn those codes. When all stakeholders grasp the existential nature of this work and provide students with the opportunities for making sustained, substantive meaning through language, then students will have greater agency in how they shape their identity through language. Furthermore, they will bring a critical eye to the printed and other texts of their lives, reading the language used therein in terms of their own identities and intentions.

Inquiry Is a Vital Pedagogical Tool

We mean this statement in a variety of ways. To begin, all stakeholders can acknowledge that adolescents are capable of conducting substantive inquiry and critique in general and, in particular, of doing so into the nature and impact of language in their lives. This notion flies in the face of stereotypes of adolescents as being disinterested in language and language learning or even capable of conducting systematic and extended exploration. Furthermore, all stakeholders need to acknowledge the power and possibility of teachers inquiring into their own classrooms, of seeing where they teach as transactional spaces where they can create new texts of their teaching practice as well as shape the existing educational canon. In addition, it would help if all concerned widened paradigmatic views on what counts as research and who gets to inquire.

Again, we call for a Bakhtinian dialogue on inquiry, one that acknowledges a need for a range of perspectives and a multiplicity of views, one that is polyphonic, one that understands that no view is privileged. In doing so, we hope to create conditions that would support a range of inquiry projects conducted by a range of stakeholders. So, of course, there is an expectation that students will inquire into a range of texts and raise questions through their inquiry. But the same expectation holds for teachers. The three of us were able to inquire into our classrooms because we were part of vibrant, supportive educational communities—the Bread Loaf Teachers Network in the cases of Bette and Renee and the National Writing Project in the case of Bob. Unfortunately, too few teachers have access to such communities and we need to envision school, district, and state networks that would support inquiries within and across stakeholders in order to begin to see inquiry as the work of all rather than the privilege of a few.

Providing Time and Opportunity for Language Inquiry

A final and crucial implication for practice is that crossing boundaries—whether they be racial, expectational, or personal—takes concerted time and opportunity. Depth of classroom inquiry and discussion evolves over the course of the year. Serious and lengthy discussions around race and language come only as a result of continued forays into and retreats from the topics over time. Students begin to question their own gaps between belief and action only when they have had ample opportunity to examine those beliefs and actions.

In effect, two inquiries take place simultaneously. The first of these is centered about the named subject of investigation; in all our classrooms, these were our inquiries into language. At the same time, a second and more tacit inquiry is being conducted. All members of the class are looking into the seriousness and safety of the class; the students and teachers are taking the measure of each other to see how much they can risk of themselves, what can be put on the table for discussion, and what might be rejected. The movement is in small increments across the whole of a year and needs time and multiple opportunities to prosper. Any classroom that expects students to risk their anonymity and the security it brings needs to understand that such risk is the product of an inquiry into the supportive ethos of the class. This inquiry can be conducted only over time and with much possibility of gathering more supportive evidence.

Extending the Dialogue

Although we three who authored this text all have our beliefs fall within a certain range of mutual acceptance, we recognize that a range does exist. For example, terms such as *mainstream power codes*, *homes codes*, and *street codes* get unpacked in different ways by each of us and have different implications for the user. As Bakhtin (1981) noted, language is half ours and half that of others, and speakers are forever striving to clarify meaning. In this text, we have only scratched the surface of our understandings of these ideas and, although we share some common vision, we also each bring our individual experience to bear.

Because we see that language and language acquisition are complex and nuanced, we realize that a completely unified stance would be foolish and perhaps even hypocritical, given our belief in dialogue. For example, although this chapter does argue that adolescents have many valid reasons for struggling with and resisting mainstream conceptions of language and literacy, the three of us remain in dialogue about those reasons. One line of reasoning offers that because language is first learned in the home and then in the neighborhood, it is very much tied to identity. When associations with mainstream power codes also are linked to a history of oppression, learners from marginalized cultures may show reluctance to acquire language that too closely ties them to visions and conceptions of the oppressor. If Gee (1996) is to be believed, acquisition of a discourse involves mutual acquisition of the mores and values of the progenitors of that discourse. This possibility of having to alter one's core belief in order to speak acceptably in mainstream settings either consciously or subconsciously can act as a deterrent toward literacy and language acquisition by learners whose language markedly differs from the mainstream.

Of the three of us, Bob is more inclined to accept this line of reasoning as being the key factor as to why marginalized students—for example, poor and rural Whites, urban African Americans living in racially isolated neighborhoods, Latino/Latinas trying to negotiate language and cultural differences—might resist code switching into dominant discourse. Bette, although accepting of this argument to a point, feels other mitigating factors such as habit and access need to be factored into the equation. Renee, somewhat less vocal on the issue, seems to fall somewhere between these views. However, no matter what our range of thoughts on these concerns, we do agree that educators should no longer—or should have ever—chalk up these struggles with mainstream power codes as an inability to learn.

Nor, however, can educators ignore the dominance of mainstream power codes in our society. Delpit (1995), although she called on educators to appreciate the language and literacy of the home, implored us to find ways to engage students in these codes of power in order to avoid continued marginalization. Teachers of students whose home languages differ markedly from the standard need to acknowledge those differences and to incorporate discussions about such differences into the fabric of the classroom. If students are aware of these differences that exist between the languages of their lives and the privileged mainstream dialect, they can make appropriate choices about accessing that privileged dialect and controlling the effects of such access on their sense of self and sense of membership in larger identifying cultures of race and class. However, again as Delpit (1995) cautioned, we must be careful that we teach in ways that don't blindly reify these codes, that students and teachers alike understand that no language code is innately superior or inferior, that all are forms of dialect, and all bring richness to our daily language use and learning.

A classroom where inquiry is the primary approach to learning is best suited, in our opinion, for allowing such investigation, discussion, and choice to take place. It allows for a conception of adolescent language learning that is complex, one that acknowledges what Bakhtin (1981) described as being multivoiced. In such a class, teachers and students call the mainstream power codes and their own language use into question in order to develop newer and deeper understandings of the import of language in their lives. In doing so, they gain insight into the complicated ways their personal language is a multivocal mix of a range of codes. Until students are actively engaged in such critique about the language and literacy that is so much a part of their lives, they will be at the mercy of those educational tools rather than masters of their complex, but much rewarding craft. As this chapter represents the second published installment of an ongoing dialogue about these issues, we encourage the larger educational community to join the circle and be heard.

Notes

1   Although Bob now prefers using terms like *mainstream power codes*, *home codes*, and *Black Vernaculars*, he has elected to remain with the terms *standard English* and *Black English* in this section because these are the terms that were used in his class at the time of the study.
2   Some redundant or summary turns have been edited from this transcript to save space and improve readability.

References

Angelou, M. (1970). *I know why the caged bird sings*. New York: Random House.

Bakhtin, M. (1981). Discourse in the novel. In M. H. C. Emerson (Ed.), *The dialogic imagination: Four essays by M. M. Bakhtin* (pp. 259–422). Austin, TX: University of Texas Press.

Ball, A. (2000). Empowering pedagogies that enhance the learning of multicultural students. [Electronic version] *Teachers College Record, 102*(6), 1006–1034.

Brown, C. (1989). *My left foot*. United States: Miramax Films.

Cazden, C. (1988). *Classroom discourse: The language of teaching*. Portsmouth, NH: Heinemann.

Clark, R., & Ivanic, R. (1998). *The politics of writing*. London, UK: Routledge.

Delpit, L. (1988). The silenced dialogue: Power and pedagogy in educating other people's children. *Harvard Educational Review, 58*(3), 280–298.

Delpit, L. (1995). *Other people's children: Cultural conflict in the classroom*. New York: The New Press.

Fecho, B. (2004). *"Is this English?" Race, language and culture in the classroom*. New York, NY: Teachers College Press.

Freire, P. (1993). *Pedagogy of the oppressed*. New York: Continuum. (Original work published 1970.)

Gee, J. P. (1996). *Social linguistics and literacies: Ideology in discourse* (2nd ed.). London, UK: RoutledgeFalmer.

Gibson, W. (1957). *The miracle worker*. New York: Knopf.

Gilyard, K. (1991). *Voices of the self*. Detroit: Wayne State University Press.

Giovanni, N. (1971). Beautiful Black men. In D. Randall (Ed.), *The Black poets* (pp. 320–321). New York: Bantam.

Gordon, L. (2000). *Existentia Africana: Understanding African existential thought*. London, UK: Routledge.

Kinkaid, J. (1993). Girl. In T. Wolfe (Ed.), *The Vintage book of contemporary American short stories* (pp. 306–307). New York: Vintage.

Ladson-Billings, G. (1992). Liberatory consequences of literacy: A case of culturally relevant instruction for African American students. *Journal of Negro Education, 61*(3), 378–391.

Lindfors, J. W. (1999). *Children's inquiry: Using language to make sense of the world*. New York: Teachers College Press.

Martin, N. (1983). *Mostly about writing*. Upper Montclair, NJ: Boynton/Cook.

Rosenblatt, L. (1995). *Literature as exploration*. New York: The Modern Language Association.

Smitherman, G. (1983). Language and liberation. *Journal of Negro Education, 52*(1), 15–23.

Wilson, A. (1986). *Fences*. New York: New American Library.

Wright, R. (1945). *Black boy: A record of childhood and youth*. New York: Harper Brothers.

10

RE-WRITING THE STOCK STORIES OF URBAN ADOLESCENTS

Autobiography as a Social and Performative Practice at the Intersections of Identities

Kelly Wissman and Lalitha Vasudevan

In this chapter we draw from our work in two separate research contexts to explore how young people claimed autobiography as a social and performative practice with personal and socially transformative impulses and outcomes. Kelly's research explores the literacy and artistic practices of young women of color enrolled in an in-school poetry and photography course named Sistahs, while Lalitha's work documents the experiences of young men of color involved in a drama-based elective called Insight within an alternative to incarceration program. In our work, we were both drawn to a re-envisioning of educational spaces with urban adolescents as a "practice of freedom" that "connects the will to know with the will to become" (hooks, 1994). Within both research spaces, young people were involved in autobiographical explorations and collective meaning-making through the arts and literacies with each other and with adults. In both cases, young people also re-wrote the "stock stories" that surround them as urban adolescents.

In the development of our inquiry-based and participatory contexts designed with and for adolescents, our approach stands in contrast to the cultural construction of adolescents (Lesko, 1996, 2001) in which they are always and already known as "out-of-control and needing direction, knowledge, and discipline from adults" (Lesko, 1994, p. 147). This "biologically-determined view" (Lesko, 1994) of adolescence as a developmental stage and as a way station to adulthood most often translates into the creation of educational spaces and practices designed to contain and control. As Lesko (2001) contends:

> Static ideas about youth have helped to keep in place a range of assumptions and actions in and out of secondary schools. For example, since

adolescents have raging hormones, they cannot be expected to do sustained and critical thinking, reason many educators. Since adolescents are immature, they cannot be given substantive responsibilities in school, at work or at home.

(pp. 189–190)

Concerns about adolescents' "raging hormones" have also translated into rationales for the creation of single sex educational spaces in which young people, presumed heterosexual, will be free of distraction and temptation. While the contexts we explore in this chapter primarily involve young people who share the same gender identity, these contexts were not created in order to keep out the opposite sex based on fears of out-of-control sexuality; rather, they were designed (in Kelly's case with young women) or emerged (in Lalitha's case with young men) in an effort to explore deeply and in a shared, collective way, the lived experiences of young people across the intersections of their identities. As we explore below, the invitation to engage in personal storytelling within these spaces opened up opportunities for young people to explore and question the construction and representation of identities through multiple modalities and to use the arts to talk back to distorted, sensationalized, and simplistic representations of their lives and identities as urban adolescents.

Framing Autobiography: Critical Race Theories, Single Stories, and Counterstories

Cultural scripts about youth are among the narratives on which decisions about pedagogy and assessment, as well as schooling more broadly, are made. These scripts reflect what Adichie (2009) has described as a "single story," and too often the single story about the literacies and identities of adolescents is one rooted in deficiency. Critical race scholars propose counterstories (Delgado, 1995; Duncan, 2005) as a call to action in response to the singular stories, or stock stories, that are circulated across space and time, through the use of words as well as images and sounds in order to communicate a set of "common sense" understandings about young people's literate lives, among other world phenomena. Counterstories can be understood as narratives that offer insights, depict realities, and render historical accounts told by individuals and groups whose perspectives are underrepresented in the broader social imagination, including academic and popular literature. The pursuit and inclusion of counterstories composed about and by adolescents is important for challenging these stock stories in the discourses that circulate about their educational and literate lives. Autobiography, as this chapter will show, is both a local practice of illuminating the contours of one's identities and a practice that can profoundly connect personal stories with global tropes.

Background to Our Studies

Kelly's study draws from data collected over one academic year within an in-school elective course she taught exploring the arts, poetry, and social change within the literacy and artistic traditions of African American women poets, songwriters, photographers, and artists. The course was created with and for adolescent girls in a large urban school district. The majority of the students self-identified as African American; three students identified respectively as Puerto Rican, multi-racial, and Black/Grenadian. The students ranged in age from 14–16. Data sources include fieldnotes, interviews, student work, and transcripts from class discussions.

Lalitha's study of the Insight Theater Project is part of a larger, five-year study of literacies, educational trajectories, and storytelling within the Alternative to Incarceration Program (ATIP), one of several incarceration alternatives that participants are mandated by a judge to attend following an arrest. Unlike some other programs, ATIP also requires that the participants agree to attend the program, thereby encouraging agency and engagement on the part of the youth from the onset. The participant makeup of Insight reflected that of ATIP overall: most of the participants identified as Black, Latino, or Hispanic; four of the 33 participants were young women. Lalitha documented three cycles of Insight and focuses on data from the first cycle for this chapter, which includes fieldnotes, formal interviews and informal conversation transcripts, and transcripts from actor talk-backs following public performances of a play.

In what follows, we each provide description and analysis of the ways in which the young people in our studies took up opportunities to make meaning through the creation and sharing of autobiographical artifacts, including poetry, photographs, improvisations, and scripts. While our contexts were unique, both engaged young people in autobiographical meaning-making that drew upon individual stories to support collective inquiries and both provide insight into autobiography as a performative, social, and embodied act with personal and social significance.

Self-Definition as a Performative and Social Act with Adolescent Girls

In response to my (Kelly's) question about what poem she was most proud of writing during the time she spent in the Sistahs course, Jasmyn pointed to her "I Seem to Be" poem, explaining that it gave her an opportunity to, as she said, "flip the script." In her poem, Jasmyn both names and refutes the stigmatized images of young women of color that paint her as "fresh," materialistic, and a "booty shaking smut," claiming she "will not be held captive" by these false understandings. She uses the space of the poem to reveal herself instead as a young woman of self-determination, creatively employing her self-described tactics of "Beauty-N-Brains" to move through and make sense of her world and her place within it. Like Jasmyn, many of the young women in the course pursued autobiographical work centered around a key theme of self-definition, offering insights into their lived experiences and perspectives that are often unrecognized, distorted, or devalued in broader public discourses. In doing so, their work has a strong resonance with Black Feminist Epistemology in which self-definition is a central tenet. As Collins (2000) also argues:

> By insisting on self-definition, Black women question not only what has been said about African-American women but the credibility and the intentions of those possessing the power to define. When Black women define ourselves, we clearly reject the assumption that those in positions granting them the authority to interpret our reality are entitled to do so.
>
> *(p. 114)*

This claiming of the right to self-define is not without complications, however. In her analysis of the rhetorical practices of African American women essayists, Royster (2000) argues that African American women must work to "shift the ground of rhetorical engagement" (p. 65) to engage with language on their own terms and for their own purposes. To consider how literacy practices support acts of self-definition and social action, Royster (2000) invokes the concept of "ethos formation" to describe how writers take on writerly identities. Defining ethos as "a way of being in the world, that permits the writer to create and present to the world a dynamic speaking and writing self" (p. 168), Royster draws attention to the need to clear a space from which to speak and to write, to establish an identity as a person with communicative intent. Given dominant ideologies reflecting and reinforcing historical legacies of oppression and inequities, Royster (2000) argues that the formation of ethos can be fraught with difficulties, but that it also holds the most promise for the very transformation of those ideologies. The rhetorical task, then, is not only to resist and critique prevailing regimes of truth and image-making, but also to craft an alternative space where new and more socially just images, arguments, and social practices may emerge.

Within previous analyses of my students' literacy and artistic practices, I have highlighted how they claimed poetry and photography as creative pursuits for self-definition and social analysis. In textual analyses of their writing, for example, I argued that their poems of self-definition were "autobiographical acts" (Hesford, 1999) of social analysis and resistance; of imagination and possibility; and of sharing and collectivity (Wissman, 2009). Here, I consider more closely how the writing community we created within the course shaped the students' emerging ethos formations as writers who wrote the "social self" (Yagelski, 1999). In further analysis of classroom transcripts, I more fully realized the integral role the social space of the classroom played in the students' ethos formation, encouraging and supporting the students' efforts "to create and present to the world a dynamic speaking and writing self" (Royster, 2000, p. 168). Sharing this work, in turn, enhanced the sense of validation that can come from writing poems of self-definition. What interests me here are the performative and social dimensions of autobiographical writing within this inquiry community exploring complex issues of identity, literacy, and the arts. Drawing on transcript excerpts to suggest the meaning-making within the group, I explore how writing poems not only created opportunities for the performance of identity, but also how sharing them became a central component of ethos formation and a key inspiration for the continued writing of new poems that challenged and refuted the stock stories of urban young women of color.

"Can We Hurry Up? Because I Want to Share My Poem": Writing Poems to be Shared

Many of our class sessions started by the reading of a poem by such writers as June Jordan, Sonia Sanchez, or Maya Angelou and an invitation for students to write poems in response. Many chose to emulate the style and form of the poems shared in the course. June Jordan's (1989) poem, "A short note to my well-beloved and critical friends and comrades," was the first poem to spark these autobiographical acts reflective of and resistant to multiple social discourses. In this poem, Jordan provides a rich and slightly humorous meditation on the complexities and possibilities of self-representation. She starts the poem by writing, "First they said..." and then repeatedly uses the line, "Then they said..." to suggest the contradictory ways in which multiple messages are relayed through discourses laden with judgments and expectations related to race, gender, sexuality, and other social identities.

Renee, who self-identifies as multi-racial and names her racial identity as "Irish, Dominican, Black, and Cherokee Indian," told me that she composed her poem as a way to reflect the multiple messages she has received about this identity. She writes:

> First they said I was skinny
> Then they said I was a nice size
> Then they asked me what I was mixed with
> Then I said many things.
> Then they said, Oh, that's why your hair is like that.
> Then I said, Don't worry on how my hair is, but make sure your hair is nice.
> Then they said I got a big head.
> And then I said look at yours.
>
> People have a lot to say about other people
> But really they need to worry about themselves.

In her poem, Renee calls attention to and resists discourses related to body size, skin color, and hair that surround her as a multi-racial young woman.

When I decided to ground the Sistahs course in the literacy tradition of African American women, I anticipated that there would be numerous opportunities for students both to read and write within this tradition in the way that Renee did, but I did not anticipate the extent to which the students' sharing of their own poems aloud would become such a defining feature of the class. For Serena and many other students, the prospect of sharing the work in the community actually became a fundamental part of the writing process. Serena, in fact, consistently encouraged other students to hurry so she could share her work; her urgency was most pronounced in relation to her poem written in response to June Jordan's poem. I include here a series of sections from a class transcript to demonstrate the impulse to share as a driving poetic force as well as how the sharing of the poems in class suggested their performative nature:

SERENA: Can we hurry up? Because I want to share my poem. I got something
     to say.
[laughter]
JOY: Go ahead. Go ahead, girl. I want to listen to that.
[As time passes, Serena becomes increasingly anxious to read her poem.]
SERENA: Can I read mine?
KELLY: Just one more minute. Give people a chance to finish.
SERENA: Come on, y'all. Finish writing!
ANGELIQUE: Can I read mines?
KELLY: Just a couple more seconds. Thirty seconds.
…
KELLY: OK. Ready to share?
SERENA: I'm first.
ANGELIQUE: I am.
JOY: I'm second.
SERENA: All right, *listen.*
ANGELIQUE: I'm third.
SERENA: Listen!
     First they said I was too big.
     Then they said I was too grown.
     Then they said I was too short.
     Then they said I was too mean.
     Then they said I was too friendly.
     Then they said I was too opinionated.
     Open up your eyes they said. Are you retarded or are you smart? Are you
          happy or you sad? (I used her [Jordan's] last line). Are you straight or are
          you gay?
     And I said, "Hey, don't you ask me no more questions about me, me, me."

After emphatically imploring her classmates to "listen" two times, Serena finally read her poem; the students responded with a great deal of laughter and discussion about her last line. Joy then immediately started to read her poem at the earliest indication she would be able to be heard. In her reading, she not only read the lines she had written in her journal, but also added direct and playfully indignant commentary to members of the class (represented in parentheses below):

JOY: First they said I was too short. (that's when I was younger)
    Then they said I was too tall (that's now)
    Then they said I was too mean (that was back then)
    Then they said I was too nice (I'm not nice no more)
    Then they said I talked too much
    Then they said I talked too little (I didn't ask you)
    Then they said I was too weak
    Then they said I was too strong
    Then they talked about it
    Then after that I got tired of it
    Then I smacked all of them in the face.
    I'm me, and I'm not changing for none of y'all.
    [group laughter]

Joy's reading of her poem with the parenthetical commentary called even further attention to her authorial presence and confidence in the poem and in the reading of it. When voicing the parenthetical additions, she looked directly at members of the class as if to assert that she was not only the self-possessed writer of the poem, but also that she was the one asserting control in how her writing would be understood by her audience.

In these series of transcript excerpts, it is evident that the students not only grasped the opportunity to write, but also to share those writings with each other. The class itself became a key sounding board and audience to the written words. Often, the students did not request extensive feedback or commentary on their poems or give extensive responses to the poems they heard read aloud. Rather than prolonged discussions, often the responses came in the form of exclamations, laughter, nods, smiles, and sometimes tears. Both Serena's insistence on sharing her poem so soon after its composition and her cajoling of her fellow classmates ("Come on, y'all! Finish writing!") and Joy's embodied reading of her poem suggest the social and performative aspects of the autobiographical within this context.

"Damn, I Look Good": Personal Stories and Collective Meaning-Making

June Jordan (1995) writes that poetry can "build a revolution in which speaking and listening to somebody becomes the first and last purpose to every social encounter" (p. 3). It is this simple, yet transformational, power of speaking and listening that I see evidenced further in another classroom discussion featuring the students' poems. In this section I explore the social and performative dimensions of autobiographical poetry as the students discuss the importance of sharing their work with each other. During a section of the course where the students were creating self-portraits with digital cameras and poetry writing, I brought to class a book of poems and photographs by teenage girls (Franco, 2001). After noticing a poem entitled "Damn, I Look Good" in the book, the students asked if they could write poems of the same title. The "Damn, I Look Good" poems had a large impact on subsequent classes and were frequently discussed. A close look at a classroom transcript further illustrates their impact and provides additional insight into the student-directed process of ethos formation of the course as a writing community.

In the first portion of the excerpt, Janelle has just finished sharing an autobiographical poem she had written a few weeks earlier and the other students try to convince her rather unsuccessfully to read her "Damn, I look good" poem. Although there are many places in my data where the young women can barely wait to share their poems and need no coaxing whatsoever to do so, I choose to highlight this particular transcript excerpt because it reveals the levels of intimacy, playfulness, high expectations, and respect among the young women in the group, as well as the agency they claimed to make this in-school space a space to meet their own needs. In addition, it helps to provide insight into how the young women consistently held each other accountable in this space, to participate in what Mia calls "an expression type class."

In this excerpt, the young women playfully and insistently try to persuade Janelle to read her "Damn, I look good" poem:

RENEE: We all read ours.
JASMYN: Why don't you want to read your "Damn, I look good"?
JANELLE: I don't want y'all to hear it.
JASMYN: Why?
JANELLE: It's too beautiful for y'all.
JASMYN: What?
RENEE: It's too beautiful?! [laughs]
MIA: Go ahead, Janelle!
JANELLE: No, y'all, I don't want to read it.
JASMYN: Why not?
JANELLE: 'Cause. I got to write it again.
RENEE: All right. We gotta learn how to, how to share our stuff with each other.
JANELLE: I just got done sharing with y'all!

A short time later, the students try again to persuade Janelle to read. I quote the resulting exchange for three reasons: to suggest the high level of engagement and participation by many members in the group evidenced by the multitude of voices speaking here; to call attention to the ways in which the students themselves explicitly describe what they expect to occur in this setting; and to illuminate the particularly influential (almost teacherly) role of Jasmyn in this exchange. All three purposes suggest the emergence of particular habits of being, social practices, and relationships that characterized the group's ethos as a writing community. As such, this excerpt provides additional evidence of the growing "sense of authority, agency, and power" (Royster, 2000, p. 168) the students claimed in the space.

JANELLE: I'm trying to learn about these numbers [pretending to do math homework].
RENEE: This is Sistahs.
MIA: This is an expression type class.
RENEE: You have to learn how to express yourself.
JANELLE: OK. Let me look at it, let me look at it.
JASMYN: You know what you wrote!
[group laughter]
RENEE: Jasmyn, has broken out, y'all. She is getting annoyed.
MAYA: She is crazy.
JASMYN: I like mines.
JANELLE: Well, I don't like mines. It doesn't sound right.
JASMYN: Well, how you know if it sound right?
JANELLE: Y'alls sound better than mine.
JASMYN: How do you know?
MAYA: You didn't hear ours!
JANELLE: I heard Jasmyn, and I heard…oh! Hers!
JASMYN: Whose?
MAYA: Lynn's! Yeah, it was good.
…
JANELLE: You got it now?
LYNN: [laughs] It's on the computer.
JANELLE: Well, print it out. You finish typing it up?
LYNN: Yeah.
JASMYN: Um, she'll print hers out if you read yours.
MAYA: Yeah. Yeah. We're making a deal. If you read yours, you can get a copy, as much copies as you want.
JANELLE: No, I'm chillin'.
MAYA: All right. Go ahead, chill.

Near the end of the class, Janelle finally did read her poem after she first managed to strike her own deal: Jasmyn and Maya agreed to sing a song for her if she read her poem. Janelle's poem and the singing were greeted with much applause.

Janelle's initial resistance reflects concerns and anxieties common to many writers: that her writing "didn't sound right," that poems written by other students were better than hers, that her poem was not polished enough yet to share. Jasmyn, the primary instigator in this exchange—and perhaps one could say Janelle's primary advocate—is persistent in finding out why Janelle doesn't want to read and challenging her to reconsider. Most intriguingly, I believe, is Jasmyn's response to Janelle when she says her poem doesn't "sound right." By asking, "How you know if it sound right?" Jasmyn is suggesting that this cannot be determined until Janelle shares it with the group. In this way, Jasmyn is contributing to the development of the ethos of the group where the community of writers support each other and produce knowledge themselves about the value of each other's writing. In other words, the students claim their own power and agency to construct knowledge in this space, rather than relying on some external validation or assessment process.

In addition to revealing how the young women understood the nature of Sistahs as a context for, in June Jordan's (1995) words, "speaking and listening to somebody" (p. 3) the whole group effort to persuade Janelle to read through a range of arguments and incentives also reveals the significant impact that the students' own autobiographical poetry had on this context. Student perspectives such as "This is an expression type class" and "You've got to learn how to express yourself" also suggest the identity this course took on as a writing community. In creating their own opportunities for ethos formation and for creating habits of being in the group that met their own needs as writers and members of this literacy community, the students were clearly asserting themselves by inventing conditions and processes to strengthen their "sense of authority, agency, and power" (Royster, 2000, p. 168) as writers of autobiographical poetry.

You Seem to Be Poems: Performing as a Collective

In the process of working on the self-portraits project, we read quite a few poems from *Voices of Our Own* (Deutsch, 2001), a book that includes writing and artwork created by teenage girls and women in the Tenderloin district of San Francisco, California. The girls in my class were particularly intrigued by a group of poems in the collection entitled "I seem to be" and suggested we write poems with the same title. Like the "First they said" poems, these poems invited an acknowledgement of, and meditation on, individual and societal perceptions and also afforded an opportunity to write back to, clarify, and often times contradict these perceptions and stock stories. As I noted above, these poems also provided Jasmyn an opportunity to "flip the script." After the students completed the individual "I seem to be" poems, I invited the students to analyze their poems and to brainstorm what they perceived to be the most common misperceptions of young women of color (represented in all capitals in the poem below). The girls first wrote individual rebuttals to these stereotypes and misperceptions. Three girls then combined their responses into a group poem. The following week, the girls chose to read their individual poems and the group poem at the school-wide Poetry Jam in front of their family and friends. Here is their poem:

> YOU SEEM TO BE TOO LOUD
> JASMYN: But really I'm just louder than you
> SONIA: But really that's just the way I talk
> JOY: But really I talk with a passion
>
> YOU SEEM TO BE TOO GROWN
> JASMYN: But really I've grown to be a beautiful young lady
> SONIA: But really I'm all grown up and responsible
> JOY: But really I'm growing up to be an adult
>
> YOU SEEM TO BE UNEDUCATED
> JASMYN: But really I'm just not educated to the fullest extent
> SONIA: But really I'm still trying to get my education for your information
> JOY: But really I'm educated to the fullest
>
> YOU SEEM LIKELY TO BECOME A TEEN MOM
> JASMYN: But really I'm a teen Magnificent-Outreaching-Marvel
> SONIA: But really I'm a teen who is trying to reach her goals
> JOY: But really I'm doing nothing at all to be into that
> Predicament

This collaborative poem invited an acknowledgement of, and meditation on, individual and societal perceptions and also afforded an opportunity to write back to, clarify, and often times contradict these perceptions. As critical readers of the world around them, the students talked back to and resisted harmful images and assumptions. The student poets have faith in the possibilities and power of language to supplant limiting, damaging, and restraining images with affirmative, dynamic, and generative ones. By composing this poem and sharing it in a public arena, the students expressed a strong sense of determination to use writing and performance as a way to challenge these misperceptions. The language practices in evidence here reveal the young women's creative and analytical interventions into dominant discourses and ideologies and a re-writing of the stock stories circulating about their lives and identities.

Autobiographical Performances and Collective Storytelling

Many of the court-involved young people I (Lalitha) have spent time with over the last several years—including those who are incarcerated, enrolled in incarceration alternative programs, currently on probation or parole—have described a persistent awareness of surveillance across the institutions they move through regularly. One formerly incarcerated young man, EJ, who has been a part of my research team for the last two and half years, recently observed that in his experience some adults characterize court-involved youth as being "criminal and animal-like." His words echo those of another young man, Robert, who recalled the term "animal-escents" being used by correction officers at the jail where he was incarcerated for several weeks before being transferred to ATIP. According to Robert and other youth participants at the program, this was a commonly used term that reflected how the youth felt they were perceived and treated by adults in positions of authority at the jail. Their observations resonate strongly with the critiques of social institutions as being filled with dehumanizing practices inflicted by adults onto children and youth in the form of labels that bring with them the weight of policies that can significantly affect future trajectories (e.g., Duncan, 2005; Ferguson, 2000). Missing from many adolescents' schooling experiences are opportunities for their expressive practices and narratives to be nurtured, and to be recognized as people with "personal and powerful" stories to share with multiple and varying audiences (Stornaiuolo, Hull, & Nelson, 2009). Thus, for the young men of the Insight Theater Project, encountering stock stories was a daily occurrence. The invitation to reclaim the right to story[1] that Insight offered was embraced by its participants in different ways, as I map out using glimpses of conversation, performances, and reflection in this section.

The Insight Project was born out of a collaborative desire between two ATIP teachers, Dan and Gabriel, to provide a venue for youth to engage in storytelling and dramatic performance, and also for those stories to find diverse and interested audiences. They imagined a space for the mostly Black and Latino young men to compose and share counterstories that did not only resist the prevalent narratives about them, but that also suggested new sites of understanding about their lived realities (Roberts, Bell, & Murphy, 2008; Yosso, 2006). With financial support garnered from an external grant and internal institutional funds, these two teachers piloted the theater initiative in the spring of 2008. Each cycle of Insight was facilitated as a two-phase program for which participants first had to audition. Nearly everyone who auditioned was accepted into phase one, where they were introduced to drama through a series of improvisations, the use of masks, and several sessions dedicated to sharing stories. Participants who demonstrated both interest and regular attendance were invited to participate in the second phase, for which they also received a modest weekly stipend.

Between 2008 and 2009, there were three cycles of Insight offered, during which time 33 participants were involved, two complete plays were written and performed for audiences totaling over five hundred people. The multiple sites of authoring and pedagogical dimensions of this project have been explored in previous writing (Vasudevan, Stageman, Rodriguez, Fernandez, & Dattatreyan, 2010). In this story of Insight, I will focus on the participants' varying autobiographical storytelling within the first cycle in which the play *Bird's eye view* (BEV) was written. During this cycle, 20 participants started and 13 completed phase one; seven started and five completed phase two. (Of the seven participants who initially started the second phase, one participant chose to accept more shifts at his job and another participant could not continue due to a conflict with an internship.) Both phases included a series of public performances including semi-public improvisation sessions, rehearsals for invited guests, and final performances. All of the participants in this cycle, including the facilitators, were male, with the exception of a costume designer, a graduate student who occasionally helped to document the project, and me; the space was largely free from female presence. In contrast with the second cycle that featured a coed cast, the making of BEV focused on issues—like relationships, family, life crossroads—in ways that foregrounded the contours of masculinity that the participants encountered in their daily lives.

"We Did Our Own Way": Sharing Personal Stories for Collective Storytelling

Early in the second phase of the first cycle, Dan asked the participants to think about codes or rules they live by and to share these with the group. Following several weeks of improvs and structured storytelling sessions, the group of seven young men was starting to coalesce around a theme for the play they would be co-writing and performing at the end of the 13-week cycle. With the exception of a few elementary school play experiences, all of the participants were new to acting as young adults and all expressed varying degrees of performance anxiety, even following the showcase they performed for their teachers and counselors at the end of phase one. Taking this trepidation into account, Dan and his co-facilitators Gabriel and Todd, a playwright, actor and longtime friend of Dan's, provided story-based scaffolds throughout the process. For example, Todd would suggest a framing scenario to set an improvisation in motion and often these scaffolds were crafted directly from the young men's stories. By asking the participants to share their "personal codes of honor," as the exercise came to be known in subsequent interviews and conversations, the Insight facilitators reinforced the narrative space of Insight as being *of* and *for* the young men involved with the project. BEV was in part a composite of the participants' stories, including people in their lives, situations they had encountered in the past or that they were working through at the time of their participation in Insight.

The script was reflective, also, of the participants' critical engagement with their own and one another's stories, wherein the obvious or seemingly inevitable resolution to a dilemma or conflict was questioned, re-interpreted, and given new possible directions throughout the various moments of the playwriting process. The tension of this duality is most visible in the penultimate scene in BEV. David, the protagonist in the play, is asleep and seated on a bench, visibly spent after a long day of caring for his aging uncle and making life-changing decisions.

He is approached by two other young men who are known by their street names, Big Baby and Slim Bag, who have been sent by their boss, a mid-level drug dealer, to shoot him in retribution for David's desire to cease his participation in the drug game. In what Clarence, the participant who played the character of Slim Bag, described at one point as an "unrealistic" turn of events, the two boys have a change of heart when instead of seeing their target sitting on the park bench, they see their childhood friend, David. When performing this reflective moment on stage, both actors in character remove the masks they are wearing and call each other by their given names, Lawrence and Maurice, and hastily turn away—but not before a playful tap that causes David to wake up in a state of confusion.

Most of the Insight participants agreed that this change of heart would not be the predictable ending to the story they were co-authoring. And while the suggestion to move beyond the predictable or obvious ending was initially suggested by Dan and Todd, it was a suggestion that was consistent with the practice that the group had developed of reflecting collectively on individuals' experiences, perceptions, and interpretations. As noted earlier, it was important to the facilitators that the stories that were to reach a wider audience did so with the autobiographical authority of the young men of Insight behind them. Participants' authority to claim their own stories (Dyson, 2002) was cultivated by creating conditions for their words and meanings to be received by attentive and engaged audiences: each other and the other audiences present at various key moments of the devising process, including ATIP staff who stopped by rehearsals, those of us documenting the project, and the mix of people they had invited to the open rehearsal a few weeks before the official opening of the play.

Here again the invitations to story foregrounded the young men as knowledgeable about their lives, as in when they were asked to identify personal codes of honor. During this discussion, one of the young men said that the code he lives by is "family first." His response was met with nods and guttural expressions of agreement from the rest of the group seated in a circle. This code did not remain the purview of the original storyteller alone. Instead it became one of several that were explored through improvisations that were used to scaffold participants' practices of storytelling and scene development. Todd would craft a scenario initially based on the code, in this case "family first." Dan describes the process this way:

> Each one of them came up with, you know, "this is a rule this I live by...." And there was a range, you know, one of them that actually made it through into the final script was the family-first idea that comes out. But we asked them to, you know, we put them into the situation, you know, and they had the experience to improv it out.

Improvs provided unguarded and safe spaces in which to explore narrative possibilities that influenced the direction of the characters' trajectories and also resonated with the daily realities that the participants were routinely negotiating. This space of collective retellings, therefore, allowed personal narratives to become fictionalized while still retaining narrative veracity. The result was a script that was akin to McCloud's (1994) notion that representations that are degrees of abstraction apart from "the real thing" increase the points of engagement for a viewer or, in this case, a member of the audience. The process of realistic fictionalization also provided additional entry points for the young men to be fully present and engaged with the stories of the characters in the play that were reflective of their stories without exploiting their lives.

The practice of composing scenes collaboratively, negotiating meanings, and considering multiple possible interpretations and responses was reflective of the "devising theater" method that Dan had studied and with which he had framed this project. In these moments of initial improvisation and subsequent scene development, Dan and Gabriel crafted teachable moments by asking the young actors questions like, "If you really believe in family first are you going to do this or is there another option?" and "What impact is your honor code having on your character in this scene?" But these were not only pedagogical spaces that involved one storyteller. By engaging all of the young men performatively with one another's codes and resulting narratives, the stories became woven into the fabric of the group. Jesse, for example, shared with the group his experience with his grandfather who was confronting the challenges of aging. Terrell somewhat hesitantly shared his challenges with finding a stable place to live even as he was involved in the project. These were among the lived realities that the group of young men considered with words and performance that ultimately found their way into the narrative plot of BEV.

Continuing to reflect on the process, Eric explained the importance of not only being heard but also being seen in the composing process:

> Todd…wrote down like nearly every move, everything that we did, he wrote down into a book and spent his time, and he wrote it into an actual play, so we—whatever we did was written in lines in the script.

Not only were participants' embodied ways of communicating meaning and conveying stories reflected in the final script, they were also used to develop characters and storylines. Clarence, for instance, came to own and more fully inhabit the character of Slim Bag/Lawrence over the course of the writing of BEV. His comedic facility and humor during initial *Bird's eye view* improv sessions helped to bring his character to life in new ways. Clarence did not merely read lines in the scenes that Todd drafted; he *became* Slim Bag and crafted a character with great physical agility, enviable comic timing, and emotional depth. Thus, Clarence's character, Slim Bag/Lawrence, was the one to flip around on the ground, occasionally break out into dance, and provide much of the comic relief for a play laden with heavy tropes.

The personal story, one's autobiography, did not remain singular. Thus, the stories that Terrell, Jesse, and the other young men shared offered variation to what might other be dismissed as a "single story" about adolescent males involved in the court system. Insight was a space in which multiple stories and the multiplicity of stories were nurtured. As such, the stories of one become the domain of many in an effort to push past the "common ending" and resist the residue of stock stories that can permeate personal narratives. Having such a space in which draw on personal experiences and also to reflect critically on those narratives allowed these young men to engage in what Hansen (2010) describes as "reflective openness to the new [alongside] a reflective loyalty to the known" (p. 17).

Autobiography as a Space for Talking Back

Building on personal story sharing and developing a collective narrative consciousness, the talkbacks following the performances offered Insight participants with another space in which to reclaim and redirect narratives about court-involved young men. This practice built upon the ongoing forms of call and response that were embedded throughout the authoring spaces of Insight and also added an important element to the overall experience: that of interacting with not only known but also unknown audiences. In addition, the talkback was another site of authoring that allowed the participants/actors to assume authority over the broader process as they engaged the questions and feedback from the audience, and it offered a space where the young men could author identities as actors and writers. Along with reflecting on their experience and responding to the questions offered by the audience, participants continued to share stories and explore a variety of themes. During a talk back following the second performance one night in late July, the five young actors sat on the stage flanked by a few of their teachers and counselors on either side. Unlike the previous night, no one was wearing the costume of their characters; the only trace of their *Bird's eye view* alter egos was found on Eric's feet on which he still wore the combination of white sport socks and black and white Adidas slip-on sandals that were a part of his portrayal of an ornery but well-meaning landlord. The young men, none of whom had acted in public before this inaugural cycle of Insight, were more relaxed than during the previous night's talkback. Their ease with the discussion and thoughtful responses to audience questions were no doubt reflective of the process they had all come through together. Moreover, sitting alongside the educators in their lives, these young men also took on the persona of pedagogues, sharing with the diverse audience of peers, family, friends, strangers, seasoned theater-goers and theater neophytes their own interpretations of the Insight. On this night, as would be repeated during each of the other talkbacks for all three cycles, a significant number of the questions directed the young men's attention to how the experience of participating in Insight affected them—what they learned, how they were affected by the process. Many of the questions seemed to assume a singular direction of impact of the Insight experience *on* the young men, an assumption that was righted during the talkbacks as the participants' narrative authority—like their autobiographical authority—was evident in their reflective responses. Embedded in these questions were assumptions about court-involved young men as individuals, as citizens who are a part of the larger society, as learners, as educated beings, and engaged or disengaged youth.

In response to an opening prompt by Dan, the ATIP staff on the stage offered the following responses that situate the young men's accomplishment in light of the larger discourses about youth:

> Miguel (Career Internship Coordinator): Well from what I saw from just from the play and watching it evolve, a lot of it was just about expressing themselves, and finding a creative way to express themselves, so this drama program has given them that opportunity, you know, to tell them, all the decisions that they face on a day to day basis, you know, with the tough decisions that they face on a day to day basis, you know, between committing a crime and not committing a crime, and helping feeding your family and not helping to feed your family, it takes a split second just to decide, I think they kinda capture that through the drama they experience.

Another teacher, Tony, echoed his colleagues' comments who noted that *Bird's eye view* offered a chance to meaningfully engage with "voices that don't get heard very often" as he observed the potential reach of these young men's authoring:

> Tony (Teacher and Artist): For once they were able to actually pretend to be in roles that they've learned to walk away from, and now they have began to express the realities of this lifestyle to an audience or to people who may not have had any inch of any idea about their experience, and so it's a learning experience.

Both Miguel's and Tony's observations were representative of those of other staff at ATIP who expressed an appreciation for seeing the Insight participants in a "new light," different from the interactions that they were often privy to in their roles as case managers, counselors, and even teachers.

As the talkback continued, the participants were asked a question about knowing the "difference between right and wrong." They engaged collectively in the response by pushing each other to consider in greater depth "what it means to be soft." The participants' responses focused on two instances that featured the masks and the characters of Slim Bag and Big Baby, particularly the scene where they decide to run away instead of shooting their childhood friend, David. What did the mask allow these characters to be? What happened when they removed their masks and connected with each other and David using their given names? In this interpretive role, the participants guided the audience through an interactive dialogue that offered a re-reading and situated understanding of the stories and characters that they had just performed.

Clarence, who had previously expressed skepticism about the play's penultimate scene, continued to wrestle with the characters' decision. When asked to consider the question of "right" and "wrong" during the talkback, after having sat with and performed the scene several times, Clarence shared some of his reflective dilemma:

> Right and wrong for Slim bag? Um, dang, I just think he confused from the beginning…if he was really putting on an act from the beginning… cause he like, really soft on the inside, but I don't understand, it's really difficult and I don't really understand the decision.

A few minutes later, while the participants continue to work through the contours of whether the characters could be called "soft" for essentially shirking their responsibilities to complete a violent act, Eric wondered aloud, "Just 'cause you did not shoot him, you're not soft. But if you shoot him, does that make you tough?" His question elicited a roaring applause from the audience and put a proud smile on Eric's face.

Insight was a space in which collective storytelling brought participants' autobiographies into the playwriting process as central texts from which to compose a narrative for multiple audiences. An ethos of viewing court-involved young men extended beyond the composing of the play and the public performances to include the talkbacks, which provided opportunities for Insight participants to assert their autobiographical authority in the form of authors and narrators, in addition to actors and performers. Likewise, it was important for me to bring a performative lens to the documentation of this project—attending to the embodied and unspoken moments of meaning making, interpretation, composing—in order to allow the young people to be seen as deliberate and deliberative in their educational engagements within Insight (Varenne, 2007). It would be simplistic to argue that the often-pathologizing narratives about young Black and Latino men within the justice system can be eradicated by the existence of a counternarrative space like the Insight Theater Project. I will simply suggest that spaces and practices that center the lived realities of youth, while providing the opportunity for sustained engagement with their own and others' stories, can move youth and their potential audiences toward more meaningful understandings of each other and possibly a blurring of the boundaries between self and other.

Conclusion

We began this chapter with perspectives from Nancy Lesko who challenges us as teachers, as researchers, and as a field to reconceptualize our understandings of adolescents. She has argued provocatively that, "When groups such as the elderly or the young are constructed as other and problematic, social regulation of these others is supported and specified by the social science experts who represent them" (Lesko, 1996, p. 156). In our estimation, these "experts" also shape the curriculum and educational spaces that are designed for adolescents in response to these constructions as "other and problematic." We take from Lesko's work and others (e.g., Gadsden, 2008; Greene, 1995; Stornaiuolo et al., 2009; Winn, 2011) continued inspiration to design educational research and teaching contexts with and for young people who are positioned as knowledge makers, artists, poets, and storytellers.

In this chapter, we have considered the possibilities that emerged in educational research and teaching spaces for knowing adolescents beyond the stock stories that circulate about them in the popular and scholarly press as well as the broader media environment. As young people were invited to draw on literacies, the arts, and aesthetics to engage with both their own and others' autobiographical stories, we were struck by the seriousness of purpose with which they undertook this work as well as the joy and lightness that often imbued the spaces as they did so. In our experiences, adolescents' ways of being can be nurtured and cultivated within spaces created for the exploration of autobiography; and likewise, the relationships between adults and youth can be re-imagined to be collective, collegial, and responsive.

We also find it important to note that these spaces invited modes of autobiography beyond the privileged and normalized modes of composing. Through multiple genres of poetry, photography, script writing, and performance, the young people presented multiple sides of themselves through multiple modalities. They also crafted their work for multiple audiences, from the immediacy of audience within the educational spaces of both Sistahs and Insight, as well as the public and semi-public performances that the young people participated in as they presented their poetry, photography, and dramatic performances. As a result, these spaces offered ways into opening up a single story, while also eliciting multiple stories from those who witnessed and engaged with the stories. In this way, the collective built on the individual narratives to form a rich, layered, fluid, and dynamic representation of experiences and identities.

Within a range of educational spaces, including schools, we see great potential in envisioning autobiography as a performative, social, and embodied practice. In conceptualizing autobiography in this way, educators may help students move beyond a notion of autobiography as an unmediated expression of self and instead conceive of the practice of personal storytelling as deeply embedded in and reflective of the social context. In this way, students may be able to pursue both creative and analytical works that consider the constructedness and rhetorical nature of texts and media representations, while also creating their own representations attuned to and aware of the possibility of autobiographical texts to intervene in dominant representations. Given the collective nature of meaning-making across our two studies, we also see value in expanding the audience for student work beyond the teacher. Clearly, we also see the great value in expanding not only the audiences for student writing and performance, but also the modes of composing that are available and valued within schools. From image to spoken word, from dramatic performance to digital storytelling, we see great potential in opening up, rather than narrowing, our definitions and practices of literacies.

As both pedagogical and research spaces, both Sistahs and Insight also suggest how a single story of adolescents can be opened up, disrupted, and fractured through the forms of documentation employed. Just as multiple modes of composing allowed youth to present various aspects of themselves to different audiences, the multimodal documentation of these narratively rich spaces also allowed the youth to help construct the stories of these spaces and their participation in the spaces. Through a performative and embodied research lens, new insights emerged related to how meaning was being made, enacted, and interpreted in each of our spaces. We therefore see the need for attention not only to the creation of spaces, but also to the documentation of those spaces as being essential to how we create new knowledge beyond the single story of adolescents. Participatory multimodal literacy research with adolescents reflects a belief about adolescents as knowledgeable, as worth listening to and listening with, and as worth seeing in ways that are not immediately recognizable or reducible to their facility with print texts. To us, moving beyond the single story of adolescents means creating the conditions, within the very practices of pedagogy and documentation themselves, to see adolescents and ourselves in new ways.

Note

1 Story is used here as a verb to signify the dynamic ways in which we make our multiple selves known to others through the various acts and actions associated with storytelling.

References

Adichie, C. (2009). Chimamanda Adichie: The danger of a single story. [Video file]. Retrieved from http://www.youtube.com/watch?v=D9Ihs241zeg.

Collins, P. H. (2000). *Black feminist thought: Knowledge, consciousness, and the politics of empowerment* (2nd ed.). New York: Routledge.

Delgado, R. (1995). *Critical race theory: The cutting edge*. Philadelphia: Temple University Press.

Deutsch, N. (2001). *Voices of our own: Mothers, daughters, and elders of the Tenderloin tell their stories*. San Francisco, CA: My Window Books.

Duncan, G. A. (2005). Critical race ethnography in education: Narrative inequality and the problem of epistemology. *Race, Ethnicity, and Education, 8*(1), 93–114.

Dyson, A. H. (2002). The drinking God factor: A writing development remix for "all" children. *Written Communication, 19*(4), 545–577.

180 Kelly Wissman and Lalitha Vasudevan

Ferguson, A. A. (2000). *Bad boys: Public schools and the making of Black masculinity.* Ann Arbor, MI: University of Michigan Press.

Franco, B. (Ed.). (2001). *Things I have to tell you: Poems and writing by teenage girls.* Cambridge, MA: Candlewick Press.

Gadsden, V. L. (2008). The arts and education: Knowledge generation, pedagogy, and the discourse of learning. *Review of Research in Education, 32,* 29–61.

Greene, M. (1995). *Releasing the imagination: Essays on education, the arts, and social change.* San Francisco, CA: Jossey-Bass Publishers.

Hansen, D.T. (2010). Cosmopolitanism and education: A view from the ground. *Teachers College Record, 112*(1), 1–30.

Hesford, W. (1999). *Framing identities: Autobiography and the politics of pedagogy.* Minneapolis: University of Minnesota Press.

hooks, b. (1994). *Teaching to transgress: Education as the practice of freedom.* New York: Routledge.

Jordan, J. (1989). A short note to my very critical and well-beloved friends and comrades. *Naming our destiny: New and selected poems.* New York: Thunder's Mouth Press.

Jordan, J. (1995). Introduction. In L. Muller (Ed.), *June Jordan's poetry for the people: A revolutionary blueprint* (pp. 1–9). New York: Routledge.

Lesko, N. (1994). Back to the future: Middle schools and the *Turning Points* report. *Theory Into Practice, 33*(3), 143–148.

Lesko, N. (1996). Denaturalizing adolescence: The politics of contemporary representations. *Youth & Society, 28*(2), 139–161.

Lesko, N. (2001). *Act your age! A cultural construction of adolescence.* New York: Routledge.

McCloud, S. (1994). *Understanding comics: The invisible art.* New York: Harper Perennial.

Roberts, R. A., Bell, L. A., & Murphy, B. (2008). Flipping the script: Analyzing youth talk about race and racism. *Anthropology and Education Quarterly, 39*(3), 334–354.

Royster, J. J. (2000). *Traces of a stream: Literacy and social change among African American women.* Pittsburgh: University of Pittsburgh Press.

Stornaiuolo, A., Hull, G., & Nelson, M. E. (2009). Mobile texts and migrant audiences: Rethinking literacy and assessment in a new media age. *Language Arts, 86*(5), 382–392.

Varenne, H. (2007). Difficult collective deliberations: Anthropological notes toward a theory of education. *Teachers College Record, 109*(7), 1559–1588.

Vasudevan, L., Stageman, D., Rodriguez, K., Fernandez, E., & Dattatreyan, G. (2010). Authoring new narratives with youth at the intersection of the arts and justice. *Perspectives on Urban Education, 7*(1), 54–65.

Winn, M. (2011). *Girl time: Literacy, justice, and the school-to-prison pipeline.* New York: Teachers College Press.

Wissman, K. (2009). Reading and becoming living authors: Urban girls pursuing a poetry of self-definition. *English Journal, 98*(3), 39–45.

Yagelski, R. P. (1999). *Literacy matters: Reading and writing the social self.* New York: Teachers College Press.

Yosso, T. (2006). *Critical race counterstories along the Chicana/Chicano educational pipeline.* New York: Routledge.

11

"IN THIS LITTLE TOWN NOTHING MUCH EVER HAPPENS, BUT SOMEDAY SOMETHING WILL"

Reading Young Adult Literature from the Blue Ridge Foothills

Gay Ivey

Four 8th grade English teachers in a middle school in Virginia's Shenandoah Valley joined me several years ago in what seemed at that time a simple question with both theoretical and practical implications: *What would it take to arrange for every student to become an engaged reader?* The answer to that question centered largely on revamping the collection of reading materials available to students, from a limited variety of whole-class novel sets to a vast selection of edgy contemporary young adult fiction and giving students full control over selecting and responding to what they read. Little did we know what those choices and experiences would reveal about students' personal lives and their capacities for using literacy to understand themselves and the world that extended far beyond their small town. In particular, we came to question our assumptions about the cultural reputation of this region of the country versus the complex, varied identities of the students living in it.

In this chapter, I hope to shed light on some misconceptions about what drives the interests of youth here and perhaps in other geographic or ethnic spaces associated with particular practices and ways of life. I will begin by describing common perceptions about culture in this region by sharing the evolution of my own association with this area of the country, starting as a tourist, then classroom teacher, then researcher. Next, I describe the engagement-focused study that led to new ways of thinking about the kinds of texts students want to read and how they work with those texts. My purpose is to inspire others working with adolescents, in places similar to this as well as in those markedly different, to reflect on the kinds of materials available to students and on what we expect students might do with the texts they prefer to read.

Focusing the Lens on a Community and its Youth

My personal history with the Blue Ridge Mountains and Shenandoah Valley extends back to my childhood, and my professional journey has included moving into this region, out, and then back again. I use my experiences at different points in this connection to not only describe my evolving perceptions of life and youth in this community, but also to emphasize the significance of understanding the literacy-related needs of youth from the insider's vantage point I eventually gained.

Visitor in the Community

One weekend each autumn when I was a child, my family packed into our red 1966 Ford Galaxy 500 and made a two-and-a-half hour drive to the Blue Ridge Mountains to take in the fall foliage and to escape the monotony of life in our small industrial hometown just outside of Richmond, Virginia. Our excursions included no fast food stops, no side trips to the shopping mall, and no nighttime getaways to the movie theater. Instead, we looked forward to immersing our-selves in the culture and uniqueness of our destination. My mother prepared a big, hearty lunch, complete with fried chicken, ham sandwiches, and potato salad, which we ate on picnic tables along the breathtakingly beautiful Blue Ridge Parkway. Our afternoons consisted of driving from overlook to overlook and meandering through the wooded wonderland of red, yellow, and orange leaves.

Apples were a big draw during October. One of my family's strongest com-monly shared memories centers on one of these weekends during a visit to an orchard. It was only about the second weekend of the month, a time of year when Virginia is normally still experiencing the remnants of humid summer weather. But on that particular Saturday, something extraordinary happened. It started to snow. The sensation of biting into a cold, crisp, tart Winesap apple as snowflakes fell across my face against this autumn backdrop was so powerful; to this day I can close my eyes and travel back to that moment. Later that day at a gift shop, I picked up as a keepsake an apple doll, an early American tradition created by carving the shape of a face in an apple and then letting it dry.

Teacher in the Community

My perceptions of life in this part of my state—as simple, folksy, and quaint, but old-fashioned—were shaped by these annual pilgrimages. Years later, I was drawn to Cynthia Rylant's picture book *Appalachia* (1991), as it matched my ideal image of the region:

> In the summer many of the women like to can. It seems their season.... In the winter many of the men like to hunt, and this seems their season.... The children love all the seasons. They go down by the creek or into the

woods or up the dirt roads with their good dogs and they feel more important than anything else in these Appalachian mountains.…In summer if you
walk the roads you will smell honeysuckle and the odors of cows and that
gritty aroma dirt roads in the mountains send up your nose.

(p. 18–19)

Never did I imagine that years later I would land my first teaching position not
far from the eastern slopes of that mountain range I visited as a child. I remember
reading aloud to students that same Rylant picture book on one of the first days
of school, sure I had chosen something with a connection. I was met only with
blank stares and some polite, but compliant responses to my question, "What
came to your mind as I read?" I am certain they could not voice what they really
thought of this clueless rookie teacher.

Given the openness and outspokenness of middle school students, it took only
a short while to understand the range of what really occupied their minds and
their time outside of school. It was true that many of my students were comfortable with outdoorsy activities associated with rural life: jumping fully clothed into
murky swimming holes, collecting pet snakes, hunting and fishing. But their
conversations with me and with each other centered on the popular phenomena
that captivated many other adolescents during the early 1990s, for instance, television programs like *In living color* and *The Simpsons*, and musical groups like *Boys to
Men* and even hardcore bands like *Suicidal Tendencies*. They talked about broken
hearts, imprisoned parents, and dreams for the future. These kids had little interest in discussing apple picking, the smell of honeysuckle, or taking in the wonder
of nature on a dirt road walk, even though most kids were certainly familiar with
these experiences. In fact, the mention of anything "folksy" by a student would
nearly always get a "You're so *country!*" from a teasing classmate.

Researcher in the Community

I left that teaching position to complete doctoral studies in Georgia, followed by
professional moves to New Jersey and Maryland. Around 10 years ago I returned
to Virginia to live in the Shenandoah Valley, and coincidentally, in the vicinity
of where my family took those yearly autumn adventures. I have the pleasure
once again of learning from youth living in and around the Blue Ridge Mountains,
but this time not only with knowledge of students in this area I gained as a middle
school teacher, but also with greater expertise on literacy engagement and a keen
interest in how to reconceptualize their English classrooms to better attend to
students' participation, literate identities, and agency.

In recent years my home for research is a middle school in a small city that
looks up at a mountain range with access to the Appalachian Trail. The community is working-class, with a median annual household income of about $40,000.
Like other formerly sleepy towns in the region, it has seen growth in the past

decade most noticeable where the interstate highway cuts through, with access to every chain restaurant imaginable, mega retail stores Target, Home Depot, and Wal-Mart, and the most surprising new addition, Starbucks. Still, though, all of this business sits in plain view of adjacent cow pastures and rolling farmland.

The school district includes four elementary schools, one high school, and Mountain Middle School (pseudonym), where I have been privileged to study literacy learning and teaching inside classrooms of the four 8th grade English teachers. Students and teachers in this school negotiate the same tensions shared by so many others, that is, honoring student interests and teacher beliefs about literacy-based learning in the face of conflicting practices associated with high stakes testing. Eighth grade teachers in particular are committed to seeing their students develop an interest in reading even as they encounter regular reminders of raising achievement scores and all of the initiatives and directives that accompany that.

When I first came to know these English teachers and their students, they included in their daily periods for each class a self-selected reading time. They were keenly interested in finding books that resonated with students' lives. One temptation when considering books that might appeal to students would be to gather books set in the familiar surroundings of their own region of the country. As it turns out, it is rare to find books for adolescents set in any rural United States community, much less the one these kids called home. What is available is historical fiction, such as *Shades of gray* (Reeder, 1989), a Civil War story set in the Shenandoah Valley, and books focused on stereotypical phenomena linked to rural America, such as *Come sing, Jimmy Jo* (Paterson, 1985), which forefronts county music cultural traditions. These types of books are typically available in school libraries and are often used as whole-class assigned reading texts. But the teachers at Mountain Middle School found, as I had with students nearby two decades earlier, that these kinds of books held little appeal for the students they taught.

They noticed, however, that certain other kinds of books caused students to come to life, echoing the experiences of adolescents who report in research that "just plain reading" (Ivey & Broaddus, 2001) is the most motivating opportunity in English class. Eighth grade students in this small town were drawn to edgy, sometimes gritty, contemporary young adult fiction not usually associated with middle school, particularly one in a semi-rural area, and for the most part, books associated with school reading at all. Teachers' attention was first heightened after a visit from young adult author Ellen Hopkins. The popularity of *Crank* (2004) and *Burned* (2006) spread like wildfire. Students demanded more time to read and competed for access to the few copies of the books available in school. Many resorted to buying their own copies, which for some, was their first experience with bookstores.

Certainly, these teachers had seen particular books captivate student interest before, but this wave of participation, especially from kids who were not typically engaged in school learning, gave them pause. What would pull these students toward fictional narratives that appeared to be so far removed from life in a small town? *Crank*, somewhat based on Ellen Hopkins' own daughter's experiences, deals with addiction to crystal methamphetamine. *Burned* involves a teenage girl coping with abuse from her father and resistance to the family's strict Mormon religious practices. Initially apprehensive about 8th graders' readiness to take on such mature and controversial subjects, teachers selectively shared their copies of the books with students whose life experiences, though different, were not much less disturbing than the characters in the book. But as word got around from student to student, the books became popular with even the unlikeliest of audiences, and equally by males and females, students from various ethnicities and economic situations, and across achievement levels.

A Study to Build Engagement

Interest in the influence of young adult literature on students' motivation to read was high among all of the 8th grade English teachers when I was fortunate enough to be drawn into their group by one of them who had been my friend for some time. I had long been interested in the significance of prioritizing time to read in school for adolescents, and in particular, for the least experienced readers. Providing access to books that fuel students' curiosities in order to make that time worthwhile is no small matter (Ivey & Broaddus, 2001; Worthy, Moorman, & Turner, 1999).

I had a big idea, though, about seeing what it would take to facilitate engagement for every single 8th grade student. In a nutshell, here is what happened: All four English teachers committed to making student self-selected, self-paced reading of young adult literature the centerpiece of the curriculum. They completely abandoned whole-class assigned readings of common texts. This shift had three central components, ceding to the students both choice of reading material and choice of how to respond, and introducing them to many books.

The choice factor is substantial because of what it does for the will to engage. Deci & Ryan (1985) suggest that intrinsic motivation will be enhanced when particular human needs are met. They describe autonomy as the need to sense that a person's actions emerge from the authentic self rather than some outside source, relatedness as the need to feel connected to other people, and competence as the need to feel capable of accomplishing a task. In line with this theory, students' liberty to make reading choices for themselves increases the possibility that they will persevere and learn. Equally important in the classroom, though, is the role of teachers in arranging for a context in which students can feel autonomous, related, and competent. Choice matters only when the options available are good options (Katz & Assor, 2007), so having good options was central to the teachers' mission.

When making sure there were good choices for everyone, we knew, given responses to Ellen Hopkins' books early on, that what fuels 8th graders' interests involves themes that differed substantially from those associated with most teacher-constructed units that were familiar to us (e.g., coming of age, survival). We also quickly realized that most of the books that appealed to students could not be found in the school library or in English department collections. Clearly, this would be a new crop of books. On the whole, students preferred books they considered unsettling in some way or books that left them at loose ends. To some degree, these were texts that did not conform to the notion of universal theme, or at least those typically taught in middle and high school English classrooms. In general, the books students found compelling were those dealing with substance abuse and addiction (e.g., *Tweak: Growing up on methamphetamines*, Sheff, 2008), teen pregnancy (e.g., *Jumping off swings*, Knowles, 2009); the implications of gang violence (e.g., *Snitch*, Van Diepan, 2007); complex relationships (e.g., *Last night I sang to the monster*, Saenz, 2009); and bullying (e.g., *Hate list*, Brown, 2009), among other mature topics. These were not feel-good selections with neatly tied together endings. Students referred to them consistently as "disturbing." Furthermore, many of the books defied the notion of universal truth or theme, leaving students to grapple with uncertainty long after they finished the books. In the end, we learned that meeting students' needs required nearly 100 different titles per classroom at a time, with collections rotating among teachers' rooms across the year to maintain adequate choices.

We went about this process without an agenda to get students to do anything in particular with the literature, for instance, to use it as a tool for critical literacy (Lankshear, 1997) or as a bridge to New Literacies (New London Group, 1996). More fundamentally, teachers were interested in helping experienced engagement broadly. At the time, we envisioned engagement much as how Guthrie and colleagues (1998) contextualized their work, that is, as intrinsically motivated, self-regulated, strategic reading to learn. We imagined for students the experience of getting lost in an interaction with text, much akin to Csikszentmihalyi's (1990) description of "flow," or absorption in the activity. Certainly, too, not far from teachers' minds in particular was the promise of engaged reading's relationship to higher achievement (Guthrie & Wigfield, 2000).

The 90-minute English block in each of the four classrooms was divided between reading and writing. The reading portion of each day consisted of a time for independent reading (typically 20–25 minutes), teacher book talks, and student impromptu discussions of books they were reading. During student reading time most students were engrossed in reading most of the time. When teachers noticed students who were not engaged, they had the opportunity, then, to spend time with individual students, problem-solve to find reasons for lack of engagement, and help students overcome it. For instance, some students needed help finding books that captivated their interests, and others needed help figuring out unconventional formats they were encountering for the first time, such as books told in shifting perspectives.

The time between reading and writing was bridged each day by a teacher read aloud time. The novels teachers selected to read aloud were quite similar in content and style to the books students chose to read on their own. For instance, a favorite book for teacher read alouds for several years running was *The beckoners* (Mac, 2004), which takes on the issues of bullying and homophobia through the story of a 15-year-old girl brutally initiated into a gang. Passages and excerpts from the edgy books students read were used by teachers in writing mini-lessons to demonstrate and provide examples of particular aspects of writing tools and style.

Most studies featuring young adult literature in the English curriculum include teachers' selections for students and teacher-prompted responses to guide students toward particular kinds of thinking. Existing professional literature includes important and useful suggestions for how teachers might use young adult literature and its themes to deliberately arrange for particular kinds of youth development. For instance, the value of using multicultural literature that allows otherwise marginalized students to see themselves in books has been an issue explored in research for some time (e.g., Bean & Rigoni, 2001; Brooks, 2006). More recently, researchers have explored the nuances and tensions of multicultural literature use in the context of mainly white, middle class communities as a way to introduce characters whose lives differ from students' own and to challenge existing stereotypes (e.g., Ketter & Buter, 2004; Lewis & Ketter, 2008). Certain kinds of books are recommended for guiding students toward social responsibility (e.g., Wolk, 2009) and for fostering critical literacy (e.g., Bean & Moni, 2003).

However, much less is known about how students think, unprompted, and what they do with literature they select on their own and over which they exercise full control. None of the books made available to students were intended necessarily to make familiar connections, to create cultural awareness or to stimulate questions about social and political positioning. Put simply, our initial purpose was just to get students to read. However, students' experiences and uses of these texts transcended our expectations. Three trends were apparent in students' selections and their engagement. First, students experienced authentic and sustained engagement in young adult literature. Second, students made connections in a wide range of books that, on the surface, appeared out of place in their community. Third, students were engaged in books in which they could not necessarily make personal connections, and these interactions fueled critical thinking.

Student Engagement

As expected, students were absorbed in the reading, and higher standardized test scores followed. Engagement was most evident in how students talked about their reading, particularly for students for whom this was a new experience. Brady described *Give a boy a gun* (Strasser, 2000) as "the one that got me going," and further explained, "It had this thing that drove you to read it and you wanted more of it." Another sign of engagement was students' persistence even when facing dilemmas in their reading. After reading *Identical* (Hopkins, 2008), a verse novel told from the viewpoint(s) of a victim of incest whose schizophrenia is not revealed until the end of the book, Kassie confessed:

> It was really confusing, but after I read half of it over again I realized what was going on. It was one person really speaking, but it was two voices.
>   I was all about that book for like 2 months. I read it and reread it.

Relatedly, students were able to distinguish meaningful reading from the compliance they demonstrated in years past, as Jennifer noted, "Last year they made you read a book and you just skimmed it. I kind of did that before. Now I actually sit there and read the books, especially when I'm bored at home." Engagement extended beyond the English classroom and the school day as students read in other classes, at lunch, and at home. Books were passed from student to student as conversations about texts emerged spontaneously in and out of school.

Although teachers had to identify some practices to support and sustain engagement (e.g., book talks, conferring), particularly for previously inexperienced readers, it was largely a combination of a vast selection of interesting books and the freedom to choose that made the difference. As students voluntarily shared their responses to books, lingering questions, and requests for additional books, it was clear that these conditions created the possibility for more than just individual engagement or the act of just reading for pleasure. The sorts of books that captivated students, their interactions with texts, and in turn, their interactions with each other as intriguing reads created the need to talk, heightened our understandings about students' identities and opened the possibilities for expanding the notion of literacy for these students.

Unexpected Connection

"This book is about my life," is what Vanessa said after finishing *Teenie* (Grant, 2010), about a 14-year-old girl who is struggling with sexual and peer pressure. Given the subject matter, her proclamation was no surprise, but what is interesting is the fact that *Teenie* is set in Brooklyn. What is more, Teenie has strict Caribbean parents, and their home is defined by that culture. Both differ vastly from the Vanessa's current surroundings.

A benefit of having such a diverse collection of books from which students could choose was that it not only served to meet individual needs, but also to illuminate them in useful ways. Like Vanessa, Devon found in books the relationship and familiarity that she was not finding in a school community where she was living on the margins. She appeared to be insatiable for more books, and when I asked how the books had changed her, she sighed:

> Where should I begin? All of the free [verse] books have had something to do with death and relationships and I've had a bunch of that go on lately.

You hear that somebody died and it's like, that's like my book. My friends don't get me at all, and I feel like I'm the person in the book. I grew up in seven different houses so far. I don't have money. I feel like I can relate to the people in half of the books I've read in some way.

Similarly, students in a small but growing Latina/o population in the community were surprised and pleased to know there existed books with culturally familiar concepts that were previously unspoken in their classrooms. Gladys confessed:

To be honest, I wasn't really reading before. That was before. They just had American books. Now they have Hispanic characters and gangs....I'm reading *The secret story of Sonia Rodriguez* (Sitomer, 2008). I live near the library so I walked there and checked it out....Some of my friends are Mexican and they recommended the book. I don't mean to be racist or anything, but this is different because it relates to me.

There were a number of books, though, that struck a chord with the majority of students. For instance, these students agreed that *Thirteen reasons why* (Asher, 2007), a book dealing with suicide and personal responsibility toward others, could have easily been set in their area:

ANA: Like you can easily imagine people in that setting and stuff.
COLE: Yeah, I pictured a small town. I didn't see anything big about it.
CHORUS: Yes!
WENDY: When she said, like the ice cream, I was like, Kraven's (local ice cream parlor)!
ALL: Yes (laughter).
ANA: And when he was, um, at…
COLE: The café.
ANA: Yeah, the café. You know what I pictured? I pictured The Blue Diner (local restaurant).
LUCY: I pictured McCall's (local restaurant).
COLE: I pictured like The Soup Bowl (local restaurant) is what I pictured, cause it was like outside and you know how The Soup Bowl has that platform off the side…
ANA: Cause like The Blue Diner, I don't know if you guys have ever been there but in the back there's like that garden....I just pictured that.

Thirteen reasons why was voted by students as their favorite book of the year, but what students remembered most was not seeing the story in their minds, but instead lingering concerns about the implications of malicious gossip. The fact that one of the book's narrators, delivering her message through taped recordings made before taking her own life, experienced a downward emotional spiral because of a seemingly harmless rumor gave readers a reason to keep thinking. Countless times when the subject of bullying arose in other texts and in classroom conversations, students would inevitably come back to the message they carried from this book, such when Clayton admonished peers in a small group, "Remember *Thirteen reasons why*. ANY little thing you do [might devastate someone else]."

Homeboyz (Sitomer, 2007), was equally popular with students, but not set in familiar circumstances. The context is urban California, and the story centers on main character Teddy's response to the death of his younger sister, an innocent bystander in a gang-related drive-by shooting. The style and language of the text, like this description of Meeksha, the intended victim standing beside Teddy's sister, no doubt intrigues 8th graders across a wide range of communities:

> At the age of nine, Meeksha, also known as Blink, shouted, "Eat my ass!" to a teacher. At the age of eleven, she got busted for trying to shoplift a pair of brass knuckles at the Swap Meet. At the age of thirteen, she got caught in the act of stealing a car stereo out of a Toyota Camry. When the sixty-three-year-old woman who owned the car said, "Give it back," Blink responded, "Okay," and slammed the three-pound metal box directly in the white lady's face.
>
> *(p. 1)*

What maintained the interest of so many students at Mountain Middle School, however, was Teddy's anguish and emotional journey. His instinct is to seek revenge, but he has a change of heart as his family develops a relationship with a younger wayward boy, Micah, who seems destined to life in a gang without their involvement. The value of *Homeboyz* for students was not in the setting, but in the characters' pain, motives, and decisions. Brock grew deeply connected to the book's characters, lamenting after he read, "I wish the author would write another book that tells about Teddy's and Micah's lives as brothers."

None of the students lived the day-to-day challenges of urban life, but the having to decide between digging deeper into a conflict that has no chance of a good ending and redirecting your efforts toward something productive was a dilemma they all understood. A spontaneous discussion of *Homeboyz* went personal when Tasha, who had been pulled from the basketball team for fighting relentlessly with a teammate, confessed to two classmates, "If I pound her, she'll just want to pound me right back, and then it starts all over again, and it's like who's ever gonna win?" Randall linked the message he gleaned from the book to larger societal tensions. He read it around the time of Barak Obama's election to the office of President, and for him, it paralleled what he was hearing in political speeches: "I think Obama's goal is like Teddy decided at the end because he thinks we should start building up and stop tearing down." Relatable characters helped these students see past unfamiliar times and places.

The Value of Disconnection

In many cases students were drawn to books with characters not relatable to them, at least not on the surface. These were mainly books students found, as they put it, "disturbing," stories and memoirs that introduced them to situations they could not have previously imagined and that often left them feeling unsettled. Consistently, students commented about the imagined lives of characters in comparison with their own realities. They reported feelings of gratitude for what they had in response to reading about personal struggles, particularly in memoirs of child abuse and other childhood traumas. Pelzer's *A child called It* (1995) and *The lost boy* (1997), two of the most widely read selections, inspired sincere emotional reactions like this one from Blair:

> It would make you want to cry and reach out and help the little kid (Robert). His mom was cruel. I don't mean to be stereotypical, but I usually think of an abusive dad, not a mom. It talks about how he had to eat raw meat, threw it up, and then his mom made him eat it again.

Upon finishing *Three little words* (Rhodes-Courter, 2008), Blair found the author's experiences in the foster care system troubling to the point of reaching out to get more information:

> [I wondered about] the Mosses, who were a cruel foster family. I sent [Rhodes-Courter] an email and she replied back. I just said it was really interesting that she wrote her story and that it was really inspiring. I also asked her if she thought she'd make it out of the Moss family home.

Stories of personal struggle had such an impact on Rachel that she was compelled to write me a note: "Those books made me realize that the horrible things in those books really do happen, well I was aware that they were, but now I understand how horrific they really are. Thank you for opening my eyes."

As students interacted with classmates over the books, however, they learned that some of the challenges faced by characters in books and authors of memoirs were not as far from their community as they first imagined. In a conversation about *A child called It*, Chrissy wondered about why the author, David Pelzer, did not as a child tell someone at school about his mother's abuse of him. Skylar surprised classmates with her response:

> As soon as you say that at school, they're not gonna just leave you at school, cause I've been in the same situation. They're not gonna leave you at school. They gonna take you straight back home and they're gonna end up calling your parents.

But reading about hardship of others did not just increase awareness. There was also reason to believe that students were developing empathy through their involvement with characters in stories. Notice how Stella switched from "she" to "you" in her reactions to the drug-addicted main character of *Glass* (Hopkins, 2007): "She was ready to try, but she couldn't because she was addicted. You want to get over it, but you can't." Derrick stated this more explicitly after reading several of Hopkins' books: "Me, I don't use drugs. Reading it, I tried to put myself in her shoes. That's what go me interested in it." In some instances, students struggled to make sense of characters' actions, but they clearly worked hard to see past their own predispositions. *Grace* (Scott, 2010) is a dystopian novel about a girl raised to be a suicide bomber within a totalitarian government, but she then botches her mission with the primary motive of saving her own life. In *Living dead girl* (Scott, 2008), by the same author, the main character, Alice, has been abducted, held captive, sexually abused, and emotionally tormented for several years until she is faced with the opportunity of helping her kidnapper replace her with a younger girl. Kelly fixated on both stories:

> I loved *Grace*. I read it like 3 times. I just couldn't figure out why she thought the things she did. She had been raised that way and that was all she knew. It was different than Elizabeth Scott's other books, but I tried to make connections to the characters in those books. Like *Living dead girl*. Grace and Alice did what they had to do to take care of themselves, and they had to realize that in doing that, they hurt other people, but still. I had to read slow it think about it as I went along, and I read it again a few times.

Kendall and her friends were drawn to *In Ecstasy* (McCaffrey, 2009), told in the alternating perspectives of two friends, one who is popular and one who becomes addicted to the drug ecstasy when she learns it causes her popularity to surpass that of her friend. Initially put off by the books that featured drug-addicted characters they perceived as nothing like their own friends, these girls began to see things differently when, living in this book through their engagement, they were able to see new perspectives. As a result, it was increasingly difficult to see these characters or their real-life counterparts as "other." The students' fascination with addicted character Mia had them talking about the insecurities that led to her downward spiral, something they learned from reading her first person perspective:

KENDALL: I just wish Mia would have like kept where she was. Like I can see her competition….I could see Mia in my head, and she was like pretty, and she was shy….
ADDIE: She was like simple, like simple beauty.
KENDALL: Yeah. And that, that's still pretty.

ADDIE: Yeah, and there are going to be people who have, like, extravagant beauty, like exotic beauty....

KENDALL: But they don't like just show it off. Like, they're conservative.

ADDIE: Or cause some people may be like, I don't know, but, cause I was trying to like, I don't know, cause like I still can't do it, but I try to tell myself like "You don't know what that person has been through in their life that has made them like this."

KENDALL: Yeah.

ADDIE: 'Cause you're like, why does that girl wear so much makeup? Why does that girl wear low-cut shirts? Why does that girl act like a you-know-what?

KENDALL: Maybe because something happened, and you always judge them in the worst way possible.

SHEA: You don't know what's going on at home.

ADDIE: It's exactly like that. Like you never know what's gone on in anybody's past.

KENDALL: You can't judge anybody until you get to know them.

As the conversation continued, Addie saw more parallels with her own life and that of Mia from the book: "Jealousy. Yeah. Like a little green monster inside of her. And I don't really blame her. If your best friend got all the attention, like if it was me, I'd be like, 'Uh, no!'" Just seconds later, she further confessed, "Because I thought I was a nasty little ugly person when I was little, I always feel like I have to look pretty." Kendall ended up labeling this book as "dead-on" in its relevance to her life, despite the fact she had never gone near drugs.

Even when students did not adopt a critical stance on their own, their engagement in books that end with uncertainty provided a substantial opportunity to do so, particularly when student-initiated dialogue pushed some surface-level readers toward deeper thinking. Julio raved about *If I Grow Up* (Strasser, 2009), and his proclamation on several occasions that "I understood the *whole* thing" led us to infer this had been a rare experience in his other reading. This book explores gang culture by chronicling the teen years of a boy navigating life in the projects and ultimately succumbing to a life of violence and imprisonment. In a class discussion in which Julio provided a summary of the book, others were quick to point out how it related to other stories they knew and books they read:

KENNY: I have a connection, The *freedom writers diary* (Gruwell, 1999), because they had gangs and shooting. But *If I grow up*, it's the best book I've ever read and they should make it into a movie.

PAUL: That book reminds me of *Homeboyz* (Sitomer, 2007)...when the dude did the drive-by.

JULIO: And *Monster* (Myers, 1999).

The next student offered a personal connection, shifting the conversation back and forth between texts and reality:

MALIK: I have a connection to that book Carlos was reading. My cousin showed me his gun. But now he's in jail.
NATE: I got to have a gun in my house. If people come in, I can shoot them.

As expected, this shift, particularly about a topic about which students have strong opinions inspired lots of comments. But what began as mostly simple arguments about the pros and cons of gun ownership became complicated by other possibilities now available to students because of the fiction they had read. Several students mentioned characters that initially viewed a gun as a source of power, but then experienced remorse after actually using it. I observed students becoming more thoughtful and deliberate in their comments as they used textual examples to introduced new perspectives on the matter. Kenny recalled making that inference when one book's narrator describes a gun as feeling cold against his arm. William added, "In *Black and white* [Volponi, 2005], the character says that the gun feels different in his hands after he actually uses it, so he throws it in the river."

Although the teacher did not intervene in this instance, the conversation begun here is ripe with the potential to move to a more critical position. Students focused on the individual decision to use or not use a gun to exert power, but it is not clear whether they grasped the social and economic backdrop of *If I grow up* and related books. Their perspectives on guns and a range of moral matters might not be nearly as complicated as teens living in the location portrayed in the book. If the conversation had continued, perhaps someone would have pointed out that characters in the book were living in an area where drugs and guns are linked heavily to everyday survival, especially in the lives of adolescents. Perhaps, another student who had read *Fist stick knife gun* (Canada, 2010), a memoir that makes clearer this reality through the story of a young man who perceived no alternatives to guns, would contribute that perspective. Someone might also have asked students if they believed all teens living in urban areas face these same conditions, particularly teens of certain races. In any case, the disconnections, whether noted by students themselves or brought to light by teachers or peers, not only intrigued students, but also fueled their capacities to entertain multiple perspectives and to confront their own preconceptions.

Changing Times and Places

The complexity of life experiences among youth in the Blue Ridge Mountains is certainly not a new phenomenon. Access to diverse literate experiences in these 8th grade classrooms merely illuminated it. One might argue that limiting literate experiences in these or other secondary classrooms by sanctioning only certain kinds of texts and by discounting student choices has the opposite consequence, that is, it masks their identities. What is more, though, is what students do with text in conventional scenarios and how and what they think is limited.

Dutro (2010) makes a compelling case for how mandated curriculum materials favor class-privileged stories that fail to provide a space for authentic response from children living in poverty and whose experiences differ substantially from those represented in the stories. The notion of not being able to predict student responses because of variation in student experiences and identities in general and for a range of students across geographic regions and socioeconomic realities is worth considering further. It is possible that it is not just materials mandated by districts for teacher use, but also materials mandated by teachers for students' use, that present a problem. I, along with the teachers in this study, often think of the opportunities students would miss if they were limited to traditional class novels and anthologies that include less controversial, more "safe" content and language.

In locations similar to the context for my work, in rural areas and small towns, in quiet suburbs outside of metropolitan areas, I imagine there would be a substantial degree of apprehension about granting students access and the liberty to choose the provocative, edgy books described in this chapter. In conversations in which I have shared my experiences at Mountain Middle School, teachers in other areas say they worry that parents in their communities would disapprove. This is not the case in our community, as parents themselves become caught up in the texts their children bring home. One parent who asked for a list of books kept in the classroom shared, "Reading the same books and talking about some tough topics gives us something to do together." Other parents have "friended" several of the young adult fiction authors on Facebook to communicate with them and to get updates on new publications. As we rethink students' literacies with respect to their identities, we might also examine our own assumptions about the literate practices and identities of our communities.

In an end-of-the-year letter to his teacher and me, Danny reflected on how reading in 8th grade expanded his knowledge about others and about the world outside of his surroundings. He has much to think about as he contemplates what the future holds for him, as he put it, "In this little town nothing much ever happens, but someday something will." Given the depth of students' engagement with text, each other, and critical issues, I would suggest it already has.

References

Asher, J. (2007). *Thirteen reasons why*. New York: Razorbill.

Bean, T. W., & Moni, K. (2003). Developing students' critical literacy: Exploring identity construction in young adult fiction. *Journal of Adolescent & Adult Literacy, 46,* 638–648.

Bean, T. W., & Rigoni, N. (2001). Exploring the intergenerational dialogue journal discussion of a multicultural young adult novel. *Reading Research Quarterly, 36,* 232–248.

Brooks, W. (2006). Reading representations of themselves: Urban youth use culture and African American textual features to develop literary understandings. *Reading Research Quarterly, 41*, 372–392.

Brown, J. (2009). *Hate list.* New York: Little, Brown.

Canada, G. (2010). *Fist stick knife gun: A personal history of violence.* Boston, MA: Beacon Press.

Csikszentmihalyi, M. (1990). *Flow: The psychology of optimal experience.* New York: Harper and Row.

Deci, E. L., & Ryan, R. M. (1985). *Intrinsic motivation and self-determination in human behavior.* New York: Plenum.

Dutro, E. (2010). What 'hard times' means: Mandated curricula, class-privileged assumptions, and the lives of poor children. *Research in the Teaching of English, 44*, 255–291.

Grant, C. (2010). *Teenie.* New York: Alfred A. Knopf.

Gruwell, E. (1999). *The freedom writers diary.* New York: Doubleday.

Guthrie, J. T., Van Meter, P., Hancock, G., Alao, S., Anderson, E., & McCann, A. (1998). Does concept-oriented reading instruction increase strategy use and conceptual learning from text? *Journal of Educational Psychology, 90*(2), 261–278.

Guthrie, J. T., & Wigfield, A. (2000). Engagement and motivation in reading. In P. B. Mosenthal, M. L. Kamil, P. D. Pearson, & R. Barr (Ed.), *Handbook of reading research, Vol. III* (pp. 403–422). Mahway, NJ: Erlbaum.

Hopkins, E. (2004). *Crank.* New York: Simon Pulse.

Hopkins, E. (2006). *Burned.* New York: Simon Pulse.

Hopkins, E. (2007). *Glass.* NY: Margaret K. McElderry Books.

Hopkins, E. (2008). *Identical.* New York: Margaret K. McElderry.

Ivey, G., & Broaddus, K. (2001). "Just plain reading" : A survey of what makes students want to read in middle school classrooms. *Reading Research Quarterly, 36*, 350–377.

Katz, I., & Assor, A. (2007). When choice motivates and when it does not. *Educational Psychology Review, 19*, 429–442.

Ketter, J., & Buter, D. (2004). Transcending spaces: Exploring identity in a rural American middle school. *English Journal, 93*, 47–53.

Knowles, J. (2009). *Jumping off swings.* Somerset, MA: Candlewick.

Lankshear, C. (1997). *Changing literacies.* Milton Keynes: Open University Press.

Lewis, C., & Ketter, J. (2008). Encoding youth: Popular culture and multicultural literature in a rural context. *Reading & Writing Quarterly, 24*, 283–310.

Mac, C. (2004). *The beckoners.* Olympia, WA: Orca.

McCaffrey, K. (2009). *In ecstasy.* Toronto, ON: Annick Press.

Myers, W. D. (1999). *Monster.* New York: HarperCollins.

New London Group. (1996). A pedagogy of multiliteracies: Designing social futures. *Harvard Educational Review, 66*, 60–92.

Paterson, K. (1985). *Come sing, Jimmy Jo.* New York: Dutton.

Pelzer, D. (1995). *A child called "It."* Deerfield Beach, FL: Health Communications, Inc.

Pelzer, D. (1997). *The lost boy.* Deerfield Beach, FL: Health Communications, Inc.

Reeder, C. (1989). *Shades of gray.* New York: Macmillan.

Rhodes-Courter, A. (2008). *Three little words.* New York: Atheneum.

Rylant, C. (1991). *Appalachia: The voices of sleeping birds.* New York: Houghton-Mifflin.

Saenz, B. A. (2009). *Last night I sang to the monster.* El Paso, TX: Cinco Puntos Press.

Scott, E. (2010). *Grace.* New York: Dutton.

Scott, E. (2008). *Living dead girl.* New York: Simon Pulse.

Sheff, N. (2008). *Tweak: Growing up on methamphetamines.* New York: Ginee Seo Books.

Sitomer, A. (2007). *Homeboyz*. New York: Hyperion.

Sitomer, A. (2008). *The secret story of Sonia Rodriguez*. New York: Hyperion.

Strasser, T. (2000). *Give a boy a gun*. New York: Simon & Schuster.

Strasser, T. (2009). *If I grow up*. NY: Simon & Schuster.

Van Diepan, A. (2007). *Snitch*. New York: Simon Pulse.

Volponi, P. (2005). *Black and white*. New York: Viking Juvenile.

Wolk, W. (2009). Reading for a better world: Teaching for social responsibility. *Journal of Adolescent & Adult Literacy, 52*, 664–673.

Worthy, J., Moorman, M., & Turner, M. (1999). What Johnny likes to read is hard to find in school. *Reading Research Quarterly, 34*, 12–27.

12

TEACHER RESPONSE

Addressing Sociocultural and Identity Issues
in Adolescents' Literacy Lives

Justin Claypool and George White

The following email exchanges between Justin Claypool and George White are in response to the three chapters in Part III. Justin and George teach at Morningside Middle School in North Charleston, South Carolina.

From: JUSTIN_CLAYPOOL
Sent: Monday, April 18, 2011 7:45 AM
To: GEORGE_WHITE
Subject: Power Codes?

George,

I was reading the chapter by Bob Fecho, Bette Davis, and Renee Moore last night and was forced to stop in confusion. What do they mean "power codes"? It says: "Students need to be taught mainstream power codes in ways that critique those codes and open them to further expansion and greater inclusion." I'd expect to see the term "power codes" in *The Lord of The Rings*, not in a textbook. Can you explain it? I do not get all the "codes," "switching codes," etc.

Justin

From: GEORGE_WHITE
Sent: Monday, April 18, 2011 8:13 AM
To: JUSTIN_CLAYPOOL
Subject: Re: Power Codes?

Hey, I can't talk during planning (parent conference), but I thought I'd send you this quick email because I didn't get that either at first. The idea of *codes* brings about a fascinating conversation about the differences within American culture. For me, *codes* are a source of communicating with familiarity. I understand the *codes* of the African American, just as an Asian American would understand the *codes* from their culture. It is a method of being connected to others, like you, and, in turn, yourself.

Cynthia described it best—she said that "power codes" are ways of communicating associated with the social/economic group who is *in control* within a culture. In America, think about those who have the most money, the most influence: Ben Bernanke, Donald Trump, members of congress, etc. Think about the way they greet each other and talk—with a firm handshake and proper grammar. Think about how they dress—conservative suit and tie. These are verbal and non-verbal "codes" of interaction created and maintained by the social and economic class who have traditionally pulled all the strings in America—the wealthy, upper class, white male.

And, though that may be changing (with Barack Obama for example), think of how our students don't understand this code—or for some reason don't want to be a part of it. One part I highlighted in that chapter was this: "[I]gnorance of [the codes of power] nullified otherwise bright and vibrant lives."

George

From: JUSTIN_CLAYPOOL
Sent: Monday, April 18, 2011 2:45 PM
To: GEORGE_WHITE
Subject: Re: Re: Power Codes?

Ohhhhhhhhhh! I get it! Our students definitely don't use those "codes." For example, some of the slang they use has always seemed like a made-up language to me, a white boy from middle-class Georgia. On a job interview a boss expects a handshake greeting while looking eye-to-eye. What happens when the interview ends with a *dap*? Oniqua asked me yesterday, "Why do you wear a tie?" I found out that she had never seen any of the males she knew wear a tie. "Why don't you just take the thing off if it's uncomfortable?" she asked.

We really have to strategically teach these ways of communication and even how to switch back and forth. The authors say "for students whose home codes differ markedly from the mainstream power codes, such approaches to language learning are crucial." Now I understand what the fuss was all about. How are they going to know any other way?

Justin

From: GEORGE_WHITE
Sent: Wednesday, April 20, 2011 7:54 AM
To: JUSTIN_CLAYPOOL
Subject: Switching Codes

You're right—teaching our students to switch from code to code is a necessity—the real question is how do we teach this? Not only is the "language of the power of culture" almost completely alien to them, they don't want to understand it. In the chapter it said students "expressed resentment that they needed to shift into language forms, that, for one reason or another, did not seem to represent them." Our middle school female students would describe using proper grammar as "just not me." And, if they feel something does not represent them, it's hard for adolescents to embrace. We must force them to question: What *does* represent me and why?

George

From: JUSTIN_CLAYPOOL
Sent: Wednesday, April 20, 2011 3:03 PM
To: GEORGE_WHITE
Subject: Re: Switching Codes

George,

I'm blown away by this quote from Chapter 7: "classrooms are the nexus where home and personal codes transact with mainstream power codes toward the reshaping of new codes." Think about it, for our students few will scrutinize language anywhere else but in our classrooms! Maybe they may not identify with the power codes, but we gotta try to teach them to respect (or at least use) the power codes, to "play the game."

Justin

PS: Do you really feel like "English is a weapon of oppression"? Do you think switching codes is equivalent to being "white" (as that one student said)? Is it mocking African American heritage/ancestry to switch codes? Growing up in white, middle-class suburbia I have never truly been forced to think about it. But, after teaching in North Charleston, I can understand why someone might say that. As you are an African American male, I was interested to know what you think.

Justin

From: GEORGE_WHITE
Sent: Thursday, April 20, 2011 4:06 PM
To: JUSTIN_CLAYPOOL
Subject: IT'S LANGUAGE!

Justin, as an African American, the concern of mocking, as indicated by the reaction of students, is something that I can relate to. African Americans have always been subjected to "corrections" by others who deem their way of speaking as unintelligible and unmatched to the "standard" way of speaking; of which their Caucasian counterparts are revered as mastering. Of course this is a mere perception from those who are still reeling from an era of mistrust and doubt; however, this has carried over to the next generation who still see a residue of "corrections" within aspects of society. This new generation sees that the dialect that they use is often portrayed as a "funny" or "comical" conversation tool; a method of energizing those who are not immersed in the culture to laugh and be entertained. It is otherwise similar to the "shuckin' and jivin'" that was expected of most African Americans to provide amusement to the affluent population of the mid-20th century.

You know there are African Americans, such as myself, who demonstrate their pride of the rich language, culture, and heritage that helps to define them today. As a teacher, I have the privilege of working with African American students who are still searching for the connections between themselves and those who have come before them. They are still developing an understanding that their culture is a reflection of multiple variations that have helped to shape its current form. Should my African American students be ashamed of how they speak, act, or walk? Should I tell them that Standard American English (SAE) is what is the "norm" and that their learned practice, which is associated with what they have been accustomed to since birth, is merely a faux pas and provides no real support for their future? I am obligated to teach them how to maneuver using the tools that will engage their understanding of the world; however, I am also obligated in allowing them to express themselves freely through use of their accustomed traditions. It is what they are used to. I am also obligated to help them develop pride in themselves and their culture; fostering their need to feel as though they belong and that their customs give root to a bigger societal structure.

George

From: JUSTIN_CLAYPOOL
Sent: Wednesday, April 20, 2011 8:12 PM
To: GEORGE_WHITE
Subject: Re: IT'S LANGUAGE!

George!

I read this part tonight about "Bob's Classroom" and what happened when he focused on the language: "a discussion ensued…about the appropriateness of the racial invective *nigger*." Maybe this is the right idea. We (perhaps wrongly) plow straight ahead into civil rights, Langston Hughes, Malcolm X, MLK…we focus on *race* when it should be *LANGUAGE!* Let the race and "codes of power" discussions come from that!

What do you think?

Justin

From: GEORGE_WHITE
Sent: Thursday, April 21, 2011 4:06 PM
To: JUSTIN_CLAYPOOL
Subject: Re: Re: IT'S LANGUAGE!

You might be on to something. I was skimming for that part you quoted when I re-read this: "students then wrote autobiographies deal[ing] with a way in which language had affected their lives. It was during this project that students broke through many of the barriers." I really like this student autobiography project where a large chunk of it is focused on examining the role of language in their lives. We have to force them to see the world through their lens—using language. We also have to leave our own "lens" behind. It also might be easier for our girls to explore the use of language in a more objective, at arm's length, way—then it may safely become more personalized and insightful. The autobiography project is brilliant: "How Does Language Affect Your Lives?"

George

From: JUSTIN_CLAYPOOL
Sent: Friday, April 22, 2011 7:41 AM
To: GEORGE_WHITE
Subject: Autobiography

George,

Yeah, I think we *should* do that. "The more one is marginalized from the mainstream power codes,…the more one needs to write about and make sense of their lives, to find purpose beyond reality." Our students start off "marginalized" from the "culture of power," but it doesn't have to stay that way. And we can still do it in a way that respects and "saves" their traditional codes. I like that. As teachers, we must push students to "make sense of their lives, to find purpose beyond reality." I mean, that's what it's all about, right?

From: JUSTIN_CLAYPOOL
Sent: Friday, April 22, 2011 7:41 AM
To: GEORGE_WHITE
Subject: "In This Town Nothing Much Ever Happens…"

Hey George, did you read the chapter by Gay Ivey, yet? She brings up some great points about choosing reading materials, giving students choice, and how it impacts engagement—as well as hints at a necessary rethinking of the "classics."

A mistake made in the selection of novels is not so easily undone. Believe me, I don't think I'll ever hear the end of the complaints about *The Pearl*. We should just let the kids choose! It will make them happy, and, because giving choice has been proven to raise the level of engagement (especially with teens), it will make *teachers* happy. I mean, I can't even predict what novel *I'm* going to love! I think about my own choices in reading—do I stay up late with my face buried in a book because of the symbolism, the figurative language? No. I pick books on a myriad of reasons: the author, the summary on the back, the genre, and (of course) the picture on the cover.

A huge collection of materials is almost impossible with our school's budget. However, if we can't give complete choice, we could at least give *some* choice. I've had some incredible success with presenting four different titles as possible picks. As instructors (and sometimes cheerleaders) of reading we are going to necessarily be plugged in to what's popular in young adult fiction. You'll probably be surprised at what's selling—as Ivey was when her students were "drawn to edgy, sometimes gritty, contemporary young adult fiction not usually associated with middle school."

Which brings me to the next piece of advice: we need to change our perception of what exactly is "school reading." Recently in a graduate class the professor had us examine the idea of the traditional literary canon. "Who has read *Moby Dick*?" he asked. A few raised their hands (not me). "Who has read *The Grapes of Wrath*?" he asked again. I raised mine with about three others. Then he pointed to me and asked me, "Are you a lesser person, *a bad person*, because you've never read *Moby Dick*?" My answer was, "Of course not." There are *great books* being published right now that could get kids active in reading, but many teachers won't use them because *they* were taught *Animal Farm* (which they despised reading then). "*Thirteen Reasons Why* was voted by students as their favorite book of the year," writes Ivey, "But what students remembered most was not seeing the story in their minds, but instead lingering concerns about the implications of malicious gossip." You see, you don't have to necessarily use *Hamlet* to teach theme.

Justin

From: GEORGE_WHITE
Sent: Thursday, April 20, 2011 4:06 PM
To: JUSTIN_CLAYPOOL
Subject: "Stock Stories"

Justin,

Good points you made. Here are some of my observations from reading "Stock Stories" [in the chapter by Kelly Wissman and Lalitha Vasudevan]. Mostly, I was glad to see the emphasis on the worthwhile task to connect adolescents with the world and have them interpret their feelings about how the world perceives them. It is this perception that generates such an enormous complexity with young minority men and women. Their outlook on life is reflected in how society has portrayed them in television, movies, music and literature. In some cases, they are condemned to believe that they will only amount to the limitation presented in these venues.

The five-year study that includes the Insight Theater Project intrigues me because it allows these individuals to engage literacy at a level that expresses their own concerns. For the young women, they are combating a society that has already condemned them to a life of "booty shakin'". I see this within my own female students, who become more expressive when given the opportunity to "vent" on concerns that involve how people perceive them. For the boys, they fight a similar battle and we see their perceptions through their actions. The theater allows for them to provide us visions of their thoughts. Surely we can provide for our own students. We must allow students to create their stories through venues that allow them free expression.

As an African American educator, I am drawn to advocate for a comfortable stage for our students (minorities). By giving them this stage, they are free to combat the voices of those that deny them the right to feel as though they can amount to success. Our female students can commandeer the false teachings that captivate society into thinking that they are not credible enough to master complex occupational operations; they are more than the deceptions that have been broadcast by mass media.

Justin, we need to pay close attention to how our students react to the minority elite, Barack Obama, Colin Powell, Maya Angelou, Oprah Winfrey, Justice Sotomayor, etc. I have integrated these individuals, as well as others, into the curriculum of written expression as a way to give compliment to the many minority individuals who are making moves in today's modern society. I don't want our students to only see stories about struggle and triumph; I want them to read about the experiences of the *working world*. I want them to feel a part of these narratives, so they too can build their story as an experience rather than a struggle.

George

PART IV
Changing Teachers, Teaching Changes

13

TOUCHSTONE CHAPTER ADOLESCENTS' MULTIPLE IDENTITIES AND TEACHER PROFESSIONAL DEVELOPMENT

Alfred W. Tatum

On one point, therefore, there can be no question—no hesitation: unless we develop our full capabilities, we cannot survive. If [black men] are to be trained grudgingly and suspiciously; trained not with reference to what we can be, but with sole reference to what somebody wants us to be; if instead of following the methods pointed out by the accumulated wisdom of the world for the development of full human power, we simply are trying to follow the line of least resistance and teach black men only such things and by such methods as are momentarily popular, then my fellow teachers, we are going to fail ignominiously in our attempt to raise the black race to its full humanity and with that failure falls the fairest and fullest dream of a great united humanity.

(Du Bois, 2001, p. 26)

Once I had read enough, learned enough to identify that process, I then had to reconstruct myself as a decent and worthy child of God, painfully peeling away the layers of filth that covered me. This deniggerization, this de-savaging of my soul, began with Shakespeare; it continued in my voracious exploration of literature. Authors as disparate as Mark Twain and W. E. B. Du Bois, Carter G. Woodson and Victor Hugo, Malcolm X and Maya Angelou challenged me, inspired me, and taught me endless lessons. Through them I have found the soul I had thought forever lost.

(Upchurch, 1996, p. xii)

These two quotes suggest that literacy development extends beyond cognitive domains that focus on learning how to read text, that is, "educational texts, visual, printed and electronically mediated, [which] typically seem and claim to speak in one voice, for all possible perspectives and with competence and comprehensiveness" (Freebody, 2003, p. 180). Du Bois (2001) suggested that the development of African Americans is connected to larger goals of humanity and that wisdom is required to move beyond things that are momentarily popular to develop full human power. Upchurch (1996), a once troubled African American teenager who spent his teenage years in and out of the criminal justice system after quitting school while in the 4th grade, suggests that his literacy development led to a reconstruction of self. He refers to the reconstruction as a "deniggeriza-tion" process that occurred after he read the words and ideas of authors, play-wrights, and poets who taught him endless lessons that permeated his soul. He was then able to peel away painful layers of filth that covered him. He asserted that the layers of filth accumulated because of his feelings of invisibility connected to his upbringing in the Philadelphia ghetto where his identity was shaped. Later in his autobiographical text, he states:

> Everything I had experienced in my childhood was the opposite of what I needed to survive socially, intellectually, and psychologically at school…I was socialized at home under the most negative emotional conditions; as a result, my socialization in school felt like an assault to my culture and values.
>
> *(p. 17)*

The major goal of this chapter is to discuss how students' identities and subjec-tivities interplay with their literacy development. The discussion centers on the identity/subjectivity of African American adolescents, particularly the ones living in impoverished communities in the United States and attending low-achieving schools. The discussion is anchored by a case study of teacher professional devel-opment conducted over a 19-month period in one of Chicago's lowest perform-ing schools where I supported one 7th and one 8th grade teacher to honor students' adolescent and cultural identities as part of the literacy instruction they provided. Many of the students were in need of developing the human power DuBois said needs to be developed and the social, intellectual, and psychological development that was missing in Upchurch's life. These teachers share how their students' literacy behaviors shifted and how their own beliefs about literacy instruction changed when they made pedagogical shifts that honored their stu-dents' identities. Before proceeding with details from the qualitative case study, I share the rationale for honoring the identities of adolescents, particularly stu-dents of color, and the potential this honoring has on their literacy development and life outcomes.

Honoring Students' Multiple Identities and Literacy Development

Identity development is critical for adolescents. Identity has been defined as the "presentation of self in a matrix of social relationships—a pattern of social assertion that significant others recognize and come to expect" (Davidson, 1996, p. 2). The concept of identity "is a complex one shaped by individual character- istics, family dynamics, historical factors, and social and political contexts" (Tatum, 1997, p. 18). Researchers have found that adolescents of color are more likely to be actively engaged in an exploration of their racial and ethnic identity than are White students, and that examinations of one's racial identity, often triggered by environmental cues, may begin as early as junior high school (see Tatum, 1997 for a more detailed explanation).

Although identity construction is central to one's literacy development, many teachers responsible for teaching adolescent students of color are unaware of their students' multiple identities and how these identities can be used or should be built on during literacy instruction. This holds true for teachers who share the same cultural and racial identity traits as their students because many of these teachers have had their own identity construction marginalized or overlooked by curricula orientations in schools that defined their education. For example, Gay (2000) explained, "If educators continue to be ignorant of, ignore, impugn, and silence the cultural orientations, values, and performance styles of ethnically dif- ferent students, they will persist in imposing cultural hegemony, personal denigra- tion, educational inequity, and academic underachievement upon them" (p. 25).

The lack of preparation in using knowledge of students' multiple identities during literacy instruction was visible in the school where I conducted this study. When asked to recall the aspects of his teacher education program that had pre- pared him to teach African American adolescents, Mr. Tuscany, a 7th grade teacher, explained, "It was pretty much directed to students. I cannot pinpoint anything that would necessarily say it was for older students…[or] anything specifically cul- turally relevant." In the remainder of this chapter, I describe how I became involved in a project to provide professional development support that led two teachers to honor students' identities as part of the literacy instruction they provided.

The Radnus Elementary School Professional Development Project

Believing that academic failure is not inevitable for African American adolescents attending public schools located in poor, urban communities, I had chosen to become a teacher of adolescents seven years before my involvement in the Radnus Elementary School Professional Development Project. Early on in my teaching career, I sought ways to break down barriers that disenfranchised my African American adolescent students, many of whom were from economically disadvantaged homes and reading several years below grade level (Tatum, 2000). Eventually, I enrolled in a doctoral program that pulled me away from teaching adolescent students for close to three years. However, I continued to regard ado- lescence as a pivotal period for literacy development, particularly for those who struggle with print.

In the spring of 2001, I received an email notice from a university listserv about a position that propelled me back into working with adolescents, not as a classroom teacher, but as a reading specialist, where I was responsible for providing professional development support to a group of teachers in Grades 6–8. I understood that helping teachers develop professionally in a low-achieving school was not a well-trodden area, and that the process would have to occur without a blueprint guaranteeing success. However, I applied for and accepted the reading specialist position in Radnus Elementary School, one of the lowest performing elementary schools in its district.

Radnus Elementary School was stamped with probationary status by its district's office of accountability. Eighty-two percent of the students were reading below grade level at the beginning of the 2001–2002 academic school year based on data from the Iowa Test of Basic Skills. Only 22% of the 7th grade students and 21% of the 8th grade students were reading at or above grade level. Being placed on probation caused tensions for many teachers and administrators who were uncertain about their futures in a school on probation. This uncertainty created considerable pressure to increase students' test scores. The high premium placed on increasing test scores influenced the instructional decisions the teachers made as reflected in their use of test preparation materials and publisher's skill-oriented worksheets. Teachers were using a *momentarily popular* approach to improve test scores.

The First Professional Development Approach

I initially provided professional development support guided by a literacy framework largely derived from research on effective elementary teachers (Allington, 2002; Allington & Cunningham, 1996; Pressley, 1998). The literacy framework involved read-alouds, word study and vocabulary development, guided reading practices, independent reading, and writing. Although the literacy framework was research-based and had both the human and material resources to move it forward, it needed to be expanded. The teachers, who had been involved for five years prior to my involvement in professional development efforts that placed an emphasis on instructional strategies with little success in increasing test scores, did not believe in the efficacy of instructional strategies to resolve the dilemmas faced by teachers and students in a school with a chronic pattern of school failure.

An Anatomically Complete Model of Professional Development

The initial literacy framework was expanded to provide what I characterized as an anatomically complete model of professional development support. In this model (Figure 13.1), students' adolescent identities and cultural identities were centralized. Although I was the reading specialist for teachers in Grades 6 through 8, this model focused on adolescent identities and cultural identities for students in

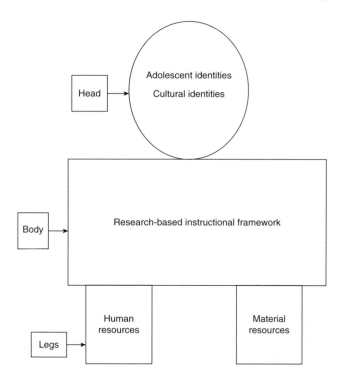

FIGURE 13.1 Anatomically complete model of professional development support.

Grades 7 and 8 because of my interest with that age group, and the 7th and 8th grade teachers' consent to participate in the study. Radnus Elementary School had one 7th grade teacher and one 8th grade teacher. My work with these teachers, who are described later, is the focus of this chapter.

The head of the anatomically complete model was conceptualized based on the following:

1. Professional development support needs to be built on the knowledge of effective teachers of African Americans (Ladson-Billings, 1991; Lipman, 1995). Gay (2000) explains:

    > A very different pedagogical paradigm is needed to improve the performance of underachieving students from various ethnic groups—one that teaches to and through their personal and cultural strengths, their intellectual capacities, and their prior accomplishments. Culturally responsive teaching is this kind of paradigm....It filters curriculum content and teaching strengths through cultural frames of reference to make content more personally meaningful and easier to master.
    >
    > (p. 24)

2. The concept of adolescent literacy is undergoing a productive reconceptu-
    alization (Alvermann, Hinchman, Moore, Phelps, & Waff, 1998). The focus
    on the literacy development of adolescents now moves beyond cognitive
    approaches and encompasses social and complex conceptions of literacy not
    limited to in-school literacy. Narrowly conceived cognitive approaches are
    insufficient for a growing population of linguistically, culturally, and socio-
    economically diverse students (Moje, Young, Readence, & Moore, 2000;
    Schoenbach, Greenleaf, Cziko, & Hurwitz, 1999).

Several texts have been written in the past couple of years that bring attention
to the promise and potential of honoring students' inside- and outside-of-school
identities as an approach to advance their multiple literacies, literacies that shape
their lives (Hull & Schultz, 2002; Mahiri, 2004; Rymes, 2001). Effectively
addressing the multiple literacy needs of adolescents requires a hybridization of
literacy practices that balance the literacies that students develop out of school
with literacies that develop in school (Finders & Tatum, 2005).

Out-of-School Literacy Overload and In-School Literacy Underload

Many students of color suffer from what I refer to as an imbalance between "out-
of-school literacy overload" and "in-school literacy underload." This imbalance
often shapes a trajectory of negative life outcomes, particularly for African American
adolescent males because in-school literacy instruction fails to answer the question,
"What am I going to do with the rest of my life?" (Tatum, 2003a). Many students'
academic performance and lives are shaped by the images of their communities
and the associated possibilities they imagine for themselves as a result of the surrounding images. Ogbu (1998) referred to these images or products of sociocultural adaptation located within the minority community as *community* forces.

The community of Radnus Elementary School can be accurately described as
low-income and inner city. The median income is about $23,000. There are
signs in the front of convenience stores that read, "Government LINK cards
accepted." The immediate area of Radnus Elementary is home to several liquor
stores, several vacant carwash lots, and blocks of vacant lots where homes once
stood. The lots are dotted with abandoned cars and are used as short-cut paths for
children walking to school. Gang and drug warfare is part of the fabric of the
community. These images, coupled with the class-based, race-based experiences
taking place inside their homes, can lead many students to surrender their life
chances before they come to know their life choices (Tatum, 2005). These factors and images contribute to the students' out-of-school literacy overload. This
out-of-school literacy overload can be characterized as a discourse community
that works like an identity kit that comes already equipped with ways of seeing,
acting, thinking, and talking in the world (Gee, 1991).

Without a counterbalance of effective in-school literacy instruction that points adolescents toward new and better realities for themselves or moves them toward a new discourse (Gee, 1991), adolescents' identities and subjectivities are in large part shaped by the overload in their out-of-school literacies. On the other hand, students at Radnus Elementary School were experiencing an in-school literacy underload because of the teachers' focus on test scores and use of test preparation materials. Their chances for encountering "touchstone texts" (Neilsen, Chapter 1, this volume), texts that can potentially help nurture students' identities and reshape the trajectory of their life outcomes, were significantly reduced. Observing the imbalance between the out-of-school literacy overload and in-school literacy underload, I conceptualized professional development support for two teachers informed by the community forces and school factors impacting the literacy development of the students.

The Two Teachers

Mr. Tuscany

Mr. Tuscany, an African American male, had been teaching for 16 years, 15 of those years at Radnus Elementary. He was teaching 7th grade students for the first time during the year of the case study. The major challenge of teaching for Mr. Tuscany was motivating students and increasing their scores on standardized assessments despite some of their disruptive behaviors. There were also professional-based challenges. He explained, "Being on probation, we have tried numerous programs and you know [we] have to be open to allow people to come in [our classrooms] to observe." He felt bombarded by the various workshops when professional developers gave him things to try or to do in his classroom.

Mrs. Garden

Mrs. Garden was a veteran African American teacher who had been teaching for 26 years. She was teaching 7th and 8th grade students for the ninth year at the time of the study. When asked to describe the major challenges she had faced over the past five years teaching at Radnus, her first comment was, "God, we would never finish if I talked about the major challenges." She believed the biggest challenge was teaching kids who lack self-confidence, kids who cannot see beyond their neighborhood. Both teachers' comments and dispositions reflected that the students and their "families seemed to be immersed in hostile educational and community [setting]" (Garcia, 2002, p. 139).

The Professional Development Support

My professional development support was designed to move the teachers toward instructional practices that would grant their students entrée into literacy instruction that extended beyond a sole indoctrination of basic skills aimed at minimum requirements on a standardized instrument. The support focused on several dominant themes for the teachers that included helping them to:

1. Engage their students with authentic text and in authentic discussions where the students could analyze their realities and discuss strategies for overcoming academic and societal barriers.
2. Use meaningful literacy activities that took into account students' adolescent and cultural identities.
3. Acknowledge that skill development, increasing test scores, and nurturing students' identities are fundamentally compatible.
4. Legitimatize African American students' culture and make it a reference for learning.

These themes anchored all of the professional development activities, which included whole-group staff sessions, grade-level meetings, post-observation conferences, sharing of professional readings in the form of books and articles, personal conversations, and various materials I shared with the two teachers. Throughout the professional development project, teachers were encouraged to think about the role of literacy instruction for the students they were teaching. Here I provide, as an example, a two-page letter I distributed to the teachers in April 2002 that expressed concerns for teaching students who lived in an environment where schooling has failed to live up to the promises of quality education for most of the members living in their communities. This letter (Figure 13.2) provides a rich snapshot of the types of dialogue held throughout many of the professional development activities that focused on students' identities:

The following is part of the follow-up conversation with Mrs. Garden and Mr. Tuscany about the contents of the letter at a grade-level meeting during the first week of May 2002. I asked them to help me understand my thinking about literacy instruction in the context of Radnus Elementary School and its surrounding community.

TATUM: There were some things I put in [the letter] that hopefully you and Mrs. Garden can help me figure out. One of the things placed in the letter was the issue of culturally responsive teaching versus a neutral form of teaching.... I want both of you to help me understand if our students' identities matter, and if there are cultural considerations for providing a better quality education.

MR. TUSCANY: I think culture definitely matters because there are particular surroundings that [the students] are involved with. By making it culturally relevant when we are teaching, if they do not understand exactly what we are teaching they still have something to draw from because it touches their lives.

TATUM: What about you, Mrs. Garden?

Teachers,

I was approached by a member of the faculty yesterday who encouraged me to think deeply about the issue of educating the children at Radnus. The issues of culturally relevant teaching versus teaching as a neutral discipline that ignores the issue of student's culture were discussed. (Why can't we just teach children as children?) We spoke honestly and candidly about the differences and did not leave with a consensus.

However, during the course of the conversation high expectations, communication patterns with students and parents, curriculum selection, discipline, and the larger ecology that pollutes the educational experiences of our children were discussed. I offered that schooling for many of our children has become a ritualistic indoctrination of failure predicated by many circumstances beyond our control; however, there are certain aspects within the teachers' realms of control. I also offered that instructional approaches in and of themselves are limited because they fail to address other competencies that are beyond the reach of identifying details, making inferences, making predictions, etc. Education has always been more than the A, B, Cs.

Solely focusing on instructional approaches ignores the strengthening of students' identities. This is important because many of our students live lives in contradiction. It is communicated to them in their homes that schooling is the pathway to promises that they do not readily witness. A feeling of inferiority is endemic for many of our students. They still associate being smart and being wealthy as being white. Focusing on instructional approaches or a student's skill-base leaves these issues uncovered, ultimately leading to the reproduction of the status quo. We will fail miserably if we do not nurture our students' identities, push them towards academic excellence, and utilize their culture as a vehicle for learning to build cultural competence.

Here, I do not speak of the KKK culture—tell them they are born of African Kings, make sure they know about Martin Luther King, and discuss the seven principles of Kwanzaa. These K's have been used as add-ons or cultural feel goods but have led to the debasement of an authentic form of culturally responsive pedagogy. Culturally relevant pedagogy is a pedagogy of opposition that encourages students to read between the lines and beyond the pages and is designed to have students examine the society in which they live. But, in order for them to read between the lines requires that there is strong instructional support in a caring community to teach them to read. For many of our students, "it is less about what's on the lines and pages than what is between the lines and beyond the pages."

The idea is not to expose our children to cultural artifacts and historical facts about African Americans in isolation, but to expose them to a conceptualization that there is a positive uniqueness about being Black in hopes that this uniqueness allows them to interact with other cultural groups more fully, an inevitability in society. "I Too, Am America." Make the teaching efforts explicit when exposing them to the *dialect* of Standard English (the *dialect* of power in these United States), and other forms of power in the United States. Our students' exposure must be wide and varied and grounded in the belief that these kids can learn just as much and more than any group of children.

FIGURE 13.2 Letter distributed to teachers.

MRS. GARDEN: I agree whole-heartedly. The reason I say this is because I think you were here when we started reading Dick Gregory's novel, *Nigger* (1995). The kids really enjoyed the book because they were familiar with the language....They said it was because they could relate to things.

MR. TUSCANY: I also feel by making it culturally relevant, it empowers the kids to a certain degree because it's not like [they] are sitting around knowing totally nothing about it. By making it culturally relevant, they can identify with something in there, which means they don't feel left out.

TATUM: We know they can relate. We know the students buy into it. But, are these the things making them better readers in your estimation? Is this going to lead to higher reading achievement? I think it is a dichotomy. We can invite them in and motivate them and empower them with ideas and feelings, but are we increasing their reading achievement?

MR. TUSCANY: To a degree. I think it is, for the simple fact it's going to allow them to get into it. When you want to achieve something, you practice towards that goal. If it is something that I don't like, I'm not going to practice, which means I am not going to reach my goal. If I like it or can get into it, then I am apt to do a little bit more, which in the end it is going to raise the achievement. I think it is going to lead to better achievement based on the simple fact that they will read it now.

MRS. GARDEN: That's an excellent point, Tuscany. I think the primary reason they were having so much trouble with other texts, and I use that term openly, is maybe they didn't fully understand what they were reading. But since we have been reading a lot of books by a lot of different authors and bringing in things that are culturally relevant to the students—I think now when I bring in stuff to them—now they say it's easy.

MR. TUSCANY: It's opened the door. At first the door was not opened. Now the door is opened.

The reflections of the teachers throughout the study suggested a reconceptualization in their literacy instruction that moved closer toward an intersection of improving students' reading scores and nurturing students' identities. Mr. Tuscany mentioned in March 2002 that his goal was "to make sure [the students] move at least one year." He also mentioned, "I just want to make them knowledgeable." After seven months of placing emphasis on curriculum orientations and a culturally responsive approach to literacy teaching, Mr. Tuscany explained how the professional development support had affected his beliefs about teaching literacy: "I've always known that success was possible, but it's helping me believe that more success is possible….I mean, you hear that this will work, that will work, but by doing it the way we are doing it [focusing on students' identities] we actually get to see some success stories." Mrs. Garden, in a separate conversation, explained how the professional development support had impacted her teaching of African American adolescents: "We are now dealing with culture in our school. We are dealing with issues that pertain specifically to us, and what we are going to do about it in this area. That's an eye-opener for them and me."

Curriculum Orientations

I had the autonomy and financial resources provided through a grant to select curriculum materials to support Mrs. Garden and Mr. Tuscany, the only teachers

Babbitt, N. (1975). *Tuck everlasting.* Farrar, Strauss & Giroux Cushman, K. (1995). *The Midwife's Apprentice.* New York: HarperTrophy.

Gregory, D. (1995) *Nigger: An autobiography.* New York: Mass Market.

Hamilton, V. (1990). *Cousins.* New York: Scholastic.

Hinton, S. E. (1967). *The outsiders.* New York: Puffin.

Johnson, A. (1998). *Heaven.* New York: Aladdin.

Kunjufu, J. (1987). *Lessons from history.* Chicago: African American Images.

Lowry, L. (1989). *Number the stars.* New York: Yearling.

Lowry, L. (1993). *The giver.* New York: Yearling.

McKissack, P. (1992). *The dark thirty: Southern tales of the supernatural.* New York: Knopf.

Myers, W. D. (1993). *Malcolm X: By any means necessary.* New York: Scholastic.

Myers, W. D. (1988). *Scorpions.* New York: HarperTrophy.

Myers, W. D. (1996). *Slam.* New York: Scholastic.

Naylor, P. R. (2000). *Shiloh.* New York: Aladdin.

Sachar, L. (1998). *Holes.* New York: Yearling.

Taylor, M. D. (1976). *Roll of thunder, hear my cry.* New York: Dial.

Washington, B. T. (2000). *Up from slavery.* New York: Signet.

Woodson, J. (1994). *I hadn't meant to tell you this.* New York: Laurel Leaf.

Wright, R. (1994). *Rites of passage.* New York: HarperTrophy.

FIGURE 13.3. Curriculum materials selected for classroom instruction.

at Radnus Elementary who did not use a basal reader during the 2001–2002 school year. I decided not to select a basal reader and opted for young adolescent (YA) literature for both the 7th and 8th grades, and a literature anthology, *African American literature: Voices in tradition* (1998) for the 8th grade. (See Figure 13.3 for a list of the YA literature used.)

There were several reasons for this. I wanted to select curriculum materials that would lead the teachers toward the following:

1. Striking a balance between students' out-of-school literacy development and in-school literacy development.
2. Using a culturally responsive approach for teaching literacy to help reshape students' views of who they are and what they can become.
3. Using and discussing literature appropriate for adolescents.

During the professional development project, culturally relevant literature anchored the culturally responsive approach. I selected curriculum materials, a large percentage written by African American authors or with African American characters, that I thought could help the students think about ways to plan their futures and shape a positive trajectory for their lives, lives "not limiting the space in which the self can roam" (Achebe, 1988, p. 53). For example, *Slam* (Myers, 1996) was selected for Mr. Tuscany's class because it provided opportunities to discuss making sound academic decisions and examining the consequences when inappropriate decisions are made. Slam, the main character in Myers' novel, is consumed by dreams that his basketball talents will remove him from the stings of poverty. His dreams are continually challenged. He neglects his studies at a magnet high school, is faced with the reality of his grandmother dying and his father's drunkenness, and has friends selling drugs. Slam is able to make great decisions on the basketball court, but is challenged to make good decisions off the court.

While discussing the curriculum materials selected for their classroom instruction, the teachers reflected on the usefulness of the materials for advancing their students' literacies. After three months of using the materials, Mrs. Garden said:

> Oh, those readings that you have given me—every book that you have thrown in my hand...has been a blessing. Especially the African American literature because I never had that approach with my students before. I always tried to feel that I had to do readings with this, that, or the other. And, those [other] readings are fine, but I think for our African American students that there are a lot of things going on that they are missing [but which they get] with the literature you are giving us now.

The two teachers found a culturally responsive approach to literacy teaching as one of the useful aspects for helping them to advance their students' literacies. Using students' adolescent and cultural identities as frames of reference allowed teachers to facilitate learning and address concerns specific to their students. Mr. Tuscany, commenting on the curriculum materials that anchored the culturally responsive approach, stated:

> Each of the topics we seemed to cover with our novels I thought were things that should be talked about with adolescents because of the things that were going on. I felt those were actually choices that one day may present themselves to them in their own lives. We went through gang-related things all the way through relatives, then we took them to new heights in terms of fantasy. Then we came back and went through a lot of genres. In *Toning the sweep* (Johnson, 1993), we talked about relationships between a mother and a grandchild. All the way back down to trust and what you should do [about] inappropriate advances by somebody [a reference to the novel, *I hadn't meant to tell you this* (Woodson, 1995)]. So those were all suitable topic, topics that as a teacher I think you need to be comfortable to teach.

The curriculum materials also allowed students to connect their out-of-school and in-school literacies as Mr. Tuscany illustrates:

> I think back to Cousins (Hamilton, 1992). [The students] compared some of their relationships to a relative in terms of some of the things we were

discussing.…Basically, things like that in their lives, their relationships with other family members, especially grandmothers.

Mrs. Garden, when reflecting on the curriculum materials, added:

> First of all, we started with the African American literature book, which is something considering we're teaching African American students. You also brought in independent reading books that dealt with African Americans, which is something we never had in the past. You gave the kids a sense of being. Going back to…Jesse Jackson's old saying—"I am Somebody." I think whether they say it, the kids started seeing it. I am somebody. This is my community. These are my people I associate with on a daily basis. [With this curriculum] they can be attuned with themselves and know [that] whatever is good for somebody else can be good for them.

Student Achievement and Literacy Shifts

Mrs. Garden, in her final interview, shared the following:

> Mr. Tatum, Tonya came up to me and I'll never forget it as long as I live, the look on her face when she just held me. She locked me in a lock and held me and looked me dead smack in the face and said, "Mrs. Garden, we did it." I asked, "What are you talking about, we did it?" She said, "We made a lie out of my grandmother. My grandmother said that I would never be able to graduate and we did it."

Tonya was not the only success story. By the end of the study, 39% of the 7th grade students were reading at or above grade level and 57% of the 8th grade students were reading at or above grade level, up from 22% and 21% respectively prior to my involvement. These were the highest percentages achieved over at least the previous five years at Radnus Elementary. From a cognitive perspective, the test data, along with teachers' reports of students' frequent independent strategy use, indicate that there was growth in students' reading abilities. However, the improvement in students' literacies extended beyond standardized test scores. There were shifts in students' literacy behaviors observed by the teachers that fit within a sociocultural view of literacy instruction, namely students' confidence levels, student expectations of themselves as literacy learners, students' connection of literacy to real-world learning, and students' positive responses to literature. This was suggested by teachers' comments that meshed with my observations.

MR. TUSCANY: I found that, through some of our discussions, the students wanted to take books home. In the past nobody—well, we weren't [reading] novels—but nobody wanted to do extra reading. When I asked them to read from A to B, that was it. But now I am finding them wanting to go on. They're already telling me, discussing the book with me, telling me what happened here and there.

MRS. GARDEN: They're reading more. I have kids who have been literally non-readers raising their hands to respond….[Student] was basically a nonreader for a couple of years in a row. He's even reading more now. He has confidence in himself since we brought about this Black—I don't know if it's the Black literature or the approach that I have with him with the Black literature.

MR. TUSCANY: Some of them I couldn't get to pay attention (at the beginning of the year). [Student] is doing better now. Before, he wouldn't cause me problems, but he wouldn't pay attention. Now I am finding them getting into the stories. Now they will try to defend their answers. "Look I found—it says so and so," and they take me back to the spot where they found certain things. I see their confidence level building.

The teachers shared their reasons why a culturally responsive approach to literacy teaching helped them advance their students' literacies. The most salient explanation converged on the idea that the approach provided an inviting pathway for student participation, namely, students' voices were awakened because the literature had familiar contexts that allowed them to make personal responses based on their experiences with the content of curriculum materials. This led to increased student participation, which in turn contributed to their literacy growth. Mrs. Garden stated, "The things that we're doing invite in the knowledge that they already bring to the table. So, I think that's how it's helping them."

The results from this study (see Tatum, 2003b for complete study) suggest that a professional development model that took into account students' adolescent and cultural identities by using texts selected with consideration for those identities helped the teachers advance the literacies of economically disadvantaged adolescents struggling with reading. Planning professional development supports based on considerations for multifaceted dilemmas related to students' identities (e.g., African American adolescent struggling readers), institutional constraints, and strong embedded historical realities that reached "beyond simply educating the child…[to] shaping the child" (Rymes, 2001, p. 90) was central to the 7th and 8th grade teachers at Radnus Elementary. This broader view for providing professional development moved toward an examination of factors both outside and inside of schools that influence literacy outcomes.

Literacy instruction that takes into account students' identities, shaped by historical and current circumstances and a vision for the future, can be viewed as a seed of optimism. Ignoring students' historical and contemporary circumstances can render an uncritical approach to literacy development that allows traditional instructional approaches to remain largely unchallenged and unchanged. At Radnus Elementary, moving beyond an emphasis solely on instructional strategies influenced the teachers' desires to develop professionally and to invest energy to change curriculum orientations and place emphasis on students' identities. Throughout the professional development project, a high premium was placed on addressing the varied needs of adolescents and redressing some of the inadequacies in education experienced by adolescent students in low-achieving schools. As a result, efforts were made to have the teachers not only provide explicit strategy instruction, but to also include YA literature, strive to use a culturally responsive approach to literacy teaching, honor students' identities, create supportive classroom environments, and engage students in discussion where they could analyze their realities in the context of the curriculum.

This experience suggests that there is a need to reconceptualize the roles of professional development support targeted toward improving the reading achievement of African American adolescents. Professional development must fit with the current concepts of adolescents' multiple literacies and must include pedagogy that has been found to be effective with African American students. There are several potential benefits related to such a reconceptualization:

1. Professional development support for teachers of African American adolescents can be built on a conceptual basis that includes theoretical, instructional, and professional considerations.
2. A cohesive system of professional development support will include considerations for educating adolescents, educating African Americans, students' literacies, and teachers' literacies.
3. Professional development support can be analyzed for its effectiveness in narrowing the literacy gap between African American adolescents and other students.

This qualitative case study provided research-based evidence that when teachers honor students' multiple identities as a critical part of the literacy instruction they provide, students show growth in traditional cognitive domains as reflected in test scores. As more research on adolescent literacy research is conducted, it will be productive to include a focus on the complexity inherent in the multiple identities that adolescents bring to our nation's classrooms (e.g., cultural, gender, racial) and to examine how the honoring of these identities can be used to advance the literacies of all adolescents. Wrestling with the complexities associated with student's multiple identities may not be *momentarily popular* in school environments where quick solutions to raise test scores are being sought, but may hold out the most promise of not only advancing students' literacies, but shaping the lives of many students who are in desperate need of full human development.

References

Achebe, C. (1988). *Hopes and impediments*. New York: Doubleday.

African American literature: Voices in tradition. (1998). New York: Holt Rinehart Winston.

Allington, R. L. (2002). What I've learned about effective reading instruction from a decade of studying exemplary classroom teachers. *Phi Delta Kappan, 83*, 740–747.

Allington, R. L., & Cunningham, P. M. (1996). *Schools that work: Where all children read and write*. New York: Addison Wesley Longman.

Alvermann, D., Hinchman, K., Moore, D., Phelps, S., & Waff, D. (Eds.). (1998). *Reconceptualizing the literacies in adolescents' lives* (1st ed.). Mahwah, NJ: Lawrence Erlbaum Associates.

Davidson, A. L. (1996). *Making and molding identity in schools: Student narratives on race, gender and academic engagement*. New York: SUNY Press.

Du Bois, W. E. B. (2001). *The education of Black people: Ten critiques, 1906–1960*. New York: Monthly Review Press.

Finders, M., & Tatum, A. W. (2005). Hybridization of literacy practices: A review of *What they don't learn in schools: Literacy in the lives of urban youth*. *Reading Research Quarterly, 40*(3), 388–397.

Freebody, P. (2003). *Qualitative research in education: Interaction and practice*. Thousand Oaks, CA: Sage.

Garcia, E. (2002). *Student cultural diversity: Understanding and meeting the challenge*. Boston: Houghton Mifflin.

Gay, G. (2000). *Culturally responsive teaching: Theory, research, and practice*. New York: Teachers College Press.

Gee, J. (1991). *Social linguistics and literacies: Ideology in discourses*. London: The Falmer Press.

Gregory, D. (1995) *Nigger: An autobiography*. New York: Mass Market Paperback.

Hamilton, V. (1992). *Cousins*. New York: Scholastic.

Hull, G., & Schultz, K. (2002). *School's out: Bridging out-of-school literacies with classroom practice*. New York: Teachers College Press.

Johnson, A. (1993). *Toning the sweep*. New York: Scholastic.

Ladson-Billings, G. (1991). Returning to the source: Implications for educating teachers of Black students. In M. Foster (Ed.), *Readings in equal education: Qualitative investigations into schools and schooling* (Vol. 11; pp. 227–243). New York: AMS Press.

Lipman, P. (1995). "Bringing out the best in them": The contribution of culturally relevant teachers in educational reform. *Theory Into Practice, 34*, 202–208.

Mahiri, J. (2004). *What they don't learn in school: Literacy in the lives of urban youth*. New York: Peter Lang.

Moje, E., Young, J., Readence, J., & Moore, D. (2000). Reinventing adolescent literacy for new times: Perennial and millennial issues. *Journal of Adolescent & Adult Literacy, 43*, 400–410.

Myers, W. D. (1996). *Slam*. New York: Scholastic.

Ogbu, J. (1998). Voluntary and involuntary minorities: A cultural–ecological theory of school performance with some implications for education. *Anthropology and Education Quarterly, 29*, 155–188.

Pressley, M. (1998). *Reading instruction that works: The case for balanced teaching*. New York: Guilford.

Rymes, B. (2001). *Conversational borderlands: Language and identity in an alternative urban high school*. New York: Teachers College Press.

Schoenbach, R., Greenleaf, C., Cziko, C., & Hurwitz, C. (1999). *Reading for understanding: A guide to improving reading in middle and high school classrooms—The reading apprenticeship guidebook.* San Francisco: Jossey-Bass.

Tatum, A. W. (2000). Breaking down barriers that disenfranchise African American adolescent readers. *Journal of Adolescent & Adult Literacy, 44*(1), 52–64.

Tatum, A. W. (2003a). All degreed up and no where to go: Black male literacy education and beyond. *Journal of Adolescent & Adult Literacy, 46*(8), 620–623.

Tatum, A. W. (2003b). *Advancing the literacies of African American adolescents: A case study of professional development.* Unpublished doctoral dissertation. University of Illinois-Chicago.

Tatum, A. W. (2005). *Teaching reading to black adolescent males: Closing the achievement gap.* Portland, ME: Stenhouse.

Tatum, B. D. (1997). *"Why are all the black kids sitting together in the cafeteria?" And other conversations about race.* New York: Basic Books.

Upchurch, C. (1996). *Convicted in the womb: One man's journey from prisoner to peacemaker.* New York: Bantam Books.

Woodson, J. (1995). *I hadn't meant to tell you this.* New York: Laurel Leaf.

Wright, R. (1994). *Rites of passage.* New York: HarperTrophy.

14

RECONCEPTUALIZING TOGETHER

Exploring Participatory and Productive Critical Media Literacies in a Collaborative Teacher Research Group

Eli Tucker-Raymond, Daisy Torres-Petrovich, Keith Dumbleton, and Ellen Damlich

This chapter describes how teachers' collaborative inquiry into Critical Media Literacy (CML) pedagogies can lead to reconceptualizations of what it means to teach and learn literacies in middle school contexts. A team of three teachers from a Chicago public middle school and a university researcher met biweekly during one school year to study CML through individual and collaborative action research inquiry projects. In presenting snapshots of our group discussions and classroom activities, we describe how collaboration mediated competing goals, values, and practices—creating opportunities for learning as we tried to implement CML in teachers' classrooms. Stemming from our collaborative inquiry into the complex commitments of critical literacy, tensions between critical deconstruction and creative production as goals for literacy practices were central to our group discussions and teachers' classroom projects. We argue that the collaborative negotiation of such tensions served as spaces for learning in which teachers developed new conceptual resources for changing their teaching in ways that led to more humanizing pedagogies.

Collaborative Action Team

The collaborative action research group, what we later came to call the Collaborative Action Team, was composed of three volunteer teachers and one university researcher: Daisy, a 7th–8th grade self-contained cross categorical special education teacher; Keith, a pullout special education resource teacher and reading, writing, and math specialist for 7th–8th grade students who were also Spanish-dominant speakers; and Ellen, the school librarian, serving all classes for one or two two-week blocks each year. Eli, an educational researcher from a nearby public university, and former middle school teacher, was the initiator of the group. Daisy was Puerto Rican. Eli, Ellen, and Keith were Anglos. The teachers had all been teaching for four or five years in total, and fewer in their current positions at Palmer School.

A public middle school in Chicago, Illinois, Palmer School (pseudonym) served about 800 7th and 8th grade students during the year of the study. Palmer had an ethnolinguistically diverse faculty and staff of about 60. The school was located in a mostly working class Latino neighborhood that had reputations for both collective community activism and gang activity. Public transportation was limited to buses and inexpensive grocery stores were few. Social services were visibly present, as were vacant lots. In the year of the study, 90% of the student population identified as Latino/a. Ninety-eight percent of students' families were low income. About 12% were considered Limited English Proficient, and approximately 18% received some form of special education services. The principal was supportive of our group just as she was supportive of at least 26 other partnerships with outside groups working in the school. After finding a time that the four of us could attend, beginning in October, we met for an hour or two after school every other Tuesday for the rest of the school year and into the summer time, totaling 17 meetings.

As each meeting could cover several topics of conversation, we also engaged in a number of tasks to develop our own perspectives on CML and to support the teachers in carrying out their own inquiries. Among other tasks, we talked about events that happened in the classroom or school that day, discussed specific media texts, articles on critical literacy, media literacy, and teacher inquiry, examined classroom discourse, developed a curriculum that included CML, and collaborated on teachers' individual inquiries.

Why Critical Media Literacy?

It is important to recognize that media texts are significant cultural tools employed by children in learning about the world (e.g., Lee, 2007). As noted above, young people spend at least as much time learning about the world via media outside of school as they do via the school curriculum within it (Rideout, Roberts, & Foehr, 2005; Xu, Sawyer, & Zunich, L. 2005). According to a recent study, in the United States young people aged 8–18 spend 6.5–8.5 hours a day engaged with electronic media (Rideout et al., 2005). Put simply, media—as texts, tools, practices, companies, and multi-leveled systems—are a large part of U.S. teenagers' lives. To ignore children's engagement with media while they are behind school doors is to disregard a significant portion of the resources they use in developing their understandings of the world. It is to ignore them as people.

Tatum's chapter (this volume) explores culturally relevant pedagogies that address the interplay between adolescents' dynamic and multifaceted ethnic, racial, and literate identities. CML is a culturally relevant pedagogy that addresses students' identities based in their dynamic and multifaceted interactions with media culture, and helps academically marginalized students succeed in more traditionally academic settings (Alvermann, 2001; Morrell, 2004). Children's identities, or how they and others conceive of them as certain kinds of people, may be more than ever tied to their experiences with a multidimensional media culture rather than ethnic, institutional, or geographic affiliations, although those dimensions of self and identity continue to be relevant (Dolby & Rizvi, 2007; McCarthy, Giardina, Harewood, & Park, 2003).

One way to address and integrate children's lives with media in a school curriculum is for teachers to conduct collaborative inquiries around the development and implementation of CML curricular content. Through analysis and production of a wide range of texts, including books, magazines, films, videos, advertisements, music, and television, CML attempts to deconstruct ideologies and reconstruct alternative representations of the world, offering both critique of inequity, marginalization, and oppression and hope for humanity, pluralism, and freedom (e.g., Alvermann & Hagood, 2000; Kellner & Share, 2007). But the point of critical literacy is not merely to describe social practices that dominate, restrict, and oppress people. The goal is also to change those practices by also changing our own practices as teachers, learners, and knowers so that they are more humanizing.

Tensions and Boundary Crossings

Collaboration involves people working together toward a common goal or set of goals. However, even though people work together, individuals may have nuanced ideas about what those goals are and, at the same time, those individuals may also be trying to simultaneously satisfy multiple goals for themselves. For instance, as teachers attempt to educate the children in their room their goals may include for children to pass standardized tests *and* to develop life-long identities as readers and writers. As teachers in a collaborative group learn about CML, they may have as goals to help the others in their group and to figure out what works best in their classroom. Competition among goals creates tensions. People's attempted resolution of these tensions drive learning and transformation (e.g., Engeström & Sannino, 2010). To resolve tensions, people create new responses, for instance, by seeking out new tools of practice, such as more information on a topic; experimenting with practice; or changing positions by deemphasizing one goal to pursue another. When new goals, tools, or positionalities are introduced in the negotiation of these tensions, people create new practices and cross previously existing boundaries of practice.

For instance, group members had multiple reasons for joining. Even though a common agenda was made explicit by Eli and agreed to by the teachers, our conceptualizations of "critical" and our diverse positionalities as teachers and human beings meant we had different goals for what we wanted to accomplish. Keith was primarily looking for support for his own continued learning about teaching. He thought the group would help "push" him through the year (Interview 2). Daisy thought the group would be a good place to brainstorm and get new ideas for her classroom (Interview 2) and Ellen thought the group would help her address issues of information and media literacy, important in library sciences (Interview 2). Eli hoped teachers would research students' media practices and use them to build a coherent curriculum that addressed injustice in and beyond students' lives. Although our individual goals and actions may have been different, creating tensions, our collaborative work together, accomplished mainly through talk, helped teachers to step out of the ways in which they had taught previously and create new practices in their classrooms.

People boundary cross when they do something new, including think from a new perspective. For instance, when the teachers joined the group they crossed a boundary into a new type of professional learning. When teachers tried out ideas, such as giving their students more power in determining the content of the curriculum, they crossed boundaries of practice. Boundary crossing is a social phenomenon because it involves people in joint actions that create new resources for understanding and participating in the world, even if that world is one's classroom. Boundary crossing "is essentially a creative endeavor which requires new conceptual resources. In this sense, boundary crossing involves collective concept formation" (Engeström, Engeström, & Karkkainen, 1995; p. 333). In our group, our general orientation toward the collaborative, critical exploration of media topics served as a boundary zone, the social interaction that allowed for boundary crossing, or the practicing of new practices. As a tool in the boundary zone of our study group, a CML perspective allowed all of us to cross into new territory and explore new pedagogies consonant with contemporary youth media engagement. Through our participation in a collaborative group we created new conceptual resources—new ways of thinking about teaching and learning, including what the goals of classroom activities were. When they change the goals of their classroom activities, teachers also change their practices and thus their own relationships to students. At the same time opportunities open up for students to transform themselves, their relationships to learning, and to the community at large.

Collaboration as a Foundation for Boundary Crossing

So how do teachers learn about what CML is and how to teach it? Pappas (2005) argues Collaborative Action Research (CAR) is a fruitful form of teacher learning because it: 1) involves dialogue with other colleagues, inviting fresh perspectives; 2) contributes to sharing of power, and the transformation of power/knowledge relationships (Foucault, 1980; p. 3) is based in classroom practice; and 4) builds theory about learning and teaching. Furthermore, as a methodology for learning, CAR is compatible with the goals of critical literacies to transform relationships of knowledge and power.

Most educational research is either for the consumption of teachers or is conducted on them. It is still a comparatively small, but active and growing group of teachers who participate in "producing" research (e.g., Duncan-Andrade & Morrell, 2008; Fecho, 2004; Pappas & Zecker, 2001). CAR is one kind of space for teacher research that allows for teachers to negotiate their own research participation with others and to produce research themselves (Oja & Smulyan, 1989). That is, collaborative research facilitates the co-construction of knowledge with teachers rather than for or on them.

In our group, teachers acted as students of pedagogy and media, principal investigators in their own classrooms, curriculum developers, and collaborators on the inquiries of other teachers and on the project as a whole. As part of the research, teachers developed inquiry questions about their own classrooms that they then pursued for the school year. Eli made several visits to everyone's classroom, collecting data, writing notes, and offering feedback. Teachers, although they did not visit each other's classrooms for research purposes, did design curricula together, and in the group, helped one another think through issues that came up in implementation. In this way, collaborative inquiry served as a model of learning for both teachers and children that encouraged perspectival plurality (Wells, 2001) and humanizing stances toward teaching and learning.

The group's collaborative relationships emerged over the course of the study. We worked together to identify areas of study pertaining to students, curricula, and critical perspectives and then to come up with possible responses. We also worked together in a number of different interpersonal configurations. We all collaborated with each other within group meetings, talking through issues group members brought up. Eli collaborated with teachers on their projects, planning with them, visiting their classrooms, and at times leading some of the classes. Teachers also collaborated with each other in their classroom spaces, especially Daisy and Ellen, but also Ellen and Keith.

Collaboration allowed us to trust and support one another so that teachers felt safe to take risks and try new ways of teaching in their classrooms. In addition to the intellectual support that served to create new ideas, collaboration served as an emotional and moral support. Meeting and talking with others was, as Ellen said, "cathartic" (Group Meeting June) and helped the teachers cope with the multiple demands placed on them.

> Oh, the benefits of being in this group. It was nice to actually bounce ideas off of each other. It's just nice to discuss curriculum on a regular basis and how we can do things in our classroom. And not feel like I'm being attacked. It's just nice to be able to discuss your shortcomings or your issues sometimes and hear your feedback without somebody criticizing you. It's nice being in a not critical environment.
>
> *(Ellen, Group Meeting, June)*

From the teachers' perspectives, as Ellen spoke about in the excerpt above, our group was successful because we operated non-judgmentally. "Bouncing ideas off of each other" signified that we were responsive to one another, and group members were able to talk about "shortcomings...and hear your feedback without somebody criticizing you." That is, the teachers felt safe talking about their classrooms and were open to hearing suggestions for practice.

In talking about providing support for one another, Daisy spoke about herself, others, and the group as a whole, as interchangeable agents,

> What I like about this group, again, we're a small group and probably that adds to being open and laid back, and I'm not afraid to say, what you really feel like saying. Maybe we should do this, what do you think?...Open to new ideas.
>
> *(Group Meeting, June).*

In the preceding quote, Daisy switched pronouns from "I," to "we," to "you" and even left an unmarked subject preceding the phrase "open to new ideas." In this short comment, Daisy began with herself, but then fluidly substituted singular others and the group as a whole as the subject who "was not afraid to say." In her statement was a recognition that she was able to say what she felt like saying, but also that the group acted together and as we sought out each other's advice were interconnected and interdependent. We were a cohesive group that had as a goal to help one another. We were able to cultivate trust with one another. For Daisy that took time, but Ellen said she felt free to openly discuss school and critical media literacy issues from the first meeting. What was important was that we created a supportive space that allowed us to collectively build on what we individually brought to the group. Such collaboration, collectivity, and interdependence were what allowed teachers to take risks and cross boundaries.

The group also served as a way for the teachers to rejuvenate their commitment to experimenting with their practice.

Discourse Excerpt 1. Group Meeting 7.

1. Keith: And that's the thing that coming—participating in this project is helping me do—because every time I think, "Oh, this is horrible, it's not working, they're not learning anything," I come back and talk to you guys....It's keeping me motivated....It feels like we should meet for four hours.
2. Eli: Good. Any time you feel like you want to stop, you're welcome to stop.
3. Keith: I mean to, I want to do it. I want to do it right.
4. Eli: There's no *right*. There's no *right*.
5. Keith: As close to my ideal as possible.

Even though Keith and the others were struggling with the new ideas they were trying out in their classrooms, coming and talking in the group helped them to see what students may have been learning that they had missed in the moment, or where there was room for tweaking and improving the ways in which they were leading the learning in their classrooms. Keith felt that the meetings kept him on track, made him try to change an idea before giving up on it completely, as he would have previously, and helped push him forward.

Another example of the ways in which we helped one another to keep trying occurred in Group Meeting 12 when Daisy offered some words of encouragement to Ellen: "There are sometimes that we try new things and the first time it doesn't work, but that is not a reason to just stop doing it completely. We just do a turn here and a turn there." Such examples of encouragement, or statements of renewed motivation, occurred throughout our meetings. The teachers cared about each other's success.

The power we developed to cross boundaries came from the group itself. It was the collaborative creation of a dialogic space where the teachers could talk in exploratory ways, bounce ideas off of the other group members and receive feedback. Those relationships required listening first, and leading second. They meant that we tied others' futures and ideas about the future in with our own as we took action towards that future through our collaboration. Our group changed through our realization of that power in returning again and again to talk with one another, build, and learn.

CML as Critical Deconstruction and Creative Production

In this section, we describe how CML emerged from our collaboration to encompass critical deconstruction and creative production. Different aspects of CML in teachers' classrooms were highlighted at different times, interacting with the texts we had to work with, the ways in which our actions and talk were integrated with our developing critical consciousness. Teachers' inquiries lasted different lengths of time, depending on what they felt was useful in their classrooms. They formulated questions, created curricula, collected and analyzed data, and eventually presented their experiences to their principal and other teachers in their school. Students' inquiries lasted for a curricular unit and were enacted differently in each class. They all presented their work to the school as part of a math, fine arts, and multimedia fair at the end of the school year. At the fair, student projects from the three teachers' classrooms were the only multimedia entries.

Our group talk and teachers' inquiries in their classrooms focused on media texts because we believed they were so much a part of students' lives. But we did not merely talk about students' consumption of texts. Even as we talked about the ways in which youth watched movies or listened to music, we foregrounded the ways in which youth actively engaged with and wanted to produce media texts. It was something that the teachers recognized easily through their daily interactions with students and that took Eli almost the whole year to realize.

Unpacking Youth Identity Engagement in Media

In an early meeting in October, we made an attempt to critically deconstruct media texts we found problematic. We discussed young people's exposure to violence and their desensitization to violence and sex, particularly the kinds found in horror films. Ellen and Daisy stated that "current" horror movies, such as those from the *A nightmare on Elm Street* (Shaye & Craven, 1984) series, were very different from the ones they grew up watching. Such movies, beginning with *A nightmare on Elm Street* (Shaye & Craven, 1984) or *Friday the 13th* (Cunningham, 1980), were much more graphic. What we talked about did not question normative perceptions of the ravages of media culture. Our talk was much like dominant media discourses about the harm popular culture could do to youth. Such evaluation of media culture and texts had led to the movie ratings system and parental advisory stickers on albums. Perhaps those references, to horror films already more than twenty years old, dated Daisy and Ellen, but what was important to Daisy was that students filled their own creative writing with violence and that they identified with the perpetrators of the violence and not the victims.

Discourse Excerpt 2. Group Meeting 2, October.
1. Daisy: You know what I think is the sad part? That they don't identify anymore with the victim. They identify with the murderer or the victimizer.
2. Eli: Why do you think that? Why?
3. Daisy: They don't want to be hurt.
4. Ellen: That's interesting.
5. Daisy: They don't want to be hurt. They don't want to be the victims anymore. They want to be the ones with the power. They want to be the ones in control. And if you ask them "Which one is your favorite character?" They're not going to tell you one of the good guys. They are going to tell you one of the bad guys. Cause that's the ones who seem to be the ones with the power. With control.

In some ways, much of the talk was reminiscent of other adults lamenting the negative influences of youth media culture. However, Daisy also articulated a nuanced view of young people's positionalities and their media interactions. She brought to the fore a different perspective about what young people might be thinking, how they might actively engage with media, and why they might be drawn to certain kinds of genres. In so doing, Daisy recognized the powerlessness that many young people felt and the ways in which media texts, be they video games or horror movies, provided outlets for young people to feel powerful.

Such a view required Daisy's active endeavor to understand what students might be going through—from their perspective—and viewed them, not as passive dummies, basking in the radioactive overglow of media sex and violence, but as people who actively constructed their responses to media based on their own life circumstances. That is, she argued that it was not the simple exposure to violence that made children empathize with violent characters, but the ways in which they accommodated their viewing of such violence into their own general perceived lack of power and the tactical outlets they saw for finding some powerful ground from which to act. It was Daisy's willingness to inquire with her students collaboratively, from their perspectives, that enabled such insights, and it was the group's own dialogical structure that enabled Daisy to share with and teach the rest of us.

Build and Destroy: Creating Critical Curriculum

As we continued throughout the year, the teachers decided that CML did not just include talking to students about media, but included providing opportunities for them to actively participate in the creation of texts. As we talked about how teachers' inquiries engaged concepts of power, including disrupting inequality, Ellen said, "There's also the concept of power—understanding how to use and manipulate the technology and the media is empowering" (Group Meeting 5, December). Knowledge is power, Ellen felt, and technical knowledge would allow students to be empowered to cross boundaries by being able participate in media culture in new ways. Yet, when we began talking about what a project that allowed students to manipulate technology and the media might look like, Ellen was still unsure how to proceed. She wanted to do a project that utilized her new computers, but also one in which students were able to pursue a topic of their choice. In the beginning of the conversation, she was thinking about addressing Internet safety issues with students, another dominant discourse about youth media participation in adult worlds (Herring, 2008). But that was where the group began, and much of our talk can be characterized as exploratory and sense making in the moment. In the following excerpt Ellen and Eli discussed creative production and critical deconstruction in her classroom project.

Discourse Excerpt 3. Group Meeting 5, December.
1. Ellen: I don't know. I was thinking if there was a blog about it then they could evaluate that. Or even like other teenagers' blogs or multimedia things, you know? "This is too revealing. I don't know if I'd put that up there about myself. This is interesting, this isn't. I learned something from…." I don't know, I'm still formulating.
2. Eli: Yeah…[very long pause]…so…I'm just trying to think what are the parameters that you set for kids in terms of what it is they're

choosing to do. I mean, I think this is always a constant tension, right, but what are the guidelines you set up for kids?

...

3. Ellen: Right. I would probably say, "Come up with a topic and it's subject to my approval." I'm pretty open-minded. You know, there might be a few things. I want to know where you're going to go with it.

4. Eli: I'm also thinking...about the subject...what it has to do with, for instance, racism in online sources.

5. Ellen: Right.

6. Eli: Or sexism in online sources or....

7. Ellen: So it could be a social problem. They could, if you want to, focus on a social problem. Like that's how I would frame something like that. I'd like you to think about a social problem that you could easily document in your community. Or something like that....There's a lot of things like the subway doesn't come out here, there's busses but...there's no book store, there's all kinds of social problems.

8. Eli: So looking at the community.

9. Ellen: There's poverty, there's housing issues, gentrification, but I didn't decide necessarily it was going to be a social problem, but that's one option if somebody wanted.

10. Eli: And so you're thinking you would use the media as a tool to investigate, right?

11. Ellen: Mmhmm.

12. Eli: What about the media as a content?

13. Ellen: The existing media. Yeah! They could do some research on that. They could find a couple of conflicting texts about things....It could be something about a current event though. Conflicting views of a current event. And that would be an easy way to do it. And they could still create a slide show and document different views of the same events, different interpretations of it.

Even though Ellen thought of students' manipulating technology and media texts and their choice in topics as empowering, she had not been thinking about how their projects might address inequity or oppression. At this point, Eli had been focusing less on students' empowerment through participation in the creation of media texts and more on addressing inequity in their communities, encouraging the teachers to think of CML as he did—the deconstruction of media's complicity in oppression through representation (line 4). Ellen seemed to be still thinking about media more as a tool for study and investigation, rather than media as a topic of critical analysis (line 1). Although media texts were objects of critical conversations for us in the group, they were not yet considered such in teachers' classroom conversations with students. Our talk in the group was exploratory; we were trying to understand what it was we were doing and what CML meant.

Through conversation and brainstorming, Ellen and Eli were able to include for her consideration an investigation of media content alongside the use of media as a tool for empowerment (line 12).

In the next meeting (Group Meeting 6, January), Ellen and Eli discussed including images of poverty as part of the "deconstruction" component in her inquiry. The idea was that students would critique photographs of poverty in a way that would help them to think about how to take photographs for their own photo essay projects about their communities. We both discussed how celebrities, such as Angelina Jolie and Brad Pitt, were romanticized by the media, and how attention to their personal, individual exploits, such as giving money to fund a hospital or adopting children from impoverished nations took people's attention from systemic causes of poverty such as unequal distribution of wealth. This conversation helped Ellen come up with a number of CML questions to discuss with her students, including, "Who produces media texts?" "Whose perspectives of poverty are portrayed?" "What ideologies do they serve?" "In whose interest are they?" and possible social action, "What do you do to fight poverty?" In this way, our discussion of Ellen's inquiry moved from empowerment through the use of media tools, such as cameras and digital imaging software, to asking specific questions that included critical deconstruction of media content as well as documenting and proposing possible ways to address social issues.

Critical Consumerism

As we worked out what CML meant in our group and in the classroom, the tension between deconstructing inequality in media representations and creating media productions also interacted with teachers' focus on the outcomes of what a CML perspective would provide for students—a tool for making choices. For example, in a group meeting from April, we all wrote and shared statements about what we thought CML was. Teachers did not address the topic of student production, rather, they focused on critical consumption. For instance, Ellen said she wanted students to become "critical consumers." Keith said CML was important so that, "we become aware of attempts to manipulate our thinking, our emotions, and our desires so that we can make choices, political choices, consumer choices." And Daisy said that CML was "a tool, or a way to become aware of how the media influences our lives and our decisions...the possible danger the media may bring...but also how it can be beneficial." That is, there was not the feeling, as in Group Meeting 2, that youth engagement with media culture led to negative consequences, but that it depended on the choices students made. The teachers hoped to be able to provide students with tools for those choices. However, such an orientation toward media, also emphasized the "critical consumer" who made "political" and "consumer" choices. There was not the sense that such choices were part of a cooperative effort to disrupt inequality, but that an informed critical perspective would benefit individuals who needed to make their own ways in the world. In a place where teachers felt their students had very little control over what happened in the world, such individual empowerment was much more salient for the teachers than the deconstruction of systemic inequities.

Boundary Crossing through Curriculum

Daisy's inquiry question was focused on how she could help her students, in a 7th–8th grade cross-categorical special education class, cross the emotional boundaries of negative self-perception so that they could cross the social and academic boundaries wrought from their placement in segregated special education classrooms. In an April group meeting, Daisy read aloud from an article (De Gourville, 2002) she had read as part of a jigsaw activity in which Eli had asked everyone to each read a different article from a book and share what we had learned: "When we begin to see our students as creators of culture, rather than as passive consumers, we develop not only a healthy respect for them as individuals having agency, but also apply the necessary insights into how they read the world" (p. 77). She then compared De Gourville's writing to what she was doing with her students,

> That is what we [her class] are working on. We are looking for the meaning according to them. For example, they did the silhouette [an activity in which they represented themselves by placing words and images within a silhouette of their torso] and they have an idea about how people, and how they, see themselves. Now we can talk about how we can help others see us as we see ourselves.

Daisy believed that when students had an understanding of how images were created, they could manipulate images of themselves to help others see them differently. In the excerpt from Daisy, the consumption and production of media were not separate paths but were intertwined in a single act of rewriting the world, recognizing boundaries and then breaching them.

Daisy's special education class was self-contained, but many of her students were placed in general education classes at different times throughout the day. In those classrooms and in the hallways they reported being constantly called names ("slow" and "dumb" were common), and left out of activities, purposely by other students and inadvertently by teachers. Her first curricular unit, developed in part before she joined the group, was on "Insiders and Outsiders" and focused on relationships between group memberships and individual identities. Daisy felt that her students, segregated into special education, in many ways were outsiders in school, their community, and even at home. She wanted her students to investigate identities and positionings in various locations: books, media texts such as magazines, and daily interactions in the world. She wanted them to be aware of social constructs and how dimensions of exclusion and inclusion were heavily embedded in their positioning. More than that, she wanted students to investigate themselves, and in doing so, change the way others perceived them.

Yesenia had just been placed in Daisy's classroom that year. Daisy reported that she had previously been one of the students in the general education classrooms who had made fun of her students. When she was placed in Daisy's class, Yesenia cried for two weeks, refusing to do anything,

> I had [Yesenia] telling me the other day, "Oh, I just want to be able to read!" But she was really frustrated and this was the first time she finally spoke. See last year she wasn't with me. She was in the regular ed. classroom and she wasn't working with the resource teacher very much. She was giving him a hard time. And this year, she accepts that…and she went the other way. The opposite way. And last year she used to make fun of my kids. Like the others, you know. Peer pressure. They're like, "Ahahaha, they're the dumb kids." What happened? She was put in my classroom. So, the thing is that I had her the first week in school crying. All day. Since she walked in, until she left. Crying. Her eyes were all swollen every single day for a week. And then, I just said, "Show me that you can do the work, I'll start having you go more and more to the regular classroom." And now, it's kind of funny because there are some times that she doesn't want to leave the room.
>
> *(Group Meeting January)*

In the beginning of the year, Yesenia hated the special education classroom and was heartbroken by her placement in it. She did not see it as a place where she could get help, but as punishment for failing 7th grade. As the year progressed and Daisy talked to Yesenia more, Yesenia opened up, at one point telling Daisy that she wanted to learn how to read. It was a breakthrough for both Yesenia and Daisy, and Daisy started an after-school "reading club" three days a week to help her three students most in need, including Yesenia.

What was worse for Yesenia, the girls who she thought were her friends rejected her because of her placement in Daisy's class. Yesenia, like many other students in the class, was so uncomfortable in the general education classes that she did not want to physically leave Daisy's room. Her transformation from September to January, from not wanting to be in the room to not wanting to leave it, showed what can happen to special education students once they become segregated based on imposed classifications of learning abilities. Their placement in special education served to make them outsiders even in their own school.

Although images of disability were not foregrounded in the beginning of her students' inquiries in the classroom, Daisy and her students did address issues of image, identity, and representation in the media, school, and her classroom. She was able to pursue questions about helping her students and others to see themselves in more "positive" and "productive" ways by looking at media images more generally, but also by having her students produce media texts.

As she thought more about it, Daisy said that the purpose of the inquiry was to help her students "be aware of their situations....I want them to be their own advocates, help them help themselves" (Group Meeting January). She thought it was important that students learn how to help themselves, because they could not count on anyone else to do it, especially as they moved to larger institutions.

> Not all of them but I still have some that see themselves as the way that others see them....And that's the sad part to me. That's what I want to change. And I want them to make that change so others change too.
>
> *(Group Meeting February)*

For Daisy, her children's development as people who viewed themselves positively and were able to take care of themselves was more important than any critical media literacy or academic literacy they might pick up in school. Media systems and texts for Daisy served as important sites, but there were many others as well, in which her students had to make choices about identity, representation, and membership.

Daisy's students then studied "Our America" which was based around a National Public Radio special produced by two young African American men, Lloyd and LeAlan, who reported on growing up in the Ida B. Wells public housing projects in Chicago (Jones & Newman, 1993). Daisy wanted to continue her own inquiry question, helping her students to change the way they saw themselves, as well as the way others saw them. Daisy and her students investigated their own lives, interviewed their parents, and wrote about themselves, finally producing a book, *Our Chicago* using Comic Life® software, which they shared with the school at the student Math, Fine Arts, and Multimedia Exposition (an end-of-the-year, school-wide celebration of student projects in the related subject areas).

As an example of one page of students' literacies produced in the book, we share a two-voice poem written by Yesenia that told others very clearly there were differences between how others perceived her and how she perceived herself. Additionally, Yesenia's Comic Life® page included different posed pictures, including one of her and and a friend with the dialogue bubble, "Look we are models" and one by herself, "I'm a rock star. Let's rock."

Table 14.1. Yesenia's Two-Voice Poem in Our Chicago book

How do people see me	*How do I see myself*
Please see me as shy, quiet but I don't let anyone take advantage of me.	I am a loner.
They see me as gothic.	I see myself as a rock star.
People see me as sweet.	I have my own style.
People see me very bossy.	I see myself happy.
People see me as serious.	I'm unique.

In her two-voice poem and on her multimedia page, Yesenia was able to "announce" how she saw herself, and let others see what Daisy called "the inside voice, the real ME" (Daisy, Introduction, *Our Chicago*). Through the book, students were able to name themselves, an about face from others constantly telling them they were "dumb," "slow," and "educably mentally retarded."

The same students who constantly called Daisy's students names in the hallway, the lunch room, and in their classes left notes in a comment book for the book's authors:

> "I think that this book is cool because it talks about our community and what students think."
>
> "I think this book is very interesting and I love the poses and pictures that yall took. This was a nice thing to look at."
>
> "It is cool and everyone was cool, even Moises. And is good book. Ok. Bye."
>
> *(Comment Book, May)*

Daisy's students *only* received positive responses from the students and staff of the school. As students who had been positioned at the bottom of the school hierarchy, they were now positioned as "cool" and what they had done was "cool" too. The students in Daisy's class had been able to reposition themselves—to cross boundaries—through their work. They had named their worlds and themselves and, as Yesenia showed in a two-voice poem that had been included in the book, she was not "shy" but "a loner" and not "gothic" but "a rock star." She had denounced the names others had given her and announced herself on her own terms. And these "announcings," "denouncings," and "namings" redefined for others who she and her classmates were and what they could do.

Daisy's research question asked how she could get her students to see themselves in more positive ways. In our last meeting, Ellen asked Daisy what her students said about how they had changed over the year. Daisy said that through their activities she saw some change in them little by little, at least some difference in the way that they were doing things and in the way they carried themselves. They were proud of themselves when they saw the reaction from other people about their book project, which carried over into other activities in school.

> They felt like "Wow! We can do this." It's just amazing how the first year I had them, their self-esteem was so low. "Oh, we can't do this. We can't do that. We're dumb. We're dumb." And the second year [they saw themselves differently].

Through their participation in critical media literacy that focused on critical deconstruction and creative production, students in Daisy's class were able to investigate multiple perspectives, connecting "identity, individuality, community, and society" (Daisy, Written Research Summary). They also used computer software in their projects. Access to digital technologies helped to motivate them and engage in the project. However, it was also the inclusion of "open discussions of topics geared towards…peers" that not only allowed students to "demonstrate their abilities and boost their self-esteem" but also demonstrate "to themselves and to other people that they possess many abilities that were hidden and surfaced throughout their projects" (Daisy, Written Summary, July). Through creative production of texts about themselves they repositioned themselves in the larger school community as knowers, doers, and cool.

Points for Learning: Humanizing Pedagogies

Essentially, the making of the group was guided by tensions inherent in negotiating our multiple goals. Eli, the university researcher, wanted teachers to pursue teaching through a critical media literacy lens and the teachers agreed, they had joined the group because of the focus on CML. Although we all agreed to study CML, what we each thought that meant informed our individual goals for what we wanted to accomplish, our different developmental paths for understanding, and our collaborative work together. Satisfying each of our goals together created driving, forward-looking tensions from which we had to negotiate and learn.

A central object of inquiry for critically-oriented education, such as we put forth in this chapter, involves recognizing, building on, and creating capacity for humanizing relationships in which teachers, students, and sociopolitical worlds are entailed in one another as they work towards liberation (Bartolomé, 1994; Gutierrez, 2008). Such humanizing relationships are collaborative and as such require a certain degree of intersubjectivity, or shared understanding, about what is to be accomplished. But shared understanding does not imply total agreement (Matusov, 1996). Tensions abound, within and between institutions and individuals, about what constitutes good teaching, good researching, good collegiality, and good critical media literacy.

In this chapter, we examined one tension in teachers' emerging conceptualizations of CML, that between critical deconstruction and creative production and some of the ways that tension allowed students to cross social, emotional, and academic boundaries. The tensions entailed participants' boundary crossing, characterized by the creation of new practices for teacher learning, in the form of our continued study together, and student participation in school as creators of representations, meanings, and new relationships.

The teachers all believed that student participation and their subsequent creative productions constituted the part of their work that most resembled CML. Students were engaged in the teachers' classes as they never had been before. For instance, a young woman in Keith's class who did not speak in a whole class discussion all year wanted to read the credits at the end of the presentation; a student in Ellen's class who had been suspended, but still wanted to complete the project, did so on her own time, and clandestinely returned to school during her suspension to hand in her project; and Daisy's students who re-created their identities through a book that showed others how they wished to be seen, all found new ways to participate in school.

For the most part, students were engaged with tools for media creation. They gave PowerPoint presentations, made slideshows, and produced multimodal books. These were genres of communication that other teachers have used in classrooms—although not these teachers and not these students. There is nothing inherently critical about any of these forms of communication. It might be argued that reading the names from a list or taking pictures of a neighborhood do not qualify as disrupting, questioning, or transforming inequitable realities and relationships; they might even reinscribe an inequitable or oppressive status quo. In terms of larger social relations, those activities were not critical. Decontextualized, just reading a list might be viewed as one of the least critical activities in education. From that perspective, we missed many opportunities to enact CML. But for the teachers, their students' participation in their classrooms, precipitated by teachers' involvement in the group, was a boundary crossing. It was a disruption of their students' relationships to school. Students' usual silence, whether it was the physical silence of not talking in the classroom, or not showing up to school, or the metaphorical silence of not completing assignments, was disrupted—and transformed into voice. By giving students choices and trusting them to make meaning, teachers allowed students to become agents of change in their own education in ways that they had not previously. As a result of the collaborative approaches to learning through which teachers began to trust the knowledge and knowledge-building capacities of their students, teachers developed different kinds of relationships with students. By changing their relationships and sharing decision-making power, teachers' classrooms were more critical (Pappas & Zecker, 2001).

In Keith's and in Ellen's class, students also tackled issues of oppression that operated in society. For instance, in Keith's class the students decided to include information on racism and discrimination so that they could tell the story of the Chicago African American Renaissance. They were critical producers of culture, selecting the context of injustice and racism against which to build the counter-stories of artists such as Chicago's Mahalia Jackson and Ray Charles. They also began to question representations of, and discourses about, immigration of Latinos to the United States and relationships between African American and Latino experiences in the United States. Students in Ellen's class focused on the physical environment of the neighborhood, such as litter, police surveillance cameras, and contrasts among conditions of various buildings, as well as the people in the neighborhood who represented to them aspects of social issues that were positive (e.g., people playing sports) and negative (e.g., alcohol and drug abuse).

The humanizing process of student and teacher relationships was also a crucial aspect of our developing CML. Such a relationship is part of the commitment of critical literacy. It is a critical act to think of one's students before anything else. It is a contrary act that disrupts dominant discourses of test scores as the ultimate measure of progress and not the students themselves or the conditions in which they live their lives. As we focus on each other as people, we can begin to understand the ways in which our conditions and practice shape us. As teachers, we can ask in what ways we put our students, our children, at the center of our curricula. But a child-centered curriculum is not humanizing simply because it focuses on individuals. It is humanizing because it connects individuals to larger cultural-historical systems with political and institutional relations of power. It is humanizing because it describes us as humans, as cultural beings involved in complex activities that provide us with differential access to resources. Within such activities we can ask why conditions for success are inequitable and we can do something about it. CML that pays attention to the participatory power of creative production is one such way to act.

Although Daisy foregrounded the individuality of her students, she nonetheless recognized the ways in which they were labeled special education by the school system, and the ways that such labeling separated and ghettoized them as second class citizens in their own school. She wanted her students to be advocates for themselves because she believed that the institutions and systems within which they had to live would not help them otherwise. An emphasis on production rather than deconstruction does not make her stance uncritical, but complicates and expands what it means to do critical literacy work in schools. Daisy's project was critical because her students made real change through the production of their book. Their peers found them cool. The principal cried when she read the book. Other teachers expressed surprise and were impressed at this simple act of literacy. Students' insertion in the public space of school, their own point of view on who they were, gave others the chance to see, in a public forum, what they were capable of, changed the way they were viewed by others, and thus they themselves more than anyone changed their relationships to the school, students, staff, and administration alike. They not only crossed boundaries, they moved them.

Finally, what the teachers pushed (and pulled) Eli to realize was that critical literacy, for their students, was about being able to participate in the world. Eli had begun with the idea that educators should include design as a part of critical literacy, but he was concerned with opening up spaces for deconstruction first. However, deconstruction is not what engaged students or their teachers. Students became engaged in the inquiry projects because they were able to create cultural texts. Through creative production students were able to voice themselves and what they valued. Shifting views of youth literacies requires a reconceptualization of youth culture from problematic to productive and youth as contributors to the cultural worlds of us all. Thus, rather than deconstruction leading production, critical literacy might work better the other way around. First, as educators, we should give young people the chance to show us what they can do. Then, we can ask them if they want to think about alternatives.

References

Alvermann, D. E. (2001). Effective literacy instruction for adolescents. *National Reading Conference white paper.* Retrieved March 23, 2004 from: http://www.nrconline.org/.

Alvermann, D. E., & Hagood, M. C. (2000). Critical media literacy: Research, theory, and practice in "New Times." *Journal of Educational Research, 93*(3).

Bartolomé, L. I. (1994). Beyond the methods fetish: Toward a humanizing pedagogy *Harvard Educational Review, 64*(2), 173–194.

Cunningham, S. S. (Producer/Director). (1980). *Friday the 13th.* [Motion Picture]. USA: Paramount Pictures.

De Gourville, R. E. (2002). Urban Black school identities views through popular media: Lessons in semiotic representation. In L. M. Semali (Ed.), *Transmediation in the classroom: A semiotic-based media literacy framework* (pp. 71–85). New York: Peter Lang.

Dolby, N., & Rizvi, F. (2007). *Youth moves: Identities and education in global perspective.* New York: Routledge.

Duncan-Andrade, J., & Morrell, E. (2008). *The art of critical pedagogy.* New York: Peter Lang.

Engeström, Y., Engeström, R., & Karkkainen, M. (1995). Polycontextuality and boundary crossing in expert cognition: Learning and problem solving in complex work activities, *Learning and Instruction, 5*(4), pp. 319–336.

Engeström, Y., & Sannino, A. (2010). Studies of expansive learning: Foundations, findings, and future challenges. *Educational Research Review, 5*, pp. 1–24.

Fecho, B. (2004). *Is this English? Race, language, and culture in the classroom.* New York: Teachers College Press.

Foucault, M. (1980). *Power/knowledge: Selected interviews and other writings 1972–1977.* New York: Pantheon.

Gutierrez, K. D. (2008). Developing a sociocritical literacy in the third space. *Reading Research Quarterly, 43*, 148–164.

Herring, S. C. (2008). Questioning the generational divide: Technological exoticism and adult constructions of online youth identity. In D. Buckingham (Ed.), *Youth, Identity, and Digital Media* (pp. 71–92). Cambridge, MA: MIT Press.

Jones, L., & Newman, L. (1993, May 18). Ghetto life 101. [Radio Documentary Program]. In D. Isay, L. Jones, & L. Newman (Producers), *Chicago matters.* Chicago: Chicago Public Radio.

Kellner, D., & Share, J. (2007). Critical media literacy, democracy, and the reconstruction of education. In D. Macedo & S. Steinberg (Eds.), *Media literacy: A reader* (pp. 193–205). New York: Peter Lang.

Lee, C. D. (2007). *The role of culture in learning academic literacies: Conducting our blooming in the midst of the whirlwind.* New York: Teachers College Press.

Matusov, E. (1996). Intersubjectivity without agreement. *Mind, Culture, and Activity, 3*, 25–45.

McCarthy, C., Giardina, M. D., Harewood, S. J., & Park, J-K. (2003). Contesting culture: Identity and curriculum dilemmas in the age of globalization, postcolonialsm, and multiplicity. *Harvard Educational Review, 73*, 449–465.

Morrell, E. (2004). *Becoming critical researchers: Literacy and empowerment for urban youth.* New York: Peter Lang.

Oja, S. N., & Smulyan, L. (1989). *Collaborative action research: A developmental approach.* New York: Falmer

Pappas, C. C. (2005). Making "collaboration" problematic in collaborative school-university research: Studying with urban teacher researchers to transform literacy curriculum genres. In J. Flood, S.B. Heath, & D. Lapp (Eds.), *Handbook of teaching on literacy through the communicative and visual arts* (2nd ed., pp. 215–231). New York: Simon and Schuster Macmillan.

Pappas, C. C., & Zecker, L. B. (2001). *Teacher inquiries in literacy teaching–learning: Learning to collaborate in elementary urban classrooms.* Mahwah, NJ: Lawrence Erlbaum Associates.

Rideout, V., Roberts, D. F., & Foehr, U. G. (2005). *Generation M: Media in the lives of 8–18 year olds.* Menlo Park, CA: Kaiser Family Foundation. Accessed September 9, 2007 at http://www.kff.org/entmedia/entmedia030905pkg.cfm.

Shaye, R. (Producer), & Craven, W. (Director). (1984). *A nightmare on Elm Street* [Motion Picture]. USA: New Line Cinema.

Wells, G. (1994). *Changing schools from within: Creating communities of inquiry.* Toronto: OISE.

Wells, G. (2001). The development of a community of inquirers. In G. Wells, (Ed.). *Action talk and text: Learning and teaching through inquiry* (pp. 1–22). New York: Teachers College Press.

Xu, S. H., Sawyer, R., & Zunich, L. (2005). *Trading cards to comic strips: Popular culture texts and literacy learning in grades K–8.* Newark, DE: International Reading Association.

15

MIDDLE SCHOOL TEACHERS' SUCCESSES AND CHALLENGES IN NAVIGATING WEB 2.0 TECHNOLOGIES IN A WEB 1.0 MIDDLE SCHOOL

Margaret C. Hagood

Ubiquitous media content and access to information has impacted the field of literacy and the kinds of content and methods of instruction that need to be included and taught in schools. Studies in recent years have shown how media uses, especially those related to social networking and online life, are central components of adolescents' literacies (Lenhart, Madden, MacGill, & Smith, 2007). Research in the areas of digital literacies, pop culture, features of Web 2.0 technologies, and participatory culture has brought awareness to educators' roles and responsibilities to design classroom contexts of meaningful literacies where students and teachers engage in collaborative learning that builds on their varied backgrounds and expertise (Alvermann, 2010; Bitz, 2010; Carrington & Robinson, 2009; Davies & Merchant, 2009; Gainer & Lapp, 2010; Guzzetti, Elliott, & Welsch, 2010; Hagood, 2009).

However, as with most current content, school curricula can't keep pace with the ever-moving and expanding access to digital media outside of school (Lankshear & Knobel, 2003). Nonetheless, many teachers are doing their parts to learn about new forms and uses of literacies, and schools are working to develop these literacies in meaningful and relevant ways despite lack of funding and infrastructure. In this chapter, I discuss how a group of middle school teachers in a yearlong professional development community explored digital technologies to affect their content knowledge and methods in their content area instruction.[1]

Relevant Research

Two areas of research inform this study. The first area, content, includes two subparts that address the expanded views of literacies: digital literacies and pop culture. The second area, sharing of content, includes both the ways that information is created and the portals for knowledge sharing in the forms of participatory culture and Web 2.0 technologies. These four subparts are briefly described below.

Digital Literacies

Digital literacies encompass the variety of texts that are read or composed multimodally.

> In multimodal composing and reading, ideas and concepts are represented with print texts, visual texts (photographs, videos, animations), audio texts (music, audio narration, sound effects), and even dramatic or other artistic performances (drama, dance, spoken word) .... [D]igital literacies [are] socially situated practices supported by skills, strategies, and stances that enable the representation and understanding of ideas using a range of modalities enabled by digital tools. Digitally literate people not only represent an idea by selecting modes and tools but also plan how to spatially and temporally juxtapose multimodal texts to best represent ideas. Digital literacies enable the bridging and complementing of traditional print literacies with other media.
>
> (O'Brien & Scharber, 2008, pp. 66–67)

Changes in broadband access in recent years have produced a convergence of old and new media content (Jenkins, 2008). Digital literacies are now integrally tied to forms of social interaction whereby users create their own content, share it with others, and use content to engage others' attention, conversation, and friendship in both face-to-face and online contexts. Adolescents' uses of digital literacies are seen in the amount of time they spend on social software such as MySpace and Facebook (Ito et al., 2010; Williams, 2009).

Pop Culture

Pop culture describes mass-generated texts that are enjoyed by large groups of people. They involve multiple modes of delivery, including linguistic, visual, aural, and performative (Hagood, Alvermann, & Heron-Hruby, 2010). Pop culture texts reveal how users' interests are tied to their constant negotiations of identities (Bitz, 2009; Gainer, 2008) and are related to the literacies they choose to use on a day-to-day basis (Vasudevan, 2006).

Participatory Culture

Participatory culture describes the ways users engage in digital literacies, predominantly with online media (Jenkins, 2006). Characteristics of a participatory culture include:

- relatively low barriers to artistic expression and civic engagement;

- strong support for producing and sharing one's creations;
- informal mentorship between those with more experience and novices;
- members who believe their contributions matter;
- members who share social connections and care about what others think of their creations.

Web 2.0 Technologies

The shifts on the Internet from a static Web 1.0 design to an collaborative Web 2.0 environment has changed the ways that people interact online (O'Reilly, 2005). There are four key features of Web 2.0 technologies (Davies & Merchant, 2009):

- Presence: Active online identities, profiles, avatars that regularly interact, and status updates help the user develop a sense of self across online spaces.
- Modification: Users can personalize online spaces, such as the design of a home page or the development of an online avatar, and have the capability to link one space to another.
- User-generated content: Users both generate and consume content rather than strictly receiving content from a site creator.
- Social participation: Users give and receive feedback through ratings, rankings, and commenting functions, which situates users as both performers and audience.

Adolescents spend the majority of their free time engaged in digital literacies that build on Web 2.0 features and participatory cultures that serve their immediate needs for just-in-time learning, such as in the writing of fan fiction (Black, 2008) and the drawing of *manga* (Bitz, 2009). For example, adolescents interested in Harry Potter might engage in fan fiction writing on a site like http://www.harrypotterfanfiction.com/ and become a member of a Harry Potter facebook page where they can participate in an online community with others who share similar interests.

Working With Digital Literacies in Professional Development

Nine middle school teachers (grades 6–8) volunteered to be a part of a yearlong professional development group to study the content of pop culture and digital technologies and to design classroom instruction to incorporate these areas into their content area instruction. The professional development group met bi-monthly for two-hour sessions at Chaho Middle School (all names are pseudonyms), where all of the teachers taught and met in one participant's, Anna's, classroom. Chaho is one of 13 middle schools in a medium-sized school district in the southeast.

I constructed the initial outline for the professional development course (PDC), and then tweaked it using the teachers' stated interests and feedback. The PDC included several components:

1. To expose teachers to content in four areas, including pop culture, digital literacies, Web 2.0 technologies, and participatory culture, and to study and reflect upon these areas in their own lives.
2. To explore areas of students' interests in these four areas.
3. To engage with digital technologies specifically unfamiliar to them, including hardware (such as flip cameras, computer and handheld tablets, mp3 players, ereaders, scribing pens/notebooks) and software/applications (such as video recording, tablet applications, websites, and Web 2.0 enabled applications on the Internet).
4. To develop and implement an inquiry project to connect their learning of these areas into their content area instruction.

The first half of the year focused on the teachers' exploration of the areas in their own lives and in their students' lives. The second half of the year involved the design and implementation of a project in their content area that connected these literacies to state-mandated content standards.

The content for the PDC included a variety of print and non-print materials: a primary text, *Bring it to class* (Hagood et al., 2010); supplemental scholarly articles; relevant current events and news articles, blogs, Youtube videos, and websites; a webinar on copyright law (Hobbs, 2010); a PBS Frontline documentary entitled *Digital nation: Life on the virtual frontier* (Rushkoff, 2010); echalk (the school district's Learning Management Software); and an online wiki (created through PBWorks) where the course content was housed and participants could network and share their work. Teachers were also given an array of digital technologies, and access to software and applications for their exploration and use.

Eight females and one male participated, and their teaching experiences ranged from first year to veteran (47 years). Content areas taught included English/language arts, health, math, reading intervention programs, social studies, and Spanish. One teacher taught special education. Two of the nine teachers had participated in a previous yearlong professional development course I taught related to new literacies/digital technologies content (Table 15.1).

Data were drawn from fieldnotes from PDC meetings, whole group and individual interviews, voice memo transcriptions of class meetings, email correspondence, artifacts from instructional practices (including videos, lesson plans, reflection activities), and the course wiki. Data were analyzed using inductive coding to collapse data, to identify patterns, and to create themes (Bogdan & Biklen, 1998). Themes were then deductively connected back to the data to develop connections to related theories (Dey, 1993).

Table 15.1 Participant descriptions

Name Number of years teaching Content area(s) & and grade level	Describe your knowledge of new/digital literacies before Professional Development Community	What is your current definition of new/digital literacies AND how do you use new/digital literacies in your classroom now?
Anna★ 47 Academy of Reading/ Math (Intervention program)	Before PD, definition of new literacies did not include anything digital or technical. Literacies to me meant anything in printed books, magazines, newspapers, etc.	Since PD, my vision of literacies has expanded exponentially to include the Internet, blogging, emailing, tweeting-- all forms of technology. I feel I have been enriched as an educator and in turn I have enriched my students' experiences while they are assigned to me.
Mariah 1 8th grade Social Studies-SC History	Strengths: Internet, applications on iPad, iPod, etc. Weaknesses: Implementing uses into classroom	My definition of new/digital literacies is anything that one reads or encounters in their day-to-day life that expands their knowledge. This can be electronically, culturally, or socially. I have had students use Flip cameras to document material (skits, songs) and used the videos for test review. I am working on having students go into their community to find "texts" that relate to our curriculum this year.
Maggie★ 13 Spanish 1st-8th grade Intro Spanish (quarterly)–7th grade World Cultures (SS)-6th grade	I was conversant in a number of literacies prior to my earliest new literacies professional development class (Tweets, Fb, texting). I developed an awareness of how these literacies were educational tools. I also learned the existence of things I was unaware of (Glogster, pbworks, etc.).	New literacies: ways to communicate/motivate others in any medium that may be a preference and/or interest. Generally, the 'new' involves digital or non-book/paper information. Can include non-writing but textually rich sources such as songs, drama, video, etc. I use it extensively-- if we lose power, I would still find ways to reach students in their 'literacies.' Eventually I would convert them to add 'old' literacies to their repertoires.
Kathy 5 Tier 3 Reading Interventions (6th, 7th, and 8th grade)	Navigating and using the Internet as a resource, know how to use iPod, digital camera, and have taken some Smartboard courses.	New literacies PD has definitely helped me realize that there are all sorts of ways to use technology in the classroom other than the basics (Internet, Smartboard, computer...). My students have truly enjoyed using the Flip camera as a learning tool, and I look forward to using more technology as it becomes available to me. I think next year I would like to implement ebooks, too.

Teacher	Self-rated expertise	Initial view	New/digital literacies view
Debbie 21 6th Grade Math/6th Honors Math	Expert–Computer/Technology Novice–Wikispace, iPad		New literacies can be anything textual, visual, that is read, spoke, or written. I use it a variety of ways in the classroom such as incorporating music in my warm ups. Students know the time is up because the song is over. Students use echalk and email to communicate. I send weekly notes via email.
Shelley# 6 8th grade ELA honors 8th grade ELA inclusion		I have always recognized the value of digital literacies; however, my mind set did not include them as a form of literacy, and I was overwhelmed with figuring out how to include them.	New literacy is using all forms (songs, movies, art, pictures, commercials, etc.) to bring literacy alive. I now have found ways to include all of these forms into my classroom.
Jerry# 3 8th English Inclusion 8th math inclusion 8th pullout resource		Before the start of the new/digital literacies PD, I was an eager beginner with this stuff. I enjoyed using the technologies, yet I was unaware of the ways to apply them in an educational setting.	New/digital literacies are "portals to another world," which allow teachers and students the ability to access, apply, and create a multifaceted text brouhaha.
Sheryl		I was like the kids. I thought that text was really only text messaging, and then everything else was a book. So, yeah, I now think of text as everything that we use to communicate.	I can use pop culture and digital literacies in most of my content about health. We have a lot of standards that connect media and healthy lifestyles, and I love pop culture, so it's really easy for me to include that in my lessons.
Kris 15 8th grade ELA		Email and navigating the web—pretty confident. I would learn what I needed to get by—as I go.	My view on text has really expanded to just about anything and I feel I have a better grasp on new media as well. I feel more comfortable experimenting with technology and have aquired some resources of where to look when I need help. A new world has opened up for me since this PD and I feel excited about embracing the future with these new literacies.

* Participated in Professional Development on new literacies in previous year.
# Team teachers.

Learning From Our Work in Professional Development

Balancing Act: Digital Literacies and Pop Culture

The PDC allowed teachers to explore their own views and uses of digital literacies and pop culture, and those of their students. Within their self-study they documented their own pop culture interests and their uses of digital texts, and they developed deeper understandings of the relevance of an array of print and nonprint texts in their lives and of the skills necessary to read, write, speak, listen, view, and design with digital literacies.

In just a few months, the teachers felt the shifts in their own knowledge building and experienced how digital literacies impacted their own lives. For example, when Deb, Maggie, and Kris (all with strong technology skills) explored the iPad and Kindle, they were surprised that the tools didn't come with manuals. The following exchange occurred at the beginning of a PDC meeting:

DEB: There are no directions! I plugged it in, thinking it would charge all night, and it would come up and everything would be wonderful in the technology world. And it didn't. It came up to that iTunes thing. So I brought it in and the kids looked at it and were like, I have an iPod at home, I'll show you how to do it. So by then four or five kids had come up and here it is. I know that it's all online [the directions], but I need a book. I need something that's hands on. I'm not into reading online; I have a hard time with that.

MAGGIE: Ditto on that. When you are at a certain age you need things in print. I like to have it in hand and be able to write notes in it. I know that you can highlight with Diigo and all of that, but it's the kinesthetic part of it that I want.

Several weeks later, I brought a copy of *iPad: The missing manual* (Biersdorfer, 2010) for their perusal and offered to buy copies of the text. None of them wanted it.

MAGGIE: I've watched my students with the Flip cameras. They didn't have a manual. I have begun to learn how my students learned. And what I have found is um, that for me to dive in and just fool around and try to figure out is a waste of my time. But that's just for me. Going to the iTunes website and watching the videos work. Going to the iTunes website and pulling up the written documentation, I don't have the patience to read that. But I, I learn a lot from the video, and then I do the kinesthetic. Actually do it and try it and go back and forth. Not everybody will learn that way, but I'm beginning to appreciate the variety of ways you can learn something, and this certainly is a literacy for me.

DEB: I agree.

MARGARET: Really?

ANNA: Mmhmm. You have to know your product. You have to know what it's capable of doing. You play with it a little bit, but you do have to have some instruction. Either a video or directions or something.

DEB: Well I just went on iTunes and from there I found lots of little video clips, and I'm trying to watch them and do them and I'm also thinking about how I can use it in my classroom. Playing around with it really helps.

ANNA: Or having the manual or good friend.

MARGARET: And that friendship part, that connection with somebody else?

KRIS: Makes a big difference, yes.

SHELLEY: Makes a big difference. Somebody that you can call and say, do you have this app? Or do you know of any free apps I could get? …

DEB: And [we] found a tutorial that that went through everything—kind of like the wiki space kind of thing. If you're having this problem then you should do this and took you through the whole video right there and said "okay well you should go, there's a reset button."

JERRY: And then think about all the literacies that are involved in trying to learn a new literacy.

MAGGIE: Right! And how quote unquote "new literacies," how technologies are so important now to learn anything new.

The teachers, who had been reading about the incorporation of multimodal texts (such as audio and visual texts) in digital literacies, saw this play out in their own work. They assumed that the digital tool should come with a printed text, a written manual that would tell them all that they would need to use the tool. However, they quickly learned that through their knowledge building of multimodal texts online, and through collaboration with others, they no longer needed (nor sought) a printed text to answer their questions. Their exploration of digital tools (the iPad and Kindle) impacted their developing digital literacies.

Other shifts in perceptions about digital tools and pop culture happened serendipitously as well. For instance, Shelley, who swore in September that she didn't want any tool on her cell phone beyond calling capabilities, "fell in love" in December with the Smartphone she received as a gift from her husband that gave her a suite of communicating tools, including texting and the Internet. And, after seeing the PBS Frontline video on virtual life, Maggie reported that listened to a radio story on NPR about a convention for folks who met through online dating. She marveled, "Wow! The world really has changed because I used to think that that [online dating sites] was for losers, and now I'm thinking that it's probably for winners!"

The teachers also implemented pop culture and digital tools in their classroom content area instruction, designing instruction that incorporated the tools in order to develop their students' digital literacies. Most often the inclusion of these texts related to two areas: (1) the melding of individual and collective action;

and (2) real world application of standards in students' lives. Building upon their understandings of collaborative knowledge building in a participatory culture, the teachers often took risks and tried out new tools without being fully familiar with them, knowing that students who were digital natives in the class would enjoy being more knowledgeable about them (Prensky, 2005).

Yet the teachers' uses of digital tools and pop culture were not without critique. They wondered how the changing faces of literacies might impair knowledge growth, about how much online time is too much, about how people will have to learn to choose to fill their time from the expanse of texts available through all forms of media (books and printed texts, visual texts, and audio texts), and about teaching all of the requisite skills of traditional literacies while also incorporating digital literacies and pop culture. They worried that it was all too much.

MAGGIE: And, you know, we change over time. Like we don't need the appendix any more [when reading a pdf]. We're in such a state of flux. That whatever is right today, is not going to be right tomorrow. And that nothing that we are learning from anybody sticks because we are learning so much. And not only that, but it will be proven wrong tomorrow. I'm sure people who created MAP [the district-approved testing] thought it was the cat's meow, but it has so many detractors now. What it was originally used for, what it's currently being used for, what might replace it and be better? And a week from now that will be different too.

JERRY: I think it all still requires work. You just have to be motivated to do work and that's the biggest challenge that we're seeing is that everything's at [students'] fingertips, but are they willing to push the button to figure it out? And so maybe not having to work as hard to gain the information is leading them to be crippled versus the muscles strengthened. You know, like the academic muscles strengthened versus, it's like academic atrophy.

ANNA: [Using digital tools] is also a faster way of doing things. I remember typing college papers on a typewriter. Of course, when erasable paper came out, it was a big thing! So, to make, I think it's so remarkable that you can write your text, make revisions, insert this and that. I think it's phenomenal! It gives [students] so many opportunities to really go above and beyond and do outstanding work, because everything is at their fingertips. It's easy to manipulate, easy to use, user-friendly.

SHELLEY: Well, at some point someone said everyone has to know how to build a fire. We can't just depend on doing this. But millions of us don't know how to build a fire. I mean isn't that progressing?

ANNA: I don't think it hurts for them to know both [how to use literacies with and without digital tools].

SHELLEY: I don't think it hurts either, but we have so much more knowledge that eventually some of those knowledges are going to be dropped.

Table 15.2 Teacher Uses of Digital Tools and Pop Culture in Content Area Instruction

Participant and content area taught	Examples of uses of digital literacies & pop culture in classrooms
Anna★ (Academy of Reading)	Uses of Photostory to create personal narratives to work on writing skills.
Mariah (Social Studies)	Making connections between reading visual images and understanding history.
Maggie★ (World Culture and Spanish I)	Student created digital stories using glogster (www.glogster.com). "These are look like Uno cards. But they're actually Spanish verbs…. These are great and connect to kids' interests in gaming, and games are a form of literacy…It's not an electronic one, but still it's a game."
Kathy (Reading Intervention)	Use of flip cameras for students to record their Spanish discussions and to critique them as whole class on the Smartboard. Reading *Bud not Buddy* on audio iPod to develop reading fluency. Producing digital storytelling using Flip cameras, Movie Maker, and Readers' Theatre to create synopsis of book.
Deb (Math)	Music to connect to math standards related to Roman Numerals; iPad apps to teach students importance of symmetry for three-dimensional designs.
Kris (ELA)	ereaders in classroom (Kindles, Nooks, iPads, smartphone apps) to teach students to highlight and to access and study popular quotes highlighted by others.
Shelley# (ELA)	"We have a Ban-on-books' week, so this week you can't put books on the SAT Spotter [daily exercise in class where students enter SAT words into collaborative Word doc to show connections to their lives]. Now, the students only put music, or TV, or a movie spot and show where they have heard used an SAT word in a different form."
Jerry# (Special Education ELA)	Quizlet (www.quizlet.com) for student study of and online class connections to SAT vocabulary words.
Sheryl (Health)	"I watch a lot of TV and listen to a lot of music. Its funny: media influences is a big part of health. It's in our standards and indicators, how does media influence with your health. I throw in pop culture references all the time, they say, "how do you know about that?" Like I'll talk about L'il Wayne or we'll talk about marijuana and how different, I guess the stigma or the social norms are, and they're always like, "How do you know who Little Wayne is?" "Are you serious, I'm ten years older than you." But, they're always surprised when I throw in things like that, and they like it, they're in to it. It perks their ears up a little bit…and I actually have to teach and how media influences children's perceptions. So I keep up with it. I mean, I like it anyway…For alcohol, for example, I take a list of as many songs that they can think of that have to do with alcohol, and they list a lot. We talk about, "well what does that mean?" How does that shape your ideas about the drug and like what to do?"

★ Participated in professional development on new literacies in previous year.
Team teaches.

This friendly banter about the melding of traditional and new literacies was woven throughout the professional development meetings. Teachers grappled with balancing it all: that, with progress and changes stemming from digital tools, other literacies would fall away.

Teachers also encountered infrastructure problems that made it difficult to use pop culture and digital literacies—such as the lack of wifi to connect to the Internet, bandwidth issues, FERPA laws, and the district filters that blocked particular sites. For example, one day Anna said, "To tell you how crazy we have gotten with privacy and with filters, one of the students saw my wallpaper [on my computer] and said, 'Is that New York?' and I said, 'No, that is Paris, and it's taken from the Eiffel Tower,' and he asked, 'What is the Eiffel Tower?' So I went on the Internet to get a picture of it, and the first website I went to, 'access denied'. How stupid is that!" The group spent some of their time in the PDC meetings reporting their concerns to Maggie (who was on a district-wide Technology Committee). She, in turn, was always quick to remind them that change, if at all, would come slowly.

But, rather than spend valuable time lamenting these hurdles *ad nauseum* and relinquishing their ideas fully, the teachers more often strategized during PDC to creatively circumvent the issues and to solve the problems themselves. For example, after Shelley expanded her definition of text beyond print, she began to include visual and nonprint texts, especially ones related to pop culture, in her ELA classes to illustrate real connections to content standards that addressed figurative language and vocabulary (especially words from the SAT list, which students often felt was disconnected from their daily lives). After the school server blocked several email attachments she sent to herself with such content, she began using her Flip camera to record television and movie clips at home and then connected the camera to her classroom computer to share these examples with students. She noted, "The way I'm using it [the Flip camera] is absolutely not what it's supposed to be used for! But these are examples that help my students see connections to their lives. So, it's worth it. The picture and sound aren't bad, other than me telling my kids [at home], 'Shhh! I'm recording.'"

Similarly, from Kris's explorations of ereaders, she decided to incorporate them into her ELA classroom. The school policy stated that cell phones had to either be turned off or housed in students' lockers; in other words, they had to be kept totally out of sight. Rather than mention that, she told students that they were allowed to bring any ereader device to the classroom. In this way, she navigated around the school policy, defining the technology (whatever that might be—as iPod, iPad, iTouch, Kindle, Nook, or cell phone) as an ereader.

Sharing Content: A Hybrid Approach

The PDC meetings were shaped by the collective group. During the meeting, participants fell into a routine that consistently followed this order: (1) sharing new content and digital tools that they had explored on their own; (2) explaining how students had responded to various content/assignments involving digital tools; (3) passing around student work samples of uses of digital literacies and pop culture; (4) reporting on successes and challenges of using various technologies both with students and in the school; and (5) brainstorming ideas related to issues raised by the group.

The teachers embraced a participatory culture, especially as it related to their work together in the PDC. They freely engaged in the discussions, shared ideas and gave feedback on implementation of digital tools and pop culture in content areas, provided mentorship to novices in the group (such as to Mariah, a first year teacher, and to Kathy, a late-comer to the PDC) in relation to expertise with technologies. Each member shared that not only did they want to come, but they needed to come to the PDC. One day Deb noted that when she wasn't feeling well a colleague recommended that she go home after school. She quickly responded, "No. I can't. I have [the PDC course] today. Others are counting on me to be there."

Related to Web 2.0 technologies, all of the participants used social software (such as facebook.com) to some degree in their own personal lives—in out-of-school contexts. As they learned of the characteristics of Web 2.0 features in the PDC, they built them into their projects with students (such as Mariah teaching students how to use glogster.com to create South Carolina (SC) history projects and how to comment on each others' work, and the group's forays with their students on quizlet.com to get them to compete with each other for improved vocabulary scores). But, somewhat surprising to me, they didn't fully realize the potential of Web 2.0 interface of the PDC wiki for a variety of reasons. The teachers often associated time on the PDC wiki as unnecessary work rather than as pleasure and preferred, and felt that they benefited more from, face-to-face contact.

It was common practice for teachers to come to the PDC with content to share with colleagues (new iPad apps, websites, uses for Flip cameras, etc.). In the meetings ideas were shared easily and folks had sincere interests in others' content and instruction. Folks regularly stayed after the allotted time so that they could pull up information on the LCD for everyone to see. One such example occurred during a meeting where participants were sharing their learning in small groups. Maggie had walked up to the computer and opened Microsoft Word and began demonstrating for Anna, Shelley, and Deb how to use the comments feature to give feedback on students' work. Soon, everyone in the room became interested in their discussion, dropped their own small group discussions, and joined in with those using the Smartboard to share tips about Microsoft Word. The demonstration (which lasted about 20 minutes) ultimately included bits of information from several folks, demonstrating how the comments and track changes features work and showing how to share the document in students' individual folders on echalk (the school's Learning Management Software). Everyone was elated about this information and brainstormed ways to use it in their own classroom work to become more efficient in their correspondence on student work, to solve a paper printing/copy budgetary issue, and to engage digital tools.

This group was consistently exuberant about content and equally good at and interested in problem solving how to share the content in their own courses. When I asked them about their interest in this topic, they responded:

JERRY: But it's just as engaging to be face-to-face and learn about a 1.0 sort of low-tech technology, Microsoft Word, that you've always used, but features of it that you're like, 'Wow, that could really open up my world!'

ANNA: Well, this [use of tracking and comments function] is a solution to a problem we've encountered and that is the budget and the paper and the copies. So this is another solution. It's been on our minds, "What are we going to do? How are we going to do it? How are we going to teach our classes?" And so this was a good solution for a lot of people.

MAGGIE: And, for all of these reasons, like working together, sharing content, doesn't that move it a little bit out of 1.0? I mean Microsoft Word, when you're doing that?

The teachers were quick to reinvent their understanding of a seemingly old "low tech" technology that didn't seem to have the features of 2.0 technologies with those of participatory culture where they could collaborate, produce, and share their creations.

On this particular day, I was surprised by how much information they had to share because I had seen little dialogue and posting onto the PDC wiki. I wondered aloud, comparing the differences I saw in the face-to-face interaction of collaboration and production of content compared to a rarely-used course wiki. The following dialogue took place:

JERRY: I just need human engagement. I struggle with the interface of [the course] wiki. I like to talk to people. I like to be engaged with another human. I like to, I have to be moving around…I mean, you're stuck behind the computer, it's like, "Aw man I can't get engaged." So I'm totally disengaged. And so I need to try to fix that because I know kids are, that's why I have trouble with kids being on the computer so much. I don't care that they're on it. I just don't understand how they're that engaged. I mean I'm, like I'd much rather just have a conversation with you than to be on Facebook.

MARGARET: K. What do others think?

ANNA: You know in the day-to-day course of things, the things that we do, do not seem very important. And you do them, and you just move on to the next thing. Like Maggie was sharing Quizlet with me and, and I had heard it before, and I had gone on there, but hadn't done anything. So I tried with my kids and they loved it. So, it was a spur of the moment thing. She said, "Look what I'm doing." So we shared it. But I think if we went that extra step and wrote it up [on the wiki] I think, "Well maybe they're already doing it and they have no interest in knowing that I'm doing it." You know?…The face-to-face interaction is nice 'cause then I can ask questions and get immediate responses. How does this work? How'd you do this? And what not.

MARIAH: For me, it's just the energy being around people or at least other adults and for a little while, like it makes you actually want to have a conversation.

MAGGIE: It's like responding to dated information. Which is different than the kids when they do the chat.…I feel that in the teaching profession we're at one hundred and fifty percent capacity.…So am I going to go on the wiki and write something later? No way. And so because it's not live, meaning in front of me at the time, which *this* [PDC] is live, I can say to myself, "I'll get to that eventually." But eventually very often doesn't happen because on my list of priorities the wiki is lower than the other things.

KATHY: Right.

KRIS: Well, and I'll piggy back on that because I have started putting things on the wiki but that's only because Sally [clinical practice intern] has been teaching so I had that time to kind of go that extra step, and I'm thinking, "Oh, maybe that will be nice to share with everybody. I think I'll do that" because I have 15 extra minutes that I can sit and do that. But before, yea, I felt the exact same way.

MAGGIE: But I think our kids probably would. They're used to communicating that way. I mean, they can be standing two feet from each other and text each other. I mean that's, it's all about the, this verbiage going back and forth and um and I guess that separates us from that generation. We don't view it in the same way.

MARIAH: Yea.

DEB: I'll piggy back on that. I think that I agree with all of those things. I think that if I want to talk to Jerry I don't have to log in and go to a site and then type something in it and say, "Hey Jerry. How are you doing?" I can look him in the face and say, "Hey Jerry. How are you doing?" And it's that immediate response. And often times as teachers we do whatever is happening at the moment and time, and that's what we focus on. And so we all came in here we were focusing on one thing at a time and what was going on with each other's personal things. And so we became engaged in what was happening in that moment [the tools of Microsoft Word].

SHELLEY: It takes me a lot longer to do it [to post on the wiki] 'cause I'm much more critical of myself in print than I am speaking. I call way more parents than I email. Because when I email it I'm evaluating how are they going to take each word? Do they do that sentence? Did I say that? I'll take forever

writing an email. I'll pick up on the phone and talk to them. I would much
rather talk to them in person 'cause I can hear how they're taking it. I can
change it. I don't have to anticipate are they going to take it this way or take
it that way. I analyze it to death. The same thing with the wiki. I'm looking
at it, is that how, is that going to sound like I do too much? Does that sound
like I don't do enough?

KATHY: I do the same thing.

SHERYL: Yes, me too. I overanalyze stuff in print.

MAGGIE: And I because I'm not in industry anymore and I'm back in teaching,
I suspect that if I were in a work group and one of us worked at home and
the other one worked some place else, I would do a lot more of that immediate feedback back and forth where we're commenting on documents. Um,
and I don't, I guess I don't feel the need to do it here.

To the teachers, Web 2.0 technologies in the uses of a shared wiki space for the
PDC seemed superfluous and perhaps an unnecessary add-on to their already
busy lives and schedules. They found this digital tool difficult to connect to based
upon their perceptions of how it worked. It wasn't live (as in others weren't on
it simultaneously), and so the responses were not immediate for them. It didn't
give them the personal interaction that they desired from a professional development group, and they were critical of themselves in their communications (Is the
content of interest to others? Did I spell it correctly?). Although they used Web
2.0 tools such as quizlet.com and glogster.com with their students, they preferred
meeting and the participatory culture they created over the online community of
the course wiki.

Yet, they utilized the characteristics of Web 2.0 features in a face-to-face
format. They were concerned with building and shaping their identities as teachers interested in content learning and in using pop culture and digital literacies to
engage students. At all the PDC meetings, they were productive and consistently
collaborative. During sessions the teachers shared content, modified their thinking, and acted as both producers of content and as audience for others. Their
rationale for their sharing face-to-face rather than later in an online format
stemmed predominantly from lack of time. As Anna noted, "an extra step"
detracted from the idea of using just-in-time learning, which was more productive for them in a PDC face-to-face context. Deb noted that, as teachers, "we do
whatever is happening at the moment and time and that's what we focus on."

Making Headway

What began in the PDC as a desire to share information to become better teachers of course content morphed into a meeting place where teachers developed a
participatory culture whereby they envisioned uses of digital tools and pop culture that worked for them personally and professionally—in their schools and in

their classrooms. The PDC became much more than a course on information technology. Instead teachers became seekers of knowledge rather than technology implementers.

Judith Langer (2011) explained that knowledge construction constitutes more than a litany of facts about a topic. "It includes understanding how these facts interrelate with one another, how they interrelate with other knowledge, and what belongs (as well as what doesn't belong) in that construct" (p. 1). She described several characteristics of knowledge:

- crafted and honed;
- includes an understanding of social and disciplinary conventions;
- relational;
- requires active and probing mind;
- requires background of context, content, and conventions of a domain;
- goes beyond information and is much deeper;
- knowledge development moves beyond receiving to ownership through a process of "focusing, narrowing, searching, considering, questioning, judging, tuning, and rejecting" (p. 2).

The PDC meetings provided a space for teachers to dig deep and to develop their knowledge about digital tools and pop culture. In this space the teachers, as learners, confidently took risks to explore their own ideas and to envision how to implement them in their classrooms. The bi-monthly meeting space was much more central to knowledge building than was the wiki space. And although a wiki provides features that allow for the construction of knowledge, the course wiki wasn't as captivating as face-to-face interactions.

Web 1.5? Baby Steps Toward Web 2.0

It is interesting to consider how the PDC wiki didn't flourish as expected. All the conditions were ripe for such work. The teachers were building knowledge, they supported one another, they were dedicated learners, they were familiar with digital tools, and they had information to share. They even designed projects for students that included Web 2.0 characteristics. Yet, they walked with slight trepidation around the Web 2.0 components in their work with one another. Maggie clearly articulated the dilemma:

> It's important to put it in context [our inconsistent use of the wiki]. You can't do everything at once. I think it [digital literacies and the teachers' hybrid uses of Web 1.0 and 2.0 tools] steps nicely 'cause what you do is baby steps in the classroom. It's going to be a long time before we straighten out all the separate regulations and protecting kids with Web 2.0 technologies in the classroom.

Maggie's stance isn't one of defeat, but rather a realistic approach to categorizing information and to making changes to the sharing of content in classroom instruction. Working within these constraints, the teachers incorporated the following instructional practices in their implementation of digital literacies and pop culture:

1. Capitalize on students' own interests and their status as digital natives.
2. Instruction founded on participatory culture where students created projects focused on collaboration, the melding of traditional and digital literacies, mentorship of novices and experts, and a sharing of those projects in a nurturing and supportive environment.
3. Small strides to bridge Web 1.0 and 2.0 features in assignments.

Throughout the PDC teachers referenced the changes in literacy they encountered both in their personal lives and with students. And they connected these changes with new forms of teaching and learning, which addressed both old and new media and traditional and new literacies. As Jerry explained, and the other teachers agreed, "Content needs to be shared not delivered."

Working in this collaborative model, participants became produsers as they focused on just-in-time learning (Bruns, 2007). Produsers are informed folks who realize that an industrial model of content delivery—where a person produces something (a concept, an idea, a resource) and others consume it—no longer works. Produsers understand that customizability and individualisability are crucial for keeping pace with the amounts of content available. Thus, for produsers, content—usually in the form of ideas—"takes place in a collaborative, participatory environment which breaks down the boundaries between producers and consumers and instead enables all participants to be users as well as producers of information and knowledge" (p. 3). Similar to a participatory culture, produsage is collaborative and continuous, but produsage emphasizes the extension of existing content knowledge for improvement on an as-needed basis.

Produsers realize that both information and knowledge are important and that new iterations and revisions of existing content result in temporary artifacts. This idea begins to address teachers' concern about the ever-changing state of literacy. Thus, instead of trying to be proficient with all aspects of a literacy, produsers become knowledgeable about how to use them and join in communities, such as a PDC, to explore collaborative practices of engagement, finding and using content that is just-in-time and relevant to their needs and desires at a particular moment. This social participation allows the produsers to align, identify, and be identified with other like-minded folks and projects.

Moving On

The successes and challenges of this PDC stem from the option extended to teachers to participate. As volunteers, the participants had a vested interest in the topics covered. They built a community where they aligned themselves and identified with other like-minded folks and projects. They found having a stake in the collaborative learning process meaningful because it related to their own learning goals and to their students' identified needs.

Often, descriptions of work with digital tools as ICTs (Information and Communication Technologies) strip away components that lead to the formation of participatory culture and to the development of produsers. Rather than focus solely on the informational side of ICTs—the facts, the how tos—it is just as crucial and productive for teachers to perceive digital literacies as both informational and knowledge technologies.

Jenkins (2006) noted that "Media change is affecting every aspect of our contemporary experience, and as a consequence, every school discipline needs to take responsibility for helping students to master the skills and knowledge they need to function in a hypermediated environment" (p. 57). To be sure, Jenkins's stance is a means to reconceptualizing adolescents' literacies. However, before schools can provide this instruction for students, teachers need to have opportunities to dig deeply into content that is of interest to them and to become knowledgeable users of the content. Mariah and Shelley explained this point well one day, when leaving at the end of a productive PDC meeting:

MARIAH: What's frustrating to me as a teacher is that I spend so much time doing all the paperwork stuff and being in the classroom that I don't get this time with other adults when we're bouncing ideas back and forth, and this is when I really learn how to do it better. But this time isn't built into our schedule.
SHELLEY: It should be. It should be! I mean this is the part that makes teaching fun. You know, when you hear those ideas and you apply them. But there's no time for this [self-chosen professional development].

The nine educators in this study are exemplars of produsers who have incorporated individual accountability and collaboration across content areas in an educational setting to benefit both teachers and students. Teachers across subject areas readily incorporated digital tools and pop culture and incorporated digital literacies into their content area instruction, enlivening the content and making relevant the subject matter. At this point, regulatory issues at the school and district level continue to keep teachers from moving into fully integrated Web 2.0 worlds. If schools are to be the places where students are going to be prepared for the future, teachers need the technological support (both in infrastructure and formal or informal professional development) that is just-in-time to their own stated needs and desires to ensure that it happens.

And, while formalized Professional Development Communities are immensely helpful, they aren't always readily available to teachers as part of the school day or academic year. Teachers interested in incorporating digital technologies into their instruction need only to consider the characteristics of participatory culture and implement them in either a face-to-face or online context with likeminded learners. Collaboration, creativity, and mentorship can be found within communities of teachers to assist in the development of ideas so that teachers can bring together traditional and digital literacies in their classroom instruction. But teachers need also to consider how students can be valuable members of such a learning community. Within such collaboration, teachers and students can work together to develop a participatory culture to develop digital literacies that are mutually beneficial and rewarding.

Note

1   This research is part of a five-year grant that offers professional development in digital/ new literacies with middle school teachers funded by the South Carolina Commission of Higher Education.

References

Alvermann, D. E. (Ed.). (2010). *Adolescents' online literacies: Connecting classrooms, digital media, and popular culture.* New York: Teachers College Press.

Biersdorfer, J. (2010). *iPad: The missing manual.* Sebastopol, CA: O'Reilly Media.

Bitz, M. (2010). *When commas meet Kryptonite: Classroom lessons from the Comic Book Project.* New York: Teachers College Press.

Bitz, M. (2009). *Manga high: Literacy, identity, and coming of age in an urban high school.* Cambridge, MA: Harvard University Press.

Black, R. (2008). *Adolescents and online fan fiction.* New York: Peter Lang.

Bogdan, R., & Biklen, S. (1998). *Qualitative research for education: An introduction to theory and practice.* Needham Heights, Massachusetts: Allyn and Bacon.

Bruns, A. (2007). *Produsage: Towards a broader framework for user-led content creation.* Paper presented at Creativity & Cognition Conference, Washington D.C., USA, June 13–15, 2007.

Carrington, V., & Robinson, M. (Ed.). (2009). *Digital literacies: Social learning and classroom practices.* Los Angeles: Sage.

Davies, J., & Merchant, G. (2009). *Web 2.0 for schools: Learning and social participation.* New York: Peter Lang.

Dey, I. (1993). *Qualitative data analysis: A user friendly guide for social scientists.* London: Routledge.

Gainer, J., & Lapp, D. (2010). *Literacy remix: Bridging adolescents' in and out of school literacies.* Newark, NJ: International Reading Association.

Gainer, J. S. (2008). Who is DeAndre?: Tapping the power of popular culture in literacy learning. *Voices From Middle School, 16*(1), 23–30.

Guzzetti, B., Elliot, K., & Welsch, D. (2010). *DIY Media in the classroom: New literacies across content areas.* New York: Teachers College Press.

Hagood, M. C., Alvermann, D. E., & Heron-Hruby, A. (2010). *Bring it to class: Unpacking pop culture in literacy learning.* New York: Teachers College Press.

Hagood, M. C. (Ed.). (2009). *New literacies practices: Designing literacy learning.* New York: Peter Lang.

Hobbs, R. (2010, Nov. 10). *Copyright clarity: Can my students use images in their writing?* Retrieved July 19, 2011 from www.mediaeducationlab.com/copyright-clarity-can-my-students-use-images-their-writing.

Ito, M., Baumer, S., Bittanti, M., Boyd, D., Cody, R., Herr-Stephenson, B., et al. (2010). *Hanging around, and geeking out: Kids living and learning with new media.* Cambridge, MA: MIT Press.

Jenkins, H. (2008). *Convergence culture: Where old and new media collide.* New York: NYU Press.

Jenkins, H. (2006). *Confronting the challenges of participatory culture: Media education for the 21st century.* Chicago: The MacArthur Foundation.

Langer, J. (2011). *Envisioning knowledge: Building literacy in the academic disciplines.* New York: Teachers College Press.

Lankshear, C., & Knobel, M. (2003). *New literacies: Changing knowledge and classroom learning.* Buckingham: Open University Press.

Lenhart, A., Madden, M., MacGill, A., & Smith, A. (2007). *Teens and social media.* Washington, D.C.: Pew Internet & American Life Project.

O'Brien, D., & Scharber, C. (2008). Digital literacies go to school: Potholes and possibilities. *Journal of Adolescent & Adult Literacy, 52*(1), 66–68.

O'Reilly, T. (2005). *What Is Web 2.0? Design patterns and business models for the next generation of software.* Retrieved March 4, 2011, from http://oreilly.com/lpt/a/6228

Prensky, M. (2005/2006) Listen to the natives. *Educational Leadership, 63* (4), 8–13.

Rushkoff, D. (2010). *Digital nation: Life on the virtual frontier.* Retrieved March 4, 2011 from www.pbs.org/wgbh/pages/frontline/digitalnation/view/.

Vasudevan, L. (2006). Looking for angels: Knowing adolescents by engaging with their multimodal literacy practices. *Journal of Adolescent & Adult Literacy, 50*(4), 252–256.

Williams, B. T. (2009). *Shimmering literacies: Popular culture and reading and writing online.* New York: Peter Lang.

16

TEACHER RESPONSE

Professional Development to Reconceptualize Literacy Instruction

Maryanne Desmond Barrett and Elizabeth G. Mascia

We, middle school English language arts teaching colleagues Maryanne and Liz, met to discuss *Part IV: Changing Teachers, Teaching Changes*. We were asked to respond as a contribution to the new edition of *Reconceptualizing the Literacies in Adolescents' Lives*. The text that follows attempts to capture our most salient impressions of these three chapters. We responded to the articles in light of our own professional journeys. Because we are close colleagues, our journeys sometimes intersect; at other times, they diverge. Nevertheless, as we talked, we were of one mind about the factors that we deem important for the effective implementation of professional development in today's educational climate.

MARYANNE AND LIZ: The chapters in *Changing Teachers, Teaching Changes* underscore the transformative role professional development can play in supporting teachers as they explore ways to meet their students'—and their own—literacy learning needs and demands. But for all those involved in professional development, it is necessary to identify the conditions that render it effective. This is especially true in this time of budgetary constraints when professional development funds have been reduced or eliminated and teachers must find their own ways to develop their understandings and practice. From our experiences and from the chapters in this section, we can identify components that successful professional development seems to require. Four essential conditions emerge: Professional development must be rooted in student need; it must be afforded sufficient time to be realized and sustained; it demands opportunities for collaboration; it ultimately relies upon systemic support. Absent any of these conditions, professional development falters.

LIZ: Taken together, the three chapters demonstrate that successful professional development must have its genesis in student need. In each case, teachers identified what was necessary for student achievement and worked to supply what was wanting in their practice. The author–researchers all provided accounts of pedagogical changes made to meet student needs. Tatum reported on two teachers bringing to their students, African-American youth in an impoverished, low-achieving school, culturally responsive young adult literature that honored their identities and thereby fostered their literacy development. Hagood provided an account of nine middle school teachers educating themselves in new technologies to bridge the gap between their students' out-of-school and in-school media uses. Tucker-Raymond and three middle school practitioners incorporated Critical Media Literacy (CML) into instructional planning, individualizing the theory and its implementation for their students' growth.

MARYANNE: Liz, quality and successful professional development only exists due to student need. Student progress is contingent upon our pedagogies, methods and strategies used to move students from point A to point B. As students' enthusiasms and needs change over time, we must recognize and reflect upon changing ourselves. How does this occur? By reconceptualizing our own identities as educators through recognition of student need, reflection, and staying educable. For example, the teachers in Hagood's study sensed their knowledge shifting as they studied the ways they experienced digital literacies in their own lives. This shift enabled participants to obtain a deeper understanding of the relevance, function, and skills necessary for digital illiteracies. In turn, this knowledge transferred into the participants' professional lives as digital illiteracies came to play a larger role in the classroom setting. It is important to remember that professional development is not all about us.

LIZ: I certainly read the articles in light of the myriad professional development experiences I have had during my teaching career, first as a high school English teacher, then as a Grade 8 language arts teacher, and, now as a literacy specialist working with Grade 7 and Grade 8 students who struggle to meet state and local reading and writing standards. I chose many of the experiences; others were mandated. Many were easily forgotten; a few provoked lasting, substantive changes in my understandings and practice, and, therefore, in my students' learning opportunities. The latter were, in other words, occasions for true *reconceptualizations*, similar, perhaps, to the experiences of the teachers in Hagood, Tatum, and Tucker-Raymond and colleagues' studies.

What was it that distinguished these experiences, one from another? For me, the answer is clear. The impetus for any of the professional development that produced significant change in my practice was student need. In each case, I was dissatisfied with my students' engagement and achievement, knew we had arrived at a point where I had to begin to think differently about their learning and my teaching, and, therefore, sought answers. On the other hand, those professional development experiences that left my thinking and practice untouched were, however intellectually worthy, unrelated at the time to the immediate wants, needs, or enthusiasms of my students. Invariably, they were the enthusiasms of someone rather distant from my classroom, perhaps an administrator or supervisor.

I can pinpoint sharp turns in my practice that all started with the terrible, stomach-churning realizations that things were not as they should be in my classroom and something had to change. And so in a lower track sophomore English class, we abandoned the mandated anthology for a reading and writing workshop when it was clear that the reading selections were leaving my students less than impressed or excited. Similarly, my middle school students and I eschewed whole- class novels and formed books clubs after a 7th grader confessed one Monday morning, " I accidentally finished it [the class novel] over the weekend"; everyone reading the same novel at the same lock-step pace was not working! The groups got even better when students suggested that they, not just I, suggest titles we might read. In my small intervention groups, we learned we had to identify comprehension obstacles in specific genres and develop strategies for getting over or around them. From such experiences stems my belief that student needs and enthusiasms are the foundation for significant change in teacher thinking and practice.

MARYANNE: Liz, on the other hand, how often have we experienced professional development that seemed distant from what was happening in our classroom! I can pinpoint the stand still moments in my practice where an outsider infiltrated the school for a day promising to share the magic trick that would solve all of our classroom needs. While these so called "Professional Development" days were a change of pace to the school week, the knowledge I took away had little to no impact on my practice. The foundation of this type of professional development was not built upon students needs. It is important to recognize that without authentic purpose for professional development, teachers will lack motivation, participation and accountability. Inevitably a professional development experience can neglect and hinder student progress.

LIZ: I tend to believe that the participants in the studies conducted by Tatum, Hagood, and Tucker-Raymond and colleagues felt similarly about change for their students and, therefore, volunteered for the professional development opportunities the researchers proffered. Participants in Tatum's study found themselves in perhaps the most compelling situation. Their students' learning and community environments were said to be hostile to academic achievement and the promise of a better future. The culturally responsive curriculum alternative offered by Tatum broke with previous approaches.

Its implementation succeeded in improving students' reading test scores and literacy behaviors. The teachers in Hagood's study faced a question that intrigues and, not infrequently, bewilders most teachers today. How might the enthusiasm and competence students have with out-of-school digital literacies be harnessed for in-school purposes? Each participant moved forward in her knowledge and instructional implementation of new literacy tools. Participants in Tucker-Raymond and colleagues' study kept their students' needs at the center of their professional development effort in a somewhat different way. In joining the study, they seemed less moved by a specific student need than by a desire to grow as practitioners. Once the inquiry was underway, however, student need took over as the teachers resisted Eli's definition of CML and conceptualized and implemented it in ways they deemed would benefit their students most.

MARYANNE: We agree the foundation of effective professional development lies in the needs of our students, but we both know in order to keep momentum and sustain growth other conditions are necessary. The circumstances in the three articles presented a unique opportunity because resources including systemic support, time and collaboration were readily available. Systemic support or the school district temporarily allowed researchers from a university to work with willing educators for a professional development opportunity. The researcher provided a framework where time, collaboration and resources were provided to the teachers over a specified period. Every educator does not have this good fortune. According to Hagood, in order to support reconceptualizing adolescent's illiteracies, teachers need opportunities to become knowledgeable of content. To dig deeply, educators need resources, time and collaboration. In reality, these factors aren't always available.

LIZ: Maryanne, you are right in seeing the circumstances of the professional development experiences described in the three chapters as rare. More common seems to be the situation of teachers piecing together their own professional growth. Of course, there can be an up side to this situation. If teachers can accept the challenge of initiating and managing their own professional development as you have, there is a strong chance that their efforts will be focused on issues of immediate significance to their students.

MARYANNE: Yes, Liz. The case you described of the teacher piecing together his or her own professional development sounds like my situation. My journey began from the difficulty of ignoring students' expertise and appetite for Web 2.0 tools in the classroom. Theirs was the expertise that Hagood wanted the teachers in her study to exploit for student learning. Many online experiences offer students a space for their voice to be heard where they fell mute in the classroom. With this new online space comes a responsibility to be respectful citizens that many students neglect or are naïve to. An obvious student need for an online space to build community, cultivate an individual voice, and learn the rules of being a citizen of this online community formed in my 7th grade classroom. During the 2010–2011 school year I participated in a year-long professional growth plan to set up this online community through the use of a blog. Originally, I wanted to create a blog to share and model reading responses. The blog transformed into an interactive reading journal per the student's request. A blog that was teacher centered soon transformed into a student driven community revolving around the conversation of text.

At the onset of my journey I was equipped with the basic resources. Previous experience with creating a blog provided me with knowledge to build on. Access to computers and the Internet enabled the use of the blog during the school day for the students and I. My journey took a detour when I found myself struggling with technological issues. My time was spent surfing the Internet for solutions. Unlike the participants in Hagood, Tatum and Tucker-Raymond's study, I did not have the resources or an expert at my disposal. If this were the case, I could have dedicated more time to restructuring the use of the blog in the classroom and better meet the needs of my students. Instead, much of my time was spent searching for the answers to my questions.

Lack of resources was not the only roadblock I faced. Questions and issues about blogging in the classroom seemed to dominate my journey. When the Internet didn't have answers, I asked colleagues for advice. However, their knowledge and experience with blogging were on a different level. The students were the ones I found myself collaborating with. This strengthened our classroom community, but I wasn't receiving the professional knowledge, opinions or exchange I was seeking. I soon found myself stranded alone on my own "blogging" island with no one to talk to.

LIZ: Maryanne, I can imagine how difficult this experience must have been for you, but you were absolutely on the right track. Your account includes a sentence that shines for me. You write of the blog giving a voice to students who had hitherto been "mute" in your classroom community. Multiple means for our students to construct and share meanings for texts are critically important. Alone, you went exactly where Hagood hoped to journey with her study group. We just have to remember that the blog may not be every student's choice, but an option that responds to many students' enthusiasm for digital communication.

MARYANNE: I quickly learned that time was not always on my side during this professional development voyage. A mandatory meeting time was not set aside, so free time presented opportunity to focus on the blog. However, once time was restricted, my focus deviated elsewhere leaving the blog untouched until time was available again. The lack of accountability hurt the progression of a growing online classroom community and my own professional development. This year-long commitment is not sufficient to dig as deeply as needed. In an effort to continue to dig and plant the seeds of blogging in the classroom, I plan on continuing the professional growth plan another year. I, along with two other educators, will continue to work towards fine-tuning the blog in the classroom.

As educators, we need to understand the hurdles of a typical professional development opportunity and be equipped to handle the roadblocks along the way. Reconceptualizing students' literacies begins with the educator's journey in understanding student needs, finding the resources available to dig deep within the content, collaborating with others and setting aside time to sustain the development needed to continue on.

LIZ: Maryanne, your experience illustrates the components we agree are necessary for lasting professional development. You acknowledged the time necessary to bring real change to one's practice and, thereby, to one's students. You reached out to others to accompany you on your journey, took advantage of a professional growth structure that the school offered, and persevered despite disappointments. It makes me wonder what happened with the teachers in the three studies. After the studies, were they able to sustain and build upon their reconceptualizations?

MARYANNE AND LIZ: We all continuously tweak our practices, adding a strategy, experimenting with a technique or activity, refreshing our tried-and-true texts. However, these modifications are not true change. Real change involves the deep reconceptualizations that truly alter our understandings and practice. This is hard, unsettling work. There seems but one motivation sufficiently strong to move us to take on the task. That motivation is genuine student growth. Furthermore, significant change is not a task we teachers can accomplish quickly or by ourselves. We must argue for adequate time and the systemic support necessary for professional growth. We must forge collaborative relationships with like-minded colleagues. Only when these pieces are in place can true change be realized for our students and ourselves.

AFTERWORD

Donna E. Alvermann and Kathleen A. Hinchman

If this book is as stimulating to read as it was to assemble, then we have fulfilled our purpose as editors. The third edition of *Reconceptualizing the Literacies in Adolescents' Lives* merges six classroom teachers' voices and a school media specialist's perspective on what it takes to bridge adolescents' everyday literacies with literacy practices common to subject matter learning in an era of Common Core State Standards and high-stakes assessment. Engaging with popular media and digital networking on a global level are but two everyday literacies that many young people know how to tap and use to enhance their own learning. When this know-how becomes part of the literacy practices common to subject matter learning, exciting things can happen. The curriculum expands, students "show us their stuff" (to paraphrase a colleague), and we educators beam with enthusiasm.

Currently, while one need not be Dorothy experiencing the land of Oz to detect a change in conditions, acknowledging this change is important in terms of what it means for us as educators and the textual choices we make when designing classroom literacy instruction. Text messages, music, videos, comics, graphic novels, games, personal web pages, podcasts, and virtual environments that foster social networking are ubiquitous texts in young people's everyday lives. So, too, are the classics, young adult novels, poetry slam performances, and student writing: texts of every kind. Yet textual use alone does not represent the full complement of the literacies in adolescents' lives. Classroom discussions about texts that invite a critical look at race, language, and culture take their place alongside teacher–student conferencing in out-of-school spaces, each having impact on young people's literacies. And behind the scenes are the ever-important professional development communities that ignite teachers' interests in broadening their own expertise, but just as importantly, their knowledge and appreciation of young people's everyday literacies.

The chapter authors in this book demonstrate an awareness of the need to take into account adolescents' everyday literacies and to use them in calling up the academic literacies that will enrich their students' lives. Why these connections are necessary and how to orchestrate them are front and center in each chapter. What bears further investigation, however, is how institutional structures may sometimes erect hurdles that teachers and school media specialists must jump over in their effort to connect students' everyday literacies with the literacy practices common to subject matter learning. We wonder, what is it about school buildings, college campuses, classrooms, and other nonphysical structures, such as curricular guidelines, policies, standards, and assessments, that make students' everyday literacies largely invisible to the very people who most need to be on the "inside" and knowledgeable?

Is There a Prevailing Sentiment that Multimodal Digital Texts Distract?

Although sufficient research exists to support students' use of multimodal digital texts in constructing meaning (e.g., Kress, 2003; Unsworth & Cléirigh, 2009), schools in the United States have been slow to make these texts part of their regular curricula. We believe this is unfortunate, especially given the various affordances they provide in teaching critical media literacy. As Lemke (2009) reminds us, "Media mediate not just among us as we play with our identities, but also between us and the interests of large-scale producers" (p. 150). Opportunities for teaching critical media literacy aside, the prevailing sentiment in many secondary schools and schools of teacher education in the United States is to ignore what adolescents are doing with 21st century texts outside school in their spare time (Alvermann, 2011). The rationale for ignoring an important element in young people's everyday literacies goes something like this: The curriculum and school day are already crowded. Young people are already immersed in using multimodal digital texts in their free time. Thus, why invite them to bring in distractions from the outside?

Immersed they are. According to a recent Kaiser Family Foundation report (Rideout, Foehr, & Roberts, 2010), youth between the ages of 8 and 18 spend an average of 7 hours and 38 minutes daily (7 days a week) using popular media to portray meaning through images, sounds, icons, gestures, print texts, performances, and other multimodal forms of communication. But that's not all. When you add in the time they spend using two or more media forms simultaneously (as they multitask their way through the day), the total number of hours of media exposure rises to 10 hours and 45 minutes per day. A comparatively small segment of that time is spent reading print texts, such as books (25 minutes a day), magazines (9 minutes a day), and newspapers (3 minutes a day). By far the largest chunk of time per day is spent on multimodal texts in the form of TV content, music/audio, websites, video games, and movies.

Are There Needless and Artificial Dichotomies at Play?

In an effort to point out why schools are becoming less important in an era where home schooling, distance education, Internet cafés, and web-based learning communities are revolutionizing how people identify as learners, Collins (2010) offered the following contrasts (which have been slightly adapted for use here) between learning as it occurs in traditional schooling and as it occurs in virtual space:

- Uniform school learning vs. customized online learning.
- Teacher controlled school learning vs. learner controlled online learning.
- In schools, teachers are the experts vs. online, there are multiple experts.
- Schools rely on standardized assessments vs. Internet enables area specializations.
- Schools value head-knowledge vs. Internet values creative uses of web resources.
- Schooling is learning by absorption vs. online, it is learning by doing.
- Schools support just-in-case learning vs. Internet supports just-in-time learning.

Although Collins (2010) relied on these dichotomies to make his point, one could argue that reifying monolithic categories, such as in-school and out-of-school, makes it that much easier for adolescents' everyday literacies to remain largely invisible and thus unavailable for making connections to academic learning. Needless and artificial dichotomies that detract from the very work the authors in this volume set out to do—and succeeded in doing—are unacceptable. Fortunately, new interactive communication technologies and a definitional broadening of *text* to include moving and still images, words, sounds, gestures, and performances support the folding of literacy practices, regardless of their place of origin.

What Happens When Awareness Building Stops Short of Action?

Chapter authors in the third edition of *Reconceptualizing the Literacies in Adolescents' Lives* illustrate clearly how young people's literacies are enacted, situated, and mediated in today's schools and the rapidly changing world outside of school. Having studied adolescents' enactments of everyday literacies in both formal and informal learning environments, the authors in this volume recognize and respect the mediating influence of texts (broadly defined) on such enactments. They also bring to their work a diverse set of experiences that enable them to write with cultural and historical awareness of adolescent literacy. We use the term *adolescent literacy* advisedly, acknowledging that the label *adolescent* can reference pejorative views of youth to which we do not subscribe. Following Hinchman and Sheridan-Thomas (2008), we use *adolescent literacy* to focus a reader's gaze on young people's "full complement of in-school and out-of-school literacy practices instead of on the narrower concerns suggested by…content-area literacy" (p. xiv) and other such descriptors. Throughout the book, the authors, too, have aligned their work with this latter, more encompassing, connotation of adolescent literacy.

Making adolescents' everyday literacy practices visible to teachers and school media specialists, especially those open to connecting everyday literacies to academic learning, requires that literacy teacher educators do more than develop an awareness of the forward looking work featured in *Reconceptualizing the Literacies in Adolescents' Lives*. Awareness is one thing; acting on that awareness is quite another. We know this from our own experiences as adolescent literacy educators for well over two decades. Acting on what the authors in this volume are advocating will equate to modifying some of our own pedagogical approaches—to letting go of tired practices, to exploring the affordances of new forms of text, and to reaching out to classroom teachers and school media specialists whose motivations for enrolling in our adolescent literacy courses cannot be squandered or slighted in the least degree.

Where is the Balance Point in Institutional Authority and Youth Identity Politics?

Gaps between adolescents' everyday literacy practices and the critical skills required for subject matter learning are prevalent in the research literature (Burn, Buckingham, Parry, & Powell, 2010; Hagood, 2009). Equally prevalent are studies (e.g., Humphrey, 2006) that show, similar to some of the research reported in this volume, that young people are not quite the socially aware political activists that popular media (e.g., "I am Australian" http://www.youtube.com/watch?v= OGoNbrODq8U) would have us believe. This is especially the case when perceptions of a school's institutional authority clash with youth's perceptions of their right to a certain degree of autonomy from adult surveillance. In other words, what teachers and school media specialists might view as their "right to know" about their students' everyday literacy practices might be the very information that politically savvy youth would seek to conceal.

Just as the seemingly contradictory discourses that embed a teacher's right-to-know stance versus a student's right-to-conceal stance can lead to misunderstandings about an intended goal, so, too, can a school's perception of the (in)appropriateness of youth identity politics in a highly regimented curriculum. If that perception is acted upon (e.g., new school policies aimed at heightening adult supervision are interpreted by students as inconsiderate and disrespectful of their needs), then the likelihood of teachers and school media specialists having access to adolescents' everyday literacy practices would diminish or disappear completely.

Where to, Next?

To date, the relative invisibility of adolescents' everyday literacy practices suggests that certain institutional structures are in place that make it difficult for teachers and school media specialists to connect those practices to the official curriculum. While instances of breaking through those structures—for example, witness the successes demonstrated in this third edition of *Reconceptualizing the Literacies in Adolescents' Lives*—are encouraging, they are small in number and subject to the critique of qualitative research findings in general. Skepticism aside, we would contend that the six teacher responders and the one school media specialist saw the potential for making connections between adolescents' everyday literacies and academic learning. Their insights, coupled with our own enthusiastic response to what the chapter authors have accomplished, would argue for moving ahead with the agenda that launched this third edition of *Reconceptualizing the Literacies in Adolescents' Lives*.

Onward.

References

Alvermann, D. E. (2011). Moving on, keeping pace: Youth's literate identities and multimodal digital texts. In S. Abrams & J. Rowsell (Eds.), *Rethinking identity and literacy education in the 21st century. National Society for the Study of Education Yearbook, 110*(1) 109–128.

Burn, A., Buckingham, D., Parry, B., Powell, M. (2010). Minding the gaps: Teachers' cultures, students' cultures. In D. E. Alvermann (Ed.), *Adolescents' online literacies: Connecting classrooms, digital media, & popular culture* (pp. 183—201). New York: Peter Lang.

Collins, A. (2010, June 11). *Rethinking education in the age of technology.* Paper presented at the Games, Learning, and Society (GLS) Conference, Madison, WI.

Hagood, M. C. (Ed.). (2009). *New literacies practices: Designing literacy learning.* New York: Peter Lang.

Hinchman, K. A., & Sheridan-Thomas, H. K. (Eds.). (2008). *Best practices in adolescent literacy instruction.* New York: Guilford.

Humphrey, S. (2006). "Getting the Reader On Side": Exploring adolescent online political discourse. *E-learning, 3*(2), 143–157. Retrieved May 25, 2011, from www.wwwords. co.uk/elea/content/pdfs/3/issue3_2.asp#3. doi: 10.2304/elea.2006.3.2.143.

Kress, G. (2003). *Literacy in the new media age.* London: Routledge.

Lemke, J. (2009). Multimodality, identity, and time. In C. Jewitt (Ed.), *The Routledge handbook of multimodal analysis* (pp. 140–150). New York: Routledge.

Rideout, V. J., Foehr, U. G., & Roberts, D. F. (2010). *Generation M2: Media in the lives of 8- to 18-year-olds.* Menlo Park, CA: The Kaiser Family Foundation. Retrieved May 22, 2011 from www.kff.org/entmedia/8010.cfm.

Unsworth, L., & Cléirigh, C. (2009). Multimodality and reading: The construction of meaning through image-text interaction. In C. Jewitt (Ed.), *The Routledge handbook of multimodal analysis* (pp. 151–163). New York: Routledge.

Variety Club Youth Choir Flash Mob. (2011, February 2). 'I am Australian' (Storyteller Media). Retrieved May 27, 2011, from www.youtube.com/watch?v=OGoNbrODq8U.

CONTRIBUTORS

Donna E. Alvermann University of Georgia

Randy Bomer The University of Texas at Austin

Stergios G. Botzakis University of Tennessee

Anne Bulcher Cario Middle School, Mt. Pleasant, SC

Justin Claypool Morningside Middle School, Charleston, SC

Ellen Damlich Chicago Public Schools

Bette Davis William Carey College

Maryanne Desmond Barrett Jamesville-Dewitt Middle School, Syracuse, NY

Keith Dumbleton Chicago Public Schools

Bob Fecho University of Georgia

Barbara Guzzetti Arizona State University

Marcelle M. Haddix Syracuse University

Margaret C. Hagood College of Charleston

Kathleen A. Hinchman Syracuse University

Gay Ivey James Madison University

Marcia Mardis Florida State University

Elizabeth G. Mascia Jamesville-Dewitt Middle School, Syracuse, NY

Renee Moore Broad Street High School, Cleveland, MS

Margaret Moran Cario Middle Schoo, Mt. Pleasant, SC

Lorri Neilsen Glenn Mount Saint Vincent University

David O'Brien University of Minnesota

Eliane Rubinstein-Ávila University of Arizona

Alfred W. Tatum University of Illinois at Chicago

Daisy Torres-Petrovich Chicago Public Schools

Eli Tucker-Raymond Chèche Konnen Center at TERC

Lalitha Vasudevan Teachers College, Columbia University

McKenzie Weaver Collins Hill High School, Suwanee, GA

George White Morningside Middle School, Charleston, SC

Kelly Wissman University at Albany, State University of New York

INDEX